Praise for
THE CASE OF THE MURDEROUS DR. CREAM

"*The Case of the Murderous Dr. Cream* is a tour de force of storytell̲i̲ ... n-drous example of creative nonfiction ar ... is year. Dean Jobb has brought to life not j ... s Thomas Neill Cream, but [also] Cream ... d how they lived. And all the while blendi ... e fictional detectives being created, of the ... the loose. This book is both chilling and, for fans like me of creative nonfiction, thrilling."

—**LOUISE PENNY**, author of the *New York Times* bestselling
Chief Inspector Gamache novels

"Deeply researched and rich in grisly detail, *The Case of the Murderous Dr. Cream* fuses the blow-by-blow efforts to catch a serial killer with the larger picture of crime and detection in the late nineteenth century. A fine piece of social history as well as an extraordinary story, it engrossed me right up to its deeply satisfying conclusion."

—**CHARLOTTE GRAY**, author of eleven nonfiction bestsellers,
including *The Massey Murder* and *Murdered Midas*

"Tense, atmospheric, and effortlessly readable, *The Case of the Murderous Dr. Cream* has all the sinister elegance of a hansom cab emerging from a late Victorian London smog."

—**PAUL WILLETTS**, author of *King Con:
The Bizarre Adventures of the Jazz Age's Greatest Impostor*

"A brilliant evocation of an age and a fascinating dissection of a serial killer's crimes. Dean Jobb is a first-rate storyteller and historical detective. A real page-turner."

—**LINDSEY FITZHARRIS**, author of *The Butchering Art:
Joseph Lister's Quest to Transform the Grisly World of Victorian Medicine*

"The definitive retelling of a story about a devious doctor, the dogged investigators who hunted him, and the murders that shocked the world. Dr. Cream's story comes to life in Jobb's spellbinding tale."

—**KATE WINKLER DAWSON**, author of *American Sherlock:
Murder, Forensics, and the Birth of American CSI*

THE CASE OF
THE MURDEROUS DR. CREAM

Thomas Neill Cream in 1874, when he was a medical student at McGill University in Montreal (McCord Museum I-99949)

THE CASE OF THE MURDEROUS DR. CREAM

THE HUNT FOR A
VICTORIAN ERA SERIAL KILLER

DEAN JOBB

HARPER**AVENUE**
An imprint of HarperCollins*Publishers Ltd*

Published by Harper Avenue, an imprint of HarperCollins Publishers Ltd,
by arrangement with Algonquin Books of Chapel Hill,
a division of Workman Publishing Company, Inc., New York.

First Canadian edition

HarperCollins books may be purchased for educational, business,
or sales promotional use through our Special Markets Department.

HarperCollins Publishers Ltd
Bay Adelaide Centre, East Tower
22 Adelaide Street West, 41st Floor
Toronto, Ontario, Canada
M5H 4E3

www.harpercollins.ca

Library and Archives Canada Cataloguing in Publication

Title: The case of the murderous Dr. Cream : the hunt for a Victorian era serial killer / Dean Jobb.
Other titles: Case of the murderous Doctor Cream
Names: Jobb, Dean, 1958- author.
Description: First edition. | Includes bibliographical references and index.
Identifiers: Canadiana (print) 20210143088 | Canadiana (ebook) 20210143185
ISBN 9781443453325 (softcover) | ISBN 9781443453349 (ebook)
Subjects: LCSH: Cream, Thomas Neill, 1850-1892. | LCSH: Serial murderers—England—London—
Biography. | LCSH: Physicians—England—London—Biography. | LCSH: Serial murders—
England—London—Case studies. | LCSH: Serial murders—United States—Case studies. |
LCSH: Serial murders—Canada—Case studies. | LCGFT: Biographies.
Classification: LCC HV6535.G6 L6368 2021 | DDC 364.152/32092—dc23

Maps by Mary Rostad

Printed and bound in the United States of America
LSC/H 9 8 7 6 5 4 3 2 1

For Kerry

When a doctor does go wrong he is the first of criminals.
He has nerve and he has knowledge.
—SHERLOCK HOLMES, IN ARTHUR CONAN DOYLE,
"THE ADVENTURE OF THE SPECKLED BAND," 1892

Dr. Thomas Neill Cream must surely be the greatest monster
of iniquity the century has seen.
—NEWS OF THE WORLD (LONDON), OCTOBER 23, 1892

CONTENTS

A Note to Readers

This is the true story of a serial killer who preyed on women in London, Chicago, and Canada more than a century ago. None of the dialogue, scenes, or details have been invented or embellished. Every word enclosed in quotation marks is drawn from a court or police file; a newspaper report, memoir, or historical study; or a letter or other document preserved in an archive or museum. Wording and spellings within quotations have been preserved, uncorrected, so the past can speak directly to the present.

———

PROLOGUE

GHOSTS

{JOLIET, ILLINOIS • JULY 1891}

THE IRON DOOR OF THE ILLINOIS STATE PENITENTIARY in Joliet groaned open and spat a haggard-looking man into the world he had left almost a decade earlier. It was the final day of July 1891, a clear-sky Friday. High above the man's head, atop the gray limestone walls of the penitentiary forty miles southwest of Chicago, men in blue coats toting Winchester rifles watched him walk away. If this had been an escape, a single guard could have pumped sixteen bullets into his back without reloading.

Thomas Neill Cream's hollow cheeks and sharp-edged features were the legacy of years at hard labor and stints in the mind-crushing hell of solitary confinement. He had traded his zebra-striped prison uniform for a new suit—a modest gift, like the ten dollars in his pocket, from the State of Illinois. His few belongings were stuffed into a pillowcase. He was also entitled to a train ticket to his place of conviction, but it's unlikely he had a desire to return to Belvidere, a city in northern Illinois. Staff at the prison—known as Joliet—stopped cropping an inmate's hair in the weeks before release and the men could grow a mustache or beard, helping them blend in. But the practice had made little difference to Cream, who was almost completely bald. Besides, after marching day after day in lockstep with fellow inmates—pressed together, single file, inching along like a giant striped caterpillar—many walked with the shuffling gait that betrayed them as former inmates. "The stripes," noted Joliet's warden, Robert McClaughry, "show through his citizen's clothes."

THE ILLINOIS STATE PENITENTIARY IN JOLIET (AUTHOR COLLECTION)

Cream had been inside for nine years and 273 days. Chester Arthur had just become president, replacing the assassinated James Garfield, when he began serving his sentence in November 1881. Grover Cleveland had won and lost the presidency in the meantime and now Benjamin Harrison occupied the White House. People who peered into the eyepiece of a prototype of Edison's kinetoscope, unveiled a few weeks earlier, were astounded to see moving images. The telephone, a novelty in the early 1880s, was now installed in almost a quarter-million American homes and offices. In Springfield, Massachusetts, brothers Charles and J. Frank Duryea were tinkering with a prototype they called the "Motor Wagon"—America's first gasoline-powered automobile.

Even crime fighting had changed during Cream's confinement. A few years before his release, an array of odd-looking calipers and measuring sticks had arrived at Joliet. Calibrated in centimeters and millimeters—metric-system increments rarely used in the United States—the devices were designed to precisely record the size of specific parts of the body. This pioneering system of identifying criminals bore a name as strange and foreign as the tools it required: bertillonage.

The system was based on eleven measurements, including a person's overall height, the width of the head, the dimensions of the ear, the size of the left foot and the forearm, and the length of the middle and ring fingers. Subjects were also measured in a sitting position and with their arms outstretched. While two men might be found to have the same-sized foot, the chances of multiple measurements being identical were remote, and the odds of finding two subjects with identical sets of all eleven measurements was estimated at one in more than four million. To make a misidentification even more unlikely, the subject's face was photographed, and eye color and any tattoos or scars were recorded. The system "renders the identification of felons and chronic law breakers . . . an absolute certainty," claimed Joliet's records clerk, Sidney Wetmore. "Mistake is impossible."

Bertillonage was touted as a scientific solution to a challenge that had long faced the police and the courts: how to identify recidivists, ensuring they did not receive the more lenient treatment afforded first-time offenders. Some police forces and prison officials had already begun to photograph those arrested or incarcerated. Police in Birmingham, England, had led the way in the 1850s, marching suspects to a photographic studio to pose for some of the earliest mug shots. The practice was well established at Joliet by the time Cream arrived in 1881, and his photograph was added to the prison's ever-expanding rogues' gallery. Illinois law demanded that repeat offenders be identified and punished accordingly—a conviction for a second serious offense carried a minimum fifteen-year prison term, while third offenders faced at least twenty years. But photographs were not a foolproof method for keeping tabs on criminals. Facial features changed as an offender aged, and growing a mustache or beard might be enough to alter a man's appearance and make identification difficult. Since mug shots were filed under the offender's name, an enterprising criminal could simply adopt an alias, and many did.

Enter Alphonse Bertillon, a clerk at the headquarters of the Paris police who grew weary of filing reports containing brief and vague references to an offender's appearance. Thanks to his father, a noted anthropologist, Bertillon was familiar with anthropometry, the scientific study of the measurements and proportions of the human body. One day in 1879, as he shuffled paper, he realized that recording a criminal's exact anthropometric measurements should make it easy to identify repeat offenders. His superiors, however, scoffed at the idea that science could be used to fight crime. Three years passed before Bertillon was permitted to begin taking measurements of suspects to test his theory. Within a year he had identified enough recidivists to prove the system worked. France's national prison system adopted bertillonage in 1885; police forces and penal institutions in other European countries soon signed on.

Robert McClaughry, Joliet's forward-thinking warden, brought bertillonage to the United States. Recording body measurements became part of Joliet's intake routine for new inmates in 1887, and McClaughry encouraged other prisons to adopt the system to catch repeat offenders. "It substitutes certainty for uncertainty," he asserted, "a thoroughly reliable identification for the shrewd guess of the detective, or the scarcely more reliable testimony of the photograph." Police forces and prison officials across the country embraced the new crime-fighting technology. Within a decade, 150 American police forces and prisons were using the system. Possessing a set of Bertillon's tools, one American criminologist would note, "became the distinguishing mark of the modern police organization."

But bertillonage had its drawbacks—and its detractors. Carefully measuring feet, ears, and fingers of offenders like Thomas Neill Cream was a time-consuming process and skilled, trained technicians were needed to ensure the results were accurate. Tools became worn or bent through constant use, producing results that could match an innocent man to the crimes of someone of similar size and build. Since the premise underlying the entire system was that bone size remained constant, bertillonage could not be used to keep track of offenders who had not reached maturity. And there was no central registry, making it difficult to trace a suspect who refused to reveal where he had lived or worked before his arrest. Some prison officials also questioned the fairness of keeping detailed records of men who had served their time and might never break the law again. McClaughry's counterargument, that the records were checked only when a former inmate reoffended, highlighted the system's most serious flaw—finding matching measurements simply proved that a suspect in custody had a criminal record. Unlike fingerprints, which were still years away from being accepted as a forensic tool, Bertillon records could not link an unknown offender to the scene of a crime. "No man can be pursued by the police or by any detective," McClaughry admitted at a national meeting of wardens in 1890, "by means of this system."

When Cream emerged from behind the walls of Joliet in the summer of 1891, there was little to connect him with his dark, murderous past. He was a doctor from Canada who had earned a license to practice from one of the world's most respected medical colleges. He was also a new kind of killer, choosing victims at random and killing without remorse. A cold-blooded fiend who murdered, the *Chicago Daily Tribune* would later declare in disbelief, "simply for the sake of murder." A serial killer, and one of the most brutal and prolific in history. Herman Webster Mudgett, a doctor who went by the name H. H. Holmes, killed at least nine people and would come to be considered one of America's first serial killers. But by the time Holmes claimed his first victim in 1891, and long before the infamous Jack the Ripper terrorized London in 1888, Cream was suspected of killing as many as six people, most of them deliberately poisoned with tainted medicine. His latest victim had been the husband of his mistress, and this was the murder that had consigned him to a hovel-like cell in Joliet. His earlier victims—two in Canada, including his wife, and three more in Chicago—were young women who were pregnant and desperate to induce an abortion; they had made the tragic mistake of trusting their doctor with their lives.

THOMAS NEILL CREAM SHORTLY AFTER HIS RELEASE FROM PRISON IN 1891
(SCIENCE AND SOCIETY PICTURE LIBRARY, LONDON, IMAGE 10658277)

In an era when police investigations were often cursory and forensic science was in its infancy, detectives lacked the tools and expertise needed to track down such a formidable foe. Few could imagine such monsters existed. But this only partly explains how Cream had gotten away with murder in two countries before he finally had been locked up in Joliet. Cream's credentials and professional status, bungled investigations, corrupt police and justice officials, failed prosecutions, and missed opportunities allowed him to kill, again and again.

The thin paper trail documenting Cream's shocking crimes was scattered from small-town Canada to Illinois, with only fading memories, forgotten court files, and yellowing newspaper clippings to connect the dots. The Bertillon identification system, cutting-edge technology for its time, was powerless to prevent a convicted criminal from vanishing like a ghost. If a former inmate wanted to disappear after his release, to hide his past—as Cream most certainly did—all he had to do was change his name.

I

"The First of Criminals"

London • 1891

I

"A GREAT SIN-STRICKEN CITY"

A MAN CLAD IN A MACKINTOSH TO OUTSMART THE DAY'S showers, a top hat covering his bald head, turned up at the door of a townhouse at 103 Lambeth Palace Road. His name was Thomas Neill, he told the landlady, and he was in search of lodgings. He took the upper-floor room at the back. It was October 7, 1891, and Cream was back in Lambeth, a downtrodden maze of grimy slums and smoky factories across the Thames from the Gothic splendor of the Houses of Parliament. It was a London neighborhood he knew well: his rooming house stood opposite St. Thomas' Hospital, where he had been a medical student more than a decade earlier. He could not help but notice that a new building, just downriver from the tower of Big Ben, had been erected since his last visit. Faced with bands of red brick and white stone and set on a foundation of granite quarried by inmates of Dartmoor and other prisons, it was the new headquarters of the Metropolitan Police, better known as Scotland Yard.

Cream was in the heart of the world's largest city, the capital of an empire at its zenith. Swaths of scarlet on globes and maps staked Britain's claim to the far-flung colonies and territories—and tens of millions of people—under Queen Victoria's rule. London was a sprawling metropolis of more than five million, a glittering bastion of wealth and power built on a foundation of poverty, crime, and desperation. Church spires and the giant teapot dome of St. Paul's Cathedral pointed skyward from a sea of slate roofs and chimneys belching black coal smoke. A chaos of carriages, freight wagons, and horse-drawn omnibuses clogged the main streets. At night, the sidewalks became a sea of bowlers and wide-brimmed feathered hats as men and women passed like ghosts through a netherworld of flickering gaslight and sinister fog. Pickpockets shouldered their way into the crowds in search of watches and billfolds. Prostitutes scanned the audiences at West End theaters and music halls in search of customers or strolled the adjacent Strand, transforming the busy thoroughfare, one observer lamented, into "one of the scandals of London." Enclaves of the rich and privileged rubbed shoulders with foul, dangerous slums like Whitechapel where, just three years before, the notorious Jack the Ripper had brutally murdered five women. To an editor at the city's *Daily Chronicle*, London was a modern Sodom and Gomorrah, "a great sin-stricken city."

THE STRAND IN 1890. THE BUSY THOROUGHFARE BECAME ONE OF CREAM'S LONDON HAUNTS. (SCIENCE AND SOCIETY PICTURE LIBRARY, LONDON, IMAGE 10436070)

Lambeth rivaled Whitechapel as one of the city's poorest, dirtiest, and most crime-ridden neighborhoods. Not even the police were safe—one bobby, a rookie on one of his first patrols, confronted a group of Lambeth thugs and was thrown through a plate-glass window. When the journalist Henry Mayhew set out to expose London's nineteenth-century underworld, he headed for the "well-known rookery of young thieves in London." Children as young as five, he discovered, roamed the streets in ragged clothing, stealing to survive. "Fagin, Bill Sikes, and Oliver Twist would have all seemed quite at home in Victorian Lambeth," the celebrated author Simon Winchester has written. "This was Dickensian London writ large."

Lambeth's industries choked the air with smoke and soot. Maudslay's foundry forged parts for the steam engines, pumps, and other mechanical marvels that powered the Victorian Age. Earthenware jugs, chimney pots, and drainpipes were fired in Henry Doulton's famous pottery works. Overhead, trains puffed and clacked on elevated rail lines that sliced through the heart of the neighborhood. Their destination was Waterloo Station, one of the city's major terminals. Thousands of people—commuters who worked in the city, travelers bound for points in southern England, steamship passengers newly arrived from abroad via Southampton—passed through its doors every day. Even the dead disturbed the living. London's cemeteries were so overcrowded that a special railway, the Necropolis line, shunted corpses from a local station to graveyards south of the city. Lambeth, the London historian Peter Ackroyd would note, "was, in every sense, a dumping ground."

It was also considered the "most lurid and beastly" of the city's red-light districts. The neighborhood surrounding Waterloo Station, a magnet for streetwalkers, became known as Whoreterloo. Brickwork supports for the station's elevated tracks offered secluded spots where business could be transacted—the succession of "dark, damp arches," one resident complained, "encouraged the more disreputable of the population."

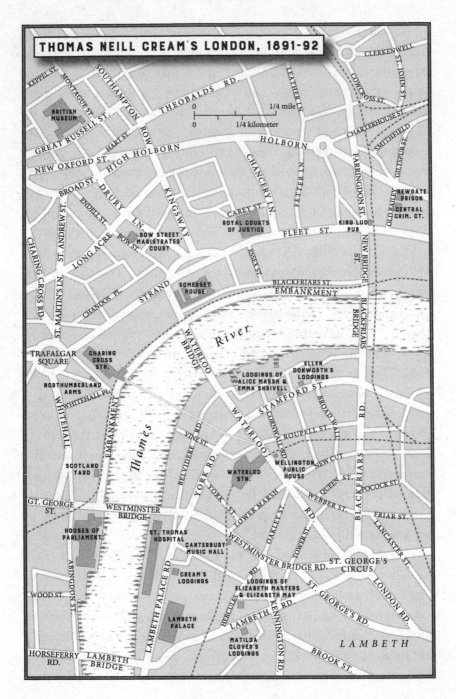

Prostitutes were described as "unfortunates" in the press, but some of the women working in the brothels, propositioning men on the street, or picking up clients at the Canterbury, Gatti's, and other Lambeth music halls considered themselves fortunate. Life was precarious for young women from poor, struggling families. A sudden misfortune—the death of a parent or husband, the breakup of a marriage or relationship, losing a low-paying job as a maid or toiling in a factory—could leave them to fend for themselves. Some working-class women turned to prostitution, the British academic Kathryn Hughes noted in an exploration of Victorian life and attitudes, when "the usual ways in which they got an income from their bodies—by working as a milliner, or a domestic or a factory hand—had come up short." Selling sex, even for a few weeks or months, might be their only option, and it offered something most women, regardless of their social standing, were denied in the Victorian world: income and independence. One Lambeth prostitute told Mayhew she earned as much as four pounds a week, far more than she had made "workin' and slavin'" as a servant in Birmingham.

Prostitutes seemed to be everywhere in Lambeth. There were "more women in the street than ever, and they are more brazen and persistent," complained Rev. G. E. Asker of St. Andrew's Church. Even he was being propositioned as he walked through the neighborhood. "The brothels are many of the perfect hells," Asker added. "Shrieks and cries, 'murder' and so on, frequently are heard."

For Lambeth's newest resident, it would be a perfect hunting ground.

⬦⬦⬦⬦⬦

MARY Cream was only fourteen when her oldest brother left home to attend medical school. She remembered fragments of his troubled life—mentions of his stints as a doctor in Ontario and Chicago, his conviction for murder. When she saw him again in Quebec City in the summer of 1891, for the first time in close to two decades, she could scarcely believe what he had become. "He was most wild and excitable," she remembered. "Not right in his mind."

Cream had arrived in Quebec City on August 2, shortly after his release from Joliet. His family had emigrated from Scotland to Canada when he was four and settled in the capital of the province of Quebec. His father, William Cream, had managed a major timber exporting firm, amassing a fortune by the time of his death in 1887. Cream spent almost six weeks in the city, staying at the home of his brother Daniel. Relatives began calling him Thomas Neill. "He wished and decided to drop the Cream," noted Thomas Davidson, a Quebec businessman and family friend, "on account of his unfortunate troubles." No one seemed to suspect he might have other motives for changing his name.

"His actions at times were that of an unsound mind," Jessie Read, Daniel Cream's wife, would recall. "He would change countenance and appear as another man," excited and manic at one moment, quiet and vacant-eyed the next. Davidson, who attributed Cream's "mental derangement" and "unbalanced" mind to his long imprisonment, was appalled when Thomas lashed out "in a most scandalous manner" at one of his sisters, possibly Mary Cream, calling her a streetwalker and a liar. These "atrocious slanders," Davidson later noted, were repeated in a letter Thomas fired off to his sister's friends.

Davidson and Daniel Cream devised a plan to send him abroad. A fresh start, they reasoned, might improve Thomas's mental as well as physical health. It would, at least, free them from the strain of dealing with his erratic and abusive behavior. As executors of William Cream's will, Daniel and Davidson withdrew a sum from the estate—the equivalent of twenty-three thousand US dollars today—that would help get Thomas back on his feet. Daniel considered sending him to Glasgow, near his birthplace in Barony, perhaps to visit relatives there. They settled on London, a city Cream knew from his days at St. Thomas' Hospital in the late 1870s. A transatlantic steamer could deliver him to Liverpool in just over a week, but they opted to dispatch him on a slower, sail-powered ship. "We believed," Davidson explained later, "that the long sea voyage and the complete change of scene would restore him to both mental and bodily health."

On September 9, the night before he was to sail to England, Cream wrote a will. He claimed to be "of sound mind" and, oddly, named his sister-in-law, Jessie Read, as his executor and sole heir. In the event of his death, she would inherit all his property as well as anything he might be owed from the estates of his deceased parents. Did Cream feel a sense of imminent doom, that he would not be returning from England? The two-paragraph will, written in the neat, upright lettering that would soon be familiar to Scotland Yard detectives, offered no insights into his motives.

He left Quebec City the next morning. On October 1, after a twenty-day voyage, he scribbled a note to Daniel Cream, announcing his arrival in England.

◇◇◇◇◇

CREAM became a regular at Gatti's Adelaide Gallery Restaurant on the Strand. The restaurant's decor was elegant—vaulted ceilings, stained glass, ornate plasterwork, a palette of blue and gold—and it was a favorite of the theater crowd. Actors and playwrights from nearby playhouses claimed many of its marble-top tables. One day, when most of the seats were taken, he shared a table with another man.

He introduced himself as Thomas Neill. He was educated, tastefully dressed, and "well informed and travelled, as men go," the other diner recalled. They shared meals many times, with Cream preferring bread and cheese, washed down with beer or gin, to the plovers' eggs and other delicacies on the menu. He spoke about how much he enjoyed attending the city's music halls. He talked about money and seemed obsessed with poisons. But most of the time, he talked about women.

"His language about them was far from tolerable or agreeable," his dining companion had to admit. Cream carried around a collection of pornographic photographs, which he delighted in showing to his new friend and to other diners. He was restless and fidgety and could not stand still, even when drinking at the restaurant's bar. And he was always chewing something—gum, tobacco, or the end of a cigar, his jaws "moving mechanically like a cow chewing the cud." He seemed wary of every patron and waiter who approached his table. He rarely smiled, and his laugh sounded forced and fake, as if he were the villain in a melodrama. And people could not help but notice that his left eye turned inward, giving him a crazed, sinister look. Cream later claimed he had come to London to consult an eye specialist, and one of his first stops after his arrival had been the office of a Fleet Street optician. James Aitchison diagnosed his condition as hypermetropia, or farsightedness—his eyes focused improperly, blurring his vision and causing severe headaches. Cream had been suffering from the condition since childhood, Aitchison concluded, and had needed glasses for years. He supplied two pairs of spectacles to correct his vision.

The more his dining companion learned about Cream, the more troubled he became. "He was exceedingly vicious, and seemed to live for nothing but the gratification of his passions," he remembered. "His tastes and habits were of the most depraved order." And he made no secret of his drug use. Cream was constantly taking pills, three or four at a time, that he said contained cocaine and morphine as well as strychnine, a deadly poison used in minute quantities as a stimulant in medicines. The pills relieved his headaches, he said. They were also, he seemed delighted to add, an aphrodisiac.

Getting narcotics and poisons in London, Cream had discovered, was easy. He called at a chemist's shop on Parliament Street—just around the corner from Scotland Yard's new headquarters—and identified himself as a doctor from America, visiting the city to take courses at St. Thomas' Hospital. The clerk, John Kirkby, could not find the name Thomas Neill in the shop's register of licensed physicians. "I am not in the habit of selling poisons to persons whose names I cannot find in the register," he would say later. Access to poisons was restricted by law, and if Cream could not prove he was a doctor, he should have been required to produce someone known to the pharmacist to vouch for him. But Kirkby made an exception and took this new customer at his word. He filled Cream's orders for opium and strychnine several times that fall. When Cream asked for empty gelatin capsules of a size not in general use in Britain, Kirkby helpfully tracked them down from a supplier. Doctors and druggists filled them with medicine too bitter tasting to be taken on its own.

Cream did not say how he intended to use the strychnine or the hard-to-find capsules. Kirkby did not ask.

2

"DETECTIVE-FEVER"

DO YOU FEEL AN UNCOMFORTABLE HEAT AT THE PIT OF your stomach, Sir? and a nasty thumping at the top of your head? . . ." Gabriel Betteredge, the head servant in the household of Lady Verinder, asks another character in the 1868 novel *The Moonstone*. "You're certain to catch it. . . . I call it the detective-fever."

Wilkie Collins's story of intrigue and a priceless stolen diamond (the Moonstone of the title) introduced one of the earliest professional detectives in English literature, Sergeant Cuff of the London police. "When it comes to unraveling a mystery there isn't the equal in England," readers are assured, and his first order of business in *The Moonstone* is a meticulous examination of the room where the gem had been stored. "In all my experience along the dirtiest ways of this dirty little world," he snaps when a colleague doubts the value of a piece of evidence, "I have never met with such a thing as a trifle yet." "I don't suspect," he states with confidence at another point in his investigation. "I know." Betteredge, who observes Cuff as he makes his inquiries, is soon infected with the mystery-solving bug.

So was the Victorian public. Crime and murder were obsessions in the nineteenth century. "Nothing," proclaimed one London news dealer, "beats a stunning good murder." Readers craved "sensations" and the vicarious thrill of peering into an abyss of wickedness and scandal at a safe distance. One British social historian has likened it to a form of pornography—a guilty pleasure that could be indulged in newspapers, books, and plays. Writers scrambled to produce novels based on the latest outrage, while London's theater promoters sometimes brought crimes to the stage before the real-life offender had stood trial. Souvenir hunters could buy ceramic figurines depicting killers and victims. The mainstream press, taking its cue from the *Illustrated Police News* and other lucrative crime-filled publications, offered lurid accounts of brutal deaths and the trials that followed. Apologies might be offered if readers had to make do with disappointing accounts of "commonplace murders." In 1861 one London publication, *The Spectator*, surveyed the previous week's highlights in the British courts: accounts of two women poisoning their children; a lodger who murdered his landlady; a doctor who performed a fatal abortion; and a man accused of trying to kill his son in a dispute over an inheritance. Otherwise, the paper noted, "the week has been a dull one."

Murder was a spectacle that could be enjoyed in person as well. People flocked to crime scenes, hoping to catch a glimpse of the house or alley where a murder had been committed. They descended on London's Central Criminal Court, the Old Bailey, jostling for seats so they could witness the ritual of trial and conviction. The satirical magazine *Punch* poked fun at the voyeurism of the times, publishing a mock dispatch from a trial in progress: "Dear me! If it isn't more exciting than the Opera," a woman exclaimed to a friend. "What makes it more delightful, it's all true."

Tens of thousands often turned out to witness the final act in the tragedy—the execution of the offender. These morbid vigils persisted even after public hangings were banned in Britain in 1868. Raucous crowds continued to gather outside prisons on the day of an execution and erupted into cheers when a murderer's demise was confirmed. Those denied a chance to see the culprit hang could visit Madame Tussaud's London museum, where the Chamber of Horrors featured the wax likenesses of infamous murderers. The English essayist Thomas De Quincey satirized the bloodlust in an essay with the provocative title "On Murder Considered as One of the Fine Arts." "Something more goes to the composition of a fine murder than two blockheads to kill and be killed—a knife—a purse—and a dark lane," he wrote in *Blackwood's Magazine*. The masses might be satisfied by "a copious effusion of blood," but "the enlightened connoisseur is more refined in his taste."

◇◇◇◇◇

THE creation of London's Metropolitan Police in 1829 and its detective branch in the 1840s introduced a new player to this spectacle of crime and punishment: the professional investigator. Charles Dickens had been the first to popularize the work of Scotland Yard's detectives. He lauded their "unusual intelligence" and their powers of "keen observation and quick perception" in an 1850 magazine article. One, Inspector Charles Field, became the model for Mr. Bucket, the investigator featured a few years later in Dickens's novel *Bleak House*. The "steady-looking, sharp-eyed" Bucket sized up situations and read people with ease. "Nothing," Dickens wrote, "escapes him."

Wilkie Collins, too, found inspiration in the ranks of the detective branch. Sergeant Cuff was modeled on Detective Inspector Jonathan Whicher of Scotland Yard—they even shared a passion for gardening— and the plot of *The Moonstone* was based on one of Whicher's most famous and puzzling cases, the murder of a child in 1860 at a country estate, Road Hill House. But Dickens and Collins were latecomers to the detective story. Edgar Allan Poe had created the genre in the early 1840s, as the first detectives were hitting the streets of London, in "The Murders in the Rue Morgue" and other stories featuring C. Auguste Dupin, an amateur sleuth who used logic and reason to solve mysteries and crimes. But the greatest fictional detective of them all emerged in the 1880s, from the imagination of an Edinburgh-born doctor determined to carve out a new career as a writer. Arthur Conan

Doyle combined the logical mind of Poe's Dupin with the observational skills and rapid-fire deductions of a real-life doctor, Joseph Bell, who had been one of his instructors in medical school. He embodied his "new idea of the detective" in an iconic character the world would soon know as Sherlock Holmes.

DOCTOR TURNED WRITER ARTHUR CONAN DOYLE CREATED HIS ICONIC CHARACTER SHERLOCK HOLMES—"A NEW IDEA OF THE DETECTIVE"—IN THE MID-1880S. (AUTHOR COLLECTION)

Holmes and his crime-solving partner, Dr. John Watson, made their debut in 1887 in *A Study in Scarlet*, a murder mystery first published in the magazine *Beeton's Christmas Annual* and later released as a book. A critic in the Edinburgh newspaper *The Scotsman* hailed it as an entrancing tale that proved "the true detective should work by observation and deduction." The story established the universe that would become familiar to millions of readers. Holmes and Dr. Watson, who serves as narrator, share a flat at 221B Baker Street, where they hold court for a succession of desperate clients and befuddled Scotland Yard detectives. Holmes displays his formidable powers of observation and reveals details about his visitors before they have a chance to speak. He describes himself as a "consulting detective": when the police are stumped in their efforts to solve a crime, they come to him for help. "They lay all the evidence before me, and I am generally able," he assures Dr. Watson, "by the help of my knowledge of the history of crime, to set them straight."

A second Holmes adventure, *The Sign of the Four* (a title later shortened to *The Sign of Four*), was a tale of murder, betrayal, and lost treasure published in England and the United States in 1890. "Among detective stories," an American reviewer correctly predicted, it was "bound to become a classic." By now readers knew that Holmes was an expert in chemicals and poisons, had published a book on the arcane subject of distinguishing varieties of cigar ash, and maintained an encyclopedia-like index of crimes and criminals. They had tagged along as he scoured crime scenes, magnifying glass in hand, in search of boot prints, traces of mud and blood, and other clues. Most of all, they watched him upstage the hapless Inspector Lestrade and other plodding Scotland Yard detectives. When London's police were "out of their depths"—which, Holmes observes with disdain in *The Sign of the Four*, was "their normal state"—he comes to the rescue. "You have brought detection as near an exact science," notes Watson, "as it ever will be brought in this world."

Conan Doyle revived Holmes and Dr. Watson in the summer of

1891, shortly before Thomas Neill Cream's arrival in London, for a series of short stories published in the *Strand Magazine*. The wide audience and serialized approach made Holmes a sensation. The public's appetite for murder and detective stories, the crime fiction expert John Curran would note, became "almost insatiable." Newsstands and booksellers were besieged by readers eager to pay sixpence for the latest issue and the latest Holmes adventure. "The scenes at the railway bookstalls," one onlooker recalled, "were worse than anything I ever saw at a bargain sale." Libraries adjusted their hours to accommodate the growing legions of Holmes fans, staying open late on the third Thursday of the month, the *Strand*'s publication day, so patrons could devour the latest adventure. By one estimate, two million people—out of a literate population of about seventeen million in England at the time—were reading the *Strand*. Major newspapers across the United States republished each installment, earning the detective an American following.

Holmes was the perfect fictional hero for an era when unraveling mysteries became a guilty pleasure. Readers were "less interested in what crimes were committed," the British historian and literary critic Judith Flanders has noted, "than in how they were solved." Cream, who would soon take a keen interest in the work of London detectives, may have been among the many readers who caught "detective-fever" from the pages of *The Moonstone*, *Bleak House*, and Poe's stories—all were on the shelves of the Illinois State Penitentiary's library.

~~~~~

WHILE Dickens and Collins had portrayed Scotland Yard detectives as clever, even heroic figures, Conan Doyle's Lestrade helped perpetuate a new stereotype: the policeman as the bumbling fool. In story after story the detective overlooked clues, chased the wrong suspect, or appealed to Holmes—the self-proclaimed "last and highest court of appeal in detection"—for help in solving a baffling case. In one *Strand Magazine* offering, Holmes berates the inspector for allowing onlookers to tramp around the body of a murder victim "like a herd of buffalo," almost obliterating the killer's boot prints. Advertisements for the *Strand* stories, reinforcing the image that the "official police" were incompetent, touted Holmes's ability to solve cases that "defied the best talent of Scotland Yard—a 'talent' for which he had a considerable amount of contempt." Others heaped scorn on the police. In productions staged in London's music halls, officers were portrayed as villains or made the butt of jokes. The press was often hostile, especially if an investigation into a high-profile crime appeared to stall. Outraged editorials and angry letters to the editor demanded arrests and questioned the competence of the police. *Punch* ridiculed Scotland Yard's "Defective Department" while the *Pall Mall Gazette* questioned the intelligence of detectives and "muddled-headed" bobbies alike.

Scotland Yard detectives bristled when they read or heard the name Sherlock Holmes. Historians of the force record their resentment at being depicted as "inept bunglers with a chronic need for the help of a consulting detective," which gave the impression that "fools flourished at Scotland Yard." The *Police Review*, a pro-police trade journal weary of Conan Doyle's persistent "sarcasm at the expense of Scotland Yard," chided the author for "circulating mischievous popular fallacies" about the methods and competence of its detectives. Conan Doyle, for his part, seemed to realize the impact of his stories and, privately at least, defended the Yard's image. "My experience of British police," he once noted, "is that they are *much* more efficient than they seem."

The adventures of Holmes and Dr. Watson made detection look easy, like a genteel parlor game anyone could play. Catching criminals in the real world, however, required more than "the exercise of pure reason," a knack for spotting details, or "flashing deductions," grumbled Frederick Wensley, who joined the Metropolitan Police in the late 1880s as a constable in Lambeth and who rose to the rank of inspector. It took hard work, patience and resourcefulness to gather evidence and build a case that would stand up in court. "It is in getting *all* the facts," Wensley insisted, "that a detective proves himself."

◇◇◇◇◇

FICTION would soon collide with fact as a doctor from America returned to his old haunts in London. Thomas Neill Cream would become one of the era's greatest sensations and challenge the investigative skills of Scotland Yard's detectives. In "The Adventure of the Speckled Band," one of the Sherlock Holmes stories featured in the *Strand Magazine* in the winter of 1891–92, Dr. Grimesby Roylott trains a venomous yellow snake with brown spots (the "speckled band" of the title) to enter a locked room, kill his stepdaughter, and escape without leaving a trace. Only a medical man with knowledge of toxins and their deadly effects, Holmes believes, could plan and execute such a near-perfect crime. "When a doctor does go wrong he is the first of criminals," he tells Watson. "He has nerve and he has knowledge."

Holmes's observation that doctors who kill were "the first of criminals" was about to prove eerily prophetic.

3

ELLEN DONWORTH

{LONDON • OCTOBER 13, 1891}

SHE WAS LEANING AGAINST A WALL ON LAMBETH'S Waterloo Road, opposite the redbrick turret of the Wellington public house. A steady stream of people crossed in front of her, emerging from Waterloo Station or rushing in the opposite direction to catch a train. It was a wet, bone-chilling October night. Gales and heavy rain had battered London all day, ripping boats from their moorings along the Thames and uprooting trees in city parks. But Ellen Donworth seemed to take no notice of the weather. Men stopped, spoke to her, and then accompanied her to a house a few steps away on a side street. After fifteen minutes or so, she was back at her post.

James Styles was standing outside the pub at a quarter till eight when Donworth pitched forward onto the pavement. He ran to help. Her face was cut and bruised from the fall. A passing bobby stopped as well and asked if she needed medical attention. "I want to get home," she said. Styles walked her to her room at 8 Duke Street. She was in pain and staggered as they walked the third of a mile, past the tenement blocks lining Stamford Street. Her body trembled. Her face twitched.

The spasms continued after she was put to bed. Donworth's landlady and Annie Clements, a fellow lodger, came to her aid. Sometimes she was "perfectly sensible," Styles recalled. Sometimes it took the three of them to hold her arms and legs as her body shook and lurched.

"A tall, dark, cross-eyed man gave me something to drink," Donworth told Clements. The bottle contained "some white stuff."

John Johnson, a medical assistant summoned from a nearby clinic, thought he recognized the cause of the severe, intermittent convulsions. Strychnine poisoning. "She had all the symptoms of it," he recalled. She had to be taken to the hospital. Immediately. "Let me die at home," Donworth protested. She was bundled into a cab for the half-mile ride to St. Thomas'. By the time the carriage arrived, she was dead.

George Percival Wyatt, coroner for the counties of London and Surrey, convened an inquest at the hospital two days later, on October 15. A picture emerged of a short, hard life. Donworth was only nineteen, the jury was told, the daughter of a laborer. Pregnant at sixteen, she had left home to live with the child's father, Ernest Linnell, who was a teenager as well. The child died soon after it was born. Linnell worked odd jobs; Donworth was hired to paste labels onto bottles in one of Lambeth's factories. But by the fall of 1891 both had been unemployed for months.

What did they live on? Wyatt asked as Linnell told his story. "She used to walk the streets," he confessed, "and bring the money home." The revelation set off murmurs in the hearing room. Not only was Donworth a prostitute, one newspaper noted with disdain, but in addition Linnell had been living on "the proceeds of the girl's degradation."

An autopsy revealed no obvious cause of death. The inquest was adjourned to allow Dr. Thomas Kelloch, the house physician at St. Thomas', to test the contents of Donworth's stomach.

◇◇◇◇◇

L Division of the Metropolitan Police, which patrolled the Lambeth district, opened a file on the case on October 19. Officers questioned prostitutes who had seen Donworth enter the house near Waterloo Station with three men in the hour before she collapsed. All three looked like tradesmen, and none resembled Donworth's description of the man who gave her a drink. "Police have ascertained that she could not be in the company of a tall dark man," Chief Inspector Colin Chisholm noted, "from the time she left home until she was found in Waterloo Road."

THE HOUSES OF PARLIAMENT AND WESTMINSTER BRIDGE FROM THE LAMBETH SIDE OF THE THAMES. ST. THOMAS' HOSPITAL IS ON THE RIGHT. (AUTHOR COLLECTION)

When the inquest resumed on October 22, Dr. Kelloch confirmed she had been poisoned. His analysis of her stomach found strychnine and traces of morphine. A few more details emerged about the tall, cross-eyed man. Annie Clements said Donworth had received two letters from him, and he had arranged to meet her the night she died. The letters had disappeared—Clements believed the man had asked Donworth to return them. The writing on the envelopes was neat, she testified, "more like a lady's than a gentleman's."

Coroner Wyatt did not realize it yet, but he had seen the same handwriting a few days earlier. He had received a strange letter claiming Donworth had been murdered:

To G. P. Wyatt, Esq., Coroner,

I am writing to say that if you and your satellites fail to bring the murderer of Ellen Donworth, alias Ellen Linnell, late of 8, Duke Street, to justice, I am willing to give you such assistance as will bring the murderer to justice, provided your Government is willing to pay me £300,000 for my services; no pay unless successful.

It was signed A. O'Brien, Detective. Three hundred thousand pounds was a ludicrous figure—tens of millions of dollars in today's terms. Wyatt assumed the letter must be the work of a prankster. He filed it away and made no mention of it at the inquest.

With the testimony complete, the jurors agreed on a verdict. "Deceased died from strychnine and morphia poisoning," the foreman announced, "but how administered there was no evidence to show."

To Scotland Yard, there was only one possible explanation. "There is little doubt that she took the poison herself, knowingly," Chief Inspector Chisholm reported to his superiors. Donworth had been depressed since the death of her child, and resorting to a life of prostitution "no doubt preyed upon her mind." After the inquest Chisholm spoke with some of the jurors, who had reached the same conclusion—she had known she was dying, they reasoned, because she had taken poison to kill herself. There was no tall, cross-eyed man. Superintendent James Brannan of L Division agreed. "I do not think that there is the slightest evidence of foul play," he noted after reviewing Chisholm's report.

Robert Anderson, the assistant commissioner of the Metropolitan Police, reviewed the file at Scotland Yard headquarters and agreed. "Clearly," he noted, "a case of Suicide." But one question, he added, remained unanswered. How had Donworth managed to obtain strychnine, a poison sold only to physicians?

◇◇◇◇◇

WILLIAM Slater claimed he was joking. The forty-five-year-old jeweler took a woman he knew, Annie Bowden, for a drink at a pub near King's Cross Station, a couple of miles north of Lambeth. He ordered glasses of ale, then pulled a bottle from his pocket. It contained a whitish liquid.

"This is the poison I intend taking. It will kill fifty people," he declared. "Will you have some?" He pressed the opened bottle to his lips, then held it over Bowden's glass. Far from amused, she lodged a complaint with the police. Slater was charged with attempted murder.

Inspector George Harvey of L Division took notice. Just three days after Donworth's death was chalked up to suicide, a man had been arrested for trying to add a whitish liquid, possibly poison, to a woman's drink. Harvey reopened the case and attended Slater's arraignment on November 3, accompanied by witnesses who had seen the men Donworth was with on the night she died. One, Constance Linfield, picked Slater out of a police lineup. "That is the man," she said. "I think."

Slater was charged with murdering Ellen Donworth. "Supposed Capture of the Lambeth Poisoner," read one headline. But the case against him was weak. Another woman who had seen Donworth and her customers that night did not recognize Slater. On November 21, the prosecuting attorney asked magistrate Horace Smith to dismiss the murder charge. The allegation rested solely on Linfield's testimony—police had failed to find any other evidence linking Slater to Donworth. "There was too much doubt," the prosecutor conceded, "for it to be expected that a jury would find the prisoner guilty on the testimony of this woman." The charge of murdering Donworth was dismissed, but Slater was ordered to stand trial for the attempted murder of Annie Bowden, even though there was no evidence that the whitish liquid he had brandished at the King's Cross pub was poison. His lawyer insisted he was "merely guilty of foolish conduct." When a jury acquitted Slater a few weeks later, the presiding judge chastised the authorities for pursuing "a ridiculous prosecution."

Back in Lambeth, the police file on Ellen Donworth's death was once again closed.

4

MATILDA CLOVER

{LONDON • OCTOBER 21, 1891}

SCREAMS PIERCED THE NIGHTTIME STILLNESS, CLAWING their way into Lucy Rose's dreams. In an instant, she was awake. The screams were real, coming from the room above—Matilda Clover's room. Rose, a live-in maid, summoned landlady Emma Phillips from her room, and they rushed upstairs. Clover was lying across the foot of the bed, writhing, screaming, and "all of a twitch," as Rose later put it. Her brown eyes "rolled about terribly" and her long, dark brown hair was a tangled mass. Her body tensed and shook in violent spasms.

"That man Fred has poisoned me," Clover gasped after one of the fits subsided. "He gave me some pills." Taking four of the pills before going to bed, the man had told her, "would prevent me catching the disease"—a reference, no doubt, to venereal disease.

Rose stayed at her bedside, offering what comfort she could. The fits came in waves, subsiding for a short time until the next seizure gripped her body. "In her moments of relief," Rose said, "she was quite calm and collected." Clover had a two-year-old son. "Bring me my baby," she begged Rose at one point. "I think I am dying."

Phillips left to fetch a doctor. She unlocked the front door of 27 Lambeth Road, shielded herself against the heavy rain, and hurried through darkened, odd-angled streets. By the time she rapped on the door of the home of Robert Graham, Clover's doctor, it was half past four. He was out, she was told, attending to a patient. When she returned two hours later, she caught Graham as he was leaving on another call, this time to assist a woman in labor.

"You had better call in another medical man," he said. "I cannot come." A doctor's assistant, Francis Coppin, finally agreed to make a house call. It was now about seven o'clock. Clover had been writhing in pain for more than three hours.

Coppin was ushered into the bedroom. "She had a quick pulse, and was bathed in perspiration, and trembling," he recalled. He stayed only ten minutes or so, long enough to witness one of the convulsions—a violent "twitching of the body." He promised to send medicine to stop her frequent vomiting.

"I concluded that she was suffering from epileptic fits, convulsions, due to alcoholic poisoning," Coppin explained later. Working as a medical assistant in Lambeth for more than a dozen years had given him "a good deal of experience of drink in its various forms," he added. "I had no doubt that this woman was suffering from excessive drink."

He was certain of something else. She did not have long to live. The convulsions and torment continued for another two hours. Clover died at fifteen minutes past nine. It was the morning of October 21, 1891.

∞∞∞

DR. GRAHAM arrived at midday. He had been treating Clover for symptoms of alcoholism, and she had been to see him several times that month. She was only twenty-seven but "not a strong woman by any means," he noted, "and her mode of life was not conducive to her health." He huddled with Coppin, who had returned, and

Phillips, the landlady. Coppin described Clover's fit during his brief examination and offered his opinion: death from alcohol poisoning. Clover had been drunk when she went to bed, Phillips added, having downed a bottle of brandy. Rose, the servant, told Phillips and Coppin that Clover had claimed to have taken some pills, but they did not seem to believe her.

Dr. Graham found a pen and drafted a death certificate. "I attended Matilda Clover during her last illness," he wrote. This, of course, was untrue. "To the best of my knowledge and belief," he added, "the cause of her death was, primarily, delirium tremens, secondly, syncope"—loss of consciousness and heart failure due to severe symptoms of alcohol withdrawal, even though he had been told she was drinking heavily the night she died. His conclusions, based on secondhand information, were incorrect. An opportunity to detect and stop a murderer had been squandered.

"I was not told," Dr. Graham would later protest, "that this last illness commenced with screaming, great agony, twitching, tetanic spasms." These tetanus-like convulsions were tell-tale signs of strychnine poisoning. Even the growing legion of Sherlock Holmes fans could recognize them, thanks to the medical expertise of Arthur Conan Doyle. In the second Holmes novel, *The Sign of the Four*, a body is found with the limbs "twisted and turned in the most fantastic fashion" and the face frozen in "a horrible smile, a fixed and unnatural grin." The victim was poisoned, Dr. Watson informs Holmes, with a "powerful vegetable alkaloid, some strychnine-like substance."

Dr. Graham had spoken briefly to Lucy Rose, but he put little stock in the young maid's description of the dying woman's statements about a man distributing poisoned pills. If he had asked, Rose would have told him something else that was important: she suspected that the man Clover called Fred had been to the house only hours before her suffering began.

Clover had brought him to the house about midevening, Rose would tell the police months later. She had let them in and had a chance to size up the man in the light of an oil lamp burning in the hallway. He was fortyish, tall and broad, with a bushy mustache. He wore a top hat and an overcoat with a cape. Clover had left him in the rooms she rented upstairs while she ducked out to buy two bottles of Bass ale, likely at the Masons' Arms pub, a few doors down. The man left sometime before ten o'clock. "Good-night," Rose heard Clover say as she let him out.

MATILDA CLOVER (*PENNY ILLUSTRATED PAPER*, OCTOBER 22, 1892)

Although Rose had never seen the man before that evening, there was nothing strange about his visit. "Clover," she allowed, "was in the habit of bringing men to 27." Addicted to alcohol and struggling to raise a child alone, she earned her living as a prostitute. Heavy drinking had aged and hardened her features, and smallpox had pitted her face, but Clover knew how to present herself. When she sat for a photographer, a flat-brimmed hat balanced like a dinner plate on her pinned-up hair, and a fashionable, high-collared jacket, with leg o' mutton sleeves and a tight bodice, flattered her five-foot-one hourglass figure. Phillips was aware how her tenant earned the rent money but considered it none of her business. "She used to receive gentlemen," she said, then further claimed she herself never saw or met them.

Rose only rarely encountered the men Clover brought home. But, as she would later reveal, she knew a lot about her last caller. Clover had told her that Fred had bought her an expensive pair of boots and offered to pay her two and a half pounds a week to keep her off the streets for the winter. And earlier that day, as she tended to Clover's child, Rose had seen a letter lying open in her room, arranging a meeting that evening at the Canterbury Music Hall. It was signed "Yours, Fred." Clover must have taken it to the meeting—when Rose searched the room after her death, it was gone.

Two other Lambeth prostitutes also knew the man in the top hat and overcoat. Elizabeth Masters and Elizabeth May lived around the corner from Clover in the Orient Buildings, a block of apartments on Hercules Road. A few days before Clover's death, Masters had met him at Ludgate Circus, a busy intersection near St. Paul's Cathedral. He had bought her a glass of wine at the King Lud pub, which faced the roundabout, and she had taken him back to Lambeth, to her three-room flat. Afterward, they went to Gatti's Music Hall, a short walk away on Westminster Bridge Road, where Masters had arranged to meet her friend, Elizabeth May. "I noticed a peculiar look in his eyes," Masters said. "He had a squint."

The man sent Masters a letter a few days later, arranging a time for them to meet again. When the day came, Masters and May sat at their second-floor windows and scanned Hercules Road, waiting for him to arrive. A woman they had seen in the neighborhood passed by, carrying a basket and wearing a white apron over her gray dress. It was Matilda Clover, likely coming from the market. They saw her turn and smile at a man in a top hat who was walking behind her. It was the man they were waiting for, but he continued along the street. Masters and May grabbed their hats and followed them to the corner. Clover entered no. 27 Lambeth Road, with the man close behind.

CREAM TOOK A LAMBETH PROSTITUTE, ELIZABETH MASTERS, TO THE KING LUD PUB AT LUDGATE CIRCUS. (SCIENCE AND SOCIETY PICTURE LIBRARY, LONDON, IMAGE 10436065)

◇◇◇◇

CLOVER was buried on October 27, six days after her sudden death. The parish council paid for her burial in Tooting Cemetery, six miles southwest of Lambeth. The lid of her coffin bore a metal plate, inscribed "M. Clover, 27 years." Fourteen other caskets were stacked above hers in "Grave No 2215H." Her short life and agonizing death were soon forgotten. One London newspaper would later dismiss her as "a miserable street outcast, whose life was of no particular value to anybody."

Dr. Graham's certificate attributing Clover's death to heart failure and not foul play made it unnecessary to notify the local coroner or the police. There would be no inquest. For now, Lucy Rose told no one about Clover's last visitor. Elizabeth Masters and Elizabeth May heard talk in the neighborhood that Clover had died not long after they saw her on the street. But they gave no more thought to the man who had stood them up and followed her into her lodgings.

5

"A HUMAN 'WERE-WOLF'"

L ONDON'S NIGHTMARE HAD BEGUN ON THE LAST DAY OF
August 1888, when the body of Mary Ann Nichols was found
on a street in the Whitechapel district of the East End. An
assailant armed with a large knife had slit her throat and slashed her
abdomen. Annie Chapman was next, found a week later in a backyard with her throat cut and similar wounds to her body. Three weeks
would pass before two more women, Elisabeth Stride and Catherine
Eddowes, were slaughtered on the same night and this time, the murderer horribly mutilated Eddowes's body.

Terror gripped one of the city's poorest neighborhoods.
"Whitechapel," the panicked *Observer* reported, "is at this moment
virtually at the mercy of a human 'were-wolf.'" Days before the murders of Stride and Eddowes, a London news agency received a letter written in red ink, addressed "Dear Boss." The writer taunted
Scotland Yard and added a warning: "I am down on whores and I shant
quit ripping them." It was signed Jack the Ripper. The Whitechapel
murderer—the police and the public alike assumed the killings must
be the work of a single assailant—had a name. The Ripper, the
London press was quick to point out, was targeting "women of the
unfortunate class" who lived "immoral" or "intemperate, irregular and

OXFORD COUNTY LIBRARY

vicious" lives. All were poor and struggling to make a living, but the British social historian Hallie Rubenhold has made a compelling case that contrary to popular belief then and now, not all were prostitutes: three of the five victims, she concluded, had no involvement in the sex trade. Every woman in Whitechapel, one resident told the press in October 1888, was living in fear. "Many are actually afraid to venture a dozen yards from the door after dark without an escort."

A massive police operation was launched to stop the bloodshed. Scotland Yard had dozens of detectives working fourteen-hour days to identify the killer. Locations where the bodies had been found were cordoned off to preserve evidence—a novel practice at the time— and some of the earliest crime scene photographs were taken. The police, like the press, assumed each victim must be a prostitute, leading one Scotland Yard commander to complain about the difficulty of protecting women who made themselves easy targets. "The victims, without exception, belonged to the lowest dregs of female humanity," said Melville Macnaghten, "who avoid the police and exercise every ingenuity in order to remain in the darkest corners of the most deserted alleys."

Fear and frustration turned to anger. *Punch* published a cartoon depicting a blindfolded bobby stumbling through Whitechapel, oblivious to the shady characters in his midst. The *Times of London* printed a letter defending the police, but it offered little comfort to Londoners who feared for their lives. Scotland Yard was struggling to find the Ripper, the author contended, because they were up against "a consummate master of his art" who was too clever to leave behind clues. Attacks in the American press were scathing. The Ripper was free to kill again and again thanks to "ignorance of the elementary methods of detection," huffed the *New-York Tribune*. Thomas Byrnes, chief of the detective bureau of the New York police, bragged that he could arrest the culprit within forty-eight hours. His plan? Recruit fifty women, send them into the streets, and wait for the murderer to strike again. "Even if one fell a victim," he reasoned, without the slightest concern for the safety of the women used as bait, "I should get the murderer."

More than a month after the double murder of Stride and Eddowes, the killer struck again. The attack was the most horrific and vicious of the five. Mary Jane Kelly was found in her room, her head nearly severed and her body slashed and disemboweled. Then, ten weeks after it began, the rampage ended. Police arrested or questioned scores of suspects, from an unstable character known as Leather Apron to anyone who fit descriptions of men last seen with the women, but no one was ever charged.

◇◇◇◇◇

WHY was Scotland Yard unable to catch the madman who terrorized Whitechapel? A killer's identity tended to be obvious: a spouse, a jilted lover, a relative, someone the victim had known and trusted. And the motive could be just as transparent. Greed. Jealousy. Hatred. Revenge. "All our methods for the detection of murder are based upon certain tacit assumptions," the *Times of London* observed a few weeks after the last Ripper murder, as panic and outrage subsided. Among these was a belief that "murders will not be committed without some motive." While the senseless, "wholly abnormal" Whitechapel killings had shaken public confidence in Scotland Yard, the failure to arrest the murderer, the paper argued, should not reflect on the skill and competence of the city's detectives. "From time to time crimes will be carried out with unusual skill and daring, aided by extraordinary good fortune, and will baffle our best detective arrangements."

The Metropolitan Police offered its recruits—its future detectives—little formal training. "A young policeman was given a few weeks' drill and then flung on a beat to pick up the elements of his trade as he might," Frederick Wensley, the inspector who started his career in Lambeth, recalled. To understand criminals and their methods, he frequented the pubs and dives where crooks gathered. He drank with them, ate with them, gained their trust, cultivated informants. "A detective must be a student of human nature," agreed William Gough, who joined the force in the 1890s and rose to the rank of inspector, "and the more understanding he has of it the higher he is likely to rise in his profession." One rite of passage was a visit to the Black Museum at headquarters, a room where weapons and other evidence from notorious cases were displayed to give recruits insights into the criminal mind. Officers compiled detailed, hand-written records of their investigations, but storage was sometimes haphazard—before the move to the new building overlooking the Thames in 1890, recalled one detective, files of unsolved cases were squirreled away "on landings and in odd cupboards." The Yard's Convict Office kept photographs of past offenders, but many detectives preferred to rely on memory and written descriptions when looking for suspects.

Late nineteenth-century detectives relied on crime-solving skills that demanded time and patience: shadowing and surveillance. Suspicious characters were followed to find out if they associated with known criminals. If a detective was patient and lucky, he might catch a burglar breaking into a house or a thief selling stolen goods. Officers worked in groups of three or more, with each man rotating in and out of view. "The average criminal is constantly on the alert, and the same figure continuously within sight, and approximately the same distance from him, would soon arouse his suspicions," explained Gough. "The shadowers are ever changing their positions, first one and then another taking the lead." Patience and endurance were also needed to stake out a street or building, in the hope that a suspect or accomplice would turn up. Officers stayed in position hour after hour, oblivious to cold, hunger, and danger. Wensley once holed up in a basement crawling with rats to catch a gang of burglars, and he watched other crooks from a railway viaduct as trains whizzed past, missing him by inches.

Sometimes more than hard work and patience was needed to crack a case. An investigation might hinge on a witness who was in the right place at the right time, an item dropped at a crime scene, or a boast overheard in a pub. "The two finest detectives," one of Gough's colleagues joked, "are 'Inspector Luck' and 'Sergeant Chance.'"

George Dilnot, a journalist and crime writer and himself a former policeman, understood the challenge of catching a killer who operated at random and acted without motive. "When a murderer steps outside the rules of logic he becomes troublesome to the detective. The whole sequence of cause and effect is destroyed," he noted in an early study of investigative methods. "The detective is faced with illimitable possibilities and no probabilities. Nothing means anything."

In the winter of 1891–92, three years after Jack the Ripper's rampage, London was once again under siege by a killer who targeted vulnerable women, a monster whose crimes defied logic.

II

THE LAMBETH POISONER

London, Quebec City, and New York State • 1891–1892

6

LOUISA HARVEY

{LONDON • LATE OCTOBER 1891}

A WOMAN IN HER MIDTWENTIES WAITED BENEATH THE Gothic facade of St. James's Hall on Regent Street, just off Piccadilly Circus, as arranged. Neatly trimmed brows arched above her large, lively eyes, and brown hair framed her delicate face. Light from gas streetlamps danced and glistened on the wet pavement, scrubbed clean by days of heavy rain. Inside the hall, theatergoers marveled at an attraction as impressive as anything on stage: "Now Illuminated Throughout," noted an advertisement, "with the Electric Light." St. James's featured the "World-Famed" Moore and Burgess Minstrels three nights a week, but the woman took no interest in the playbill on this damp October night. She was working.

A man in a black overcoat, a top hat perched on his bald head, touched the woman on the shoulder. A mustache softened the sharp features of his thin face, but what stood out were his eyes, steel gray and magnified by the thick lenses of his spectacles: they were crossed. No one would have described the man as handsome, but the woman had spotted the glint of a gold watch. And the top hat was the mark of a gentleman, a symbol of wealth and privilege—most men favored the less formal bowler, even for a night out at the theater. This was a man of means. The best kind of customer.

She had met him at the nearby Alhambra Theatre of Varieties in Leicester Square, a massive Moorish-themed hall complete with minarets that could pack more than four thousand into its galleries, standing-room sections, and bars. It was renowned as a venue for music, dance, and comedy routines—"High Class Variety Entertainment," in the words of a guide to the city's nightlife—and featured a house orchestra and a roster of 250 performers. Many of the men in the audience, however, were not there for the shows. Scantily clad dancers returned backstage to find notes from admirers in the box seats, some making what were politely called "improper proposals." Prostitutes circulated in the crowd and scanned the seats—"brazen-faced women, blazoned in tawdry finery, and curled and painted . . . enticing simpletons to drink," noted one patron who remained immune to their advances. The Alhambra's manager reckoned as many as one hundred "women of the town," as he called them, were in attendance on most nights. As long as they were clean, well dressed, and discreet—like the woman who had arranged the rendezvous on Regent Street—their presence was tolerated.

The woman and the man in the top hat walked a half-dozen blocks to the Paris Hotel on Berwick Street in Soho, a seedy enclave on the edge of the West End theater district.

He said he was a doctor at St. Thomas', across the river in Lambeth. This was not quite true—he was a medical man, but he had no affiliation with the hospital.

What was her name?

Lou Harvey, she said. It was short for Louisa. She told him she was a servant, but they both knew this was a lie.

Thomas Neill Cream did not offer his name, and she never asked. She did not need to know.

In the morning, before they left the Paris Hotel, Cream handed her three pounds, more than some prostitutes earned in a week. She had been right—he was a man of means. He suggested, apparently in jest, that she should move to America to live with him. They arranged to meet again later that day. Half past seven on the Thames Embankment, near the Charing Cross railway station. He would take her to a show. Her choice. She picked the Oxford Music Hall on Tottenham Court Road, one of the best and most popular in the city.

LOUISA HARVEY (PENNY ILLUSTRATED PAPER, JULY 16, 1892)

As they parted, he made a strange remark.

"He said I had a few spots on my forehead," Harvey would recall. "He said he would bring me some pills to take them away."

He was waiting for her when she reached the riverside that evening. They walked to the nearby Northumberland Arms public house for a glass of wine. When a woman selling flowers passed by, he bought her some roses. They strolled back to the river's edge, lined with hissing gas lamps that cast an eerie glow over the Embankment. He reached into a pocket of his waistcoat and pulled out a wad of tissue paper. Inside were two oblong light-colored pills.

"Don't bite them," he told her. "Swallow them as they are."

He pressed them into the palm of her right hand. She lifted her hand to her mouth and seemed to swallow the pills, but he wanted to be sure.

Show me your hand, he said. She did. It was empty.

He asked to see her left hand. It, too, was empty.

There was a change of plans, he announced. He had an appointment at the hospital, but she should go to the music hall on her own. He would meet her outside, and they would go back to the Paris Hotel for the night. He gave her five shillings for cab fare.

"Meet me at eleven," Cream said as he turned and walked toward Westminster Bridge in the direction of the hospital. "Good-bye for the present."

Harvey had not taken the pills. "Not liking the look of the thing," she would recall, "I pretended to put them in my mouth." In the flickering gaslight, the doctor had not noticed as she passed them from one hand to the other. When he looked away for a moment, she dropped them over the edge of the Embankment.

Harvey was wary of her generous new customer. Before heading to the Thames Embankment that evening, she had asked the man she lived with to follow her to the meeting with the doctor. Charles Harvey—she used his surname, even though they were not married—had been in the next booth as she drank wine with Cream at the Northumberland public house. He had followed them to the riverside and watched from the shadows as the doctor handed her the pills.

Hours later, at eleven o'clock, as arranged, Harvey emerged from the Oxford Music Hall. Cream was not there. She waited for half an hour, but he never showed up.

Strange, she must have thought. It was as if he had never expected her to keep their appointment.

7

BLACKMAIL

{October–December 1891}

CREAM HAD BEEN IN LONDON FOR BARELY TWO WEEKS when he poisoned Ellen Donworth and left her for dead on the sidewalk outside Waterloo Station on October 13. Matilda Clover's room on Lambeth Road, where he gave her pills on the evening of October 20, was about ten minutes' walk from his lodgings at 103 Lambeth Palace Road. A few nights later he had met Louisa Harvey at the Alhambra Theatre. He had insisted she take the pills in his presence, perhaps for the thrill of seeing with his own eyes how quickly he had earned her trust, how easy it was to kill. He had seen her swallow the pills, he was sure of that—and he was just as certain she must be dead. While there had been no mention of her death in the newspapers, there had been no press coverage of Clover's either. Both deaths, he must have assumed, had been attributed to natural causes.

Only the Donworth poisoning had attracted the attention of the authorities and the press. Cream had fired off the mischievous "Detective O'Brien" letter to George Percival Wyatt, the coroner investigating her death, offering to help identify her killer for the ridiculous sum of three hundred thousand pounds. When he learned in early November that William Slater had been charged with her murder—*his* murder—an audacious plan began to form in his warped mind. Why not accuse others of killing his victims? He could threaten to publicly accuse wealthy, prominent men of murdering prostitutes, and they would pay handsomely for his silence. If they ignored his demands, he would alert the authorities. Cream, like a puppet master, could watch with amusement as Scotland Yard's detectives rushed to accuse and arrest more innocent men.

Cream put away his strychnine and his capsules. He picked up a pen.

◇◇◇◇

ON November 6, a letter was delivered to the offices of W. H. Smith & Son, Britain's leading bookseller and news distributor. It was addressed to the firm's owner, William Frederick Danvers Smith, a member of Parliament who was known as Frederick Smith. The writer, one H. Bayne, claimed that letters incriminating Smith had been found among Ellen Donworth's effects. "If they ever become public property" or wind up in the hands of the police, they "will surely convict you," Bayne warned. "Think of the shame and disgrace it will bring on your family if you are arrested and put in prison for this crime." The writer offered a solution: if Smith retained him as a legal adviser, Bayne would shield Smith "from all exposure and shame in the matter." Enclosed was a copy of a letter purportedly sent to Donworth before her death, warning her that Frederick Smith was planning to poison her with medicine that was supposed to produce an abortion. There was enough strychnine in the medicine "to kill a horse," this second letter warned. It was in a postmarked envelope addressed to Donworth, making it appear genuine.

Smith was told to post a notice on the window of the W. H. Smith office on the Strand, stating: "Mr. Fred Smith wishes to see Mr. Bayne, the barrister, at once." If the notice appeared, the writer said he would drop by for a private interview with Smith. One of Smith's partners, Alfred Acland, consulted the company's lawyers, who notified the police. A trap was set for the blackmailer. The requested notice was posted at the W. H. Smith office, agreeing to the meeting. Officers kept watch, but no one showed up to see Smith.

FREDERICK SMITH WAS AMONG THE TARGETS OF CREAM'S BLACKMAIL CAMPAIGN. CREAM CLAIMED HE HAD PROOF THAT THE OWNER OF BOOKSELLER W. H. SMITH HAD MURDERED ELLEN DONWORTH. (*ENGLISH ILLUSTRATED MAGAZINE*, AUGUST 1892 / AUTHOR COLLECTION)

Cream decided, instead, to follow through on his threat to alert the authorities. In mid-November, the magistrate presiding over the Slater case, Horace Smith (no relation to the bookselling Smiths), received a letter from someone who identified himself as Campbell. "Slater, the man you have repeatedly remanded," the writer asserted, "is absolutely innocent"—Donworth's killer was Frederick Smith. The writer warned the magistrate not to suppress the sensational allegation. "I have evidence enough to hang Smith," the writer added, "and I will make it hot for the police if they do not do their duty in this matter." A copy of the letter to Donworth, warning her of Frederick Smith's plan to poison her, was enclosed.

Magistrate Smith showed the letters to Inspector Frank Thorpe of E Division of the Metropolitan Police, the division responsible for the King's Cross area. But Thorpe, who was unaware of the blackmail letter sent directly to Frederick Smith, saw no need to investigate. He did not alert the officers in Lambeth who had investigated Donworth's death either. The magistrate tucked the letters into a file.

Cream's next target was the eminent London cardiologist and neurologist William Broadbent, who received a letter dated November 28, accusing him of poisoning another Lambeth prostitute, Matilda Clover. The writer, who identified himself as M. Malone, knew where she had lived—27 Lambeth Road—and the poison used, strychnine. Evidence implicating Dr. Broadbent had been found in Clover's effects, Malone claimed, and would be handed over to the police unless he was paid twenty-five hundred pounds. "I am not humbugging you," Cream warned. "You know well enough that an accusation of that sort will ruin you for ever." If Dr. Broadbent wanted to suppress this evidence, he was instructed to place a notice on the front page of the *Daily Chronicle* offering to pay Malone "for his services." Dr. Broadbent contacted Scotland Yard, and another trap was set. The advertisement was inserted in the paper's classified columns on December 4, and officers staked out the Broadbent home, 34 Seymour Street in Marylebone. When no one showed up to collect the money, no further action was taken.

About the same time, Countess Mabel Russell received a letter addressed to her at the Savoy Hotel, where she was staying. The countess, an actress and singer, was in the midst of an acrimonious divorce from Earl Russell, the grandson of a former British prime minister. The writer claimed to be "in a position to obtain Lady R's divorce" with information that "would hang her husband as he had poisoned a woman named Clover." The countess showed the letter to her lawyer and was intrigued enough to send her coachman, George Rich, to make inquiries. The letter, however, said Clover had lived at 27 South Lambeth Road, and no one at that address had heard of her. Rich showed the letter to a detective at Scotland Yard, who displayed little interest. Apparently unaware of a similar allegation against Dr. Broadbent, the officer read it over, handed it back, and sent Rich on his way. "We treated the matter as unimportant," Rich would recall.

COUNTESS MABEL RUSSELL,
AN ACTRESS AND SINGER,
RECEIVED A LETTER ACCUSING
HER ESTRANGED HUSBAND OF
POISONING MATILDA CLOVER.
(*SKETCH*, MARCH 8, 1899 /
AUTHOR COLLECTION)

Why did Cream target Broadbent, Smith, and Russell in his extraordinary campaign of attempted blackmail? It was likely because all three were in the news in the fall of 1891. When Frederick Smith's father died that October, the twenty-three-year-old had succeeded him as member of Parliament for the Strand and as the head of W. H. Smith, perhaps the most recognizable corporate name in the country. "A business known," a company biographer would note, "wherever newspapers, books, journals or magazines were bought, sold, lent, or borrowed in late-Victorian Britain." Dr. Broadbent, a physician to Queen Victoria and the royal family, was treating Prince George of Wales, third in line to the throne and the future King George V, who had been stricken with typhoid fever. The doctor's name appeared in the newspapers on a daily basis during November 1891 as he updated the prince's condition. The Russell divorce case, with its shocking allegations of cruelty, was making headlines in the days before the countess received her letter.

In class-conscious Britain, aristocrats like Earl Russell, politicians like Frederick Smith, and professionals like Dr. William Broadbent were expected to set an example for others. The allegations in Cream's letters, as false and outlandish as they were, could forever taint their reputations. "To accuse a man of a number of disgraceful offenses throws a certain stigma upon him even if he is innocent," one newspaper noted in an exposé of blackmail in London. "A man often hesitates to come forward and charge some lying rascal." Smith would have been well aware of the "shame and disgrace" his illustrious family would endure if he were publicly accused of murdering a prostitute; Dr. Broadbent would have known that such an accusation, leveled at a doctor who cared for members of the royal family, would indeed ruin his career. It's remarkable that both men had the courage to bring the letters and the bogus allegations to the attention of Scotland Yard.

Cream, however, had made a mistake—a mistake that could expose him as a murderer if someone at Scotland Yard made a connection between the deaths of Clover and Donworth. In accusing others of his crimes, he had revealed details that tied him to both poisonings. Details that only the killer could know. But the officers of L Division in Lambeth were unaware of the letters that had prompted their colleagues in other parts of London to set traps for a mysterious blackmailer. The Metropolitan Police made no inquiries to find out if there was any truth to the allegations that a Lambeth woman named Matilda Clover had been poisoned in October, as the letters to Dr. Broadbent and Countess Russell claimed. For now, no one suspected she had been murdered, let alone poisoned, like Ellen Donworth, with strychnine.

⬦⬦⬦⬦⬦

ONE evening that fall, as Louisa Harvey scanned the faces of men as they walked past her in central London, she spotted Cream. It was a few weeks after their first meetings, when she had pretended to take the pills he offered to clear up her complexion. He was standing near the Regent Street entrance to Piccadilly Circus, the site of their original rendezvous. He treated her to a glass of wine at a nearby public house on Air Street. They arranged to meet again later that night. To her surprise, he seemed unaware of who she was.

"Don't you know me?" Harvey asked as they were leaving.

"No; who are you?" Cream's mind was so clouded by drug use or he had been with so many prostitutes that he failed to recognize her.

"You promised to meet me outside the Oxford Music-hall."

"I don't remember; who are you?"

"Lou Harvey."

Cream said nothing but spun around and briskly walked away. He had just seen a ghost.

◇◇◇◇◇

THAT November, Cream met Laura Sabbatini, a young woman with olive-toned skin and dark hair and eyes. She was from Berkhamsted, a town of a few thousand in the Chiltern Hills, about twenty-five miles northwest of the city, and was staying in London to learn the dressmaking trade. Cream curbed his appetite for prostitutes long enough to court her, and he proposed within a few weeks. "I shall be as faithful, loyal, constant, and true to you," he vowed, "as God ever made a man." He was twenty years her senior, but she accepted. Sabbatini knew he had been a doctor in America but little else about his past. She was aware of his opium use—he claimed he needed the narcotic to relieve his headaches, and sometimes he would pop into a drugstore to purchase some when they were out for a walk. Her mother consented to the engagement after Cream wrote her a letter, promising he would be a devoted husband and assuring her he was "free of all vicious habits." Later, when he visited Berkhamsted for the weekend and met Sabbatini's mother in person, Cream made a point of accompanying his fiancée to a service at her family's church.

The people who knew him in Quebec City, meanwhile, were receiving disturbing reports about his behavior. George Mathews, a Presbyterian minister in London who knew the family, warned Daniel Cream that his brother should be "placed under restraint" and was not "in a fit state to be at large." Thomas Davidson, the close friend of their father, conceded that sending Thomas to London had been a mistake. "He seems to have been so much weaker mentally than we supposed," Davidson noted later, and "utterly unable to resist it he fell a ready victim to the stream of vice always flowing in the Metropolis." Cream was broke—it had taken him less than two months to squander the money from his father's estate—and he seemed incapable of managing his own affairs. Davidson asked Mathews to give him fifteen pounds for a ticket back to Canada. "His friends here wish him to return at once to Quebec and remain with his brother Dan until a satisfactory change has taken place."

Cream agreed to return home in early January. He had little choice—he may have resorted to trying to blackmail prominent Londoners because he was so short of cash. He told Sabbatini he had to return to Canada to settle some matters arising from his father's estate. He asked her to write to him while he was away, at his brother Daniel's address. Two days before Christmas he drafted a new will, leaving what little property he had to his fiancée.

8

"A Bad Man
with No Refinement"

{Quebec City and New York State •
January–March 1892}

For William Sellar, it was the crossing from hell. The Montreal-based salesman booked a stateroom on SS *Sarnia* for the return trip to Canada early in the New Year. His door faced cabin no. 19, and soon after the Dominion Line steamer cleared Liverpool, just one week into the new year, he was on speaking terms with his neighbor. The man introduced himself as a doctor who had practiced in Chicago and London.

"He was very restless and excitable," Sellar recalled. And a heavy drinker. When Sellar suggested he go easy on the alcohol, Cream said he had taken opium for years but had quit. Without it, he needed liquor "to quiet his nerves." He talked incessantly about women—how he met them on London's streets and in the theaters, took them to dinner at restaurants, slept with them. He was "a bad man with no refinement," in Sellar's opinion, "and an utter absence of morality."

He was also a pest. Cream woke up Sellar at odd hours of the night, armed with a bottle of whisky and asking to come in for a drink. He could not sleep, he said, and wanted someone to talk to. Sellar opened his door and dared not turn down the requests. The man was volatile, easily annoyed, and "not quite right in his mind." He endured hour after hour of Cream's "lewd talk," to humor him. "He might be a dangerous man," Sellar feared, "if crossed."

CREAM IN A PHOTOGRAPH TAKEN ABOUT THE TIME OF HIS RETURN TO QUEBEC CITY IN 1892 (SCIENCE AND SOCIETY PICTURE LIBRARY, LONDON, IMAGE 10658278)

Other passengers had vivid memories of Cream's behavior during the voyage. He "acted in every way as a gentleman" during the first days of the voyage, said Robert Caswell, a prison chaplain from Toronto. Then he started drinking, and there were whispers he was taking morphine. "When in this condition," Caswell recalled, "he talked a great deal about the number of women he had been intimate with in his life and occasionally spoke in disparaging terms of women generally." At mealtimes he was seated at the same table as Lieutenant Colonel Leon Vohl, a former militia officer in his midfifties. "He constantly spoke about women," Vohl recalled. "He said he used to have as many women as he wished in London." Cream told Vohl he took morphine "but was giving it up" and had undertaken "a special study" of poisons. On another occasion, he casually mentioned that he had performed abortions on several women. The admissions were startling, given Vohl's job title—he had been Quebec City's chief of police for more than a decade. And John Cantle, a salesman for a Canadian oil company, remembered Cream mentioning he had information relating to a murder—something about "a woman who had been poisoned in London." None of Cream's new acquaintances took him seriously. They chalked up his boasts and erratic behavior to drink and drugs.

At one point during the voyage, Sellar recalled months later, he mentioned he was feeling unwell. Cream offered to give him a pill. Sellar declined.

∞∞∞∞

CREAM arrived in Quebec City on January 20, 1892, a day thermometers flirted with twenty below, and checked into Blanchard's Hotel. Staying with his brother was no longer an option. Daniel Cream's wife, Jessie Read, refused to allow him into their home.

One day he invited a fellow guest, salesman John McCulloch, to his room. Cream unlocked a yellow japanned trunk and produced a cashbox sized tin. Inside was a small bottle partly filled with whitish crystals the size of pinheads.

"It is poison," Cream announced.

"For God's sake," McCulloch spat out, "what do you do with that?"

"I give it to women to get them out of the family way," Cream said, then opened a bureau drawer, exposing an array of identical medicine bottles and a small cardboard box. Inside were about twenty empty gelatin capsules, each about a half inch long. "I give it to them in these." Then he reached into the yellow trunk and pulled out a fake beard, neatly parted at the chin.

"What do you use these for?" McCulloch asked when he saw the whiskers.

"To disguise my identity" when operating on women, Cream explained, "so that they would not recognize me again."

⬦⬦⬦

BLANCHARD's Hotel was in the heart of Quebec City's historical quarter, its name painted in block letters across a pair of gray-stone buildings with high-pitched roofs. It was rated as a second-class hotel, and the rooms were cheap. It was likely the best Cream could afford. He had told Chief of Police Vohl and other *Sarnia* passengers that he was coming to Quebec to collect funds from his father's estate. He would then return to England, he explained, and marry Laura Sabbatini. He produced her photograph to convince them—and, perhaps, himself—that he had a fiancée. Securing more money proved easy. Within days of his arrival, he visited William Brown of the Bank of Quebec, one of his father's executors, and came away with fourteen hundred dollars in bank shares and cash (a total of thirty thousand dollars in today's US currency). But there would be no more. "As matters now stand," as far as Brown was concerned, "he has received more than his share of the estate."

He stayed at Blanchard's for two months. Daniel Cream dropped by for occasional visits, and Cream exchanged letters with Sabbatini. McCulloch, who sold spices and coffees for the Pure Gold Manufacturing Company of Toronto, checked in for eight days, and despite Cream's disturbing claims to have poisoned women and performed abortions, they remained on good terms. One Sunday evening, they toured the city by sleigh, and Cream pointed out houses where his relatives lived and a shipyard where he had worked in his youth. Cream was drinking heavily and taking morphine—on one occasion, McCulloch found him "in a perfect stupor." And he continued to brag about his conquests. He showed McCulloch porno-graphic images and said he had "lots of fun in London," paying no more than a shilling for a prostitute and claiming he hired as many as three a night.

Then a man who could supply him with drugs and poisons walked through the hotel's front door. Martin Kingman, a salesman for the G. F. Harvey Company, a drug manufacturer in Saratoga Springs, New York, stayed at Blanchard's when he was in town. Kingman did not think much of Cream—"a loose sort of man," he thought, "con-stantly talking about women and fond of reading smutty books"—but took his order for an array of deadly narcotics and poisons, including strychnine, morphine, and opium. The drugs were delivered to him at Blanchard's. Cream soon wrote to the company, apparently pre-senting himself as a licensed doctor and offering to become its agent in England. He ordered a rectangular brown-leather carrying case for holding sample bottles of Harvey's products, which he claimed he would use to drum up sales to doctors and hospitals in London. He told McCulloch and his brother about his plans. "He expected to make a fortune out of it," McCulloch recalled.

∞∞∞∞∞

MATILDA Nadeau exchanged a word or two with Cream whenever they met at Blanchard's. He made a point of speaking to all the maids at the hotel. One day in mid-March, he told the twenty-two-year-old she needed medication and offered her two dark-colored pills.

"Take one at tea time," he said, "and be sure and take the other as you go to bed."

She took one pill and felt a burning pain in her stomach. Purple blotches erupted on her face. Her hands clenched uncontrollably. She felt an odd sensation all over her body. Glasses of milk helped soothe her stomach and she recovered. Nadeau did not take the other pill.

∞∞∞∞∞

By late March, Cream was ready to return to London. He had collected the money he had come for, and no one in his family appeared eager to have him stay in Quebec City. Before leaving, he commissioned a local printer to run off five hundred copies of a handbill. It read:

ELLEN DONWORTH's DEATH

To the Guests of the Metropole Hotel
Ladies and Gentlemen,
    I hereby notify you that the person who poisoned Ellen Donworth on the 13th last October is today in the employ of the Metropole Hotel, and your lives are in danger as long as you remain in this Hotel.

Yours respectfully,
W. H. Murray

The Metropole was a newly opened upscale hotel opposite the Charing Cross rail terminal—Cream and Louisa Harvey had strolled past its elegant facade of buff-colored stone the previous October, on the evening he had given her pills on the Thames Embankment. A new blackmail scheme was taking shape, but how he planned to use the scurrilous notice and why he singled out the Metropole was never explained. He arranged for the copies, when completed, to be forwarded to him in England.

◇◇◇◇

CREAM and Kingman traveled to Saratoga Springs, about thirty miles north of Albany, for a March 22 meeting with George Harvey, the drug company's president. Cream again asked to become the firm's London agent, but Harvey declined, saying he was concentrating on the North American market. Cream was given a discount on any medicines he ordered, however, if he wanted to resell them.

Cream picked up the leather case and drug samples he had ordered, paid the Harvey company twenty dollars, and caught a train to New York City. He claimed one of the 220 first-class cabins on SS *Britannic*, which cast off at half past one the following afternoon and soon melted into a curtain of rain and fog. The White Star liner, one of the fastest afloat, could ferry up to seventeen hundred passengers from New York to Liverpool in less than eight days. Six months earlier, Cream had taken a slow sail-powered ship to England. This time, he was in a hurry. He had a fresh supply of poison and unfinished business in Lambeth.

9

ALICE MARSH
AND EMMA SHRIVELL

{LONDON • APRIL 1892}

POLICE CONSTABLE GEORGE COMLEY WAS WALKING HIS beat when he heard a door creak open at 118 Stamford Street. A man emerged, let out by a woman who remained in the doorway. It was fifteen minutes till two, but there was nothing remarkable about a man leaving a dwelling at such a late hour, not in this part of Lambeth. Stamford Street, as one of the area's clergymen complained, was "swarming with brothels."

PC 211 made a few mental notes about this particular man. Perhaps it was because he was so well dressed, in a top hat and black overcoat. He was five foot nine, maybe five ten, Comley reckoned, and in his forties. The moon was full, and the constable was barely a dozen yards away, but he saw the man's face for only an instant—he had turned away as soon as he made his exit. The man had a mustache, and in the light of a streetlamp, Comley caught the glint of gold-rimmed glasses. He seemed to be in a hurry. "He walked away rather smartly," the officer recalled, although this was not suspicious either. "It was," he allowed, "a cold morning."

Comley was retracing his steps at about half past two when a cab pulled up in front of no. 118. As he approached, another L Division constable, William Eversfield, burst out of the building's doorway. He was carrying a young woman whose name, he soon discovered, was Emma Shrivell. "There is one more inside," shouted Eversfield, who had been summoned after the women were found shrieking and groaning in their upstairs rooms.

Comley ducked inside and found Alice Marsh lying facedown in a hallway, clad in a nightdress. He carried her to the cab, and they rushed to St. Thomas' Hospital. It was only minutes away, but Marsh was dead by the time they arrived. Dr. Cuthbert Wyman, the house physician, pumped Shrivell's stomach. Both women must have ingested "some powerful poison," he told Eversfield.

Shrivell was taken to a ward. She was able to speak and told the officers she and Marsh had spent the evening with a man who had given each of them three long, thin pills. She held up her thumb and forefinger to show their size. They had taken them and eaten tinned salmon before turning in for the night, then became so sick they could not sit or stand. She did not know the man's full name. "We call him Fred."

"Was it the gentleman you let out at a quarter to two," Comley asked, "with glasses on?"

Yes, she said. And her description of Fred—top hat, black overcoat, stout build, mustache, eyeglasses matched the man Comley had seen. She added one detail: the top of his head was bald.

Within three hours, Shrivell was also dead. Later that day, April 12, 1892, Inspector George Lowe of L Division drafted an initial report on what appeared to be an open-and-shut case. "Accidental poisoning," read the heading on File No. 77682, "supposed through eating Tinned Salmon." Lowe summarized the accounts of the two officers and other witnesses and noted that the police had collected for analysis an opened tin of salmon that they had found in the room of one of the women. Shrivell's comment about taking pills a man had provided was mentioned, but only in passing. The divisional commander, Superintendent James Brannan, reviewed the report and endorsed Lowe's assessment: "This is in all probability," he added as a postscript, "another case of poisoning by eating tinned salmon." Ptomaine poisoning from food improperly canned or not eaten promptly after opening, the officers knew, was common. The British Admiralty had recently stopped supplying canned herring to its ships after four sailors who ate the fish were poisoned. Reports in the next day's London newspapers also attributed the Lambeth deaths to tainted salmon.

Dr. Wyman was not so sure. Shrivell had endured a succession of agonizing seizures in the hours before her death—telling evidence that a specific, deadly poison might have been at work: strychnine. He revealed his suspicions when an inquest opened the next day before George Percival Wyatt, the coroner who had investigated Ellen Donworth's death six months earlier. Charlotte Vogt, the women's landlady, testified and added an important clue to the identity of Fred. Shrivell had told her about the visitor and the pills before the constables arrived.

"Do you think we are poisoned?" Shrivell had asked.

They were foolish, Vogt had told them, to take pills from a stranger.

"He is not a stranger," one of the women had protested. "He was a doctor."

Dr. Wyman had performed autopsies and preserved samples taken from the women's stomachs, livers, and kidneys in three glass jars, each sealed with red wax. The inquest was adjourned to await the results of laboratory tests.

In the meantime, L Division, based about a mile south of Waterloo Station on Kennington Lane, pursued two leads. One was the salmon—Acme Flag Brand, canned in California. While it now appeared unlikely to have poisoned the women, it might lead police to their killer. Checks with shopkeepers and wholesalers confirmed that it was not for sale in London. "This points to the probability," investigators noted in one report, "that the man brought it with him." The other lead seemed more promising. Before she died, Shrivell had said there was a letter from Fred in their rooms. Officers found a letter, signed George Clifton, arranging to meet the women the day before they died. This man, police concluded, must be the real name of the mysterious Fred. "No effort will be spared to trace Clifton," Superintendent Brannan vowed in a note appended to one report. "*Clifton*," another supervisor emphasized in the thickening police file, "must be found."

ALICE MARSH AND EMMA SHRIVELL (*ST. LOUIS POST-DISPATCH*, NOVEMBER 15, 1892)

Details emerged about the women and their paths to prostitution. Marsh was twenty-one, Shrivell just eighteen. Both were from the seaside resort city of Brighton. Marsh's real name was Alice Burgess, and her stepfather, a paperhanger, told investigators she had worked as a servant and "bore a good character." Shrivell's stepfather, a fish seller, revealed she had lived, unmarried, with a local man for about a year. The two women were close friends and had moved to Lambeth only a month before their deaths. They had pawned their possessions to pay the train fare and told relatives they had found work in a biscuit factory. Instead, they took rooms on brothel-lined Stamford Street.

Brannan sent a sergeant to Brighton to work with local police, but relatives and friends of the women had never heard of a man named Clifton. The women's bodies were shipped home for burial, and the wreaths placed on their graves were checked, on the off chance one might lead to Clifton. The letter found in their rooms was written on the letterhead of a hotel in Chatham, a port city east of London. The local constabulary was enlisted to join the search but could find no one named Clifton.

One of the officers leading the double-poisoning investigation, Inspector George Harvey, had investigated the death of Ellen Donworth. Three prostitutes poisoned in Lambeth within six months—could this be the work of one man? William Slater, the jeweler briefly accused of murdering Donworth, was once again a suspect. "Every inquiry is now being made respecting this man," noted an internal report. Comley was dispatched to the King's Cross area to meet Slater, but the constable was certain he was not the man he had seen leaving 118 Stamford Street. Slater was tall, with drooping shoulders and an unkempt beard, and looked nothing like the man in the top hat. Comley was reassigned to patrol the Strand in plainclothes, in hopes he might spot Fred looking for new victims among the prostitutes who frequented the area. He scanned face after face, to no avail.

The officers of L Division were frustrated and running out of ideas. "All efforts to trace the man seen to leave the house on the night in question by PC Comley," lead investigators Harvey and Chief Inspector John Mulvany reported on April 28, "have been at present unsuccessful."

10

BITTER MEDICINE

THREE GLASS JARS FILLED WITH A STOMACH-CHURNING mass of human organs and tissue samples were delivered to a laboratory at Guy's Hospital in Southwark, downriver from Lambeth, in mid-April 1892. One was labeled Alice Marsh; the others were marked Emma Shrivell. Dr. Thomas Stevenson, one of the top forensic investigators in Britain, broke the seal on each jar and began his work.

Over the next week he subjected the rank-smelling, partly decomposed samples—portions of stomach, liver, and kidney, stomach contents, vomit—to a battery of tests. It took days of boiling, cooling, filtering, and drying to reduce the liquid squeezed from the samples to a light-colored crystalline powder. "I proceeded in the ordinary way to test whether there was strychnine," he later explained. For the color test, he added a sulfuric acid compound; the residue turned purple-violet, indicating strychnine. The substance precipitated when added to a solution, as strychnine should. Then, Dr. Stevenson tasted the residue. The poison, he later explained, has "a distinct peculiar metallic bitter" taste, and his tongue confirmed what his tests were telling him. There was one final step. He prepared a solution using the residue from each jar and injected a small amount under the skin of several frogs. The animals quickly suffered "strong tetanic convulsions" and died.

The remnants of the salmon the women had eaten had been sent to Dr. Stevenson's lab for analysis, but it had played no role in the tragedy. Traces of fish left in the can, he reported, "were free from strychnine or other poison." Some other substance or method, he concluded, had been used to mask the strychnine's bitter taste as the two women ingested a fatal dose.

◇◇◇◇◇

THE nineteenth century was the century of the poisoner. Arsenic, the murderer's weapon of choice, was cheap, widely available—it was sold by grocers as well as druggists—and seemingly everywhere. Controlling vermin, bedbugs, and other pests was just one of its many applications. Arsenic was an ingredient in medicines used to treat a variety of ailments, from asthma to malaria, and small amounts could be found in cosmetics, dyes, paint, and wallpaper. It was also useful for eliminating an abusive or unfaithful spouse or other unwanted person, and it was so effective in hastening the deaths of wealthy parents that the French christened it *poudre de succession*—inheritance powder. In 1849 *Punch* published a cartoon with the caption "Fatal Facility; Or, Poisons for the Asking." It depicted a druggist serving a child barely able to reach a store counter, who requests "another pound and a half of arsenic for the rats."

Arsenic has no odor or taste, making it easy to add to food and drink, and the symptoms of a lethal dose—abdominal pain, vomiting, diarrhea—mimic those of food poisoning, cholera, and other illnesses. After the development of a laboratory test to detect arsenic in human tissues in the 1840s, however, it was deployed by only the most desperate or foolhardy murderers. In Britain, would-be poisoners faced a further hurdle with the introduction of the Arsenic Act in 1851. Retailers were required to record the name and address of anyone buying the poison, along with the amount purchased and its intended use—a register that became known as the Poison Book. If the buyer later became a suspect in a sudden death that appeared to be a poisoning, the police now had a paper trail to follow.

With arsenic "out of fashion," as one British politician put it, poisoners sought alternatives to their old standby. Scientists obliged by extracting a variety of plant toxins in the opening decades of the nineteenth century, including morphine from opium poppies; nicotine from tobacco leaves; and aconitine, which was derived from the monkshood plant. Strychnine, one of the most potent of poisons, was first produced from the disk-shaped seed pods of *Strychnos nux-vomica*, a tree native to India, in 1819. It attacks the central nervous system when ingested, disrupting the chemical reactions that connect the brain to the muscles. Limbs twitch and muscles tense uncontrollably in response to the slightest sensation, as if the body has become a runaway train. Strychnine was soon being used in rat poison and other pesticides and, in trace amounts, as a muscle stimulant in medicines and tonics. It was also a poisoner's dream: it was fast acting, no effective antidote was known to exist, and it was lethal even in small doses. As little as half a grain—about fifteen milligrams—was enough to kill a person. Best of all, from a murderer's perspective, it would be decades before tests were developed to detect it in human remains. "In the present state of our knowledge," Britain's leading toxicologist, Dr. Alfred Swaine Taylor, lamented in 1848, "the greater number of vegetable poisons are beyond the reach of chemical analysis."

Death by strychnine is truly horrible, as the witnesses to the violent convulsions of Cream's victims could attest. One nineteenth-century doctor offered a chilling description of the poison's effects. Within an hour or so—and sometimes within minutes—a victim finds it hard to breathe. Muscles tingle and there is often nausea and vomiting. The head, arms, and legs begin to jerk uncontrollably and "the whole frame shudders and trembles." The back muscles tighten, and the body of a reclining victim arches upwards, resting on the back of the head and the feet. Fists clench. Eyeballs bulge. The face muscles contract, stretching the mouth into the "peculiar sardonic grin" Dr. Watson described in *The Sign of the Four*. Medical men described the spasms as tetanic convulsions because they resembled the muscular contractions and contortions caused by tetanus. But there is a crucial difference: tetanus attacks are continuous, whereas in cases of strychnine poisoning, convulsions strike, subside, then strike again. Excruciating pain grips the victim and then relents, as if an unseen torturer were playing a cruel game. In the intervals between attacks, the doctor who described strychnine's effects noted, "the intellect is perfectly clear." Victims realize they are gravely ill and likely dying, compounding their horror. The convulsions become increasingly violent until the victim is no longer able to breathe or succumbs to heart failure. The poison can kill within thirty minutes, but some victims have lingered—and suffered—for two hours or more. "In the roster of truly appalling poisons," one modern-day science writer has noted, "strychnine must rank close to the top of the list."

Thomas Griffiths Wainewright, an artist and author who turned to fraud to support his extravagant lifestyle, was likely among the first to use strychnine to kill. While never charged with murder, he was suspected of poisoning as many as four people, including his sister-in-law in 1830 after taking out insurance policies on her life. Strychnine would not make its debut in a British court of law until the mid-1850s, when a doctor in the Staffordshire town of Rugeley was accused of murder. William Palmer had abandoned his medical practice to try his luck at breeding and racing horses; he also bet on races but lost more often than he won. In 1855, when a big wager paid off for a friend and fellow turf enthusiast, John Parsons Cook, Palmer saw an opportunity to seize the windfall and pay off his mounting debts. Thanks to his medical training, he knew of a poison so little understood and hard to detect that it might make it easy to get away with murder: strychnine.

Soon after Cook won at the track, he drank brandy and coffee with Palmer and became seriously ill. Palmer continued to supply him with food, drink, and medicine as his condition worsened over several days. Then, shortly after Palmer administered some pills, muscle spasms gripped Cook's body; they were so severe that his back arched upward, leaving only his head and feet touching the bed. He died within minutes. Other doctors attending to Cook suspected he had been poisoned. It was soon discovered that Palmer, who claimed the dead man's estate owed him four thousand pounds, had bought small but lethal amounts of strychnine during Cook's illness, with the final purchase made on the day his friend died. Suspicion deepened when Palmer insisted on attending the autopsy and tried to tamper with the jar containing Cook's stomach before it could be sent to London for analysis.

Palmer's access to Cook during his fatal illness, his desperate financial straits, and his clumsy attempts to cover his tracks all screamed that he was guilty. And by plying Cook with coffee and brandy, the doctor appeared to have masked strychnine's intensely bitter taste, which was essential in order to administer a fatal dose. But there was a problem. Dr. Alfred Swaine Taylor, the toxicologist who examined Cook's stomach, admitted at Palmer's trial in 1856 that his tests had failed to detect any trace of the poison. Taylor was convinced that strychnine was the cause of death, however, based on Cook's symptoms. Defense lawyers countered that tetanus could produce similar convulsions and sudden death. Palmer's strychnine purchases and suspicious behavior, however, offered the jury enough evidence to convict. As many as thirty thousand people gathered that June to watch him hang. Cook was believed to be the last of Palmer's many victims—he was suspected of poisoning his wife and brother, to collect on life insurance policies, as well as several infant children and one of his creditors.

The trial made headlines across Britain and exposed the need to develop reliable tests to detect strychnine and other plant-based poisons. A "deadly cat and mouse game" began, the American science writer Deborah Blum has noted, as murderers deployed new poisons and scientists raced to find ways to catch them. A Belgian chemist, Jean Servais Stas, had made a crucial breakthrough in 1850 when he devised a process for extracting alkaloids from human tissue. But which poison remained? Analysts bravely touched a small amount of the extract to their tongues and discovered there was enough variation in the burning and tingling sensations produced to identify some of the alkaloids. Extracts were also injected into frogs, mice, and other animals to see if their death throes mimicked the symptoms associated with a particular poison. Scientists bolstered these crude procedures over the next two decades as they devised a battery of chemical tests for tissue extracts that produced colors unique to each poison. For strychnine, it was a purple-violet hue.

As detection improved, British lawmakers took steps to restrict the distribution and sale of poisons other than arsenic. After 1869, only registered pharmacists could sell chloroform, aconitine, hydrogen cyanide (known as prussic acid), and "all poisonous vegetable alkaloids," including strychnine. Purchases were recorded in a register, and pharmacists were required to confirm the identity of any purchaser unknown to them. If another customer or someone the pharmacist knew was present to introduce the new buyer, this was sufficient. Like the Arsenic Act, it was expected to deter anyone bent on murder or suicide. In practice, however, the restrictions were little more than an inconvenience for someone determined to buy poison. A buyer rebuffed by one druggist or allowed to buy only a small amount could simply visit other shops until a clerk willing to bend the rules was found or a lethal dose had been amassed. In 1871 a woman in Brighton made a mockery of the restrictions. Christiana Edmunds, who claimed she needed strychnine to kill cats that had invaded her garden, was able to buy thirty grains of strychnine— enough to kill sixty people. She was infatuated with her doctor and tried to poison his wife with a chocolate. Then, to deflect suspicion, she distributed poisoned chocolates and food to people throughout the city, as if some madman were on the loose. Many people became ill and a child died before she was caught. To obtain the strychnine, Edmunds convinced a shopkeeper—a woman she had just met—to accompany her to a pharmacy and vouch for her, then signed the poison register using a false name. The medical journal *The Lancet* was outraged. "So dangerous an article as strychnia," it scolded, "should never be entrusted to unskilled hands."

Poisons could be just as deadly in skilled hands, as the Palmer case proved. Almost two hundred doctors were accused of homicide in Britain alone during the nineteenth century, and many poisoned their victims. "He is different from the ordinary murderer," crime writer Rupert Furneaux would argue in a book exploring the motives and methods of doctors who kill. "He knows, or should know, how to do it successfully." Doctors could buy poisons in large quantities without raising suspicions; since many practitioners formulated their own medications, druggists were accustomed to supplying them with toxins such as strychnine and arsenic. Doctors knew how much poison to administer, the symptoms to expect, and how long it would take the victim to die. They might even be able to issue a death certificate to cover their tracks. When Dr. Edward Pritchard's wife and mother-in-law succumbed to similar stomach ailments in Glasgow in 1865, he signed the paperwork attributing the deaths to natural causes. When suspicion was aroused and the bodies were exhumed, both were found to contain lethal levels of antimony, a poison used medicinally in small doses to induce vomiting. Dr. Pritchard was convicted of murder and confessed shortly before he was hanged.

A doctor's status as a respected professional was usually enough to overcome any suspicion of wrongdoing. Patients trusted their physicians with their lives, and colleagues consulted for a second opinion or recruited to conduct an autopsy had difficulty believing "a brother medical man," as one observer put it, could be capable of murder. "Of all types of murder, murder by poison is the worst, for poison is administered in secret and usually by a trusted hand," wrote Rupert Furneaux. "When that hand is the doctor's it is even more heinous."

A doctor turned killer was "the hardest man in all the world to overtake," the *Cincinnati Medical Journal* would warn before the century was out, echoing Sherlock Holmes. "He brings to bear all his knowledge of science and often chemistry, all his knowledge of human nature, to further his vicious ends."

◇◇◇◇◇

THE investigation of sudden deaths in the late nineteenth century was as much an art as a science—an art filled with uncertainty. Coroners and doctors conducting autopsies often had to make judgment calls. Stab and slash wounds that killed instantly could be indistinguishable from those inflicted after death, noted a forensics guide published in the 1870s, making it difficult to say where and when a victim was killed. The author considered suspicious bruises "the most difficult to deal with," as they could be evidence of an accidental fall rather than an assault, or marks caused by disease, decomposition, or other natural causes. If a bullet fragmented upon striking bone, a single gunshot could create multiple wounds. In one notorious case, a lead ball broke into two pieces as it passed through a man's leg, and the pieces lodged in his other leg, producing three entrance wounds, two exit holes, and a puzzle for the examining doctor.

Allegations of poisoning created further challenges. Internal organs had to be carefully removed and preserved for later chemical analysis. Doctors who performed autopsies were expected to collect samples of vomit, urine, and, if possible, any food or drink the person had consumed. To avoid contamination that could skew the test results, specimens were to be placed in clean containers and handled "with a scrupulous regard to cleanliness." Doctors were reminded not to use lime to suppress the sickening odor produced by samples and to avoid using earthenware containers, which contained lead. The 1870s forensics guide offered a cautionary tale to remind doctors how easily mistakes could be made: during one autopsy, the stomach was carelessly placed on a layer of fine sand, leading to the erroneous conclusion the victim had been murdered with powdered glass.

Murder by poison ushered a new participant—the expert witness—into the nineteenth-century courtroom. Prosecutors recruited doctors and chemists to identify the toxin used and to explain complex laboratory tests; defense lawyers rounded up medical men and scientists willing to dispute these findings. William Palmer's trial for the murder of John Parsons Cook was one of the first to become a battle between opposing experts. A scientist with the stature and authority of Dr. Alfred Swaine Taylor—lecturer in chemistry and medical jurisprudence at Guy's Hospital in London and author of a leading British textbook on poison and its detection—could tip the scales of justice. "The opinion of a distinguished man whose work was at the forefront of medical knowledge gave the jurors a sense of safety as they explored the mass of evidence before them," the historian Linda Stratmann has noted. "He provided a path they felt they could follow with confidence." But if experts could not agree on whether a man had been poisoned or had died of natural causes, whom should judges, jurors and, ultimately, the public, believe? Even Dr. Taylor, in the wake of the Palmer trial, cautioned against placing "an absolute and blind trust in chemistry, as all-sufficient to settle a disputed case of death from poison." Jurors expected to do their duty and send murderers to the gallows wanted certainty, however, not a robust scientific debate with no clear resolution.

Public confidence in the emerging field of forensic science was shaken three years after the Palmer trial when a London doctor, Thomas Smethurst, was accused of murdering his pregnant mistress. Physicians who treated the woman suspected she had been poisoned, and Dr. Taylor, called in to investigate, discovered arsenic in a bottle of medicine found in Dr. Smethurst's possession. At least he thought he had. He conducted follow-up experiments, and when the case came to trial in 1859, Dr. Taylor admitted the arsenic had come from materials used in his tests. A jury convicted Dr. Smethurst despite the botched test results, but the medical evidence was so inconclusive—other doctors believed the woman's symptoms were consistent with dysentery—that the British government took the unprecedented step of issuing a pardon. A laboratory error had, at best, allowed a murderer to walk free; at worst, it had almost sent an innocent man to his death. Dr. Taylor, the *Dublin Medical Journal* fumed, had "brought an amount of disrepute upon his branch of the profession that years will not remove." The prediction proved correct. Faith in science as a tool to fight crime was shattered and would take decades to recover. "In the eyes of the general public—from whom all juries were drawn—forensic science was now a seriously flawed product," noted one author who explored the development of crime detection.

It was left to Dr. Taylor's successor to repair the damage and lead forensic investigation into the twentieth century. Dr. Thomas Stevenson had joined the staff of Guy's Hospital in the early 1870s and before the decade was out had taken over the lectureships in chemistry and medical jurisprudence as Dr. Taylor eased into retirement. Born in Yorkshire in 1838, Dr. Stevenson had won prizes in an array of subjects, including chemistry, while in medical school. He excelled at laboratory work and became one of the first scientists appointed to ensure the purity of food and medicine sold in Britain. The Home Office, which was responsible for criminal prosecutions, recruited him in 1872 to test autopsied samples when poisoning was suspected. By 1881 he was part of the government's elite team of senior forensic analysts and enjoyed a reputation for thoroughness and precision. "He never jumped to conclusions," by one assessment, "and was never misled by appearances." And once his mind was made up, the outcome of a criminal case often hinged on his conclusions. "To the guilty he was a veritable voice of doom," noted one journalist; another was in awe of his ability to dismantle a defendant's case "with the pitiless accuracy of the expert." Years of methodical experiments with poisons gave him a talent that was perhaps unique in the annals of forensic science. After applying at least fifty different alkaloid poisons to his tongue, he claimed to be able to correctly identify many of them by taste alone.

DR. THOMAS STEVENSON,
BRITAIN'S LEADING TOXICOL-
OGIST, COULD IDENTIFY DOZ-
ENS OF POISONS BY TASTE.
(AUTHOR COLLECTION)

It was a skill that Dr. Stevenson needed in 1881 when George Henry Lamson, an American-born doctor with a practice in the English south-coast resort town of Bourne-mouth, was accused of poisoning his brother-in-law, Percy Malcolm John. Dr. Lamson was facing financial ruin when he visited John, who was disabled and lived at a boarding school in Wimbledon. The young man stood to inherit a large sum of money, but if he died before reaching the age of nineteen, fifteen hundred pounds would pass to Dr. Lamson and his wife. During the visit, the teenager swallowed a capsule the doctor assured him was harmless. John became violently ill soon after Dr. Lamson had rushed off to catch a train and was seized with convul-sions so severe that schoolmates had to hold him down on his bed. Physicians were summoned but could do nothing to save him. After writhing in agony for four hours, he died. It seemed clear the youth had been poisoned, and Dr. Lamson was the obvious suspect. He was charged with murder.

Dr. Stevenson was asked to identify the poison Dr. Lamson had employed. He used the Stas process to distill samples of the victim's internal organs, stomach contents, and vomit, then tasted the liquid produced. He reported feeling a "biting and numbing effect" on his tongue. Then he tasted aconitine, which Dr. Lamson was known to have purchased barely a week before the murder. Since there was no known chemical test for this rare poison, the taste test was essential. The aconitine, Dr. Stevenson reported, produced an identical burning, numbing sensation. Next, he injected a sample of the victim's urine under the skin of a mouse; it died within a half hour. When aconitine was injected into other mice, the animals exhibited similar symptoms as they died.

When the case went to trial, the lawyer defending Dr. Lamson tried to discredit Dr. Stevenson's findings. European scientists had recently discovered alkaloids in cadavers that were produced naturally during decomposition. Could this be the source of the burning substance recovered from John's remains? Dr. Stevenson deflected the attack. While he knew little about the new research, he said, he trusted his tongue. He was certain he had tasted aconitine. The jurors deliberated for less than an hour before returning a verdict of guilty. Dr. Lamson confessed shortly before he was executed.

Dr. Stevenson's key role in convicting Dr. Lamson burnished his growing reputation as a skilled toxicologist and forensic expert. But in the spring of 1892, more than a decade after the Lamson trial, the murders of Alice Marsh and Emma Shrivell presented Dr. Stevenson with one of the greatest forensic challenges of his career: Who was poisoning the women of Lambeth with strychnine, and how?

II

"A STRANGE CUSTOMER"

{MAY 1892}

WHEN THE INQUEST INTO THE DEATHS OF ALICE Marsh and Emma Shrivell resumed on May 5, the hearing room at St. Thomas' Hospital was so crowded that the entry door could not be closed. Peering through his glasses, a thick beard cascading onto his chest like a waterfall, Dr. Stevenson announced his findings: both victims had ingested a lethal dose of strychnine, and far more than the half grain needed to kill. He had found almost seven grains in Marsh's viscera and a little more than three grains in the samples taken from Shrivell's body.

The coroner's jury quickly agreed on a verdict: "death from strychnine—how administered there was no evidence to show." The blame for the inability to identify a suspect, the members of the coroner's jury believed, rested with Scotland Yard. "The police had not exerted nearly sufficient energy" in searching for the author of the letter found in the women's room, the jury foreman announced. L Division investigators had briefed Coroner Wyatt on their efforts to trace the man known as Fred or Clifton, however, and the coroner jumped to their defense. While he did not want to make the details public, he assured the jury that "exhaustive enquiries had been made." The foreman withdrew the censure of the investigation, but there were grumblings in the press as well. Donworth's murder was still unsolved, noted a report in *Reynolds's Newspaper*, and police seemed just as baffled by the latest Lambeth homicides. "Apparently there will be two more murders to add to the already terribly long list of the undiscoverable in London."

L Division, which had received Dr. Stevenson's findings a week before they were made public, was already searching for the source of the poison. Superintendent James Brannan circulated a notice at the end of April, asking Metropolitan Police divisions citywide to canvass drug wholesalers, retail druggists, doctors, and surgeons who might have sold elongated pills containing a strychnine compound to someone matching Fred's description. The inquiries turned up nothing. Police in Chatham, the suspected home of George Clifton, were asked to make similar inquiries but came up empty as well.

A new lead emerged when a performer at one of Lambeth's theaters came forward. Charles Burdett had spoken with Alice Marsh shortly before her death and she had told him a man—"a sea captain," she said—had asked her to live with him, "as it was a shame for a fine girl like her to be on the street." As they were out walking one day, Marsh had pointed out the man, who matched the description Shrivell and Constable Comley had given of Fred. Burdett added a few details. He had a heavy gold watch chain and a walking stick, and his face appeared weathered; he looked like a man "who spent his time out of doors."

This opened a new line of inquiry. A ship's officer or steward could have access to drugs containing strychnine or purchase the poison while overseas. And a seafarer's schedule could account for the six-month lapse between the murder of Donworth and the poisonings of Marsh and Shrivell. Efforts were made to determine which vessels had been docked in London in October, when Donworth died, and whether any of these ships was also in port on April 12. It was a massive undertaking that would take weeks to complete. Police in Liverpool were asked to make similar inquiries but were unable to help. Some three thousand vessels had arrived in the port since October, L Division was told, and it would be impossible to verify if a man matching Fred's description had been among the crews.

Then, after two weeks of frustration and dead ends, a breakthrough. An L Division sergeant, Alfred Ward, one of many officers going door to door in Lambeth in search of prostitutes who might have encountered Fred or the murdered women, knocked on the door of 88 Lambeth Road. The landlady, a Mrs. Robertson, said her maid, Lucy Rose, might be able to help—she had been working at no. 27, a short walk away, when a woman died there the previous fall. Rose was interviewed the next day, April 27, and told Ward and Inspector George Harvey about Matilda Clover's sudden death in October 1891, after she was visited by a man. A broad-shouldered man in his forties, with a mustache, who wore a top hat and an overcoat. A man named Fred.

The news flashed through the ranks. "Another case has come to our knowledge bearing materially on this one," the lead investigators, Chief Inspector John Mulvany and Inspector Harvey, told their superiors the following day. On April 30 the Home Office authorized the exhumation of Clover's body and retained Dr. Stevenson to test her remains for strychnine. Even before the results were known, the officer in charge of L Division was convinced that she, too, had been poisoned with strychnine. "Without doubt," Superintendent Brannan asserted to a colleague, all four women had been murdered "by the same individual."

⁕⁕⁕⁕⁕

SOMETIME after seven o'clock, PC George Comley stopped on Westminster Bridge Road and surveyed the crowd outside the Canterbury Music Hall. It was a warm spring evening in May 1892, and after nights of strolling the Strand in plainclothes in search of the murder suspect known as Fred, he was back on the beat in Lambeth.

People were filing into the Canterbury for the eight-fifteen performance of headliners Will Evans and Ada Luxmore, the "Musical Eccentrics." A well-dressed man wearing glasses was walking back and forth outside the entrance, surveying the crowd.

"The man," Comley would recall, "was looking at the women sharply," especially those who appeared to be prostitutes. "That excited my suspicions." And at that moment, the constable realized he had seen the man before.

It was almost midnight when he teamed up with one of his sergeants, Alfred Ward, to shadow the suspicious man. Comley was certain it was the man he had seen leaving the Stamford Street tenement the previous month, just before Alice Marsh and Emma Shrivell were poisoned. They followed the man as he accompanied a woman from the Canterbury to her lodgings. The officers kept vigil until he emerged and then tailed him to 103 Lambeth Palace Road, where the man produced a key and let himself in.

Ward visited the woman a day or two later and asked about the man. He had recently arrived from America, the man had told her, and "lived solely to indulge in women." Ward and two constables were assigned to keep the man under surveillance.

"It is important that the movements and antecedents of this Man be traced," L Division's superintendent, Brannan, scribbled on an internal report revealing the possible, long-sought breakthrough. "Careful inquiry is being made to do so."

Five nights later, on May 17, as officers watched from a distance, the man called at the lodgings of another Lambeth prostitute, Violet Beverly. He stayed for three hours and, as police politely put it, had "connection" with her. Ward followed up, to find out what she knew about the man. He claimed to be an agent for an American drug company, Beverly said, and had shown her a leather case filled with sample vials of brightly colored pills. He had also mixed her something he called "an American drink," but prudently she had declined to try it. Ward, realizing the woman's life could be in danger, explained

CREAM CARRIED A LEATHER CASE OF MEDICINE SAMPLES HE HAD BROUGHT
FROM AMERICA, INCLUDING A VIAL CONTAINING STRYCHNINE.
(SCIENCE AND SOCIETY PICTURE LIBRARY, LONDON, IMAGE 10658282)

why police were shadowing the man. Beverly had an appointment to meet him again. She promised to pass along anything more she learned about him.

Police soon had a name: A reference to "Dr. Neal" appeared for the first time in a report filed on May 19. It was soon corrected to Neill, but it would be weeks before the police discovered Cream's full name.

Was he the poisoner they were seeking? L Division had its doubts. He was a medical man and appeared to have a legitimate position as a drug salesman. The carrying case of pill samples he had shown to Beverly, investigators noted, was "exactly what a person travelling in the trade would carry." And while he consorted with Lambeth's prostitutes, this did not make him a murderer. "He is an extremely sensual individual," concluded Chief Inspector Mulvany and Inspector Harvey, "but he makes no effort to conceal his identity, and we are of opinion, that he is not the man we are seeking known as 'Fred.'" Nevertheless, Neill was "a strange customer," a supervisor noted, and appeared to be someone worthy of "any Police attention bestowed on him."

The clandestine operation to monitor Cream was soon exposed. One of the women Ward had spoken to tipped him off about the police inquiries. Mulvany and Harvey were outraged. "I know from experience how unreliable these women are," noted their superior, Brannan. "This will be our great difficulty in getting evidence."

Then, an American man named John Haynes, an unemployed ship's engineer, turned up at the Kennington Lane station to lodge a complaint. Police were harassing one of his friends, he said, a doctor he had met about a month earlier. Scotland Yard officers may have prided themselves on their ability to shadow suspects, but the constables monitoring this man's movements had been spotted. His friend's name? Dr. Thomas Neill.

He was referred to Mulvany and Harvey. Haynes, it turned out, had worked for the British government as a private detective during the 1880s, when Scotland Yard was investigating the Irish American extremists—known as the Fenians—behind a string of bombings in London. He had met Cream about a month earlier, Haynes explained to the investigators, and they often dined and drank together. At one point, Haynes realized they were under surveillance. When he asked Cream why the police might be following him, his new friend related an extraordinary tale of intrigue and murder.

A fellow lodger at 103 Lambeth Palace Road, Walter J. Harper, was a medical student at St. Thomas' Hospital and "well known among a low class of prostitutes," Cream had claimed, including Marsh and Shrivell. In fact, this student had first met them in Brighton, where he had gotten one of their friends pregnant. The student had performed an abortion, and the woman, who worked at a hotel there, had died. Harper had confessed all this to Cream because Marsh and Shrivell were blackmailing him, and he wanted "to get rid of them." He had asked Cream to buy him some strychnine. Cream had refused and claimed he had sent an anonymous note warning Shrivell of Harper's plan. There was more. Cream claimed Harper had used strychnine to poison three other women—Ellen Donworth, Matilda Clover, and Louisa Harvey. Haynes, shocked at the seriousness of the allegations, had promised to investigate.

Mulvany and Harvey could not believe their luck. They had just returned from the office of George Percival Wyatt, the coroner who had investigated the deaths of Donworth, Marsh, and Shrivell. Just before the Marsh and Shrivell inquest wrapped up on May 5, Wyatt had received a note addressed to the foreman of the coroner's jury:

Dear Sir,

I beg to inform you that one of my operators has positive proof that Walter Harper, a medical student of St. Thomas's Hospital, and a son of Dr. Harper, of Bear Street, Barnstaple, is responsible for the deaths of Alice Marsh and Emma Shrivell, he having poisoned these girls with strychnine; this proof you can have on paying my bill for services to George Clarke, Detective, 20 Cockspur Street, Charing Cross, to whom I will give the proof on his paying my bill.

Yours respectfully, Wm. H. Murray

Wyatt had ignored the letter, assuming it was the work of someone with a grudge against the Harpers who wanted the scandalous allegation made public to embarrass them. He now realized he should have handed it over to the police. There was a George Clarke detective agency in London, and Mulvany and Harvey discovered the principal, Henry John Clarke, had received a similar letter from a William Murray. If Wyatt contacted him, this letter stated, Clarke was to assure him evidence of Harper's guilt would be produced, provided the coroner agreed to pay Clarke for acting as an intermediary. Clarke had dismissed the letter as a hoax.

The letters, coupled with the information Haynes had gleaned from his new friend, shifted attention away from Cream. Police had a new suspect, Walter Harper, "who may be guilty of the Lambeth poisoning matter," a senior investigator noted on a copy of Haynes's statement. An officer was sent to Brighton to investigate the possible abortion death and any connection Harper might have with Marsh and Shrivell. Cream seemed to be off the hook. The surveillance team was disbanded. Cream's claim that Harper had also killed Clover—police had only begun investigating her death as a homicide—raised no eyebrows. "As he is frequently in the company of prostitutes in Westminster Bridge Road," Mulvany and Harvey reasoned, Cream "has doubtless heard Clover's case spoken of by them."

But cracks quickly appeared in his story. Harper had been a fellow lodger at 103 Lambeth Palace Road, police confirmed, and a student at St. Thomas' since 1889. But their landlady's daughter, Emily Sleaper, assured them Harper was "a highly respectable person," and he did not match descriptions of "Fred." The investigators' next step would be to compare the letters sent to Wyatt and Clarke to see if the writing was the same. And not everyone in L Division was as quick as Mulvany and Harvey were to eliminate Cream as a suspect. A notation was added to the file: "Get a specimen of Dr. Neill's handwriting."

12

THE SUSPECT

AS THE FOCUS OF THE INVESTIGATION SHIFTED BACK TO Cream, L Division recruited the doctor's American friend, John Haynes, as an informant. "If Haynes can be relied on," Superintendent Brannan noted, "he may render material assistance in this case." Soon, however, investigators had a more reliable source who had earned Cream's trust.

Sergeant Patrick McIntyre of the Criminal Investigation Department at Scotland Yard's headquarters was introduced to Cream in May at the Crown & Cushion public house. McIntyre, in his fifteenth year on the force, was a veteran investigator who, like Haynes, had helped foil Irish American bombing plots. Cream was in a talkative mood, describing himself as "a St. Thomas's man" who had studied medicine in Edinburgh and Dublin before moving to America. He claimed he had never operated his own practice—selling drugs for the G. F. Harvey Company, he said, paid better. Later, when Cream complained to McIntyre about the policemen shadowing him, a meeting was arranged at another pub, the Pheasant. McIntyre introduced Cream to Chief Inspector Mulvany and Inspector Harvey and said they were local officers who would review his grievance against the police. The detectives investigating the Lambeth poisonings had heard a lot about Cream, but it was the first time they had met him face-to-face.

Cream brought along his samples case, worn at the edges from use, to prove he was a drug manufacturer's agent. The only reason police might be interested in him, he suggested, was "some indecent portraits" he carried around. These, he assured the officers, had been destroyed. Cream admitted, as McIntyre recalled the conversation, that he had been "a good deal about with women"—being careful not to admit they were prostitutes—"but did not think that a crime."

SERGEANT PATRICK MCINTYRE OF SCOTLAND YARD COLLECTED A SAMPLE OF CREAM'S HANDWRITING. (AUTHOR COLLECTION)

McIntyre arranged to meet Cream at his lodgings a few days later. There, Cream repeated the story he had told Haynes, adding a new twist: he had learned of the allegations against Walter Harper from a detective named Murray. Could this be the same man who had written to Coroner Wyatt, accusing the medical student of poisoning two of the four Lambeth victims? McIntyre had no idea if this Murray existed, but he was sure of one thing: Cream knew a lot about the Lambeth poisonings.

"He talked readily about the girls," the sergeant recalled, "and I remarked he appeared to be well up in the history of the case."

Cream brushed him off, saying he had been following coverage of the deaths in the *British Medical Journal*, which was already comparing Lambeth's "poisoner of prostitutes" to Jack the Ripper. "Being a medical man," Cream said, "I take an interest in matters of this kind."

McIntyre seized the opportunity to ask for a sample of the doctor's writing. Surprisingly, Cream agreed to the request. There was a copy of the medical journal in the room, and he dictated a passage as Cream wrote it out in pencil. He used expensive stationery and McIntyre noted the watermark: Fairfield Superfine.

∞∞∞∞

ROBERT Anderson was under pressure to make an arrest in the Lambeth poisonings. Appointed assistant commissioner of the Metropolitan Police amid the Ripper killings, he had been monitoring L Division's investigation since Donworth's death the previous October. But by mid-May, when the secretary of state for the Home Office, Henry Matthews—the minister responsible for Scotland Yard—asked for an update on the investigation, Anderson had little to report. Prostitutes believed to have met Fred were being tracked down and questioned, he told the minister, with little success. "These women," as one frustrated investigator had noted in an internal report, "are so unreliable." L Division was still compiling a list of ships that had been docked in London in April and the previous October, in case Fred was a seafarer. The officer sent to Brighton could find no one who knew Harper and no evidence to support Cream's allegations against the medical student. Another officer returned empty handed from a foray to government offices in Somerset House on the Strand, where a search of London's death records turned up no reference to a Louisa Harvey. Dr. Thomas Stevenson submitted the preliminary results of his tests on the exhumed remains of Matilda Clover on May 23, adding a new sense of urgency to the investigation. He had found strychnine. The poisoner appeared to have claimed four victims—Clover, Donworth, Marsh, and Shrivell—and possibly a fifth, Harvey.

Then Cream stepped squarely into Anderson's sights. He retained the law firm Waters & Bryan to lodge a formal complaint of police harassment. He had been followed, interviewed several times, and, his lawyers claimed in a May 26 letter, threatened with arrest if he tried to leave London. "As our client is not conscious of any wrong on his part, he feels the inconvenience he is put to acutely." His business as a drug salesman had suffered. Further contact with the police, the lawyers demanded, should be handled through Cream's solicitors.

The commissioner of the Metropolitan Police referred the complaint to Anderson, who summoned McIntyre. Cream, the sergeant explained, was concerned he would be arrested if he left London to visit his fiancée, Laura Sabbatini, in Berkhamsted. "I told him I thought there was no fear of that," McIntyre said, and offered to walk with him to Scotland Yard to confirm he was free to travel. They were partway across Westminster Bridge, in sight of Metropolitan Police headquarters, when Cream backed out. He seemed to suspect McIntyre was luring him into a trap. "He would not go any further with me," McIntyre recalled, "as he thought I was not acting straight with him and that he had been advised to see a lawyer." The sergeant was surprised the incident had sparked a formal complaint.

Anderson saw an opportunity to turn the harassment allegation to Scotland Yard's advantage. The stalled Lambeth investigation, he believed, had reached a crisis point. It was time to put a new, more experienced officer in charge of the case. He contacted Cream's lawyers. "I am anxious to have the matter thoroughly sifted," he assured them, and he wanted their client's side of the story. Inspector John Bennett Tunbridge, one of his senior detectives, would investigate. Unknown to Cream, however, the detective he was about to meet was not interested in how he had been treated by the police. He was the new officer in charge of Scotland Yard's investigation into the Lambeth poisonings.

Tunbridge was a rising star at Scotland Yard. He had joined the Metropolitan Police at nineteen, earned his sergeant's stripes within four years, and was still in his twenties when he was promoted to inspector. Colleagues considered him one of the smartest detectives on the force. "As wary as a night hawk and sharp as a needle," an awestruck reporter wrote after seeing him testify. George Dilnot, the policeman turned writer, remembered him as a methodical investigator "capable of a brilliant coup from meager materials." Yet he shared his colleagues' distrust of crime-fighting innovations and introducing science to the art of detection; assigned in 1888 to review a proposal for using fingerprints to identify criminals, he concluded that collecting and comparing prints was a process too "delicate," as he put it, to be used in police work. Tunbridge was Cream's age, forty-one, but looked much younger. His carefully parted hair and the upturned ends of his thick mustache showed he was as meticulous about his appearance as he was about his investigations.

INSPECTOR JOHN BENNETT TUNBRIDGE. "AS WARY AS A NIGHT HAWK AND SHARP AS A NEEDLE." (AUTHOR COLLECTION)

Tunbridge would tackle his assignment with the open-minded, follow-the-facts approach championed by Arthur Conan Doyle's Sherlock Holmes. "It is a capital mistake to theorize before one has data," Holmes tells Dr. Watson in "A Scandal in Bohemia," the story that had launched the *Strand Magazine* series the previous July. "Insensibly one begins to twist facts to suit theories, instead of theories to suit facts." The officers of L Division had been quick to chalk up Ellen Donworth's death to suicide, only to make an abrupt about-face and accuse an innocent man of her murder. And considerable time and effort had been expended in the search for seafarers and suppliers of tinned fish that now appeared to have nothing to do with the deaths of Alice Marsh and Emma Shrivell. Tunbridge was determined to review every scrap of evidence and look at the facts with fresh eyes before making up his mind about the possible identity of the killer the press would soon christen the Lambeth Poisoner.

He reported to Superintendent Brannan at the Kennington Lane station on the afternoon of May 26. Mulvany and Harvey briefed him, then turned over the hefty investigative file for review. L Division, Tunbridge discovered, still considered Walter Harper a suspect—and, in the opinion of some investigators, the medical student was a more likely suspect than Cream. This, Tunbridge believed, was a mistake. Cream, he was convinced, had concocted the story about Harper being blackmailed and used his friend Haynes to feed it to the police, launching a new set of inquiries and buying him time.

"Assuming Haynes' statement to be true," Tunbridge wrote in his initial report on the case, "we have Neill accusing Harper of being the murderer in no uncertain terms. Now why should he do this? To me it appears to point to Neill being either mad or the murderer himself, as I do not think it can for one moment be entertained that Mr. Harper was the murderer." He scoured the eyewitness descriptions of Fred. Most mentioned he was cross-eyed or had a squint, and "Neill has this peculiarity." Something else stood out for Tunbridge—Shrivell said the man who gave her the pills was a doctor. "We have a man answering Neill's description as to size and age, he was wearing glasses and, most important of all was known as the doctor."

Tunbridge called on Cream at eleven o'clock on May 29 on the pretext of seeking more information about the complaint of harassment. Sabbatini was with him in his room. "He was in a highly nervous state," the inspector recalled, "and trembled visibly." Cream had been taking more opium and morphine than usual and seemed to be cracking under the strain of the police scrutiny. When he refused to be drawn into a discussion of the poisoning cases, Tunbridge backed off and asked him about his work as a salesman. Cream produced his samples case and described some of the medications. The G. F. Harvey Company's pills were "much more agreeable and convenient," he said, than "old-fashioned" spoonfuls of liquid medicine. One bottle caught Tunbridge's eye. The label indicated that each of the tiny pills inside contained one-sixteenth of a grain of strychnine. "It would be highly dangerous to let these articles get into the hands of the public," Cream noted. He sold them only to doctors and druggists, "who would dispense them to their patients in the proper quantities."

Tunbridge spent about an hour with Cream. When he emerged into the bright sunshine of the spring day, his mind was made up. "Under all the circumstances," he told his superiors, "I respectfully submit that suspicion points very strongly at present to Neill as the murderer."

13

"YOU HAVE GOT
THE WRONG MAN"

{JUNE 1892}

D R. JOSEPH HARPER HAD BEEN SHOCKED TO RECEIVE A letter threatening to expose his son as a murderer. It had arrived back in May, and the sender, one W. H. Murray, claimed to have "indisputable evidence" that Walter Harper had poisoned Alice Marsh and Emma Shrivell. Pay fifteen hundred pounds to suppress the information, Murray demanded, or he would alert the police. "The publication of the evidence will ruin you and your family for ever," the letter warned. Enclosed was an article clipped from *Lloyd's Weekly Newspaper*, reporting on the deaths of Marsh and Shrivell. The doctor was instructed to place an advertisement in London's *Daily Chronicle* indicating he was willing to pay Murray for his "services."

Dr. Harper, of course, had no idea Scotland Yard had recovered other letters bearing the name Murray, each one leveling the same allegation against his son. He had consulted a solicitor, but they had seen no need to contact the police. Dr. Harper kept the letter, though, and showed it to his son when he returned from medical

THE HEADQUARTERS OF SCOTLAND YARD, LOCATED DIRECTLY ACROSS THE THAMES FROM LAMBETH, IN 1891 (AUTHOR COLLECTION)

school a couple of weeks later. Walter Harper was understandably upset, but he knew nothing of the women, and he had not been in London when they died. Someone's idea of a practical joke, he thought. They heard nothing more from W. H. Murray.

Now, more than a month later, on the second day of June, a Scotland Yard detective was in Harper's home in Barnstaple, examining the letter. Tunbridge had taken a train from London to the North Devon town to find out what Dr. Harper knew about the scurrilous allegations against his son. He had not realized the Harpers had been threatened with blackmail. The instant he saw the handwriting, Tunbridge knew who had sent it.

"That Neill was the writer," he would tell his superiors. "I have no doubt." It matched the specimen Cream had provided to Sergeant

McIntyre. When Sherlock Holmes received the letter that launched the story "A Scandal in Bohemia," he checked for a watermark. So did Tunbridge. Like Cream's specimen, it was written on Fairfield Superfine stationery, a rare brand that, Tunbridge soon discovered, was not carried by London stationers. It was manufactured in the United States.

It was the evidence needed to charge Cream with extortion, an offense serious enough to carry a maximum penalty of life in prison. But he had to move fast. Haynes had caught wind of Cream's plans to leave London on the afternoon of June 4, ostensibly to visit Sabbatini's family in Berkhamsted. Tunbridge feared he was planning to skip the country. An arrest warrant must be drafted immediately, he urged his superiors. "Otherwise we may be too late."

Robert Anderson, the assistant commissioner, took the new evidence to the director of public prosecutions, Sir Augustus Stephenson, who endorsed the warrant. The Home Office was notified. After "close & careful investigation," Anderson told the secretary of state, he was certain Cream had murdered Clover, Donworth, Marsh, and Shrivell.

"The moral proof of his guilt is ample," he continued, "but my utmost efforts have so far failed to procure any direct evidence connecting him with these crimes." Scotland Yard, he explained, faced the same challenges in the Lambeth case as it had in its pursuit of Jack the Ripper—finding hard evidence and reliable witnesses. "Owing to the character & habits of the class to which his victims belonged," he noted, "Police action is beset by difficulties similar to those which proved insurmountable in the Whitechapel cases." The blackmailing charge was a first step, to prevent Cream from escaping. The murder investigation would continue with the prime suspect safely lodged in a jail cell. "I by no means abandon the hope," Anderson added, "of procuring sufficient evidence ultimately to charge him with the capital offence."

◇◇◇◇◇

TUNBRIDGE arrested Cream in his room at 103 Lambeth Palace Road at half past five on June 3. "You have got the wrong man," Cream said after the extortion charge was read. "Fire away."

Tunbridge showed him the envelope addressed to Joseph Harper.

"This," he said, "is what you are accused of sending."

"That is not my writing."

The detective pulled out the enclosed letter, which Tunbridge was certain was in Cream's handwriting.

Cream said nothing.

A search of his pockets turned up less than five pounds in coins.

He was taken to Bow Street Police Station in central London, famous as the former base of the city's first police force, the Bow Street Runners. Cream asked to contact his lawyers.

"You can send them a telegram," Tunbridge said. "I will get you a form."

"I write nothing," replied Cream, who must have regretted providing a writing sample to Sergeant McIntyre. "You can send it for me."

Cream was arraigned on the blackmailing charge the following day in Bow Street Magistrates' Court. Bail was denied—he would remain in custody as he awaited trial. Three hundred seven days after he walked out of the Illinois State Penitentiary, Cream was back behind bars.

Tunbridge arranged a meeting with a prosecutor to discuss the next steps in the investigation. If Scotland Yard was to build a murder case, inquiries would have to be made outside Britain. Documents found in the doctor's room revealed his true surname and his family connection to Quebec City. Police knew he had arrived in London from New York the previous October but little else about his background. "Enquiry should be made in the United States and Canada," Tunbridge wrote after the meeting, "to trace Neill's movements as closely as possible for some years (five at least) back." And since the drug samples case might implicate Cream in all four poisonings, it was essential to contact the G. F. Harvey Company in New York State.

"Care should be taken to get from this firm the most minute particulars of the pills etc. he was supplied with," Tunbridge noted in a report compiled on June 11, "as there is one vacant space in his Sample Wallet which might have originally been occupied by some pills containing Strychnine."

The report reached Anderson's desk on June 13. In the wake of Cream's arrest, the Home Office had issued a directive: The police must pursue "any clue they may possess in regard to this individual."

Anderson picked up his pen and appended a note. "I will send an officer to America."

III

THE
TRUSTED HAND

NEW YORK CITY, QUEBEC, ONTARIO,
ENGLAND, AND SCOTLAND •
1850–1879

14

JARVIS OF THE YARD

{New York City and Quebec • June 1892}

Inspector Frederick Smith Jarvis stepped ashore in New York City in late June. The arrival, on the steamer *Umbria*, of a man the *New York Times* considered "one of the shrewdest of the Scotland Yard detectives" did not go unnoticed. His father-in-law lived in Yonkers and he had come for a visit, the press was told. But the *Times* soon discovered his real mission—to reconstruct the past of the doctor accused of blackmail and suspected of murder.

Jarvis was sixty-four and an imposing figure, more than six feet tall and sturdily built. "The biggest man at the Yard," one journalist joked, and not just because of his height. His impressive list of investigations and arrests ranged from collaring forgers to solving a murder committed on a train bound for Brighton. And like Sergeant Patrick McIntyre and John Haynes, he had helped round up Fenian bombers. After joining the Metropolitan Police in the early 1850s, he had "devoted all his energies to one object—a thorough acquaintance with the ways of criminals," noted an account of his career. He had sat in on trials, visited prisons, mingled with crooks and lowlifes. His potential for detective work was soon spotted. He was "a rough fellow

Cities/towns where Cream lived or killed

Other major cities

Areas covered on main map

able to mix in the lowest society" and "a highly educated man able to direct the operations of others"—the perfect combination, thought one admirer, for a Scotland Yard inspector.

He was the logical choice for a complex overseas investigation. "A man of the world and of cosmopolitan character," said a fellow detective, "who knew his New York quite as well as his London." He once tracked a fraudster all the way from London to Philadelphia. Colleagues marveled at his coolness under pressure. When a murder suspect pointed a pistol at his head, he slowly closed his hand on the weapon and slipped it from his assailant's grasp. "An earthquake," claimed former policeman George Dilnot, "would not have jarred his self-possession." And he was a skilled shadower, able to hide in plain sight. "Thousands of people have seen Mr. Jarvis at work," claimed London's *Daily Telegraph*, "without ever suspecting it." Following the trail of a man already in custody and suspected of poisoning as many as five women was a different matter: Jarvis's high-profile North American investigation would generate headlines in every city he visited.

He met with Thomas Byrnes, New York City's newly appointed chief of police and the man who had bragged of catching Jack the Ripper within forty-eight hours. Byrnes assigned a pair of detectives to help, and the trio scoured police and health agency records in New York, Brooklyn, Hoboken, and Jersey City. They found no evidence that Cream had practiced medicine in the area, and "no suspicious deaths" had been documented within the past five years, Jarvis reported. The futile search was proof of how little was known about Cream. The doctor had spent, at most, a few days in the New York area.

Jarvis headed north. An overnight train whisked him across the border and into the province of Quebec at the end of June. In Quebec City, he met with Cream's brother, Daniel, and his father's close friend, Thomas Davidson, who filled in some of the details of a privileged upbringing. In Montreal, officials of McGill University confirmed that Cream had graduated with a medical degree in 1876. Then Jarvis called on Dr. Herbert Reddy, a member of the class of 1876, at his office at 999 Dorchester Street, a short walk from the McGill campus. Reddy, who had also studied with Cream at St. Thomas' Hospital in London, had plenty to say about him.

Back at his hotel that evening, Jarvis rushed to write down everything he had just heard. A fire at Cream's Montreal lodgings during his student days, likely set to collect on an insurance policy. A forced marriage, shortly after he graduated, to a young woman in Waterloo, a small town in Quebec's Eastern Townships. And, most intriguing of all, a possible arrest in Ontario in the late 1870s, after a woman's body was found near his medical office.

Arson. Insurance fraud. A long-ago marriage. And another possible murder in Canada. All this was news to Scotland Yard. Reddy did not know the details of the Ontario death, Jarvis informed his superiors, but he believed Cream had somehow "got over this matter." Jarvis would follow up these leads and others in the weeks ahead, as he crisscrossed the eastern half of the United States and Canada to uncover Cream's past.

15

"A Young Man of Rare Ability"

{Glasgow and Quebec City • 1850–1872}

EVERY GRAY-STONE, TIN-ROOFED BUILDING, EVERY STATUE and monument, every crooked street in Quebec City was steeped in history. Once the center of French power in North America, and the gateway to the St. Lawrence River and the continent beyond, it was still referred to as the "Ancient Capital" in the newspapers. On the broad Plains of Abraham at the city's edge, an eighteenth-century battle had decided the future of the continent. Buried beneath its cobblestones were the remains of fortifications where Redcoats and Canadian militiamen had repulsed an American invasion during the Revolutionary War. The châteaux-inspired architecture and narrow streets were frozen in time, remnants of Old France transplanted to North America. "Tourists in search of a city remarkable for its commercial activity, fine buildings and modern improvements," an early Canadian travel guide cautioned, "should not come to Quebec."

The city's once-thriving industries, the export of timber and the building of wooden sailing ships, were in sharp decline in the age of steam and steel. Left behind by the modern world, the city seemed to be tucked "away in a corner," as Inspector Jarvis described it in one of his official reports, "isolated from the rest of this Continent." By the last decade of the nineteenth century, all that Quebec City seemed to offer visitors was history. And history was precisely what Jarvis had come from England to find.

◇◇◇◇

WILLIAM Cream, the father of the man now lodged in a London jail cell, had been born in Ireland about 1820 and grown up in Belfast. By the time a census-taker caught up with the Creams in 1841, they had moved to Scotland and were living in Dalkeith, near Edinburgh. In June 1849 William married Mary Elder, a woman from the Glasgow area, and Thomas, their first child, was born on May 27, 1850, in Barony, just north of the city. Within a year, William Cream was working as a bill collector for the Glasgow Gas-Light Company, which produced illuminating gas from coal, and the couple were living at 60 Wellington Lane, near the city center. Two more children, Daniel and Christina, were born before the family immigrated to Britain's North American colonies, a thin strip of empire on the northern fringe of the United States and poised to form a new nation, the Dominion of Canada, in 1867.

The Creams arrived in Quebec City in 1854. One illustrious visitor, Charles Dickens, had gazed up at the city's imposing citadel atop a three-hundred-foot cliff, toured the "picturesque steep streets and frowning gateways" clinging to the slope below, and declared it the "Gibraltar of America." With a population of just over forty thousand, it was a major commercial center as well as a key military outpost. Huge rafts of timber cut in the interior of the continent were floated downstream to Quebec for sorting and export to Britain. "Every stick of square timber cut on the St. Lawrence waters," the historian Arthur Lower would observe, "found its way to Quebec." By midcentury, scores of ships were under construction, giving sections of waterfront "the appearance of one vast shipyard."

A VIEW OF QUEBEC CITY'S HARBOR AND CITADEL PUBLISHED IN 1860, WHEN CREAM WAS TEN (*HARPER'S WEEKLY*, AUGUST 25, 1860 / AUTHOR COLLECTION)

William Cream, Jarvis discovered, was hired as a clerk at Allan Gilmour's shipbuilding and timber-sorting yard in Wolfe's Cove, a mile and a half upriver from the city. Gilmour was the head of marine operations for Pollok, Gilmour & Company of Glasgow, a major player in the transatlantic timber trade. Gilmour and other owners and managers were from the Glasgow area, and when they staffed their overseas operations, they hired schoolmates and relatives—people they knew and trusted. Cream may well have been recruited for the Quebec City job before he left Glasgow.

Wolfe's Cove was a cluster of riverfront workshops, houses, and wharves at the base of a high cliff. Booms filled with massive logs jutted far into the river, waiting to be culled and manhandled into the holds of ships. New vessels in various stages of construction were propped up on slipways along the beach. The Creams moved into one of the company houses. The scent of tar and fresh-cut wood, the din of incessant hammering and raftsmen's shouts, the backdrop of tall ships and timber—this was Thomas's world until he reached the age of sixteen.

William Cream rose to the position of site manager, supervising as many as a thousand shipwrights and stevedores. He was also put in charge of timber exports from the site. When Gilmour's ships ran aground or were lost at sea, he picked up the pieces; when disputes arose with ships' captains, overseas customers, or government agents, he kept the timber moving. Predicting the next economic downturn and dodging the storms roiling the North Atlantic could be all that stood between profit and bankruptcy. "It must be desperation which drives people to lumber," one of his fellow merchants lamented, "and madness which continues them in it."

Cream's expertise caught the eye of a rival exporter. James Maclaren, another transplanted Glaswegian, was "an energetic, smart businessman" who was building a logging and sawmilling empire on the Ottawa River. They met in 1865, when Maclaren contracted the Gilmour company to sell some of his timber. When Cream assured him he could make more money if he dealt directly with British buyers, he became Maclaren's Quebec City agent. But their partnership was far from harmonious. Stubborn and easily provoked, Cream bristled when Maclaren failed to treat him as an equal. "In a recent letter you speak of me being your servant," he wrote testily during a dispute over one of their ventures. "I don't think I can be considered such."

Cream oversaw a small clerical staff at the James Maclaren & Company office at 28 St. Peter Street in Quebec City's financial district, a few steps from the riverfront docks. He shuttled to and from the Maclaren timber yard on the opposite side of the river, at Indian Cove West, where he had the use of a house that likely became a summer retreat for his family. He earned a hefty salary and often invested his own money in the company's timber shipments, entitling him to a share of the profits. William Cream was becoming one of the city's wealthiest businessmen.

⬦⬦⬦⬦⬦

THOUGH Quebec City remained rooted in its French past, English was the language of government and commerce. In the 1860s, 40 percent of the city's residents were of British descent or recent immigrants from the United Kingdom, an Anglo elite that relegated the French Canadian majority to second-class status. The layout of the city reflected the deep ethnic divide. English-speaking administrators, merchants, lawyers, and doctors lived in the Upper Town or in comfortable suburban homes on the city's outskirts. French Canadian and Irish Catholic artisans and laborers congregated in the Lower Town, the oldest part of the city, and in neighborhoods bordering the shipyards. Stevedores and timber raftsmen—"rough, powerful men who could work like horses . . . and drink and fight with equal ability"—frequented the taverns and brothels of the Lower Town. When merchants were short on crewmen for their vessels, they hired thugs known as crimps to scour the wharves and boardinghouses for sailors who could be enticed—or forced at gunpoint, if necessary—to desert their ships.

When William Cream left the Gilmour firm to work for Maclaren, he had to uproot his family. They left the chaos of Wolfe's Cove and found a new home in the suburb of St. Lewis, where three out of four residents spoke English. A city directory for 1867, when Thomas was seventeen, listed their address as 26 D'Artigny Street, at the crest of a gentle slope rising above the Upper Town. By then, Thomas was the oldest of six children. A young Irish widow was the family's live-in maid.

Thomas's father was active in his church and generous with his time and money. When an Irish Protestant Benevolent Society was established in 1859 to help newcomers from Ireland, William Cream became a founding member and served on the finance committee.

He was a devout Presbyterian—"Godfearing," as Thomas Davidson, the businessman and family friend, put it—and instilled his beliefs in his children. The Lord "hath fed me and led me all my life," he told them, and he prayed they would "serve Him in their generation." Presbyterians followed the teachings of John Calvin and John Knox and believed that sinners were born, not made. Only through self-discipline and restraint could people overcome their innate sinfulness and hope for God's forgiveness and salvation. It was a hard, demanding faith, one that the Cream children seemed to embrace. "Every one of them," Davidson later asserted, was "distinguished for exceptional integrity and uprightness . . . devoted members of the Church, Sunday School and every association of an elevating character." The family worshipped within the neo-Gothic stone walls of Chalmers Church, which proclaimed its presence with the tallest spire in the city.

THE GILMOUR COMPANY'S TIMBER YARD AT WOLFE'S COVE, WHERE CREAM GREW UP AND ATTENDED SCHOOL UNTIL HE WAS A TEENAGER (McCORD MUSEUM N-0000.193.200.2)

An incident during Thomas's youth revealed William Cream's strong views on religious matters and an unchristian-like reluctance to forgive. In May 1866 he walked out of Chalmers Church when he became "dissatisfied with choir," according to a notation in the church's archives. Thomas had a fine singing voice, and his father may have been unhappy with the son's treatment in the choir. The family joined another Presbyterian assembly, the Congregational Church. William Cream did not return to the Chalmers fold for more than fourteen years.

Thomas received his early education in Wolfe's Cove, at a school the Gilmour company operated for the children of employees. Presbyterians were fervent believers in the value of education; the ability to read and understand the Bible was considered essential to personal salvation and furthering the church's missionary work. Thomas taught Sunday school as a teenager while the Creams still worshipped at Chalmers. Given the Presbyterian emphasis on education, he must have been considered a trusted and responsible member of the congregation. He also appeared to be living up to his father's Christian ideals and high standards—Thomas Davidson was confident the young man was "incapable of anything disreputable."

〰〰〰

It was an era when death came often, and swiftly. Disease, epidemics, and poor sanitation exacted a terrible toll, especially on the young. In mid-nineteenth-century Montreal, only three of five children survived to celebrate their fifth birthday, and the average life expectancy in Canada was forty-two years. "One of the ways in which family life in the nineteenth century differed from that of our more sheltered age was in its greater familiarity with sickness and death," one historian would observe a century later. "It was necessary to be prepared, to expect that death would come, often with cruel swiftness."

The Cream family was not spared. Thomas was only five when his sister Christina, born in Glasgow shortly before the voyage to Canada, died; she was barely a year old and the cause of death was recorded as "teething." In February 1861 another sister, ten-month-old Hannah, succumbed to inflammation of the lungs. Then his mother fell seriously ill, possibly due to complications from a late pregnancy—Mary Cream gave birth for the eighth time in 1867, at age forty-three. Thomas was devastated. "His affection and anxiety for his mother during her long sickness, and his solicitude in providing her with everything that might possibly lead to her recovery," one of his teachers recalled, "was worthy of all praise." On January 17, 1870, a miserable winter's day of rain and slush, she died. Thomas was four months shy of his twentieth birthday. Brief newspaper announcements invited friends to assemble at the family home on D'Artigny Street two days later, at two o'clock, to join the funeral procession.

By now, Thomas was working as a clerk at the Baldwin shipyard in the suburb of St. Roch, bordering the St. Charles River on the city's north side. William H. Baldwin, a third-generation shipbuilder with Scottish roots, was a close friend of William Cream, which no doubt helped secure the job. Baldwin and his cousin, Peter, operated one of Quebec's busiest yards and employed as many as four hundred men. Thomas's title was confidential clerk, and his duties included bookkeeping and recording when hourly paid tradesmen arrived and departed. Men showed up for work as early as six in the morning, so it would still have been dark on most days when Thomas left his home for the twenty-five-minute walk to the shipyard. It took at least six months to complete a large ship, with most of the work undertaken in the winter months, even on the coldest days, to allow for a spring launch. Since most Quebec shipwrights were French Canadians, Thomas probably had a good command of the language.

The Baldwins were full of praise for their young employee. "A perfect young man and a good Christian," was William Baldwin's assessment. Peter Baldwin, who had taken over the business by 1870, was pleased to report that Thomas "gave every satisfaction being honest sober attentive and in every respect trustworthy."

⬦⬦⬦⬦

THEN disaster struck. A fire roared through St. Roch in May 1870 and destroyed much of the Baldwin shipyard. It was a serious blow to the city's entire shipbuilding industry. British yards had been producing iron and steel vessels for years, and Quebec builders were struggling to modernize. Baldwin was the first to use iron beams and other structural components in his designs, producing a stronger, "composite" vessel. These would outlast wooden-framed ships, one journalist noted, and "prove that Quebec could compete with the world in naval architecture." His partly built prototypes were destroyed in the fire.

Baldwin rebuilt his yard and launched more ships, all using traditional framing. No other local builder experimented with composite ships or metal construction. Steamships and steel hulls were the future, but Quebec shipyards continued to produce wooden sailing ships that fewer and fewer buyers wanted. The British market for timber was collapsing as well, dealing another blow to the city's economy. The businessmen of St. Peter Street, Thomas's father among them, began to look for new opportunities. William Cream branched into manufacturing cement, bought a pottery works, and invested in banks and insurance companies.

Thomas appeared eager to escape a dying industry. He continued to work for Baldwin for about a year after the fire. Then, in 1871, he was dispatched to Lachute, northwest of Montreal, to attend a private school founded by a Presbyterian minister. Lachute Academy offered advanced education for older students that went beyond the basics offered in the public schools. The ambitious curriculum included classes in Latin and Greek, philosophy, mathematics, and chemistry. Thomas had reached his twenties, but he would not have felt out of place—more than half the students were sixteen or older. The school expected great things from its graduates. "As a result of the Academy's influence," a former principal noted with pride, "men are to be found in every profession who must attribute their start in life and much of their later success to the instruction which they received in its classes."

He boarded with one of his teachers, who was impressed with his character and potential. Thomas was "steady, industrious, kind-hearted," James Emslie would remember, "and highly respected by all who knew him." Emslie was just as pleased with his conduct outside the classroom. "I always found him scrupulously correct in all his habits, regular in his attendance at church, and particular as to the character of his associates."

His goal, Thomas told his father, was a career in medicine. Why medicine? Inspector Jarvis put the question to Thomas Davidson as he made his inquiries. All Davidson knew was that at some point, Thomas had "expressed a desire to become a doctor." It was a suitable profession for the eldest son of a wealthy, respected family. And his helplessness during his mother's lingering illness and the loss of his infant sisters may have ignited a desire to help and heal others. He was accepted into McGill University's Faculty of Medicine in 1872.

Cream, "a young man of rare ability," left for Montreal that fall, recalled James Robertson, another family friend, "destined to make his mark in the world."

16

"THE ANIMAL SPIRITS WITHIN"

{MONTREAL • 1872–1876}

A BOISTEROUS CONTINGENT FROM McGILL UNIVERSITY converged on a Montreal courtroom on a fall day in 1875, to support a fellow medical student arrested for robbing a grave. When a fine was imposed—the offense was considered a minor one—they passed the hat and raised the money needed. Then the convicted man was hoisted on shoulders and carried through the streets by a crowd "brandishing body-snatching implements," the city's *Daily Witness* reported, "and shouting forth songs of triumph."

A shortage of cadavers was making it difficult for McGill students to learn surgical skills, the campus newspaper explained not long after the courthouse celebration. While they observed a few dissections over the course of an entire term, British medical schools staged as many as three a day. A thorough knowledge of anatomy was a crucial part of a physician's training, and there was no substitute for the real thing. "It is better to learn by dissecting the dead," noted one student grave robber, "than bungling upon the living." But it would be another decade before the province of Quebec introduced a law forcing hospitals, asylums, jails, and other public institutions to turn over unclaimed bodies to medical schools. In the meantime, McGill anatomy instructor Francis Shepherd resorted to the black market, paying up to fifty dollars for each corpse delivered to the school. The body snatchers included McGill students—they called themselves "resurrectionists"—out to earn a few dollars or seeking a ghoulish thrill.

The year Cream entered the medical school, Shepherd would later note, "nearly every subject for dissection was obtained illegally" from enterprising students and other grave robbers.

⬦⬦⬦⬦⬦

ON a damp and chilly October morning in 1872, members of the freshman class gathered to begin their medical training at McGill. Professor William Wright, who would soon teach them how to formulate medicines, addressed the doctors of the future. "May the morning you first crossed these halls of learning," he began, "be ever a red letter one in your life's calendar."

It was a day to remember for McGill as well, marking the official opening of a new home for its Faculty of Medicine. The two-story building housed a museum of anatomical models and specimens, a laboratory, and a dissection room fitted with a hygienic lead-covered floor. The arrival of Cream's class in the fall of 1872 brought enrollment in the four-year program to 154. Wright greeted them with a rousing call to arms against disease and death. A medical degree "gives you power over the ills to which flesh is heir," he declared, imploring them to be "God-like" as they stood their ground "between the living and the dead."

Cream was twenty-two when he arrived in Montreal. The city, located on an island in the middle of the St. Lawrence, had a population approaching 110,000, double that of his hometown. It was touted to would-be visitors as a "solid and progressive" city, with wide streets, spacious shops, and "new and elegant edifices." A wealthy English-speaking elite dominated the French Canadian majority, as it did in Quebec City, from an oasis of mansions known as the Golden Square Mile. The McGill campus looked down on this enclave of power from the side of the mountain—Mount Royal—which gave the city its name. The Faculty of Medicine, Canada's first medical school, was the university's marquee program. Medicine was in a state of flux when Cream embarked on his studies, as science transformed an ancient art into a modern profession. A British surgeon, Joseph Lister, was pioneering the use of carbolic acid as a disinfectant during operations. The renowned French scientist Louis Pasteur was demonstrating that bacteria were the cause of disease and infection. Chloroform, first used as an anesthetic in 1847, had replaced brandy and ether as the preferred means to spare patients the excruciating pain of surgery.

But old ways died hard. Many physicians clung to the notion that putrid air bred infection and disease, scoffing at the idea that invisible germs were killing people. When Arthur Conan Doyle began studying medicine in Edinburgh in the 1870s, he encountered skeptics who dismissed germ theory and Lister's antiseptic techniques "as an enormous fad." Older doctors, Conan Doyle remembered, regarded chloroform as "a dangerous innovation" and referred to the stethoscope, in use for half a century, as "a new fangled French toy." Druggists still stocked jars of leeches in the 1870s, even though by then most physicians realized that bloodletting would not purge the body of disease.

McGill, like the old-school doctors Conan Doyle encountered, had fallen behind the times. George Fenwick, who taught surgery and was considered the best surgeon in Montreal, wore a black frock coat spattered with dried blood as he operated. No one bothered to clean or sanitize scalpels and other surgical instruments. "With the little cleanliness used," noted Francis Shepherd, "it is a wonder any cases recovered." Few did. Postoperative infections were so deadly that physicians refused to open a patient's abdomen to remove a tumor, let alone a ruptured appendix. A compound bone fracture or a surgical amputation was usually a death sentence. McGill students dissected the limbs and muscles of cadavers to prepare for the day they would cut into the living, Shepherd recalled, but rarely explored the internal organs or the brain—there was no need to rehearse for operations they would never perform.

Cream and his classmates learned by watching and listening, rarely by doing. His cohort of instructors favored lectures over demonstrations and drew their material almost verbatim from textbooks. Students conducted dissections with little supervision. They followed doctors on their rounds at the Montreal General Hospital but were not allowed to examine or treat patients. Since surgery was often a last resort, students might observe as few as three major operations a month. To pass the obstetrics course, Cream was required to attend only a dozen births, with a midwife in charge. Many students graduated without ever seeing a physician use forceps or without assisting with a delivery.

There would be times, he discovered, when he would indeed have to play God, choosing one life over another. A lecture in obstetrics explored when and how abortions should be performed. They were "sometimes necessary," Cream would later say, "to save the mother's life." His midwifery professor revealed how doctors could tell whether an abortion had been caused by accident or disease or if it had been deliberately "provoked" and would be considered a crime. A course in medical jurisprudence—the emerging science of forensic medicine—taught Cream how to detect when a death was the result of crime rather than natural causes and precisely how a person died when hanged by the neck. He learned from another professor that chloroform was "a 2 edged sword," safe when used properly as a surgical anesthetic but lethal if administered in excessive amounts. A person forced to inhale undiluted chloroform, he was told, would soon die of cardiac arrest. Since most doctors formulated their own medicines, Professor Wright taught a course showing students how to use herbs, chemical compounds, and opium and other narcotics, and it was common to add poisons such as strychnine and arsenic, in trace amounts, to many prescription drugs. This was knowledge that could heal. Or kill.

Students became oblivious to the sight of blood, inured to the stench of death. The hospital's surgeons worked at a primitive operating table, its wooden top blackened with the blood of a succession of patients; the floor below, a student recalled, was "blood-stained and reeking with odours." In the dissecting room, they tossed coins to decide who would have the disgusting chore of cleaning out a cadaver's internal organs to expose the muscles underneath. Some students, however, eagerly joined the body-snatching forays to local cemeteries. There's no evidence that Cream took part in these nocturnal activities, but he would have known where most of the cadavers came from, and he likely knew or suspected which classmates had exhumed them. Even the school turned a blind eye to the practice, promising students an "abundance of fresh material" for dissection without specifying its origins.

Some students reveled in their macabre studies. "There is something in the atmosphere and curriculum of a medical school," one of Cream's fellow students confessed in 1874, "which, like measles, propagates its contagion from one body to another" and releases "the animal spirits within."

At McGill, for the first time in his life, Cream was living on his own. There were no dormitories. Medical students lived "where they please," Jarvis later noted in a report to his superiors at Scotland Yard as he investigated Cream's student days, with "little supervision of their private life." For those weary of poring over lecture notes and textbooks, the taverns and brothels of the city's red-light district were a twenty-minute stroll from the campus. "What man with any common sense would trust his son in the largest city in this country," the *McGill Gazette* asked in an editorial demanding on-campus housing, "knowing that there was but little restraint placed upon his actions" and he would be exposed to "the many temptations which are almost sure to beset him."

There were about 350 students at McGill in the 1870s, almost half enrolled in medicine and all of them men. It would be another decade before women were admitted. Campus life revolved around the literary society, the snow-shoeing club, and varsity sports such as football and hockey. The musically inclined formed a glee club to stage benefit concerts and, the *McGill Gazette* hoped, infuse "the spirit of song . . . into our men." Cream may have been among its members—his voice was good enough to earn him an invitation to sing at the university literary society's dinner in January 1876.

Wright, in his introductory lecture, warned the Class of 1876 to avoid "the snares of bad habits" such as smoking and drinking. "Be almost anything," he pleaded, "but a drunken doctor." Cream indulged in one of the temptations Wright railed against—he smoked a long, thin clay pipe and later switched to chewing tobacco. And like his fellow students, he undoubtedly drank heavily. Medical students of the time, noted *Harper's Magazine*, had a reputation as "lawless, exuberant, and addicted to nocturnal activities." After some boozy dinners at Montreal restaurants, drunken McGill students sometimes spilled into the streets and clashed with the police.

Cream found a room a few blocks south of the campus at the home of Jane Porter, a music teacher who took in boarders at 106 Mansfield Street. He lived there for all four of his academic years at McGill, sharing the house with a succession of bank and railway clerks and another long-term resident, a widow named Mary Blackwood. "He always conducted himself as a gentleman," Porter told Jarvis when the detective looked her up. But students and professors knew a different person—an unsavory young man who flaunted his wealth. James Bell, who was a year behind him, and Walter Sutherland, a member of the class of 1874, considered him someone to avoid. "They did not associate with him more than they could help," Jarvis noted in a report, "not liking his manners." Bell and Sutherland never explained what rubbed them the wrong way, and Jarvis confirmed that college administrators received no complaints about Cream's behavior during his time at McGill. But Cream gained a reputation for extravagance and fast living. Robert Craik, who taught chemistry at the medical school, remembered him as "rather wild and fond of ostentatious display of clothing and jewelry."

Medical students had a six-month break between academic years— from early April to the end of September—and were encouraged to use the time to take optional courses at local hospitals, to learn more about diseases and treatments. Cream chose to return to Quebec City to work for his father. In March 1874, when Thomas was in his second year of studies, William Cream remarried. Elizabeth Harbeson, the daughter of a Quebec City accountant, was fourteen years younger than her new husband. Cream had idolized his mother; his reaction to the marriage and his relationship with his stepmother are unknown.

Thomas's father gave him a good-paying job, Daniel Cream recalled, so he was "well supplied with money when at College in the winter"—money he needed to indulge his expensive tastes. He posed for a series of studio photographs while at McGill and commissioned the renowned Montreal photographer William Notman— who billed himself as "Photographer to the Queen" and catered to the politicians, businessmen, and celebrities of the day—to do the honors. He paid for at least four sittings while at McGill. In one photograph, he wore a formal frock coat, top hat, starched collar, and a striped cravat with a stick pin. For another, he ditched the coat but kept the top hat and lounged in a vest and shirt sleeves, with a pocket watch dangling at his waist, a clay pipe in one hand, and a copy of the McGill student newspaper in the other. He put on a bulky fur coat for other images, then leaned against a pillar and tucked his right hand between the buttons, Napoleon style. It was an expensive wardrobe. In 1874 Thomas took out an insurance policy on the contents of his room on Mansfield Street. The Commercial Union Insurance Company of Montreal covered his clothing and other personal items to a maximum of one thousand dollars—about eighteen thousand dollars in today's US currency.

CREAM, HOLDING A PIPE AND A COPY OF MCGILL UNIVERSITY'S STUDENT NEWSPAPER, POSES AT THE NOTMAN PHOTOGRAPHIC STUDIO IN 1874.

(MCCORD MUSEUM I-99946.1)

Even though Cream was still in his midtwenties, the photographs show his brown hair receding above the temples, leaving a tuft in the middle. Thick eyebrows and a dark complexion added intensity to his gray eyes. His most notable feature was a heavy, square chin with a slight dimple. Combined with his narrow shoulders, it made his head appear slightly too big for his body. "Stout solid build, full face and forehead . . . heavy massive jaws and chin," read one less-than-flattering assessment of his appearance. He was five foot nine, about 180 pounds, and when he bought a pair of boots, he asked for size 9. Cream wore a mustache, which became wider and thicker during his four years at McGill and, for a while, was twisted into handlebars. By the time he was twenty-six he was sporting a heavy set of auburn-tinged mutton chops as well, leaving only his dimpled chin exposed. The new look made his jaw appear smaller and balanced his face, which was likely his intent.

As his looks changed, so did his personality. It was becoming harder to find traces of the kindhearted student James Emslie had taught at Lachute Academy, or the good Christian who had taught Sunday school and later impressed his then employer, William Baldwin. He had become haughty and self-centered, a boorish young man who squandered his money. Vain about his appearance yet oblivious to how others saw him. Wild. Fast. Someone to be avoided. Professor Wright had pleaded with McGill's future doctors to lead exemplary lives, to be "gentle, kind, and genial" in their manners and to avoid "wild puerile folly." Cream had forgotten this advice, or chosen to ignore it.

◇◇◇◇◇

GRADUATION exercises for the class of 1876 began at three o'clock on March 31 in William Molson Hall, located in the west wing of McGill's main campus building. Outside, the remnants of the winter's snow were melting; inside the crowded hall, the atmosphere was stiflingly hot. Principal John William Dawson, assisted by Robert Craik—the chemistry instructor who would remember Cream as wild and foppish—handed out the degrees. Dawson, a renowned geologist who taught botany in the medical school, offered each graduate a few words of advice and encouragement as they passed. Cream and thirty-three other students were now entitled to append the letters MD, CM—doctor of medicine and master of surgery—to their names.

Speeches followed. John S. Archibald, a lecturer in the Faculty of Law, exhorted the graduates "to devote their abilities towards the attainment of the highest eminence in their chosen profession." Judge Frederick W. Torrance hoped that "the purity of their professional career might be among their best aspirations." While lawyers toiled in the glare of publicity, doctors did their work "in the privacy of the sick chamber, often away from the scrutiny of human eyes," with God

THE MCGILL MEDICAL SCHOOL'S GRADUATING CLASS OF 1876. CREAM IS AT THE CENTER OF THE PHOTOGRAPH, KNEELING IN THE SECOND ROW. (MCGILL UNIVERSITY ARCHIVES, PL007815)

alone to witness and judge their actions. "Your patient," he reminded them, was "entirely at your mercy, and is unreservedly and entirely in your hands."

Soon Cream would wield this power over life and death. He had passed final examinations, written and oral, on an array of subjects—surgery, anatomy, diseases affecting women and children, hygiene. One exam question asked, "How do poisons produce their fatal effects," and "on what tissues do they act?" Each graduate had prepared a thesis on a medical subject and had defended it before their classmates and professors. Cream's thesis has not survived. The subject was chloroform, and it may have explored an issue discussed in one of his classes—its potentially lethal effects when used improperly or in excessive concentrations. Each graduate swore an oath, in Latin, promising to "practice the art of medicine with caution, uprightness, and excellence" and "to

administer faithfully all that which pertains to the health and soundness of the diseased body." Cream added his signature to the Faculty of
Medicine's oversize, leather-bound registry book. In the class photo he
knelt in the center of the frame and posed with his right arm draped
over the shoulder of Stephen Robinson, a student from Ontario who
was crouched on the floor in front of him. In a sea of solemn and
pensive faces frozen for the long exposure, Cream was one of the few
future doctors who looked happy.

17

FLORA ELIZA BROOKS

{Waterloo, Quebec • 1876}

I T LOOKED LIKE A GOOD MATCH. HE WAS THE SON OF A wealthy, respected Quebec City merchant and would soon qualify as a doctor. She was the daughter of Lyman Brooks, proprietor of Brooks House, the best hotel in Waterloo—four stories of rust-brick Second Empire grandeur on the village's main street—and commander of the local militia company. Brooks had operated a tavern and a store before entering the hotel trade and had been the area's postmaster for almost twenty years, occupations that brought him into daily contact with neighbors and visitors. He was constantly meeting and sizing up new people. If he had any suspicions or misgivings about Thomas Neill Cream, the young man courting his daughter, Flora Eliza, in the spring of 1876, he seems to have kept them to himself.

Waterloo, about sixty miles east of Montreal, was Jarvis's next stop as he unearthed Cream's past. A lakeside village set against a backdrop of glacier-worn mountains that rose like the backs of giant slumbering beasts, it was one of the first station stops on the train ride from the city into a region known as the Eastern Townships. "As beautiful a tract of country as perhaps any on the continent,"

a visitors' guide claimed, a pastoral mix of farms, lakes, and wood-
land that "presents a scene most decidedly English in appearance."
Settled by Loyalists fleeing the American Revolution and just inside
Quebec's border with Vermont, Waterloo was named for the battle
that doomed Napoleon—proclaiming it an English foothold in a
predominantly French-speaking province. The population stood at
just twenty-five hundred residents but "a stranger visiting Waterloo,"
Cyrus Thomas, the principal of the Waterloo Academy, boasted in a
local history published in 1877, "is struck by the air of city-like elegance and substantiality of several of its public and private buildings."

CREAM'S FATHER-IN-LAW OPERATED BROOKS HOUSE IN WATERLOO, QUEBEC.
(AUTHOR COLLECTION)

Flora Brooks had met Cream in Montreal in early 1876, when
she was in the city to visit friends. She was twenty-three; he would
turn twenty-six that May. Once he had caught her eye, and she his,
the courtship rituals of the Victorian era had to be observed. A suitor
needed an invitation to call on a young woman at her home, with at
least one family member in attendance. A chaperone was expected
to tag along for forays outside the home, but with a little ingenuity

couples could arrange to spend time together without supervision. In the months that followed, Lyman Brooks recalled, Cream was "in the habit of coming to visit her" in Waterloo, and "they were looked upon as being engaged." He became a fixture at Brooks House, and the pair exchanged letters when he was back in Montreal. They discovered they had a lot in common, besides the advantages of a father's healthy income. Each was the eldest child, and both had endured the loss of a parent—Brooks's mother had died two years earlier. Her family was Anglican, so the Protestant faith was another common denominator—and, in the nineteenth century, an important one.

But Brooks knew little about her suitor, and she could never have imagined what he was capable of. That April, about two weeks after his graduation from McGill, Cream had told his landlady, Jane Porter, he was moving out of 106 Mansfield Street. He asked if he could keep his belongings in his room until he could arrange for their removal. She agreed, even after he mentioned he was also leaving a human skeleton. (Many medical students and physicians purchased skeletons, bones, or preserved organs to further their studies of anatomy.) Two days later, on April 18, a fire broke out in the room. By the time the fire brigade arrived, much of the furniture had been destroyed; the blaze appeared to have started in a bureau, which was reduced to ashes. Cream had placed the skeleton in his bed. When the firemen found it, they assumed the room's occupant had been burned to death.

Porter was able to explain the skeleton in the bed, but not how a fire had started in a bureau in an unoccupied room. She was certain no one had entered. The insurers suspected arson. When Cream filed a detailed list of lost possessions and a claim for $978.40, just shy of the maximum under his policy, the Commercial Union Insurance Company refused to pay. The dispute went to arbitration, with Cream eventually accepting a $350 settlement.

The incident foreshadowed the bizarre and destructive behavior that lay ahead. When Jarvis learned of the fire during his investigation in the summer of 1892, he was convinced that Cream must have returned to his room and set it ablaze. More disturbing questions were unasked and unanswered. Had Cream, someone capable of arson and fraud, tried to fake his own death? How did he acquire the skeleton? And whose remains were found in his burned bed?

◇◇◇◇◇

THE summer of 1876 was a scorcher in Waterloo—a stretch of hot, dry weather the local weekly, the *Waterloo Advertiser*, proclaimed "almost unequalled in the annals of Canadian experience." Streams dried up. Farmers hustled to harvest grain that ripened early. The dust was so bad that someone rigged up a cart to water down the gravel street in front of Brooks House and other businesses.

Despite the heat, there was plenty to occupy a young couple's time. The Waterloo Red Stockings played the first baseball games that summer in a village where cricket had long been the king of outdoor sports. Brooks and Cream could stroll to one of the outdoor evening concerts staged by Hubbard's Brass Band. Or they could join the groups of young people who rowed across Waterloo Lake for secluded picnics— and a chance to be free from chaperones. W. W. Cole's Circus and its clowns, daredevils, and exotic animals arrived on August 4, packed inside thirty-six railroad cars. As many as eight thousand people descended on Waterloo—filling Brooks House and other hotels—to marvel at the elephants and zebras, the chariot races, the bravery of Conklin the lion tamer. No doubt Brooks appreciated having a man on her arm; local women were complaining that tramps and drunks were insulting them on the streets. "We would advise no lady to venture out after dark without a proper escort," the editor of the *Advertiser* noted. "There are too many roughs about to make it safe."

Cream promised they would marry, and this was enough to induce Flora to consummate their relationship. Then, on the night of September 9, she was struck by a sudden, serious illness. Family members heard her cries, rushed to her bedroom, and found her in agony. Lyman Brooks called in the family physician. Dr. Cornelius Phelan's diagnosis was shocking. She had undergone an abortion, he concluded, "procured either by drugs or instruments." Phelan could not be certain of the method used, but it was obvious that Cream had been both the father and the abortionist.

Phelan broke the news to Flora's father the following day. Lyman Brooks could have gone to the authorities and pressed charges. Under Canadian law, it was a criminal offense to perform an abortion or to administer or provide any noxious substance with the intention of causing a miscarriage. Common substances used in some medicines—tansy, savin, cotton root, ergot—were widely known to have the desired effect, and it would have been easy for Cream, as a medical school graduate, to obtain and administer them. But Brooks knew a prosecution would expose his daughter to public ridicule, and for little gain. The stigma of pregnancy out of wedlock, one contemporary noted, was "a living death." In a community as small as Waterloo, her reputation would be ruined.

Lyman Brooks caught a train to Montreal, where Cream was staying at a hotel. He enlisted the help of the police but only to make sure his quarry agreed to return to Waterloo. Two officers accompanied him to Cream's hotel.

"What does all this mean?" Cream asked, startled by the presence of the policemen.

"It means that you are coming back to marry my daughter."

He was in no position to argue or refuse.

"Just what I wish to do," Cream replied. It was surely a lie.

On the afternoon of September 11, a Monday, there was a tense gathering at the Brooks home to negotiate a marriage contract. A local lawyer, Thomas Brassard, had been retained to draft the provisions. Cyrus Thomas, the local historian who was also the school principal, was present to act as a witness. The six-page agreement's legalese and businesslike tone could not mask the underlying currents of reluctance and hostility. Brassard's fluid script filled four pages before the parties acknowledged, as an afterthought, their "love and affection" for each other. Words crossed out and additions scribbled in the margins showed the document was drawn up in haste, the product of tough negotiations. Lyman Brooks signed off on the agreement; he had likely dictated its harsh terms.

There would be no community property, let alone a dowry. Cream would have no claim to his wife's existing property—itemized as one thousand dollars from her mother's estate and two hundred dollars in "wearing apparel, jewels & trinkets"—or anything she stood to inherit from her father. Cream agreed to cover her household expenditures and to provide for the maintenance and education of any children "who may be born of their intended marriage." If they did have children and Cream ever sought a divorce, he agreed to pay her ten thousand dollars—a staggering sum, almost two hundred thousand dollars in US currency today. Should Flora die childless, the offer of this generous "gift," of course, would be "null and void."

Only the formalities remained. It was evening by the time Archdeacon David Lindsay, the rector of St. Luke's Anglican Church, performed the private ceremony at the Brooks home. The bride, too weak to stand, reclined on a lounge chair during the service. The summer's heat wave had passed; nighttime temperatures were dipping toward the freezing point. The cool air outside likely matched the chilliness in the room. No one from Cream's family appears to have been present—his brother, Daniel, would later tell Inspector Jarvis he had never met Flora Brooks. The *Advertiser* published a brief announcement of the Cream–Brooks nuptials, with no hint of the drama that had played out on the eve of the ceremony.

The day after the wedding, Cream made his escape. "He was going to England for a time," he told his father-in-law, "to finish his medical education."

Lyman and Flora Brooks never saw him again.

18

STUDENT NO. 2016

{LONDON • 1876–1877}

HER MAJESTY'S PERSONAL PHYSICIAN CONSIDERED THE site unhealthy and unsuitable. "I cannot think the bank of a muddy river the best place for a hospital," Sir James Clark protested. "It may get air, but not of the best kind at any season—in the summer loaded with emanations from the river, & in the winter loaded with moisture, the smoke of the city, & the chilling east wind." His misgivings were ignored. Victoria herself presided in 1868 when the cornerstone was laid at the new site of the storied St. Thomas' Hospital, in Lambeth on the banks of the Thames. By the time the queen returned, three years later, to officially open the six-hundred-bed facility, London was as damp and smoky as ever, but fortunately a new waste-water system had cleansed the river of sewage and its nauseating odor.

One of the city's oldest hospitals, St. Thomas' traced its origins to an infirmary founded by a religious order about 1106. Student doctors were apprenticing there as early as 1550, making it one of England's first medical schools. The hospital was an early champion of vaccination and among the first to adopt chloroform as an anesthetic. When

Florence Nightingale returned from the battlefields of Crimea to establish a training school for nurses in 1860, she chose St. Thomas'. Railway construction had forced the move to the new riverside site, directly opposite the newly completed Houses of Parliament.

It was common for McGill graduates to travel overseas for additional training in Britain or Europe to learn the latest procedures and techniques or to pursue a specialty such as obstetrics or pathology. Cream settled on London and St. Thomas', and his goal was to qualify for membership in England's prestigious Royal College of Surgeons. The "MRCS" after his name promised to open doors—and patients' pocketbooks.

◇◇◇◇◇

St. Thomas' eight-building complex—"the finest hospital in Great Britain, if not in the world," in the estimation of the *British Medical Journal*—occupied a narrow half-mile strip of riverbank south of Westminster Bridge. A row of identical, four-story blocks created a series of pavilions with connecting corridors and sunlit, well-ventilated wards, a design championed by Nightingale. The medical school was housed in a smaller building at the south end of the grounds, under an Italianate tower that marked its location like a landlocked lighthouse. The school had illustrious neighbors. It backed onto the crenellated gatehouses of Lambeth Palace, the residence of the archbishop of Canterbury since medieval times. When students glanced in the opposite direction, across the Thames, they could check the time on Big Ben.

With its modern facilities and a reputation for excellence, St. Thomas' promised to make up for the shortcomings in Cream's McGill training. It was one of the city's busiest hospitals, admitting thirty-four hundred patients and treating another seventy thousand in its outpatient department every year. "All students," the medical school's prospectus promised, "have the opportunity afforded of being engaged in the performance of practical duties" and could study an array of emerging specialties, including mental illness; ailments of the eyes, skin, and teeth; and diseases affecting women and children. The move to Lambeth "was followed by a renaissance in the medical school," in the words of the hospital's official history, attracting a group of young, talented doctors who were "competent to give students a good training in all branches of medicine and surgery."

ST. THOMAS' HOSPITAL IN LAMBETH (AUTHOR COLLECTION)

An intersection of poverty, crime, and industry had made Lambeth the logical location for the new St. Thomas'. As a charity hospital, it cared for poor people who could not afford a doctor's fee or nursing care at home. "The hospital should be in a densely populated neighbourhood," explained Sydney Jones, a surgeon who lectured in the medical school, "of ready access to the masses, in proximity to factories and accident-making districts." It was. Squalid tenements and poor sanitation filled the wards of St. Thomas' hospital with the sick; victims of assaults and drunken brawls turned up at the outpatients department to have wounds mended; factories fed the hospital a steady stream of mangled workers.

There was a downside. Lambeth's streetwalkers and brothels tempted the young men studying at St. Thomas'. "That a little over-indulgence should follow on sudden liberty in a great centre of life," one medical student argued in their collective defense, "is only to be expected."

Inspector John Bennett Tunbridge, who was leading Scotland Yard's probe of the Lambeth poisonings, had confirmed Cream's connection to St. Thomas' early in the investigation. Cream had arrived in London for the first time in October 1876, at age twenty-six, and registered as student no. 2016. He was among almost two hundred "cubs," as students were known around the hospital—even the men who, like him, already had a medical degree and sought to specialize or to upgrade their qualifications. Cream focused on obstetrics, a promising and wide-open field for a young doctor, as the medical profession was only beginning to intrude into the traditional domain of the midwife. He later claimed to have seen or treated five hundred pregnant women during his two years at St. Thomas', and he assisted and advised others as they performed abortions to save the life of the mother.

Cream would emerge from St. Thomas' with an award of honor for his studies. His entry in the ledger the hospital used to keep track of student work and achievements, however, contains only a single notation, confirming that he served as a dresser. These assistants accompanied surgeons on their rounds, observed as their instructor diagnosed and assessed patients, and did the grunt work of tending wounds and changing bandages. "A good dresser," noted one doctor who trained at St. Thomas', "generally makes a good surgeon."

Students who wanted more experience were offered appointments as clerks in the wards or the outpatients department. Cream either chose not to apply for these positions or his applications were turned down. Men who had already qualified as physicians could supervise undergraduate students as they studied obstetrics, ophthalmology, and other specialties. He did not. The medical school's secretary, George Rendle, urged students to devote "as much time as they can spare from

STUDENTS PREPARE MEDICINES IN A CHEMICAL LABORATORY AT ST. THOMAS' HOSPITAL. (*GRAPHIC*, OCTOBER 2, 1886 / AUTHOR COLLECTION)

other engagements to clinical study in the wards and in the out-patients' rooms." Cream's sparse student record suggests he found other ways to occupy his free time.

He had come to London not just to boost his credentials but also out of desperation to escape his past and his forced marriage. But even in a vast city an ocean away from Canada, Cream encountered people who knew him. Four other McGill graduates were studying at St. Thomas' in the fall of 1876, including three members of his graduating class. He spent his first year avoiding one of them, Herbert Reddy, who knew about his scrapes back home. The fire at Miss Porter's boarding-house in Montreal? Reddy had heard the rumors and was convinced that Cream had torched his room to collect the insurance money. The hotelkeeper's daughter he seduced and the shotgun wedding? Reddy had heard all about that too.

Then Archdeacon David Lindsay, who had performed the marriage ceremony in Quebec, showed up in England in November 1876 after the death of his brother, a London merchant. Flora Brooks had asked him to deliver a parcel to her husband, and Cream called on Lindsay at the late brother's home in North London to collect the package. After he left, Lindsay's relatives inquired about the visitor and recognized the name: he was courting a wealthy young woman who lived in the neighborhood, a Miss Alexander. The woman soon learned Cream was married, and the relationship ended.

Within months he was pursuing the daughter of his landlady at Gough Square, a cul-de-sac just off Fleet Street where he had taken lodgings. This woman also had connections in Canada. Sometime in March 1877, she received a letter from a friend in Montreal, Charlotte Louisa Botterill, announcing that Cream had gotten a respectable girl in "trouble" and had abandoned her the day after their wedding. Cream, outraged by the revelations, retained a London lawyer and threatened to sue for libel, even though the account was accurate. Botterill apologized for her comments, ending the dispute. In the meantime, the letter no doubt ended his latest dalliance as well.

◇◇◇◇◇

THERE were nineteen medical licensing bodies in Britain, creating a "bewildering multiplicity of qualifications," as a prominent surgeon put it. The Royal College of Surgeons of England, sixteen thousand strong, was the largest and most influential. Candidates for membership had to pass one or two rounds of examinations, depending on their previous medical education and qualifications. A board of examiners composed of college fellows—all with at least six years of professional experience—oversaw the examinations and formulated the questions. The failure rate was high. In 1876, seven hundred candidates wrote the preliminary examination for membership and barely half received a passing mark. One out of four candidates failed the second examination, in surgical anatomy and the principles and practice of surgery and medicine, and were denied membership.

Cream paid the five-pound five-shilling fee and sat for an examination on the afternoon of April 16, 1877, alongside graduates of St. Bartholomew's, University College, and other London schools. College records do not indicate whether he took the preliminary test or if, based on five years of training at McGill and St. Thomas', he was eligible to write the final exam. He had three hours to answer four questions that demanded a thorough understanding of anatomy, disease, and treatments. There were only two possible results: candidates were either approved or "referred"—a polite way of saying they had failed the examination.

Cream was referred.

Candidates could rewrite the examination after a waiting period of several months, but he did not make a second attempt to enter the college. He remained in London and continued his training at St. Thomas', completing his service as a dresser in July 1877.

Students often ventured into Lambeth's slums as part of their training, to make house calls on patients unable to come to the hospital for treatment. Part of the obstetrics training was to assist midwives and, since at the time children were born at home, Cream and other students witnessed the worst conditions the neighborhood had to offer. The celebrated author W. Somerset Maugham, who trained at St. Thomas' little more than a decade after Cream, remembered nighttime forays into mazes of streets where a stranger risked being robbed or beaten. He was led down dank alleys and into filthy, crowded tenements, passing unmolested through areas "the police hesitated to enter, but in which my black bag amply protected me."

Cream, like Maugham, saw how the people of Lambeth trusted and respected a doctor. He would remember the squalor and desperation, how life in London's slums was a daily walk along a knife edge between good and evil, between life and death.

And he would remember the women who sold their bodies on Lambeth's streets.

19

A PREMATURE DEATH

{WATERLOO, QUEBEC • SUMMER 1877}

A WATERLOO NOTARY WAS SUMMONED TO THE HOME OF Lyman Brooks on a hot summer day to call on Flora. She was too ill to leave her room—and too young to be requesting this particular form of legal service. Louis Jodoin dipped his fountain pen, noted the date—July 25, 1877—at the top of a blank form, and began the ominous task.

"Being sick of body but sane of mind, memory, judgment and understanding," he wrote in his not-quite-perfect English, and "in the prospect of death," the wife of "Thomas N. Cream, Physician and Surgeon . . . hath requested us said Notary to receive and draw her Last Will and Testament."

Flora Brooks's declining health was puzzling. She had rebounded from the effects of the abortion performed almost a year earlier—"fairly recovered," as her father put it. She had not seen her husband since the day after the wedding, but she had written to him while he was studying at St. Thomas' and had dispatched a parcel when she discovered that Archdeacon Lindsay would be visiting London. Flora may have hoped that Cream would return to

Waterloo once he completed his studies and make her a doctor's wife in fact as well as in name.

Then, almost as suddenly as before, she became seriously ill. She descended into "a half state of insensibility," by one account, and "seemed almost an imbecile." It was some time before she regained the ability to speak. The family doctor, Cornelius Phelan, was called in, but he could find no explanation for her symptoms.

Then Flora admitted she had been taking medicine Cream had sent to her.

Phelan ordered her to stop taking it, and her symptoms faded away. The medicine was never tested, but the doctor was certain it contained some substance that had made her ill.

Her health, however, remained fragile. By the summer of 1877, she was near death—and dictating her will to a lawyer. She may have suspected Cream had tried to kill her with his medicine. She may have discovered his womanizing in London. Or perhaps Lyman Brooks had convinced her that her husband should not profit from her death. Whatever her reasons, she directed that her entire estate would go to her father.

She died eighteen days later, on August 12, a day the heavens dumped more than an inch of rain on Waterloo. Brooks was buried in a cemetery one block south of St. Luke's Anglican Church. A single rose was carved into the top portion of her gravestone, which bore her maiden name and described her, in a final bid to preserve her reputation, as the "Wife of Dr. T. N. Cream." The marker also recorded her exact age: twenty-four years, nine months, and three days—stark evidence of a life tragically cut short.

The news soon reached Cream. In lieu of a note of sympathy, he presented Lyman Brooks with a letter from a London law firm demanding one thousand dollars from his late wife's estate, ignoring the terms of their marriage contract and Flora's will, which left him nothing. Two more demands followed until a final missive, dated April 10, 1878, offered to settle for two hundred dollars. Jodoin advised Brooks to accept. As galling as it was, he wrote a check to his son-in-law.

FLORA ELIZA BROOKS'S HEADSTONE IN WATERLOO, QUEBEC, IDENTIFIES HER AS THE "WIFE OF DR. T. N. CREAM." (AUTHOR PHOTO)

No official death record for Flora appears to have survived. The *Waterloo Advertiser* reported that she died "after a lingering illness." Lung diseases were one of the leading causes of death in the Waterloo area in the 1870s, and Lyman Brooks later claimed his daughter had been stricken with bronchitis, then contracted consumption—the deadly disease that was only beginning to be referred to by its modern name, tuberculosis.

Was Flora Brooks murdered? Had Cream sent her medicine laced with poison? He certainly had reason to want her dead. Having a wife back in Canada had scuttled his relationships with at least two women he had courted in London. And divorce had not been an option—the marriage contract left him on the hook, for as long as she lived, for a crippling ten-thousand-dollar payout if he had tried to end the marriage. Her death was not only sudden; it was convenient.

If poison or the abortion performed the previous September had caused Flora's death, Cream could have been charged with murder. Canadian law allowed a homicide prosecution to proceed in cases where "the stroke was received or cause of death administered" within the previous year. There was a recent precedent involving another McGill graduate: Dr. Eric Sparham, who practiced in Brockville,

Ontario, had been convicted in 1875 of murdering a woman who died after he performed an abortion.

Dr. Phelan should have alerted the local coroner about Flora Brooks's baffling symptoms and the suspicious medicine Cream had sent to her from London. Instead, he said nothing. No inquiry was launched into the disturbing chain of events that culminated in her death.

It was a decision he would come to regret. Fifteen years later, he received a visit from a Scotland Yard detective. Inspector Jarvis's interviews with Lyman Brooks and Archdeacon David Lindsay revealed the abortion, the forced marriage, and the groom's escape to England to study at St. Thomas' Hospital. Then the inspector called on Dr. Phelan. He was curious to hear the doctor's opinion on the cause of Flora's untimely death. He wanted to know if she had been the first of Cream's growing list of victims.

Dr. Phelan "never saw any of the medicine Cream had sent his wife," Jarvis reported after their discussion in the summer of 1892, "but he strongly suspected him of foul play."

20

THE LICENTIATE

{EDINBURGH • APRIL 1878}

THREE TIMES EACH YEAR, MEDICAL SCHOOL GRADUATES from across Britain converged on Edinburgh. In January, April, and July, the city's two professional bodies—the Royal College of Physicians and the Royal College of Surgeons—examined candidates for a license to practice both medicine and surgery. It was the only dual certification available in the United Kingdom, and the twenty-one-pound fee for two licenses made it even more attractive. "The fees are moderate, the journey agreeable, the locality interesting and attractive," noted the author of an overview of medical education in Britain in the 1870s, "and much trouble is saved to the candidate by having to present himself at one board of examiners only." To medical students, this writer added, the Scottish capital was a place "where diplomas were cheap, and regarded as easily obtainable."

Edinburgh, the birthplace of the Scottish Enlightenment, had been a center of learning for centuries, the "Athens of the North" to its boosters. It was also dirty and polluted, mocked as "Auld Reikie"—Old Smokey—for the coal smoke in the air. The city huddled beneath an eponymous castle, which crowned a rocky outcrop like a second

Parthenon. Home to more than two hundred thousand, it was less than half the size of Glasgow, forty miles to the west, where Cream had briefly lived as a child. Edinburgh University's medical school was the largest in Britain, with a student body of thirteen hundred—at a time when London's eleven schools had a combined enrollment of less than nineteen hundred—and an international reputation for excellence. Surgical procedures were more advanced than those Cream had watched in Montreal. The operating table Edinburgh's instructors used for demonstrations was clean and covered with a sheet of waterproof material; a tray of sawdust was placed below to absorb the patient's blood. Joseph Lister's antiseptic techniques, a novelty at McGill, were in everyday use.

CREAM IN THE MID-1870S
(MCCORD MUSEUM II-24647.1)

After failing to obtain a license in London, Cream traveled north to try once again. He was just shy of his twenty-eighth birthday when he arrived in Edinburgh in the spring of 1878. He faced two rounds of written examinations, each requiring a day to complete and followed, a few days later, by a summons to appear before a panel of examiners for further evaluation and questioning. Candidates were asked to perform surgical procedures on cadavers, if enough bodies were available, and College of Physicians assessors expected the hopeful prospects to examine and correctly diagnose hospital patients "labouring under disease."

The drawn-out examination process kept Cream in Edinburgh for at least two weeks. The spring weather was cloudy and dull, with only a couple of hours of sunshine to lift the gloom on most days. At some point, he may have met or encountered Arthur Conan Doyle— the future author was completing his second year of studies at the medical school and was in the city for most of April. Cream might have downed pints or sipped sherry at Rutherford's bar on Drummond Street, a favorite haunt of Conan Doyle and other medical students.

Cream did come face-to-face with Conan Doyle's favorite medical school instructor and one of Edinburgh's most renowned physicians, Dr. Joseph Bell. He was secretary-treasurer of Edinburgh's Royal College of Surgeons in 1878, and Cream and other candidates were directed to his home at 20 Melville Street to submit their educational and training records and to pay examination fees. A wiry man with an eagle-beak nose, Dr. Bell taught surgery and amazed his students with his ability to size up patients—a crucial skill for any doctor in an era when a diagnosis was often based on little more than a person's appearance and visible symptoms. But he seemed to be able to read minds as well. Within seconds of meeting new patients, he could correctly identify where they had been born, where they lived, what they did for a living, and other personal details. Conan Doyle, who worked as Dr. Bell's assistant during his student days and, to prepare his case notes, had interviewed each patient moments before, was in awe. "His intuitive powers," he recalled, "were simply marvellous." Years later, when Conan Doyle longed to abandon medicine for a writing career and was looking for a model for a fictional detective, he would remember Dr. Bell's amazing powers of observation, how he used logic and evidence to make lightning-fast deductions. And in that instant, Sherlock Holmes would be born.

Dr. Bell's remarkable skills involved a combination of careful observation and deduction. Accents, he told his students, betrayed place of birth. Clothing revealed lives of hardship or good fortune. Hands screamed occupation. "The scars of the miner differ from those of the quarryman," he pointed out, just as the calluses built up on a carpenter's hands "are not those of the mason." Soldiers and sailors walked in different ways. Tattoos recorded voyages to distant lands. Details such as these were telling, and mattered. Never forget "the vast importance of little distinctions," he urged his students, "the endless significance of the trifles."

Dr. Bell sometimes used his deductive skills to investigate crimes, assisting Dr. Henry Littlejohn, Edinburgh's police surgeon. His inquiries cracked at least one murder case, in 1877; Bell was the only one who noticed that Eugene Chantrelle had loosened a gas pipe fitting in his Edinburgh home to make his wife's murder look like an accidental poisoning. And Bell was convinced that his methods could be used more widely in criminal investigations. Seemingly insignificant details—a suspect's gait, a spatter of mud on a murder victim's trousers—could be the key to solving a case. "It would be a great thing," he believed, "if the police generally could be trained to observe more closely."

◇◇◇◇◇

THE Edinburgh examinations began on April 2, and tested Cream's knowledge of anatomy, physiology, and chemistry. One in three candidates failed to get through this round in 1878.

This time, Cream passed.

The second-round examination covered more specialized subjects, including surgery, surgical anatomy, pharmaceuticals, the practice of medicine, and midwifery. On Saturday April 13, a few days after writing the second round, Cream appeared before six examiners for further questioning, and Dr. Bell was among the representatives of the College of Surgeons on the panel.

A quarter of the candidates who advanced to the second round that year were rejected. Cream was among the 159 granted a license.

The president of the College of Surgeons, Dr. Patrick Heron

Watson, signed off on the panel's finding that Cream had been tested on his "skill in Anatomy, Surgery and Pharmacy" and "found duly qualified to practice these arts." As a licentiate of both of Edinburgh's professional bodies, Cream was now entitled to display the professional markers LRCP Ed. (Licentiate of the Royal College of Physicians of Edinburgh) and LRCS Ed. (Licentiate of the Royal College of Surgeons of Edinburgh) after his name. The double qualification, noted a medical expert of the time, "should entitle its holder to practice all branches of the profession in any part of Her Majesty's dominions."

Dr. Bell had plenty of time during the April 13 examination to size up Cream, to glean information from his mannerisms and his appearance, to search for clues as he had done so often to the astonishment of his students. Cream never lost his Scottish accent, and Bell would have found it easy to pinpoint his Glasgow origins. From Cream's expensive clothes he may have deduced—correctly—that this scion of a wealthy Canadian family, sent overseas to burnish his medical credentials, was vain, self-absorbed, and spoiled. But not even Joseph Bell, for all his superhuman ability to observe and deduce, sensed the evil lurking within Thomas Neill Cream.

21

CATHARINE HUTCHINSON GARDNER

{LONDON, ONTARIO • 1879}

A YOUNG GIRL WALKED TOWARD THE PRIVY BEHIND Bennet's Fancy Store, her family's business. It was the first day of May, but spring had come late to the Ontario city of London that year. A stubborn frost clung to windowpanes for the third morning in a row.

Jessie Bennet opened the door.

A woman in her midtwenties was seated inside, motionless and slumped against the wall. A black straw hat, trimmed with netting and sprouting a gray ostrich feather, lay at her feet. A faded purple dress, scuffed shoes, a cheap ring with imitation garnet stone on a finger of her right hand—this was a woman of limited means. Bennet fetched her brother, who assumed the woman must be asleep or drunk. The children alerted a passing policeman. Constable William Rider touched the woman. She was dead.

On the seat beside the body was a small silk handkerchief and an upright, uncorked medicine bottle containing a colorless liquid.

Rider summoned a doctor, James Niven, who estimated she had been dead since daybreak. He detected an odor familiar to any medical man. Arthur Conan Doyle described it as "a sweetish, insidious scent." Chloroform. The woman's nose and cheeks were blotched and raw—burned, Dr. Niven suspected, from contact with the chemical.

Before the body was removed to the London General Hospital for an autopsy, another doctor showed up. His office was on an upper floor at 204 Dundas Street, above Hiscox's Livery Stable and next door to Bennet's store. A lane and outdoor stairway connected his building to the privy in the backyard. He identified the woman as a maid at the nearby Tecumseh House Hotel. He knew her name too—Kitty Gardner. She had consulted him several times. A reporter at the scene jotted down the name of this helpful bystander: Dr. Cream.

∞∞∞

INSPECTOR Jarvis visited London in mid-July 1892, following up on Dr. Herbert Reddy's tip that his McGill classmate had been implicated in a woman's death in the Ontario city more than a decade earlier. Cream, Jarvis learned, had established a practice in the city in the fall of 1878. After earning his licenses in medicine and surgery in Edinburgh, he had returned to North America in search of a city in need of a doctor. He wound up in Des Moines, a coal mining center and the capital of Iowa. "Not liking the place," as Cream later put it, he headed back to Canada and stepped off a train in London, midway between Detroit and Toronto.

The largest city in southwestern Ontario, it had enough factories and foundries on its outskirts to resemble "a miniature Pittsburgh." The population would soon top twenty thousand, and London was shedding the "raw newness and impermanence" of its early decades, noted one local historian. The Tecumseh House Hotel—grand enough for royalty and completed in time to host the future king of England in 1860—beckoned to travelers arriving at the neighboring Great Western Railway depot. But plank sidewalks and muddy streets mocked the brick-and-stone dignity of the Tecumseh and other new buildings of the commercial district.

After living in the British capital for two years, Cream encountered familiar place names in his new home. This London also straddled a Thames River, and he could once again stroll on Oxford, Regent, and Pall Mall streets. A nearby village was called Lambeth.

CREAM'S MEDICAL OFFICE IN LONDON, ONTARIO, WAS LOCATED ABOVE THE LIVERY STABLE ON THE RIGHT OF THIS PHOTOGRAPH. CATHARINE GARDNER'S BODY WAS FOUND IN A PRIVY BEHIND THE BUILDING. (McCORD MUSEUM N-0000.193.271.1-2)

Advertisements for Cream's practice began to appear on the front pages of London's papers, the *London Free Press* and the *Daily Advertiser*, in September 1878. He claimed top spot in the medical section of the classifieds, muscling out established physicians and dentists with a large notice that touted his Edinburgh credentials, his specialization in midwifery, and his training at St. Thomas'. He boarded at 250 Queens Avenue, a few minutes' walk from his office, on one of the city's finest residential streets.

Cream was active in his new community. He registered to vote in Ontario elections. He attended Park Avenue Presbyterian Church, and a local man who befriended him, James Reid, described him as a "pillar" of the congregation. He taught Sunday school each week, helping children improve their reading and writing skills as well as introducing them to the Gospels and the missionary work of the church. He joined the local chapter of the Young Men's Christian Association. Founded in the 1840s, the organization catered to young, single men like Cream. It offered "a safe Christian environment," one writer noted, to divert its members from "the temptations of alcohol, gambling, and prostitution." The London YMCA organized sporting events and camping excursions. On a Friday night, he might head to the Oddfellows' Hall for a gathering of the Bachelors' Club, a group of unattached men who had banded together to promote "social inter-course and moral improvement." And he continued to sing at public events, as he had at McGill. He was on the program in March 1879 when the Ladies' Aid Society of another Presbyterian congregation staged an evening of music and readings, and sang the French national anthem, "La Marseillaise," to an audience of about six hundred.

But there were two Thomas Neill Creams. The respectable, churchgoing, community-minded young doctor with the fine sing-ing voice seemed to vanish with the setting sun. A shadowy figure took his place, drawn to the temptations the YMCA urged young men to avoid. At night "he was always to be found with a number of London's most congenial spirits," recalled James Reid. He frequented the city's hotels "with his more intimate friends" and "indulged in excess in the flowing bowl"—a polite term, in those days, for drunk-enness. It was scandalous behavior for an educated, professional man from a prominent family—"respectable people did not get drunk," noted one study of life in the Victorian era, "or behave wildly," as Cream did. He began to live a double life. "He guarded his reputation well," Reid added, "and was never found in the day time when he was not perfectly right."

Cream was a hypocrite in an age of hypocrisy. A respectable facade could mask an appetite for drink, illicit sex, and other sins being denounced from the pulpit every Sunday. Many Victorian men who "professed allegiance to the sexual ideals of purity and self-restraint," a historian of the period has noted, "spent their nights prowling through the underworld of prostitution and sexual deviancy." Within a few years, the writer Robert Louis Stevenson would explore what he saw as the "thorough and primitive duality of man" in his classic story the *Strange Case of Dr. Jekyll and Mr. Hyde.* Physician Henry Jekyll, like Cream, enjoyed "the respect of the wise and good" but concealed his guilty pleasures. Once out of the public eye, he "laid aside restraint and plunged in shame." Jekyll concocted a drug that released a debauched and murderous inner demon. Cream was releasing a Mr. Hyde of his own.

Six months after his arrival, his professional reputation came under fire. He was hauled before police magistrate Lawrence Lawrason in February 1879 and charged under Ontario's Medical Act with practising without a license. In court, Cream claimed it was all a misunderstanding—he had submitted the required fee, but the Ontario Medical Council had failed to issue a license. The case was adjourned for a week to allow the council's inspector to follow up with his superiors in Toronto. Within a few days, both London newspapers reported that the allegation had been withdrawn. Cream "paid his registration fees and obtained his licence sometime previous to his commencing practice in this city," the *Daily Advertiser* assured its readers, "and therefore the authorities were in error in taking proceedings." The press reports were in error, however, not the medical authorities. The prosecution, indexed as Case No. 199 on the court's docket, remained active for months as Lawrason granted one adjournment after another. The local papers appear to have published no updates as the prosecution stalled. As far as the public was concerned, Cream was a licensed physician.

The allegation of illegal practice was still before the magistrate when Catharine Gardner was found dead in the privy just steps from

Cream's office. "The general opinion is that it is a case of suicide," readers were told when the *London Free Press* broke the news on May 3. It was believed the woman had been pregnant, "and to hide her shame it is conjectured she took poison."

"But the real cause," the report cautioned, "cannot be ascertained before the inquest."

◇◇◇◇◇

"IT is indeed desirable," noted William Fuller Alves Boys, an Ontario lawyer and the province's leading authority on the Office of the Coroner, that inquests into sudden, unexpected deaths "should be held with as little delay as possible; yet nothing can be more reprehensible than *unseemly* haste." Some coroners, overeager to take charge of a corpse, had been known to hover at the bedsides of dying victims of violence or accidents. Such disgraceful conduct, Boys warned, undermined the dignity of the office. "Coroners who wantonly give additional pain to that which a sudden death has already caused," he noted in his definitive work, *A Practical Treatise on the Office and Duties of Coroners in Ontario*, "cannot be too strongly condemned."

Was an inquest needed to confirm what appeared obvious—that Gardner had taken her own life? The decision rested with Dr. John R. Flock, the City of London's forty-six-year-old coroner, who had been practicing medicine for two decades. The law made his duty clear: he was to investigate any death caused by an unlawful act, negligence, or "violence or unfair means," while ignoring the victims of "mere accident or mischance." It was a tough call. A heated debate over the number of inquests and the conduct of coroners was being waged in Ontario's newspapers that year. One critic, in a scathing letter published in Canada's capital, Ottawa, argued that few inquests— only one of every one hundred, the writer claimed—were justified. Coroners were padding their fees at taxpayers' expense, and there had been "quarrels approaching to fights" as rival coroners squabbled over bodies. One small-town coroner responded with a passionate defense of the office. Unless inquiries were held to confirm or rule out murder, "there would be no safeguard for existence—men's lives would be at the mercy of the secret assassin, who could ply his deadly art with comparative immunity."

Coroners took the lead role in murder investigations for much of the nineteenth century. They were part judge, part detective—responsible for gathering evidence and presenting it to a jury, which would decide whether a crime was committed and, if possible, name those responsible. When a death was reported, they were expected to rush to the scene, as William Boys put it, "whilst the body is still fresh." They were to check the corpse for wounds, bruises, or other marks that might suggest the cause of death. They should note any bloodstains or mud on the victim's body or clothing and scour the surrounding area for traces of blood and footprints. If poisoning was suspected, "every vessel in which food has recently been prepared should be examined, and the contents reserved for analysis." If the death appeared suspicious, Boys's concerns about acting with unseemly haste vanished; an inquest should be convened as soon as possible. The coroner was in complete control of the next phase of the investigation as well, deciding who would be summoned to testify, questioning each witness, and scribbling detailed notes of their responses. If the jury concluded the victim had been murdered, the coroner had the power to order the suspect's arrest. The evidence gathered would then be forwarded to the local prosecutor, who would take the case to court. Despite the coroner's key role and demanding duties, Ontario appointees were not required to have medical or legal training. While most, like Flock, were doctors, candidates were expected only to be "of sound mind" and possess "the amount of education and mental ability necessary for the proper discharge of the duties." Knowing the right people was essential; appointments were made on the recommendation of local politicians and power brokers who had influence with the Ontario government. The legal concepts and procedures a coroner needed to grasp—from how to conduct a trial-like hearing to the distinction between murder and the less-blameworthy crime of manslaughter—were summarized in Boys's indispensable guide. Dr. Flock likely had a copy on his office desk, ready to be consulted. The coroner was to undertake his investigations "with great caution, if not scepticism," the manual advised, "always remembering that hasty conclusions or thoughtless omissions may both endanger his own reputation and the lives of his fellow creatures."

An inexperienced or careless coroner could jeopardize an investigation or allow a killer to escape unpunished. When a woman died in Sarnia, Ontario, a few days before Catharine Gardner, her stomach was removed during an autopsy, placed in a glass container, and shipped to Toronto, the provincial capital, for chemical analysis. A doctor was implicated in her death, and the authorities suspected some form of poison had been administered to produce an abortion. But the coroner or the assistant who had forwarded the evidence failed to properly seal the container, and some of the liquid inside leaked out. Ontario's deputy attorney general was incredulous. "The careless way in which the stomach and its contents were sent to the Analyst," John Scott scolded a local official, made it "utterly impossible to prove that they reached him in the same condition as they left the hands of the Coroner."

As the nineteenth century progressed, the coroner's investigative role shifted to the police. By the 1860s, police forces in Boston, New York, Chicago, and other major American cities had established detective branches and were pursuing their own homicide investigations. In England, detectives with London's Metropolitan Police, unwilling to wait for the coroner to complete his work, sometimes scooped up murder suspects and took them directly before the courts for trial. A rivalry developed as coroners and the police jostled over who would take charge of investigations; the winner sometimes depended, one British coroner complained, "upon who gets possession of the prisoner first."

In a small community such as London, Ontario, where the police force was understaffed and murders were rare, the coroner's traditional monopoly over homicide cases remained intact. The police deferred to Dr. Flock's expertise, and officers played a supporting role in his investigations—testifying at inquests if they had been at the crime scene, and helping round up witnesses. Chief of Police William T. T. Williams, who had been a detective in England, was saddled with about half the men he needed to patrol the growing city. His officers were poorly paid and poorly trained, valued more for their size and ability to subdue troublemakers than for their intelligence or investigative skills. "We can't hire gentlemen to serve as policemen," Williams acknowledged, "for $1.25 a day." Constables had their hands full as they rounded up rowdies and drunks, who accounted for almost half of all arrests the city's twenty-member force made in 1878. The week Gardner's body was discovered, patrolmen were rebuked for ignoring offenders that the press, at least, considered a serious threat to the public peace—stray cattle. "The animals roam around at night," one of the city's papers complained, "destroying the shade trees and boulevards."

Coroner Flock quickly ordered an inquest into Gardner's death, but a crucial mistake had already been made: her body had been removed from the outhouse before it could be viewed by a coroner's jury. "If possible, the body should be first viewed exactly in the position in which it was found," Boys advised the province's coroners. Dr. Flock should have escorted the jurors to the back of Bennet's Fancy Store to see the outhouse while Gardner was still inside, with the bottle of chloroform on the seat beside her. He should have drawn their attention to the burned skin on her face and any other injuries, as well as any marks on her body or clothing, before she was moved. He was supposed to point out any footprints visible in the surrounding ground—possible proof that someone else had been present.

"Murderers," Boys warned in his manual, "have been known to purposely place their victims in positions calculated to indicate accidental or suicidal death."

22

BY SOME PERSON UNKNOWN

{MAY–JULY 1879}

D R. FLOCK OPENED THE INQUEST INTO GARDNER'S DEATH in the London hospital's "dead house," as morgues were known, within hours of the discovery of her body. A jury was sworn in to view the body and hear evidence. In Ontario, such juries had to have at least twelve members—"lawful and honest men," each one under the age of sixty and literate enough to write their own name.

Constable Rider had retrieved the medicine bottle and handker-chief from the outhouse and brought them, along with two letters found in Gardner's pockets, to the inquest. Friends and coworkers at the Tecumseh House Hotel were sworn in and described the woman they knew as Kitty. Catharine Hutchinson Gardner had grown up on a farm near Kinkardine, about a hundred miles north of London. She had been feeling ill and had left the hotel a week earlier. One witness described her as "down-hearted" about being too weak to work, but no one thought she was suicidal. The bottle containing the chloroform bore the label of a local drugstore, but the owner swore the chemical was sold only to doctors.

Dr. James Niven had already completed an autopsy—coroners, even those with medical training, were required to delegate the task to the most qualified local doctor available—and he was able to reveal why Gardner had felt unwell. She had been two months pregnant. He did not, however, suspect suicide. The burns to her face showed the chloroform had been held tightly against the skin, and he doubted she could have held the handkerchief to her face long enough to kill herself. "The marks produced would lead me to believe that the poison was forcibly applied," he explained, "and could have been applied by some other person standing in front of the deceased." Catharine Gardner, in his opinion, had been murdered.

Dr. Flock adjourned the hearing so more witnesses could be summoned. He would have to trace Gardner's movements in the days before she died. He needed to identify the father of her child, and he needed to find the source of the chloroform. He was now looking for a killer.

⬦⬦⬦⬦⬦

WHEN the inquest resumed on the afternoon of May 7, two more physicians came forward to support Dr. Niven's theory. The handkerchief found beside Gardner's body was too small to absorb enough chloroform to kill her, they said. It must have been saturated and held to her face more than once. Besides, Gardner would have fallen unconscious before she could inhale a lethal dose. One of the physicians, Charles Moore, checked her hands at the morgue. "No stains of chloroform were found on them," he reported.

London was rife with rumors about who might be responsible. One name kept popping up at the inquest. Gardner was last seen alive on the Friday evening before her death, walking along Dundas Street toward Cream's office.

Sarah Long, a Tecumseh House Hotel maid who had roomed with Gardner, identified the baby's father as a man named Johnson who lived in another town. Then she shocked onlookers with a sinister tale of deceit and attempted blackmail. Gardner had gone to Cream for an abortion, but he had refused to provide drugs or perform the operation. Instead, Long claimed, Cream had urged Gardner to seduce and sleep with one of the Tecumseh's residents, a wealthy businessman named William H. Birrell. She could then accuse Birrell of being the father, and Cream, as her doctor, had promised to back her paternity claim. The plot was supposed to be a secret—Cream, Long said, had ordered Gardner "never to breathe his name."

The next witness was Birrell, who assured Flock he had never met or spoken to Gardner. Then it was Cream's turn. He had met Gardner soon after his arrival in the city—she was Presbyterian, and they may have known each other through the church—and he had treated her for minor ailments. An examination on April 5 had confirmed she was pregnant.

"She offered me $100 to make her right. I said I would not touch her for $1000," he said. "She cried in my office and said she would poison herself. I said I could do nothing for her." Three days later, he continued, a letter was slipped under his office door. Gardner's name was at the bottom, and Cream said he recognized her handwriting. He had handed it over to the coroner earlier in the day:

I called this afternoon to see you again about what I was speaking to you last Saturday but found you out. I am getting worse and getting stouter every day. . . . As I told you before Mr. W. H. Birrell is the cause of my troubles. He says he will pay you well if you make this all right for he is getting very anxious about me.

I can not get out tomorrow but will call to see you on Thursday when I hope you will consent to do what I want done.

Cream insisted he saw her for the last time on April 20 and claimed there was no chloroform in his office. Surprisingly, he was not questioned about the alleged blackmail plot.

Cream had no real alibi for the night before her body was found.

He said he had been out most of the evening, before returning to his office at eleven and sleeping there overnight. By his own admission, he had been close by as her body was placed in the outhouse. As for the letter he claimed had come from Gardner—accusing Birrell of fathering her child—it did not appear to be genuine. Sarah Long looked it over and said the signature and writing did not match other letters she had seen from Gardner. Robert Gardner, her brother, was confident he "would recognize her handwriting anywhere" and swore it had been written by someone else.

The jurors deliberated for more than ninety minutes before announcing a verdict: Catharine Gardner had been murdered—poisoned with chloroform "administered to her by some person or persons to us unknown." While they had not seen her body in the outhouse, they concluded it had been placed there after death to make the crime look like suicide. The jurors also identified Johnson as the father of Gardner's unborn child, clearing Birrell of "all blame whatsoever."

There was no exoneration for Cream, who remained the prime suspect. The *Free Press* urged Londoners to keep an open mind. While the doctor appeared to be "cognizant of some details of the transaction," an editorial cautioned two days after the verdict, "the evidence does not connect him with it in any improper way." Cream had been "resolutely opposed" to helping Gardner end her pregnancy, and there was no evidence to suggest anyone, the doctor included, had a motive to kill her. This should be borne in mind, the paper contended, "before any individual is singled out for suspicion as having committed so grave an offence as that of murder."

A day later the *Free Press* published a letter to the editor that portrayed Cream as the victim of an "extremely one-sided" inquest. If doubts remained about the letter Cream had produced, experts should be consulted to determine whether it was in Gardner's handwriting. "Fair play has not been done in this mysterious matter," the letter concluded, "nor has sufficient 'daylight' been admitted into the investigation." It was signed with the pseudonym Veritas.

Who killed Gardner? Where and when did she die? The evidence implicating Cream was circumstantial but damning. He was her doctor. She had begged him to "make her right" and, by his own admission, had offered him a hefty fee if he provided drugs or performed an abortion. When last seen alive, she had been walking toward his office. Her body was found only steps from his building, and he had been among the first people on the scene after her remains were discovered. There were whispers he had administered the chloroform as an anesthetic so that he could perform an abortion, but the chemical had killed her. Cream had then planted her body in the outhouse, staged to look like a suicide.

Coroner Flock could have consulted an expert, as the author of the Veritas letter suggested, to determine whether Gardner had written the message that conveniently identified another possible suspect in her death. Handwriting analysis had played a key role in a high-profile Boston murder trial three decades earlier, and in Britain experts were routinely consulted during criminal and civil cases when the authorship of documents was in dispute. William Boys offered advice on how to evaluate handwriting evidence in his guide for Ontario coroners: if witnesses familiar with someone's writing style expressed doubts—witnesses such as Sarah Long and Gardner's brother—this was sufficient to dismiss the document as a forgery. Boys also cautioned coroners to be wary of a witness like Cream, who seemed defensive and went to great length to exonerate himself or implicate others. "The culprit," his investigative manual observed, "is apt to betray himself by an excess of caution, or by numerous and improbable suggestions as to the cause of death."

Dr. Flock made no effort to challenge Cream's self-serving claims or to verify whether Gardner had written the letter. Fulfilling his final duty as coroner, he submitted the verdict and a transcript of the testimony to the local prosecuting attorney. The authorities, however, took no further action. Gardner's murder was never solved.

The coroner and prosecutor might have been more suspicious

and done more digging had they known about the abortion performed on Flora Brooks or about the subject of Cream's thesis at McGill: chloroform.

And no one realized how adept Cream was becoming at forging letters, deflecting blame, and plotting blackmail.

⬦⬦⬦⬦

CREAM returned to the police magistrate's court on May 27, his twenty-ninth birthday, and pleaded guilty to the charge of practising without a license. He was ordered to pay a little more than twenty-seven dollars—the minimum fine, plus court costs. No reports of his admission to practicing illegally appeared in the local papers. But his sudden notoriety, coupled with the unanswered questions about Gardner's death, made it impossible for him to remain in London. "Although he was blameless in the eyes of the law," fellow Londoner James Reid recalled, "even his friends believed him guilty, and the stigma was unremoved."

On July 5, a sweltering day in the midst of an early-summer heat wave, he left the city. He was headed west.

⬦⬦⬦⬦

THIRTEEN years later, almost to the day, a train delivered Inspector Frederick Smith Jarvis to the Ontario city. The tip he had received from the Montreal doctor Herbert Reddy proved to be correct—Reddy's former McGill classmate, Cream, had been implicated in a woman's death there. Jarvis met with the city's chief of police, who described the discovery of Catharine Gardner's body in an outbuilding behind Cream's office, the burns to her face, and the bottle of chloroform at her side. Jarvis, like the coroner's jury that investigated the case, was convinced it was murder, not suicide. "The chloroform had been held to the face for a considerable time which would be impossible for the deceased to have done," he reported to Scotland Yard. "She would have been unconscious almost immediately and consequently powerless to keep her hand to her face sufficiently long to have caused the abrasions." But Cream had denied seeing her that night, Jarvis noted, "and there was no evidence to disprove this."

Jarvis's superiors back in England, meanwhile, had been digging into Cream's past. Scotland Yard was building a case for charging Cream with one or more of the Lambeth murders, and the first step was the coroner's inquest into the death of Matilda Clover. Inspector John Bennett Tunbridge, the lead investigator, was hearing rumors that Cream had been implicated in the deaths of more women in Chicago. Then a letter arrived from the Pinkerton's National Detective Agency. Frank Murray, the superintendent of the agency's Chicago office, had read reports of Cream's arrest in the local papers, and he was certain the man who called himself Thomas Neill was a former client who had served time in the Illinois State Penitentiary for murder.

Tunbridge directed that the new information be forwarded to Jarvis "with the least possible delay." While the inquest proceeded in London, the North American phase of the investigation into the crimes of Thomas Neill Cream would soon return to the United States.

IV

INQUEST

London • June–July 1892

23

MISSING LINKS

NSPECTOR TUNBRIDGE STOPPED BY BENJAMIN PRIEST'S drugstore at 22 Parliament Street. The detective was eager to find out more about the vial of strychnine pills Cream had brought to London from America in the leather case of drug samples from the G. F. Harvey Company. He chose Priest's shop because it was close to Scotland Yard. He was in for a surprise.

"Strangely enough," he discovered, the staff knew Cream.

Clerks confirmed Cream's visits the previous fall and produced an order form filled out in his handwriting. Store records showed that Cream had bought strychnine a couple of days before Ellen Donworth's death on October 13—and an amount "sufficient," Tunbridge noted, "to cause the death of a number of persons." John Kirkby told of Cream's purchase of empty gelatin capsules and showed the inspector some that they had in stock. Tunbridge remembered Emma Shrivell's description of the "long pills" provided by Fred. The capsules were oblong, he noted, "and 'a *long pill*' would fairly describe them." Priest's records showed Cream picked up the capsules in mid-October, a few days after Donworth was poisoned. This, Tunbridge realized, would explain why he had added strychnine to a drink to kill her. By the time he killed Matilda Clover a week later, Cream had the gelatin capsules and could use them to administer the poison.

Tunbridge had stumbled on at least one of the sources of Cream's supply of strychnine. Before this discovery, officers had fanned out across London in search of a druggist, medical wholesaler, or doctor who had provided elongated pills and strychnine to a man matching Fred's description, without success. Now it turned out, the supplier they sought was almost next door to the headquarters of the Metropolitan Police. The Parliament Street shop was either missed during the inquiries or Priest's staff failed to make the connection until Tunbridge's visit.

The lead investigator on the Lambeth poisoning cases was in for a bigger shock. Within days of Cream's arrest in June, Tunbridge discovered that the blackmail letter sent to Dr. William Broadbent had been on file at Scotland Yard since the previous fall. It accused the eminent physician of poisoning Matilda Clover with strychnine. Tunbridge instantly recognized the document's significance. "The fact that Clover died of Strychnine poisoning was only known to the person who administered it until about 10 days ago," after her remains had been exhumed and tested, he noted in a June 6 report. "Therefore the writer of the letter is presumably the poisoner."

He compared the letter to samples of Cream's handwriting. They were the same. A crucial piece of evidence had been in Scotland Yard's hands—and overlooked—for months. There was a second letter, one that accused Frederick Smith, a member of Parliament, of murdering Ellen Donworth. This, too, was in Cream's writing. There were references in police files to yet another letter, to Countess Mabel Russell, accusing her husband of poisoning Clover. If Cream had written it as well, it was further evidence that he was her killer. The officer who had dealt with Russell's coachman, however, had neglected to keep the letter. The countess should be contacted and asked to hand it over, Tunbridge noted, "without delay."

A LETTER IN CREAM'S DISTINCTIVE HANDWRITING, WRITTEN TO HIS FORMER FIANCÉE, LAURA SABBATINI (SCIENCE AND SOCIETY PICTURE LIBRARY, LONDON, IMAGE 10658283)

Inquiries outside London yielded more evidence. Tunbridge interviewed Laura Sabbatini at her mother's home in Berkhamsted. Mortified to be linked to a suspected murderer and blackmailer, she was reluctant to hand over documents Cream had written. But by the time the inspector caught the train back to London, he had taken possession of Cream's will and a letter he had written when Sabbatini accepted his marriage proposal. Another lead, a slip of paper bearing the names of Alice Marsh and Emma Shrivell and their Stamford Street address, took him to Brighton. Marsh's sister, Fanny Taylor, recognized the handwriting as her sister's. The paper had been found during the search of Cream's room on Lambeth Palace Road, tucked into the pocket of a pair of trousers.

The note linked Cream to two of his victims. But Scotland Yard needed more—eyewitnesses who could identify their suspect as the mysterious Fred or, better still, had seen Cream with the murdered women. It was a slow, frustrating task. Tunbridge had arranged for Lucy Rose, the maid at Clover's lodgings, to watch Cream and other men walking along Westminster Bridge Road before his suspect was arrested, in hopes she could identify him as the man Clover was with the night before she died. Rose "took a long look" at Cream as he passed, Tunbridge reported, and said he matched Fred's "stature and general appearance." But this man was strolling in the sunshine and wearing glasses—the one she had seen in dim lamplight seven months earlier had a darker mustache, a paler complexion, and no spectacles. "Therefore," Tunbridge noted with disappointment, "she did not think it was him."

Constance Linfield, who had seen a man with Ellen Donworth the night she was poisoned, also failed to recognize Cream. Charles Burdett, the theater man and Alice Marsh's friend, identified Cream as "The Captain" he had seen on Stamford Street. But weeks earlier someone, possibly a police officer, had pointed out Cream to Burdett as a suspect in the murders, rendering his evidence useless in court. Identification lineups were arranged at the Bow Street Police Station before Cream's court appearances on the blackmailing charge. A number of newspaper reporters were enlisted for one of the viewings, and they stood alongside the man they were writing about as two witnesses filed past. Neither recognized Cream, and worse, one selected a well-known journalist and announced he was "like the man I saw."

The London papers quickly linked the blackmailing allegation to the investigation of the Lambeth murders. In the days after Cream's arraignment, there were reports that Scotland Yard was trying to connect a suspect in custody to the poisonings. "There were previous cases of poisoning which were never satisfactorily cleared up," noted the *Observer*, "and suspicion in respect of all these cases has fallen upon the man in question." The man was not named. British judges frowned on trial by newspaper and could use their contempt powers to fine or jail journalists who rushed to judgment or suggested a suspect was guilty.

To alert readers of the man's identity without ruffling judicial feathers, one paper cleverly reported the evidence pointing to the guilt of an unnamed man and then segued into an update on the blackmailing prosecution of Cream. The *Pall Mall Gazette* believed the police had evidence "pointing to systematic poisoning of women and girls," while the *Standard* assured the public that "discovery of the missing links is but a question of time." The *Daily News* was already trying to understand the murderer's twisted mind. "He is suffering from a peculiar form of mental derangement which finds exercise in a desire to take away life," the paper speculated, before comparing this killer of prostitutes to the most famous London murderer of all, Jack the Ripper. "As the history of the Whitechapel murders shows, the indulgence of this homicidal tendency upon women in a peculiarly defenceless position is not singular to the Lambeth poisoner."

In America, newspapers less circumspect than their British counterparts—and beyond the reach of the contempt powers of British judges—quickly identified Cream as a murder suspect. Headlines and stories linking him to the poisonings appeared in Philadelphia and Cincinnati barely a week after his arraignment on the blackmail charge. He was "under the most serious suspicion of having poisoned four, or possibly more, immoral girls by giving them strychnine pills," according to a London dispatch in the *Cincinnati Inquirer*. "The Scotland Yard people," the item added, "expect to bring eight crimes of this kind home to Neill." The *New York Times* named Neill as a suspect in the murders of Clover, Donworth, Shrivell, and Marsh. "The general impression is that Neill, in his attempt to levy blackmail, has got himself in a predicament that will require the utmost ingenuity to get out of," *Times* readers were told. "It is thought that a charge of willful murder will shortly be made against him." The editors of the *Buffalo Morning Express* in New York saw no need to wait for charges, let alone a conviction. An update on the evidence implicating Cream was topped with the headline "Jack the Poisoner."

Scotland Yard's chief investigator, however, was still assembling the "missing links" needed to support murder charges. The upcoming coroner's inquest into Matilda Clover's death promised to uncover fresh evidence and new leads that tied Cream to her and to the other three poisoned women. And he was determined to find Louisa Harvey, the fifth victim Cream had mentioned to John Haynes and Sergeant Patrick McIntyre. Officers in Scotland Yard divisions across the city were ordered to comb through the records of every death registered in London during the final four months of 1891. It was only a matter of time, Tunbridge was convinced, until the date of her murder was discovered.

◇◇◇◇◇

MATILDA Clover had been buried for more than six months by the time her body was exhumed in early May. Her remains were stored in a shed at Lambeth Cemetery, in the South London suburb of Tooting, for another seven weeks before a viewing was held for a coroner's jury in late June. The plate on the coffin lid still bore her name, but the corpse's face was bloated and unrecognizable. Other clues were used to confirm the body was hers: the clothing, the long brown hair and protruding front teeth, the slightly deformed nail on the right forefinger.

Their grim errand completed, the twenty-three jurors reassembled at the Vestry Hall in Tooting, a mile from the cemetery, for the inquest. While Coroner Wyatt had presided over the investigations into the deaths of Donworth, Marsh, and Shrivell, Clover's body had been exhumed and autopsied within the jurisdiction of A. Braxton Hicks, the coroner for mid-Surrey. His investigation would be far more thorough than the one years before that had failed to tie Cream to the murder of his patient Catharine Gardner in the Canadian province of Ontario. "I will do my best," Hicks promised Scotland Yard's Robert Anderson, "to elucidate this matter."

The hall could accommodate 150 people, and lawyers, witnesses, police officers, and journalists claimed many of the seats. The "chattering and laughing crowd" of Tooting residents that filled out the gallery appeared to regard the proceedings as "an entertainment especially devised for their benefit," one reporter noted. As key witnesses, one by one, were brought to the stand to testify, the rowdy spectators shushed one another. Many women had brought along their babies, and Coroner Hicks, frustrated by the crying, ordered several of these mothers to be ejected. "A coroner's court," he observed with palpable sarcasm, "was not a dry nursery."

Cream, escorted to the hearing under guard from his cell in Holloway Prison, was seated at a table at the front of the room. His lawyer was running late. Cream was offered a pencil and paper so he could take notes, but he hesitated. The police, he protested, would seize them as evidence. "I received instructions from my solicitor not to write anything at all," he said, "and since the time I was arrested on this matter I have written nothing." Hicks assured him he could retain any notes. He scribbled as witnesses testified, even after his lawyer arrived. Often, when reporters glanced his way, he was cradling his head in one hand, his eyes cast downward at his notes. He appeared calm, one reporter noted, almost defiant.

Lucy Rose, the maid at 27 Lambeth Road, and other witnesses described Clover's horrible death. Hicks zeroed in on the misdiagnosis of her symptoms and the flawed death certificate, which had allowed a murder to go undetected for months. He took Dr. Robert Graham to task for relying on the assessment of Francis Coppin, who was not a qualified physician. "If you had any accurate knowledge of the circumstances," he scolded, "you would not have given this certificate." Kirkby, the clerk at Priest's drugstore, was rebuked for selling strychnine to Cream. "In the future," Hicks advised him, "you should take a little more care."

Dr. Thomas Stevenson, the expert who had found strychnine in the bodies of Marsh and Shrivell, presented the results of his tests on Clover's remains. He had recovered a sixteenth of a grain of strychnine. While this residue was too little to kill, it indicated Clover had ingested much more before her death and "points to the administration of a fatal dose." Hicks read aloud his notes of witness descriptions of Clover's symptoms. "Not only are they consistent with, but they point to, strychnine poisoning," Dr. Stevenson confirmed, underlining Dr. Graham's negligence in certifying delirium tremens as the cause of death.

Lucy Rose, however, could not identify Cream as the man she had seen briefly in a dimly lit hallway at Clover's lodgings. Robert Taylor testified that Clover, his niece, had introduced him to a man she called Fred, a "toff" who gave her "plenty of money," at the Mason's Arms pub, and said the man bore "a strong likeness" to Cream. But he was certain the meeting had occurred at least a month before Clover's death, which was before Cream arrived in London. Emma Phillips, Clover's landlady, added to the uncertainty when she claimed Fred was the father of Clover's child and she had met him many times. She swore she had never seen Cream before.

Meanwhile, the blackmailing case also appeared to be in trouble. Cream appeared in Bow Street Magistrate's Court several times that June as prosecutors called witnesses to support the charge of blackmailing Dr. Joseph Harper. After Tunbridge's discovery of the letters sent to Dr. Broadbent and MP Frederick Smith, the prosecution announced it would pursue additional extortion charges. These letters had been read out in court on June 20, two days before the inquest opened. A handwriting expert, George Smith Inglis, testified Cream had penned every one of the letters, including three that accused Harper of murdering Marsh and Shrivell. "They are all written by one and the same individual in my opinion," he declared. Cream had tried to disguise his writing in some of the letters, he added, without success.

The magistrate, Sir John Bridge, asked if he had any doubts about his conclusions.

"None whatsoever," he replied, using two of the letters as examples. "This letter was written sloping; this one in a back hand; but they are all by the same hand."

Inglis had been analyzing handwriting for a decade. He had appeared in court to expose bogus signatures on wills and the authenticity of other disputed documents. He was, the *Strand Magazine* asserted, "the first amongst handwriting experts of the present day." But Tunbridge, who was in the courtroom, began to worry as Cream's lawyer, John Waters, conducted his cross-examination. Waters actually seemed pleased that a renowned expert believed his client had produced all the blackmail letters. "I was convinced," Tunbridge would recall, "that Inglis was wrong."

He had a hunch. After the hearing, Tunbridge obtained a sample of Laura Sabbatini's handwriting. He compared it, letter by letter, to three of the missives and "saw at once," he later reported, that all three "were undoubtedly written by her." When he confronted her at her London flat, Sabbatini admitted she had drafted them at Cream's request. Inglis submitted a revised report, acknowledging his mistake, but his credibility had been shattered.

Investigators did make inroads as the Clover inquest progressed. Tunbridge finally found the eyewitnesses he was seeking—Elizabeth Masters and Elizabeth May, the prostitutes who had met Cream the previous fall. They picked him out in a police lineup and told the coroner's inquest he was the man they had seen with Clover. Emily Sleaper, the landlady's daughter at 103 Lambeth Palace Road, testified about disturbing conversations with Cream. He had asked her to make inquiries for him at 27 Lambeth Road, Clover's former lodgings. "I know a girl there, and I think she has been poisoned," he had told her. "I want to find out if she is dead." The killer, he claimed, was Lord Russell. She had refused to run the errand. Not long after Marsh and Shrivell died, he had spoken to her again, claiming Walter Harper had killed the two women. "The scoundrel," he added, "ought to be brought to justice."

A COURTROOM ARTIST CAPTURED THE MOMENT WHEN LAURA SABBATINI
APPEARED TO TESTIFY AT THE INQUEST INTO THE DEATH OF MATILDA CLOVER.
(*PENNY ILLUSTRATED PAPER*, JULY 2, 1892)

Then Laura Sabbatini was called to testify. Murmurs rose from the spectators. Cream, who had been composed, even nonchalant as witnesses came and went, was clearly surprised and upset to see his former fiancée. Tunbridge escorted her into the hall, signaling she was cooperating with the police. She wore a black dress with small pink ribbons on the lace sleeves. Her face was veiled, but she met Cream's cold gaze for a moment before she was seated with her back to him. Her hand trembled as she held a small copy of the New Testament and swore to tell the truth. Her voice was a faint whisper. Her answers had to be repeated so the coroner and jury could hear.

She and Cream had been engaged, she confirmed, and during one of his visits to her family's home in Berkhamsted, he asked her to write letters for him. As he dictated, she drafted some of the notes accusing Walter Harper of killing Marsh and Shrivell. It was strange to sign them in the name of William Murray, she said, and she asked Cream why he was making such allegations. He brushed off the question. "Never mind," he said. "I will tell you some day."

The final witness on the inquest's third day was John Haynes, who described an incident as he rode with Cream on an omnibus in late May. They passed newsboys who were shouting, "the Stamford-street case—important arrest." Cream seemed shocked and could barely wait to get off at the Charing Cross stop to buy the newspapers. He was so nervous that Haynes had to read the item to him. "He appeared much relieved," Haynes noted, when he discovered the story referred to the prosecution of a Stamford Street theater agent accused of indecently assaulting young women who were hoping to launch stage careers. In his testimony, Haynes also mentioned Louisa Harvey's name, identifying her as one of the women Cream claimed had been poisoned. He said he had made inquiries but had been unable to trace her.

When the hearing adjourned on June 24, Scotland Yard's murder case appeared to be crumbling. While a conviction on the blackmailing charges appeared certain, the evidence Cream was a killer was weak and circumstantial. He had been seen with Clover. He had known she was poisoned before anyone else did. But no one could say for certain he had been the man killing the prostitutes of Lambeth.

Hoots and jeers greeted him as he emerged from the hall in handcuffs, flanked by his guards. Bobbies held back the crowd as he ducked into a cab. When the four-wheeled carriage pulled away for the trip across the city to Holloway Prison, a group of youths ran alongside, yelling over the clatter of hooves and wheels. Cream, wearing his top hat, looked back at them. He was smiling.

24

RESURRECTION

A WELL-DRESSED, CROSS-EYED MAN IN A TOP HAT WHO gave pills to prostitutes. The words jumped out as Louisa Harvey read a newspaper account of the coroner's inquest into the death of Matilda Clover. Could it be the doctor from America she had met the previous fall? "I was struck," she would recall, "with the resemblance." And the report's description of oblong pills—they sounded like the ones he had insisted she take to clear up her complexion. She made a point of picking up the next morning's edition of one of the London papers, the *Daily Telegraph*, to find out more about the inquest. It featured an account of the testimony of John Haynes, who described his efforts to trace a victim of the Lambeth Poisoner who was believed to have dropped dead on the street outside a music hall. Harvey was stunned. A name appeared in the newspaper's crisp font like an epitaph—her name.

Harvey was living in Brighton when she discovered that Scotland Yard detectives thought she was dead. Even Cream, the man investigators were certain had murdered her, assumed she had swallowed his pills and died within hours. She had left London and her life as a prostitute and adopted a new surname, Harris, to start over, to escape her past. On this June day, the past had reached out and found her.

She asked her partner, Charles Harvey, to write two letters. One was to Sir John Bridge, the Bow Street magistrate hearing evidence on the blackmail allegations. The other was addressed to Coroner A. Braxton Hicks. Louisa Harvey, the letters assured them, was alive. And she was willing to testify.

◇◇◇◇◇

"Louisa Harris." Few people in the Vestry Hall knew the identity of the witness called when the Clover inquest resumed on July 7. Even Cream may have been in the dark until she was sworn in and stated the name she had been using in the fall of 1891.

The fate of Louisa Harvey had been "perhaps the most mysterious element in the case," noted a reporter for London's *Daily News*. Detectives had wasted weeks searching for a death record and a grave. Now, here she was, in a bold outfit that ensured she would not be overlooked again—blue jacket, green dress trimmed in brown, her hair pinned up under a brimmed black hat decorated with scarlet roses. She was tanned, one onlooker noted, having escaped London's fogs for "sunny Brighton."

She seemed calm as she spoke, but her voice was too faint to carry far in the crowded hall. Each statement had to be repeated, amplifying its impact. Cream kept his head down and scribbled furiously, as if trying to record every word she said. He understood the significance of her testimony. She described Cream's attempt to get her to take pills that night on the Thames Embankment and how she outwitted him. They were elongated capsules, like those he had purchased from the druggist Priest, and must have contained strychnine: Why else would Cream have believed she was dead? At last, Scotland Yard had direct evidence that its prime suspect was administering pills to London prostitutes.

The powerful testimony upstaged another surprise witness, who offered one more piece of the puzzle. After Countess Mabel Russell's messy divorce was splashed across the papers, she had been reluctant to become embroiled in the allegations of murder and blackmail swirl-

THE CASE OF THE MURDEROUS DR. CREAM

ing around Cream. Sworn in, she confirmed she had received a letter the previous fall accusing her ex-husband of murder. The letter had been brought to the attention of Scotland Yard, she said, but she had been unable to find it. The purported crime had been committed "by poison," the letter said, but she could not recall if strychnine was specified. She was certain, however, that the surname of the victim mentioned in the letter was Clover.

∞∞∞∞

THE major London newspapers sent reporters to Tooting to cover the revelations at the Vestry Hall. Murder, blackmail threats against prominent persons, illicit sex, debauchery—it was the kind of scandalous, lurid tale that repulsed and titillated Victorian readers. Many papers offered verbatim accounts of the testimony, complete with sketches of the main witnesses. Journalists sought out people who knew Cream, and John Haynes proved to be a rich source of anecdotes about his friend's drug-addled, louche behavior. "His theme was solely women—morning, noon and night," Haynes told the *Star*. "Neill was crazy," he asserted in another interview. "No man could consume the enormous amount of drugs that he did, abuse his health in every way as he used to, and be sane." Other acquaintances, and prostitutes who counted him among their customers, agreed. "While at first his manners were extremely pleasant and agreeable," *Lloyd's Weekly Newspaper* reported, "on coming to know him better they thought that he was a little wrong in the head."

The British press eagerly picked up and reprinted American news reports of Cream's past. Details were sketchy, but the big picture of a doctor capable of murder and malpractice was accurate. Cream's "career of crime" in Canada and the United States, the *Illustrated Police News* reported, included the deaths of at least two women and a long stay in an American prison.

Cream's lawyer, John Waters, tried to staunch the disclosures. "Charges of a more serious character" than blackmail were likely, he complained at one Bow Street hearing, and unfounded rumors and distorted news reports might influence the jury if Cream "should have the misfortune of being sent for trial." Magistrate Bridge scolded the journalists present for failing to restrict their reports to the evidence presented in the courtroom. "Any other statement against the prisoner," he said, "is extremely unfair and improper." Many newspapers ignored the warning and continued to publish exposés of Cream's past. *Lloyd's Weekly Newspaper*, in an act of open defiance, quoted Bridge's comment, then appended the latest revelations about Cream's "vicious career" in America.

WITNESSES AND SCENES FROM THE BLACKMAILING PROSECUTION AND CLOVER INQUEST (*ILLUSTRATED POLICE NEWS*, JULY 9, 1892)

Waters also tried to keep Cream's face out of the newspapers. He objected to the publication of courtroom artists' sketches and engravings based on photographs, arguing they could influence witnesses being asked to identify his client in police lineups. Cream's photograph, however, had been presented as evidence, and Bridge pointed out that the newspapers "have the right to publish all that takes place in the court." And, he could have added, press coverage was aiding the police investigation—Louisa Harvey might never have been found if she had not seen her name in the papers. *Lloyd's Weekly Newspaper* again led the press backlash, publishing images of Cream and urging people who recognized him to come forward.

◇◇◇◇

THE inquest resumed on July 13 for a fifth and final day of testimony. Dr. Thomas Stevenson was recalled and presented the results of his tests on the bodies of Marsh and Shrivell and his analysis of the pills in Cream's samples case. As few as nine of the tiny strychnine pills would be a fatal dose, he said, and about twenty would fit inside a gelatin capsule of the size Cream had purchased. If the pills were ground into powder, each capsule would hold about thirty.

Inspector Tunbridge testified for the first time and revealed a damning piece of evidence. An envelope found in the top drawer of a bureau in Cream's room had been used to note dates and initials that corresponded to the murdered women. There was an "L. H." as well, for Louisa Harvey.

At times, Cream did not seem to appreciate the growing weight of circumstantial evidence tying him to the murders. He was smiling and cheerful as he stepped into the dock for one of his Bow Street appearances. At another point, he praised the witnesses building a case for murder charges. "Thank God, they are none of them perjuring themselves," he blurted out, as if their testimony helped his cause. He sought out Tunbridge at a break in the inquest and shook his hand. "I'm having a fair show," he declared loudly. It was a resurgence of the odd behavior observed by the people who knew him in Lambeth.

As the inquest wound down, Coroner Hicks announced that he had received a strange letter he wanted to read into the record:

Dear Sir,

The man you have in your power, Dr. Neill, is as innocent as you are. Knowing him by sight I disguised myself like him, and made the acquaintance of the girls that have been poisoned. I gave them

(187)

pills to cure them of all their earthly miseries, and they died. Miss
L. Harris has got more sense than I thought she had, but I shall
have her yet.

The letter's author, who had clearly been following the case closely, repeated the accusation that Earl Russell "had a hand in the poisoning of Clover." He closed with some advice to the coroner: "If I were you I'd release Dr. T Neill, or you might get into trouble. His innocence will be declared sooner or later. And when he is free, he might sue you for damages." The letter ended with a warning: "Beware all, I warn, warn but once."

Then Hicks read out the signature: Jack the Ripper.

The hall exploded in laughter. Even Cream laughed. It was a reminder, however, that the Lambeth poisonings were the most murderous attack on London's most vulnerable women since the Whitechapel slayings of 1888.

The final witness was supposed to be Cream. He was sworn in but refused to testify. "My instructions are not to testify in the matter at all," he said. "I decline to open my mouth." He refused to confirm his name or admit he was a doctor.

Coroner Hicks connected the dots for the jurors in his summation of the evidence. The author of the blackmail letter sent to Dr. William Broadbent knew Matilda Clover had been poisoned with strychnine months before her body was exhumed. The letter was in Cream's handwriting. He knew Clover, knew where she lived, and had been seen walking with her. "Could they have any reasonable doubt," he asked, "that Neill was the man who administered the poison, and who ought to be put upon his trial for murder?"

If there were doubts, they evaporated within twenty minutes. "We are unanimously agreed," the jurors stated in a note, read out by the coroner upon their return to the hearing room, "that Matilda Clover died of strychnine poisoning, and that the poison was administered by Thomas Neill with intent to destroy life."

Eyes flashed to Cream, but there was no hint of his reaction. Outside, a squad of nine officers faced a crowd of about a thousand that had gathered around the cab that would return him to his cell. When a few men broke through the cordon and tussled with the police, Cream's guards took advantage of the diversion, hustled him into the cab, and sped off.

The coroner's jury praised the effort the police had put into investigating Clover's murder, and Hicks noted the "exemplary" work of the investigators, singling out Tunbridge and Inspector George Harvey. But the inquest had revealed Scotland Yard's failure to investigate the blackmail letters sent to Dr. Broadbent and Russell—clues that could have led police to Clover's murderer within weeks of her death and possibly saved the lives of Marsh and Shrivell. For now, the press was in a forgiving mood. "Bit by bit," noted the *Daily News*, "the pieces of this puzzle, at first apparently insoluble, are being put together by the unfailing vigilance of the police."

The verdict ensured Cream would stand trial for at least one murder, and in the weeks ahead, Scotland Yard would gather enough additional evidence to charge him with the killings of Marsh, Shrivell, and Ellen Donworth.

Meanwhile, on the other side of the Atlantic, Inspector Frederick Smith Jarvis was piecing together Cream's years in the United States in the 1880s—an investigation that would expose more crimes and furnish even more evidence of the doctor's capacity for cruelty and murder.

V

CRIMES AND PUNISHMENT

ILLINOIS, CANADA, AND
NEW YORK STATE • 1880–1892

25

MARY ANNE MATILDA FAULKNER

{Chicago • August 1880}

FOOTSTEPS DRUMMED ALONG THE CEILING OF Elizabeth Green's flat during the night. At daybreak the upstairs tenant at 1056 West Madison Street, Hattie Mack, was seen scurrying away with her three children. Soon the sickening, unmistakable odor of death began to seep through the building. The stench grew worse in the heat of an August day. Green's husband, George, climbed the rickety fire escape to the second floor and tried the door. It was locked. He headed to Chicago's West Lake Street police station to report the smell and his neighbor's hasty departure.

By the time two blue-coated, star-badged officers arrived, people passing on the street were holding their noses. Lieutenant Edward Steele and Sergeant John Rehm broke down the door. Inside, on a blood-soaked bed, was the body of a woman. Her arms were folded serenely on her chest, but her face and neck were hideously bloated and blackened by decay. They retreated through the doorway, gasping for air.

The woman, Elizabeth Green told the officers, must be the delicate, ladylike one who had moved in with Mack about ten days earlier. Mack was known in the neighborhood as a midwife and nurse, and a doctor had visited the flat two or three times a day since her arrival. Once, when Green asked the doctor who was ill, he claimed he was treating one of the Mack children. He had handed her his business card. It bore the name Thomas Neill Cream.

Steele and Rehm found Cream at White Brothers drugstore, a few blocks away, where he lived in a rented room at the back. A search of his office at 434 West Madison, a mile and a half from Mack's flat, turned up two notes. One identified the dead woman as Mary Anne Matilda Faulkner, originally from Ottawa, Canada. The other, scrawled in pencil and riddled with grammar and spelling errors, was from the missing Hattie Mack:

> Dr. Cream Ill not be home to night Ive tryed to see you I got the key I cant take the children home till she is movved I not told any one please let me see you as quick as you can I am under a great Strain I am at my Sisters.
>
> H. M.
>
> The window is up be careful of the woman up stairs.

Cream was questioned as the officers escorted him to the station. Faulkner had been his patient, he admitted. She had come to his office to be treated for dysentery. Then he changed his mind, and said she had suffered from cervical lesions, or as he put it, "ulceration of the womb."

When police picked up Mack at her sister's house, she accused Cream of performing an abortion. She had done her best to care for the woman as her condition worsened after the operation. Confronted with Mack's statement, Cream offered yet another story: Mack, acting alone, had botched the abortion, and infection had set in. By the time he had been called in to help, he claimed, it had been too late to save Faulkner's life.

"A Brutal Case of Malpractice," screamed an August 21, 1880, headline in the *Chicago Daily News*, a day after the body was found. Both Cream and Mack were held in the West Lake Street station's cells until a coroner's jury could review the evidence and decide who was telling the truth.

<><><>

CREAM had arrived in Chicago in July 1879, soon after his hasty departure from Ontario. It had been only eight years since a massive fire had killed hundreds and reduced more than three square miles of the city's core to ashes and ruins. On the edges of the "Burnt District," the windowless shells of churches and other buildings still stood like macabre monuments to the disaster. But an ambitious reconstruction effort was under way. The downtown streets were lined with new fire-resistant stone and brick buildings, some towering seven stories high. "The city has risen up out of its own ashes," marveled a visiting British writer, Lady Duffus Hardy, "grander and statelier than ever." Others searched for the right words to capture the city's resilience and relentless growth. To the actress Sarah Bernhardt, who came to town in 1881, it was nothing less than "the pulse of America." Even German chancellor Otto von Bismarck was curious as to what all the fuss was about. "I wish I could go to America," he reputedly said, "if only to see that Chicago."

Immigrants were flooding into the city every year, many of them from Bismarck's fledgling German Empire. The population almost doubled in the decade after the fire, reaching a half million and making the reborn Chicago the fourth-largest city in the United States. In the early 1880s Lady Hardy found a city "full of energy and enterprise" and "wholly devoted to money-making." Thousands of young women joined the influx, in search of work and a fresh start in a city reinventing itself. They came from midwestern farms, from Canada, and from Europe. They found work in factories or as seamstresses, teachers, nurses, or store clerks, but most working women in 1870s America—one million across the country—were maids in private homes. Faulkner, twenty-nine when she died, had been a maid and had dutifully sent part of her earnings to her widowed mother in Canada, to help support her younger siblings. She had quit her last job, waiting tables, about six weeks before her death, telling her employer she was about to be married.

A CITY "FULL OF ENERGY AND ENTERPRISE." CHICAGO'S STATE STREET IN THE 1880S. (AUTHOR COLLECTION)

Cream, just as eager to make a fresh start, set up a practice in the city's West Side. The Illinois State Board of Health added his name to its register of licensed physicians on August 22, 1879. There should have been plenty of work for a doctor new to Chicago. The polluted water supply, drawn from sewage-fouled Lake Michigan, led to frequent outbreaks of typhoid fever and cholera. And waterborne dysentery, which caused intestinal pain and bloody diarrhea, was so common that it was known as the "summer complaint." But Cream struggled to attract patients and relocated his office several times. He had "considerable difficulty," he later confessed, "in making both ends meet."

Cream's examining room, Scotland Yard's Inspector Frederick Smith Jarvis discovered when he reached Chicago in the summer of 1892, had been located at 434 West Madison, above a barbershop and opposite a livery stable and the West End Opera House. The area was only a mile from the city center but a world away from Chicago's impressive new buildings. His office was surrounded by shabby tenements and rooming houses crammed with new arrivals and people displaced by the fire. Broken plumbing filled basements with sewage. Garbage was heaped in backyards. Neighbors closed their windows on hot summer days to keep out the smell.

The West Side was one of Chicago's most violent and dangerous areas—a "nursery for criminals," one newspaper complained shortly before Cream's arrival. Vagrants and gangs roamed the streets at night, robbing and assaulting passersby. Prostitution thrived in a city where one publisher offered a "pleasure seeker's" guide with the risqué motto: "All tastes . . . promptly satisfied, all preferences catered to." The administration of Mayor Carter Harrison, elected in 1879, allowed gambling operations and brothels—"sporting houses," as they were known—to operate openly in vice districts with names as disreputable as their establishments: Hell's Half-Acre, Bad Lands, Satan's Mile. Crime bosses and brothel operators controlled votes and bribed the police to look the other way. "Chicago is in a terrible situation," one resident lamented to a friend in New York City, "being completely in the hands of gamblers and crooks." The most powerful underworld figure, Mike McDonald, controlled a gambling empire—and, many said, the police and the city itself—from a downtown casino and headquarters known as the Store.

Faulkner and other young women like her, "cast adrift in a great city," as one newspaper described them, faced hostility and discrimination and risked being drawn—willingly or by force—into prostitution. They were paid less than men, even if they did not have the support of a husband or father. Landlords often refused to rent rooms to unmarried women, assuming they must be promiscuous. "If a girl didn't live at home," a Chicago woman of the era recalled, "we thought she was bad." Single women gravitated to the West Side and other seedy neighborhoods, where accommodations were cheap and fewer questions were asked. Mrs. Leander Stone, the president of the Woman's Christian Association, which operated a females-only boardinghouse in Chicago in the 1880s, warned of the hardships and desperation many of them faced. "They will be left for the coming winter to freeze in attics, or starve in cellars," she fearfully lamented, "or what (god forbid) is worse than death, sacrifice their honor to secure food and warmth." While pimps and madams preyed on the poor and vulnerable, there were also women who willingly turned to prostitution to escape a life of poverty and drudgery. Seamstresses and lace makers in Chicago's sweatshops worked long hours for less than three dollars a week, a tenth of what a sex worker could earn.

Single women and prostitutes who became pregnant could find an abortionist with ease. One newspaper claimed the practice was "flourishing" in the city, where "scores of self styled physicians [carried] on the work by wholesale." Some were said to offer their services for as little as two dollars, well below the going rate of ten dollars in New York and Boston. Until the nineteenth century, an abortion performed in the early weeks of a pregnancy was not considered a crime. The fetus, it was believed, was not alive until the point of "quickening"—when a woman first felt movement, about fourteen weeks after conception. By the mid-1800s, however, it was an offense to perform an abortion or to induce a miscarriage at any point during pregnancy.

Still, the belief that life began months after conception remained widespread, and many women felt they had a right to end a pregnancy in its early stages. One state board of health estimated that one-third of all pregnancies were terminated. Homemade concoctions, including a noxious mixture of turpentine and sugar, were thought to bring on a miscarriage. And newspaper advertisements for an array of patent medicines promised relief from "female irregularities" and to restore the menstrual cycle—code words for ending a pregnancy. Some suppliers included explicit warnings of the desired side effect: "Ladies who have reason to suspect pregnancy," noted the promoters of Friar's French Female Regulator, "are cautioned against using these tablets." Many women pleaded with doctors for drugs or operations. "When you are solicited to interfere for the relief of these poor wretches, pity them, pity them with your whole hearts," one physician advised his colleagues in 1875, but "meet their entreaties with prompt, decided refusal." There were practitioners, however, willing to risk prosecution. In 1880 Chicago's newspapers carried frequent reports of illegal abortions from across the United States, including many that left the woman dead and a doctor facing homicide charges.

In the desperation of pregnant women, Cream—cash strapped and struggling to build a medical practice—saw opportunity. He promoted himself as an expert in "diseases of the womb"—a clever way, it appears, of conveying his willingness to help end an unwanted pregnancy. A Mrs. Goodwin rented him office space on the West Side until she discovered the true nature of his practice and evicted him. "Producing abortions," she noted tartly, was "the best"—the most important—"part of his business." Cream eventually admitted, according to one press account, that he specialized in performing abortions for unmarried women—assisting them "over their troubles," as he put it. Hattie Mack, his alleged accomplice in Faulkner's death, claimed that Cream performed abortions for as many as fifteen prostitutes working in just one of the city's many sporting houses.

The prevailing attitude was that any unmarried, pregnant woman was to blame for her predicament, not the putative father. "So long as passion shall betray women into illicit relations with men," the *Chicago Daily Tribune* pontificated in the summer of 1880, "there will be those who seek or submit to abortion in order to escape shame or trouble."

When Mary Anne Faulkner discovered she was pregnant, she turned to a fellow Canadian for help. Her horrible death threatened to bring Cream's checkered career as a doctor to an abrupt end.

◇◇◇◇◇

THE West Lake Street police station looked as though it was under siege on the morning of August 23, a Monday, as people jockeyed for seats at the inquest. Latecomers stood outside until officers emerged to clear the sidewalk. Mack, the first witness, claimed she had been pressured into caring for Faulkner—she owed Cream money and felt she could not refuse his request. The arrangement was to be a secret. "Dr. Cream cautioned me time and again," she testified, "to keep my doors locked and let no one in." The doctor came a few times a day and during one visit took surgical instruments into Faulkner's bedroom and performed the abortion. He washed off the blood-ied instruments in her kitchen sink, she said, and she saw the fetus before he took it away. She fled the apartment after Faulkner's death and left the note for Cream, begging for his help. When she tracked him down, he said he would deal with the body.

"What will you take for your furniture?" he had asked. "I have a notion to burn it up house and all." When she refused his offer of thirty-five dollars, he mused about recruiting a couple of men to remove the body in the middle of the night. "If any one interfered with him," he said, according to her account, "he would shoot him down."

Cream was nervous when it was his chance to speak. His hands and lips were quivering and at times he had trouble speaking. After noting his Edinburgh credentials, he insisted he knew nothing of Faulkner or her condition until Mack summoned him to her apart-ment. Faulkner told him she had fallen and had a miscarriage, he said, but he suspected she was lying.

"I kept at her, urging her, for her sake and mine, to tell me if any instruments had been used," he claimed, and Mack finally admitted she had used a catheter to induce an abortion. It had been too late to save Faulkner's life, but he had done what he could, he said, prescribing the painkiller quinine. He had also asked Dr. Donald Fraser, a fellow McGill graduate with a practice on Chicago's West Side, to examine Faulkner and offer a second opinion on her condition. After she died, Cream added, he had urged Mack to go to the police and the coroner.

MIDWIFE HATTIE MACK'S NOTE WARNING CREAM SHE HAD FLED THE HOUSE WHERE POLICE LATER FOUND MARY ANNE FAULKNER'S BODY

(CASE NO. 10926, CRIMINAL COURT OF COOK COUNTY, 1880)

The Cook County deputy coroner, Major W. E. Waite, expressed surprise that Cream, a licenced physician, had failed to file a death certificate. "Don't you know that it is proper for the attending physician to furnish a certificate of death?"

"Well sir, I've only had to furnish one certificate since I came here," Cream replied, "and I didn't know just how to act."

"You've only lost one case?"

"Yes, sir," he said, adding—as if it made a difference—"and that was a child."

The autopsy report was read, confirming an abortion had been performed with instruments sharp enough to perforate the womb and cause a fatal infection. Dr. Fraser was called and confirmed he had examined Faulkner, at Cream's request, and had found her seriously ill from the aftereffects of an abortion. Surprisingly, neither physician seemed to have considered sending her to a hospital.

Dr. Fraser was shown the catheter believed to have been used on Faulkner. "A physician who would use that instrument would be a blunderer?" he was asked.

"I think that any man who goes into this kind of business at all is a blunderer."

The six men on the coroner's jury needed less than a half hour to agree on a verdict. Faulkner died of infection, foreman William Neff announced, "following an abortion committed with the knowledge and assistance of Dr Thomas N. Cream and Mrs Hattie Mack." Under Illinois law, the pair would have faced up to ten years in prison if convicted of performing an illegal abortion. But Faulkner's death during the procedure made it a capital offense. Both remained in jail to await a grand jury's indictment for murder.

In the meantime, Chicago newspapers learned of Cream's brush with the law in Ontario. "The Doctor's Record a Bad One," declared one of the headlines topping a report in the *Chicago Daily News*, although it acknowledged "there was nothing to positively connect Dr. Cream" with Catharine Gardner's death. The *Daily Tribune*, however, refused to give him the benefit of the doubt. Gardner, like Faulkner, had died after an abortion, it asserted, and Cream, hoping "to palm off the crime as suicide," had placed her body in the outhouse.

Cream tried to salvage his reputation. When journalists interviewed him in jail, he insisted "no educated physician" like himself would employ chloroform to induce an abortion. The burns to Gardner's face suggested someone "inexperienced and non-professional" had been responsible. "It had been administered by her seducer," he claimed, "to prevent her from returning to her parents, who would have made him suffer for his acts." The damage, however, appeared to be done. The "general opinion" in Chicago, one interviewer noted, was that Dr. Cream was responsible for killing Faulkner.

There was more bad press. "Cream's Crime" was a repeated headline in newspapers certain of his guilt. The *Chicago Times* toyed with his surname: "Churning Cream" appeared above one story, only to be upstaged by the headline "Cream a Tartar." Some press reports labeled him a quack or enclosed his title in quotation marks, suggesting he was not a real doctor. His name was even sullied in the pages of the *New York Times*, which ran an item naming him as implicated in a "fatal and revolting case of malpractice." His alleged victim, in contrast, was portrayed as a fallen angel. Faulkner was a respectable woman from a "poor, but honest" family, as one paper put it, not one of the sporting-house residents said to seek out Cream's services. Mack related a heartbreaking story of how Faulkner had asked for paper and pencil when she realized she was dying and then scribbled a note revealing her mother's address and the location of a trunk containing her few belongings.

When a notorious abortionist named Charles Earll was accused of murdering a patient a few days after Faulkner's death, the *Daily Tribune* demanded that the authorities crack down on the "fiendish practice." Earll, "a professional butcher," had already served a one-year prison term for manslaughter after another fatal abortion, an editorial writer harrumphed, and Cream appeared to be "an equally incompetent, unscrupulous, and callous practitioner, with previous experience in this worse than brutal pursuit." The *Tribune* demanded "merciless prosecution" of offenders. "If Earll and Cream be the guilty persons, as seems to be the case from all the evidence at hand, *let them hang!* This is the surest remedy against the prevalence of abortion as a practice."

Cream wound up sharing cell 45 at the Cook County Jail—a six-by-nine-foot box on an upper-floor tier of cells known as Murderer's Row—with the gray-bearded, grandfatherly Earll. They found "a good deal of comfort in each other's company," one newspaper reported, and were often seen chatting during the daily, hour-long exercise period, perhaps swapping ideas for their defenses. Cream was desperate to rehabilitate his reputation; however, striking up a friendship with the "professional butcher" Earll was a poor way to start. So when a *Tribune* journalist interviewed him in his cell, he went on the offensive. He produced his Edinburgh license, McGill degree, and other certificates to prove his qualifications and to refute his portrayal as a quack. "Why should I perform an abortion upon a strange woman who has neither money nor friends?" he asked. "He is confident of a triumphant acquittal from what he considers a foul charge," the reporter noted, "and says he has the sympathy of all the regular physicians of the city, any one of whom might easily be led into the same trap."

There was a reason for Cream's bravado. One of the most accomplished, controversial, and expensive lawyers in Chicago would defend him at trial, no doubt thanks to money supplied by his father. Alfred Trude, his dark hair combed back to form a peak and his eyes intense and locked on target, was thirty-four and had been practicing for a decade. Criminal law was his specialty. One journalist later reckoned he had won acquittals for "more murderers, thieves and scoundrels than any other living lawyer in Chicago." By 1880 he had defended about thirty men and women accused of murder; only a handful had been convicted and none had been hanged. His most infamous client was gambling boss Mike McDonald, who relied on Trude to keep his minions out of jail. Eloquent, sharp-tongued, and fearless in the courtroom, he once stood his ground when a judge threatened to fine him for contempt: "He could fine me only $5," Trude fired back, "while I had a million dollars' worth of contempt for him." He could be just as blunt in his attacks on prosecution witnesses, but he also knew how to win over skeptical jurors. "He is a good judge of human nature," noted one admirer, and "knows how to work upon the sympathies of a jury." He was also thorough and made a point of visiting crime scenes as he prepared his cases.

There were rumors, however, that Trude did not rely solely on convincing legal arguments and his powers of persuasion to win acquittals. Chicago's justice system was notoriously corrupt, and he appears to have played by its crooked rules as well as anyone. Within a few years, a newspaper would accuse the man who was about to defend Cream of bribing witnesses, court officials, and jurors. Trude, the *Chicago Herald* would claim, was the author of "an unprincipled series of plots against justice in the defence of gamblers, thieves and murderers."

26

"PURE CREAM"

{NOVEMBER 1880}

A SET OF CLOSE-TRIMMED BURNSIDE WHISKERS FRAMED Cream's face as he was escorted into the courtroom on November 15. Cradled in his arms were a stack of books and two rolls of paper, which turned out to be anatomical drawings of his own creation. The nervous, evasive man of the Faulkner inquest was gone. Cream carried himself with an air of professionalism and confidence, one observer noted, projecting an image of "combined intelligence and power." He was dressed in a business suit with a white tie and looked like "an associate counsel in the case," the observer thought, "rather than a man charged with a terrible crime on trial for his life."

About one hundred people were in the courtroom as the trial opened, many of them African Americans. Onlookers assumed they were present to support Hattie Mack, who was black. Separate trials had been ordered, and Mack, who had cut a deal with the prosecution, was the chief witness against Cream. The venue was the Criminal Court House on Michigan Street, a building erected three years after the fire and described as "attractive in its new and pristine whiteness." The county jail was next door, and Cream, who had been in custody for almost three months, was escorted to and from the courtroom through an elevated passageway that apprehensive inmates nicknamed the "bridge of sighs." Condemned men had been hanged within sight of the courtroom windows.

On the bench was Joseph Eaton Gary, a circuit court judge of few words who was admired for his common sense and his deep understanding of the law. "Men who are not honest fear him. Lawyers who are tricky avoid him," the *Daily Tribune* observed. He was about to turn sixty, and the weariness in his eyes suggested he had seen his share of human misery in seventeen years on the bench. He kept his trials running at a brisk clip and quickly shut down any lawyer who dared to test his patience. "Irrelevant oratorical flights," it was noted, were rare in his courtroom. Yet he would show remarkable tolerance for Alfred Trude's theatrics and bombast in defense of Cream.

It took a day to empanel a jury, as Trude and the assistant state's attorney, George Ingham, questioned candidates about their attitudes and knowledge of the case. One after another was rejected, and court officials scoured the nearby streets to round up more bodies. Trude asked the prospective jurors if they would believe "a disreputable woman," signaling his plan to attack the prosecutor's main witness. One man was deemed unsuitable for the job of passing judgment on the doctor, a reporter quipped, "because he had been guilty of reading the newspapers."

"Which, then, should be punished," Ingham asked the jurors in his opening statement, "the principal or the dupe?" It was reasonable to conclude the doctor was the abortionist, not "an ignorant colored woman," he said, and the state would call witnesses to corroborate Mack's story. The defense's position, Trude countered, was simple. Cream, a professional man with "ability possessed by few if any physicians in this city," was too skilled to have performed the crude operation that killed Faulkner.

Mack repeated her allegations against Cream, and some of the journalists in the room, at least, felt she was telling the truth. Trude subjected her to a prolonged cross-examination, with questions ranging "from the blunt to the insinuating," one reporter said, but failed to impeach her evidence "in the slightest degree." He had more success with other witnesses, who questioned whether Mack—the purported author of the damning letter to Cream—could write. And after Mack swore she had not spoken to anyone about her testimony, Trude took the bizarre step of calling the prosecutor as a witness; Ingham acknowledged he had spoken to her briefly the previous day.

Police officers bolstered Mack's evidence. Lieutenant Steele and Sergeant Rehm told of Cream's evasions after his arrest. And they described finding Mack's letter and Faulkner's jewelry and pocketbook at his office. Trude, however, had some success teasing favorable evidence from the prosecution's medical witnesses. Theodore Bluthardt, the physician for Cook County who had conducted the autopsy, believed Faulkner's injuries were the work of "an ignorant and reckless person" and acknowledged that "child-murder was largely practiced by women." Fraser, the doctor called in before she died, agreed that her injuries appeared to be the "bungling work" of an amateur.

CREAM'S LAWYER, ALFRED TRUDE, WON ACQUITTALS FOR "MORE MURDERERS, THIEVES AND SCOUNDRELS THAN ANY OTHER LIVING LAWYER IN CHICAGO." (AUTHOR COLLECTION)

Trude called a half-dozen witnesses to attest to Cream's good character, including a businessman who had known his father for years, but his star witness was his client. The jurors were shown his diplomas and licenses as he described the years of study he had undertaken in Canada and Britain to gain "a thorough knowledge of medicine." Neither Cream nor Trude needed to remind the jurors that Chicago was flooded with charlatans who promised miracle cures and took advantage of the ill and the desperate. An example was Dr. Fritz, another West Madison Street practitioner, who touted himself as "the Greatest Physician of Modern Times" and treated rabies by applying a "mad-stone" to animal bites. The newspapers were filled with advertisements for Sandford's Radical Cure, Mountain Rock Oil, and other concoctions to combat a dizzying array of ailments, from rheumatism and burns to tumors, "cerebral congestion," and low spirits. The State Board of Health and the Illinois State Medical Society were waging a well-publicized war on quacks, snake-oil salesmen, and unlicensed practitioners during 1880, exposing and prosecuting the worst offenders. Cream, with his Edinburgh license and other credentials, appeared to be—as Trude contended—one of the more qualified physicians in the city.

Cream calmly offered his side of the story. He had been summoned to examine Faulkner after the abortion and had done all he could to save her. He was unaware of the punctures to her womb, he explained, and believed she was suffering from blood poisoning. He accused Mack of setting him up to take the blame for her crude handiwork. Unrolling his drawings of the female anatomy, he illustrated for the jurors, "in a very explicit manner," a reporter noted, "the method of childbirth." Presented with medicines seized from his office and Mack's apartment—"enough to stock a small-sized drug store," according to another press account—Cream explained the contents and properties of each one. Laughter erupted when he opened a few of the bottles and took a taste. The discovery of Faulkner's pocketbook and jewelry in his office was explained away—after her death Mack had given him the "trinkets," as he called them, for safekeeping.

Ingham used his cross-examination to probe Cream's checkered past. Cream denied leaving London, Ontario, because of the woman found dead near his office. He had "never been arrested for crime in any part of the globe to this time," he said, choosing his words carefully. And "he had never performed an abortion in his life," he added, confident that no one in the courtroom had heard the name Flora Brooks.

In his closing statement, Trude accused the police of trying to frame an innocent man. Sergeant Rehm had "coached and drilled" Mack, he claimed, and it would be "monstrous" if the jurors believed her story over the sworn testimony of "a reputable physician against whom nothing had ever been charged." Cream, a highly educated and accomplished medical man "poised on the very top round of the ladder of science and learning," would never have performed the amateurish operation that killed Faulkner. Then he rolled the dice. If the jurors doubted Cream's story, they should convict him of murder. "There was no middle ground," he thundered, "for Dr. Cream was either innocent, and should be acquitted, or guilty of such a murder as could only be committed by an empiric, charlatan, and quack, and he should be hung." A few of the jurors, touched by the emotional plea, had tears in their eyes.

Then Ingham rose to his feet. Not yet thirty, he was considered one of the smartest and most talented lawyers in the city. "A conscientious, hard-working and painstaking attorney," one court watcher recalled, as no-nonsense and direct as Trude was loud and flashy. There was evidence to corroborate Mack's story, he argued, and Trude was attacking the police in desperation to shore up a weak defense. Then he offered some melodrama of his own, reminding the jurors that Faulkner had spent her final hours "friendless and alone, and, feeling the shadow of death coming upon her, wrote her name and her mother's address upon a piece of paper." One of the reporters glanced at Cream, curious to see his reaction to the description of Faulkner's death. There was "a fierce glitter in his cold, gray eyes," he noted, "and a perfectly sardonic smile upon his face."

The judge's instructions amounted to an invitation to acquit. The jurors, Gary said, should consider whether Faulkner's injuries were "the work of a skillful and educated physician or that of an unskilled and ignorant person." Cream's "good character and reputation both as a man and physician" should be taken into account. If he had operated on Faulkner or given her medicine "under an honest belief that he might do her good," he should be found not guilty. And they were cautioned about accepting Mack's evidence. They should "scrutinize closely and accept with great caution" a witness who confessed to being an accomplice to murder, especially one who, like Mack, had been granted immunity from prosecution if her testimony helped convict Cream.

The jurors filed out at half past three to begin deliberations. They were back within the hour.

"We the jury," the foreman announced, "find the Defendant Thomas Cream not guilty."

Cream was elated. He jumped to his feet when the verdict was announced and pumped Trude's hand. Then he shook hands with each of the jurors.

Trude's attacks and bluster had worked. And if the jurors had doubts about Mack and her story, Cream's impressive diplomas and licenses may have tipped the scales in his favor. Or, perhaps, there was a darker explanation for the ease and familiarity he displayed when he shook hands with the men who, only moments before, could have condemned him to death. Trude was suspected of bribing jurors to pad his record of acquittals in murder cases, and jury tampering was common in Chicago. "In these days, when a juryman is offered bribes and frequently takes them," the *Chicago Daily News* noted within days of the verdict, "it is a wonder that any convictions are had in the Criminal Court."

The state's attorney's office dropped the murder charge against Mack a day after the acquittal, even though her testimony did not yield a conviction. Both of Mary Anne Faulkner's suspected killers escaped unpunished. A headline in the *Chicago Times* reported the doctor's exoneration while cracking one last joke about his name: "Pure Cream."

∞∞∞

AFTER the trial, Cream dropped by Trude's office several times to chat. He was no doubt grateful for his lawyer's efforts, but he seemed more interested in flaunting his knowledge of medicine. "He was a most charming talker," Trude would recall, "and if he let loose on his pet theories" about medicine and people, "he would hold the listeners by the hour."

One of these pet subjects was prostitutes. "A menace to society," he called them. And Trude agreed. As he told the *Chicago Times* a few months after the trial, streetwalkers should not be "left free to spread disease and rob and plunder the unwary." He endorsed Chicago's solution, which tolerated prostitution within designated vice districts and out of the sight of respectable citizens. Cream, however, had a solution of his own. He "talked incessantly," Trude said, of "his desire to rid the earth of these unfortunate beings."

∞∞∞

ALMOST twelve years later, in the summer of 1892, Inspector Frederick Smith Jarvis stepped onto a station platform in Chicago as he continued to dig into Cream's past. A Chicago police officer named O'Hara briefed him on the doctor's reputation as an abortionist and the evidence presented at his trial for murdering Mary Anne Faulkner. Cream's acquittal had been a close call, but this courtroom victory appeared to have emboldened him. In the months ahead Cream would implicate others in suspicious poisoning deaths and become a suspect himself. And one of those killings, Jarvis would soon discover, should have been his last.

27

ELLEN STACK AND
SARAH ALICE MONTGOMERY

{MARCH–APRIL 1881}

E LLEN STACK HAD BEEN FEELING UNWELL FOR SEVERAL days when she visited a doctor's office on a March evening. Born in Ireland, she was twenty-five and worked as a maid in the household of Charles Bowler, a Chicago clothing salesman. When she returned to the Bowler home, she told her employers a doctor named Beebe had vaccinated her against smallpox. He had also written prescriptions for two medications, and she had stopped at a drugstore on West Madison Street to have them filled.

Stack took the medicine before going to bed. About one o'clock in the morning, her groans awakened Charles Bowler. She was "tossing about in her bed" when he burst into her room, he later recounted, "and apparently suffering great pain." Convulsions twisted her body and limbs. "Water," she gasped. He summoned Donald Fraser, the same doctor who had aided Cream's defense at the Faulkner trial. He lived more than three miles away, and by the time he arrived, she was dead.

Stack had not consulted a Dr. Beebe that night. She had seen another doctor, it was soon discovered, one who had treated her in the past. She had lied to her employers, knowing they would not have approved. Bowler's wife, Minnie, had told her more than once: "Have nothing more to do with Dr. Cream."

◇◇◇◇◇

AFTER his release from jail, Cream reopened his medical practice at 434 West Madison. While one newspaper suggested he emerged from the Faulkner trial "with his character unblemished," his reputation was in tatters. And he did himself no favors when he attended Dr. Charles Earll's murder trial in early December 1880, within a couple of weeks of his own acquittal. Reporters spotted him in the courtroom, and it was rumored he might testify in defense of his former cellmate, perhaps as an expert witness. He remained in the gallery, however, as Earll was convicted of the less serious offense of attempted abortion and sentenced to five years in prison.

Cream inserted a classified advertisement in the *Daily Tribune* in late January 1881 announcing, in bold type, that "DR. CREAM, Graduate of the Royal College of Physicians and Surgeons, of Edinburgh, Scotland," was back in business. To impress patients, he ordered a sheaf of prescription forms that touted his Edinburgh credentials and his training at St. Thomas' Hospital. Cream moved to new lodgings about a mile south of his office, at 105 West 13th Street, in an even seedier neighborhood that bordered the slums of Maxwell and Halstead Streets. The "Terror District," Chicago police called it, a cesspool of crime, poverty, and misery. He rented a room from a widow, Mary McClellan, and was soon engaged to marry her twenty-eight-year-old daughter, Lena.

◇◇◇◇◇

THE physician for Cook County, Theodore Bluthardt, performed an autopsy on Ellen Stack on the afternoon of March 10, 1881. "It was found that the girl had not been poisoned," one newspaper reported, "nor in any way maltreated." The journalist offered no details of the tests conducted, if any, for the presence of poison. Neither did Bluthardt, who recorded the cause of death as "a collapse, resulting from spasmodic colic"—an obstruction or inflammation of the digestive tract.

Why had she ventured out at night to consult Cream, one of Chicago's best-known abortionists? The answer seemed obvious. "Some rumors were afloat to the effect that the girl had died from an abortion," the *Chicago Times* reported. But the autopsy found no evidence she had been pregnant or undergone an abortion—Bluthardt's examination "perfectly vindicated her character," as the paper put it. Perhaps she had feared she was pregnant when she consulted Cream but had been mistaken.

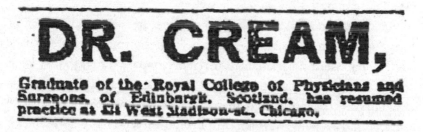

CREAM'S ADVERTISEMENT APPEARED IN THE *CHICAGO DAILY TRIBUNE* IN JANUARY 1881.

Reporters tracked down Cream, who admitted Stack had come to see him. "The girl had every symptom of the early stages of smallpox," he claimed. Fever, aches, and sometimes vomiting preceded the formation of the disease's telltale skin rash and sores, and there were isolated smallpox outbreaks in the city that year. Yes, he had vaccinated her, and yes, he had written prescriptions for two medicines. "Strange," Cream mused, "that the girl should have died within a few hours" of the visit. The medicine he had prescribed, he assured the journalists, "was not such as would cause convulsions or spasms."

He even listed the exact amount of each ingredient, as specified in his prescriptions.

Despite Bluthardt's conclusions, Cream suggested Stack had been poisoned. He pointed a finger at Frank Pyatt, a twenty-nine-year-old transplanted New Yorker whose drugstore was only two doors away from Cream's office. Cream called for a coroner's inquest and an analysis of the medicine she had taken to determine "if a mistake had not been made in putting up the prescriptions." But there was a problem. Somehow, in the confusion surrounding Stack's death, the liquid medicine and capsules Pyatt had prepared for her—the drugs Cream insisted would prove Pyatt was to blame, not him—had disappeared. "The doctor lays particular stress on the fact that these medicines cannot be found," the *Daily Tribune* reported. "He hopes that the inquest will be held at an early day and the case thoroughly investigated."

Had Pyatt made a tragic mistake? Cases of accidental poisoning from medication occasionally made headlines, prompting New York City to introduce an ordinance in 1880 requiring druggists to keep arsenic and other poisons in locked cabinets. While this was not a legal requirement in Chicago, many drugstores there took similar precautions. Errors, however, were still made. A few weeks before Stack's death, a Chicago druggist had mistakenly added morphine to a prescription. Two children died after taking the medicine, and the druggist was prosecuted for criminal negligence.

Despite Cream's allegations against Pyatt, no inquest was held. Stack was interred in Calvary Catholic Cemetery two days after the autopsy. The *Daily Tribune* backtracked within twenty-four hours of reporting Cream's claims, issuing an apology for tainting Pyatt's reputation. "There is no question," the paper declared, "that the medicines were put up in exact accordance with the prescriptions."

Chicago police already suspected Cream was capable of murder. So, too, did Bluthardt, who had examined Mary Anne Faulkner's body only a few months earlier. A pattern was emerging. Young women who consulted Cream turned up dead. He should have been the prime suspect in Stack's suspicious death. But by going public, by claiming Stack was poisoned and demanding an inquest, Cream had covered his tracks. Further examination of her body might turn up traces of poison, but without a sample of the medicine to analyze, it would be Cream's word against Pyatt's. It was a risky move, but Cream had a darker motive for taking the offensive and deflecting the blame.

On March 13, the day after Pyatt was exonerated in the pages of the *Daily Tribune*, he received a letter from Cream. "I understand you are annoyed at my making a statement in regard to Ellen Stack's death," it began. "No offence was intended." Pyatt should know, however, that he was in deep trouble:

> *I expect you will be arrested and held for Ellen Stack's death, she was poisoned and there is no doubt of it. The fact has been proved by experiment. I received this information this morning and to show my friendly disposition towards you I have written to give you the benefit of the information I received so that you can take any steps you may deem prudent in the matter. For God's sake keep quiet and trust no one, my bitter experience taught me to be suspicious of everyone I meet. I am sorry for your sake things have turned out as they have.*

The threats sounded like blackmail. They were. In a follow-up letter on March 24, Cream claimed a lawyer investigating Stack's death had interviewed him. "They are preparing to prosecute you," he warned, "and their case is a clear one against you." Pyatt's label and handwriting were on the bottle of medicine supplied to Stack, and it "*contains poison* beyond a doubt." Cream had told the newspapers the medicine had gone missing. Now he was suggesting to Pyatt that he had the bottle and the capsules and could supply them. If Pyatt recovered the incriminating evidence, he explained, "*there would then be no case*" against him. Ominously, Cream added, "If this comes out again in the papers it will kill you and your Business for ever. I have given you this information with a desire to do you a friendly turn."

Did Cream want money, or were his threats designed to ensure Pyatt's silence? And if he did have Stack's missing medicines, as the letter suggested, how had he obtained them? Pyatt did not know the answers. But the day he filled the prescription, he had watched Stack leave his store and turn in the direction of Cream's office. If she had returned to see the doctor, he would have had a chance to tamper with the medicines. And after her death, Cream had shown up at the store, accusing him of making a mistake and killing Stack. He had told the druggist to destroy the written prescription. "I asked him if he thought me a fool," Pyatt recalled, "and ordered him out of the store."

The blackmail letters that followed had convinced Pyatt that Cream was trying to frame him for murder. And he had no doubt as to who killed Ellen Stack. Cream had poisoned her "by changing the medicines in the bottles and capsules," he later alleged, then tried "to throw the blame on the druggist."

◇◇◇◇◇

A WOMAN rang the bell at the front desk of the Sheldon House on West Madison at about nine on a Saturday evening. She was in her early twenties, with a light complexion and brown hair and eyes. A black cloak was draped over her dress to ward off the early-spring chill, and a single ostrich feather made a stylish arc from her white hat. A woman of refinement and taste, hotel proprietor Samuel Sharp thought. Ladylike. She wanted a room for the night but declined to reveal her name. He handed her the key to room 43, on the top floor. She asked for a glass and a tablespoon, then headed upstairs, carrying a small leather satchel.

Within the hour, Sharp heard a woman's screams and found the guest on the floor of an upstairs hallway, writhing in pain. She was carried to her room and placed on the bed. Two doctors were summoned and administered ether to ease her suffering. They thought they recognized the cause of her violent spasms and convulsions, which matched the death throes of Ellen Stack: strychnine poisoning. Had she swallowed something? "Yes," she replied, but she was too weak to say anything more. She lost consciousness and died within minutes.

"A death surrounded by a great many suspicious and curious circumstances," the *Daily Tribune* announced the following day, April 10, 1881. "Whether murder, suicide, or poisoning through criminal carelessness or inexcusable ignorance has not yet been made known."

Chicago police and newspaper reporters quickly identified the woman and traced her movements in the hours before her death. Sarah Alice Montgomery had been a waitress in the dining room at the Illinois Eye and Ear Infirmary, a twenty-minute walk from the Sheldon House. "She was very intelligent, full of life and spirit, and a general favorite at the place," noted one newspaper. Alice—she went by her middle name—was from Illiopolis, a village near the state capital, Springfield. She had come to Chicago to be treated at the hospital, then stayed on to work in the dining room. She had turned twenty-two just days before she died.

Police searched her room and found a medicine bottle containing a dark liquid and a prescription for ergot, an alkaloid that doctors often used to induce labor. It also was known to bring on an abortion. Ergot in large doses could be lethal, but the bottle was almost full—she had taken only a spoonful or two.

Montgomery had left the infirmary the afternoon before she died, telling her roommate she was going to stay with a friend. She went instead to the hospital's superintendent, announced she had found a new job, and asked for the wages she was owed. At four o'clock she walked into H. F. Kraft's drugstore on West Madison with a prescription for ergot diluted in water. The clerk hesitated because the prescription was a copy, not the original. Montgomery explained that Dr. Donald Fraser—the doctor summoned barely a month earlier to help Ellen Stack—had prescribed the medicine to one of her friends, who had allowed her to write out a duplicate. The clerk, who likely understood why a young woman might need ergot and knew it was harmless in the dosage prescribed, prepared the medicine.

Montgomery, an autopsy revealed, had been three months pregnant. When a sample taken from her stomach was fed to a cat, the animal died within twenty minutes. The cause appeared to be the ergot mixture. A chemical analysis of the bottle's contents later confirmed it contained strychnine. But who added it, and when? Montgomery's death no longer looked like suicide or a case of a desperate woman poisoning herself by accident. "Somebody committed a fatal blunder," Chicago's *Daily Inter Ocean* newspaper was convinced, "if not murder."

The inquest, delayed while the bottle was tested, finally opened on April 23 at the J. Rogerson & Son funeral parlor, 487 West Madison. The drugstore clerk was adamant—he had not mistaken strychnine for another ingredient when filling the prescription. Then Cook County's coroner, Canute Matson, produced letters he had received after Montgomery's death. Their origins were unclear, but one, possibly in Montgomery's handwriting, accused Dr. Fraser of agreeing to perform an abortion. The doctor, who had shown up for the inquest, jumped to his feet and denied any wrongdoing. Called to testify, Dr. Fraser insisted he had never met Montgomery.

It was left to a six-man jury to sort through the confusing, conflicting evidence. Montgomery had been poisoned by strychnine, the jurors concluded, and had ingested the poison from the bottle of ergot. "We further find that the Druggist is in no way accountable for the Strychnia found in the bottle."

Key questions went unanswered. "How," the *Daily Tribune* asked, "did the strychnine get into that bottle?" And where had Montgomery been for almost five hours, between four o'clock, when the prescription was filled and her arrival at the Sheldon House? "Could Alice have got drugs from someone else, and if so was she given strychnine," the *Chicago Times* asked, "and directed to mix it in the ergot bottle?" The *Daily Tribune* summed up the inquest's findings in a two-word headline: "Very Unsatisfactory."

There should have been an obvious suspect—a West Side doctor who had been in the news less than a month earlier, tossing about allegations that Ellen Stack had been poisoned. Cream's office was two blocks from the Sheldon House, on the route Montgomery likely took on her way to Kraft's drugstore and then to the hotel. If she had stopped at his office, he could have tampered with the medicine. And he was known to the city's police as "a regular abortionist," as one officer later put it.

But the authorities in Chicago were as easily deceived by a skilled and devious murderer as their counterparts in London, Ontario, were. Coroner Matson, like Dr. John Flock before him, struggled to make sense of a web of conflicting evidence and false accusations: a young woman desperate to end a pregnancy; a bottle of medicine laced with deadly poison; mysterious letters, possibly forged, pointing the finger at another suspect. And like London's coroner, Matson seems to have received little help from the Chicago police. Patrolmen and detectives were overworked, poorly trained, and easily corrupted. "One jostles the elbow of a murderer at every angle of the street, and yet the law seems powerless to bring the evil-doers to justice," a leading Chicago businessman complained not long before the deaths of Faulkner, Stack, and Montgomery. "The police are weak and their leaders ineffi-cient." A ten-dollar bribe to an arresting officer, some offenders dis-covered, was sufficient to have charges dropped. Patrolmen in uniform brazenly patronized saloons and brothels while on duty. Gambling czar Mike McDonald made regular payments to officers of all ranks, including station captains and the superintendent of police, to shield his operations and to encourage raids on his rivals. Alfred Trude was well known as McDonald's lawyer and fixer; his vigorous courtroom defense of Cream, and his attack on the officers who investigated Faulkner's death, may have sent a message to the police that the doctor from Canada was untouchable.

If Cream had poisoned Montgomery and wanted to deflect blame, Dr. Fraser made a convenient target. He was someone Cream knew, and not just as a fellow McGill graduate or from his role as a witness in the Faulkner case. They were now neighbors—Dr. Fraser's home was two blocks from Cream's rooming house on West 13th Street. News reports suggested Dr. Fraser's arrest was imminent. The letters left him "in an exceedingly bad box," as the *Chicago Times* put it. But he was never prosecuted. No one was. "The mystery of Alice Montgomery's death," the *Daily Tribune* reported on April 24, "is a mystery still."

Months later, however, the name of Montgomery's suspected killer was finally made public. The revelation came from a surprising source: the top law enforcement official in Belvidere, a city about seventy miles to the northwest, just inside the Illinois–Wisconsin border. And Boone County's sheriff, Albert T. Ames, would not mince words. "Cream," he assured a newspaper reporter, "was the murderer of Alice Montgomery."

28

A **DESPICABLE SCHEME**

{JUNE 1881}

A LETTER CARRIER DROPPED OFF THREE POSTCARDS AT
an address on Chicago's West Side on a warm, sunny
Saturday in the summer of 1881. They were addressed to
Joseph Martin, a thirty-year-old furrier from England who lived at 129
West 13th Street with his wife, Deborah, and their two young daughters. As Martin read each message, his shock and outrage grew.

"I am obliged to inform your neighbors and employers," announced
one card, "that you, your wife and children are suffering from a loathsome disease called syphilis in order that they may protect themselves." It was signed Dr. Cream. The other messages, ending with
the initials T. N. C., singled out Deborah Martin for abuse. "You
had better learn that low vulgar wife of yours to keep her foul mouth
shut," the writer warned. "Two can play at that game. I heard on very
good authority that you had to leave England on account of a bastard
child you left behind."

Martin would have known the sender's name even if the cards
had been unsigned. He had already received two threatening letters
from Cream, who lived a few blocks away, and he recognized his

handwriting. In the letters, the doctor claimed to have obtained a prescription from a druggist that proved the family was being treated for syphilis. As disturbing as those messages were, the latest ones were worse. Anyone could read the filthy, abusive allegations scribbled on a postcard.

Before the day was out, Cream was in the custody of US marshals. He was charged with violating a federal law that made it an offense to use the postal service to distribute "indecent, lewd and obscene" messages. The allegations were serious. If convicted, Cream faced a fine of up to $5,000—the equivalent of about $120,000—and a prison term of one to ten years at hard labor. When he was arraigned on June 20, he pleaded ignorance of the law and seemed to admit he had mailed the offensive missives. "People over in Canada did this sort of thing," he protested, "and never got into trouble for it."

The charges thrust Cream back into the spotlight. The newspapers reminded readers that "the notorious Dr. Cream" had stood trial for the murder of Mary Anne Faulkner the previous year. The *Daily Tribune* was delighted to see him back before the courts, "with a prospect of being rewarded according to his deserts." Some editors once again referred to him as "'Dr.' Cream," his title in quotation marks to suggest he was a quack. Headlines mocked his name as they implied his guilt: "Whipped Cream," read one; "Off-Color 'Cream,'" another.

He hired a lawyer and was granted a one-week adjournment. Bail was set at twelve hundred dollars, and he was released when Mary McClellan, his landlady and fiancée's mother, put up her property as security. A motive for sending the offensive postcards emerged in the *Daily Tribune*. Cream claimed Martin owed him twenty dollars for medical services, the newspaper reported, and "resorted to the despicable scheme" of threats and insults to force him to pay. But Martin insisted that Cream had been paid in full. And the allegation he had contracted venereal disease and spread it to his wife and children was "infamously false."

Cream did not show up for a hearing into the allegations on Monday, June 27. Mary McClellan, who had not seen him for several days, was ordered to forfeit her bond—almost thirty thousand dollars in today's US currency. An arrest warrant was issued.

"The case against Cream is a very plain one," in the *Daily Tribune*'s opinion, "and he doubtless realizes, if he stands trial, that he will go to the Penitentiary for a year or so." But by then, a possible jail term for sending obscene messages was the least of Cream's worries.

29

DANIEL STOTT

{GARDEN PRAIRIE AND BELVIDERE, ILLINOIS •
JUNE–JULY 1881}

I T WAS LATE—TWO O'CLOCK IN THE MORNING—WHEN JULIA
Stott's train pulled in at the Chicago & North Western Railroad's
depot in Garden Prairie, a village in northern Illinois. Her husband, the stationmaster, suffered from epilepsy, and a doctor in
Chicago had prescribed remedies that eased Daniel Stott's symptoms
and seizures. She had been to the doctor's office to fetch a fresh batch
of the medicine.

The following evening, as the rumble of a thunderstorm faded in
the distance and rain gutters dripped the last of the day's downpour,
Daniel Stott used a penknife to uncork a bottle bearing the label of
Chicago druggists Buck & Rayner. He measured out a tablespoon of
the liquid and swallowed it, along with three capsules the doctor had
provided. He made a face. The bitter taste was a surprise.

About fifteen minutes later, as he lay in bed, he cried out in pain
and clutched his stomach. Julia Stott lit a lamp. "His upper lip was
drawn back," she said later, recalling that horrible night, "and his eyes
half out of his head." She tried to get him to his feet several times, but

his back snapped straight each time, leaving him writhing on the bed.

"My God," he exclaimed, "I am dying."

"No Dan—I have brought you out of spells before—try and help me."

"It is no use—you have done all you can do for me—this will finish me."

Within minutes, he was gone. Stott alerted a neighbor, who checked for a pulse or a heartbeat and confirmed he was dead.

Mourners gathered at Stott's graveside two days later, on June 14, 1881, in a cemetery on the eastern edge of the village. But his body— and the secret it contained—would not stay buried for long.

∞∞∞

A WESTERN Union messenger caught Dr. Frank Whitman at his office in the nearby town of Belvidere two days later, in time to hand over a telegram relayed from Chicago. "Want you to have Postmortem examination on body of Dan Stott Garden Prairie," the sender demanded. "Have Stomach analyzed suspect foul Play." A second cable arrived the next morning, repeating the call for an inquest and advising Dr. Whitman to take charge of medicine purchased shortly before Stott's death.

Dr. Whitman, the goateed, heavyset coroner for Boone County, was puzzled. Stott was sixty-one and prone to epileptic seizures. There had been nothing suspicious about his death, no need for an autopsy or inquest. Had the authorities missed something? And who was behind the messages? One telegram identified the sender as Doctor Crame; the other, Dr. Cram. The coroner thumbed through his copy of the Illinois directory of practicing physicians, but neither name appeared in the Chicago section. How had this mysterious doctor heard about Stott's death so quickly, he wondered, and why was he so adamant that an investigation was needed?

Dr. Whitman, who was in his early thirties, had been practicing in Belvidere, Boone County's main town, for almost a decade. He had been coroner for five years. "His skill and marked ability" as a medical man, claimed one admirer, "placed him at the head of the list." He knew when a death was suspicious. And he was just as confident he could spot the work of a prankster. Someone, he concluded, "was endeavoring to play a ghastly joke at my expense." He ignored the requests.

Then a letter arrived from Chicago, bearing the same date, June 16, as the first telegram. It repeated the demand for an inquest. Stott "did not die from natural causes," the writer insisted. "It looks as if he died from Strychnine poisoning, but that is for you to say after you have held the inquest." The local state's attorney, Reuben Coon, received a note in the same handwriting. The sender complained of the coroner's inaction and repeated the allegation that Stott, his patient, had been poisoned. "He was not suffering from any disease that would carry him off so suddenly." The letters bore a signature that finally revealed the source of the allegations—Thomas N. Cream.

That Saturday, June 18, Dr. Whitman rode the train the few miles to Garden Prairie to speak with Stott's wife. "He died of one of his old epileptic fits," she assured the coroner, "only that this was a hard enough one to kill him." Dr. Whitman took possession of the medicine bottle but saw no reason to exhume the body.

"No one here is guilty," he wrote in response to Cream's missives. "If there is any criminality it probably rests with the druggists who put up the medicine." Or perhaps the prescription "was not agreeable to the case." The state's attorney backed the coroner. Coon promised to "promptly and cheerfully" take steps "to ferret out any criminals and bring them to justice" if Cream furnished evidence that Stott had been poisoned.

Cream was infuriated. "The prescription was all right," he fired back by letter on June 20. "I have forgotten more medicine than most of the physicians of Illinois know." He threatened to go to the newspapers with his demand for an exhumation. And time was of the essence. "The weather is warmer, decomposition proceeds rapidly," he added, as if lecturing a child rather than addressing a fellow doctor, "and if you do not get to work immediately your examination will not amount to anything."

Blank No. 1.

THE WESTERN UNION TELEGRAPH COMPANY.

This Company **TRANSMITS** and **DELIVERS** messages only on conditions, limiting its liability, which have been assented to by the sender of the following message.
Errors can be guarded against only by repeating a message back to the sending station for comparison, and the Company will not hold itself liable for errors or delays in transmission or delivery of **Unrepeated Messages.**
This message is an **UNREPEATED MESSAGE** and is delivered by request of the sender, under the conditions named above.

A. R. BREWER, Sec'y.   3   NORVIN GREEN, President.

Dated *Chicago June 17* 188 *1*

Received at *1005 Awc*

To *Coroner Boone Co*

Want Dan Stotts body Garden "Hearse" taken up post mortem examination made contents stomach analyzed inquest held find out cause of death take charge medicine purchased for Statt last saturday

          Dr Cream

30 Collect 68 ¢

One of Cream's telegrams to the coroner in Belvidere, Illinois, demanding an autopsy and inquest into Daniel Stott's death (Case No. 4580, Circuit Court of Boone County, 1881)

The next day, Cream followed up with an apology for his rant—"I was in a very bad and angered state of mind"—and a suggestion: Coroner Whitman should test a tablespoon of the leftover medicine on a dog or cat. "It is possible that more Strychnine was put in the bottle than was ordered," he noted. "That mistake has been made before." And he offered a strange explanation of how he had learned of Stott's death. A woman he had never met before had come to his office the day after the funeral—a clairvoyant, who said she had been sent to tell his fortune. "I was not a believer in such nonsense," Cream explained, but he decided to test her with questions about his patients. When he mentioned Stott's name, she announced he was dead and had been poisoned. It was not unusual for someone to consult a fortune-teller. As many as a dozen clairvoyants advertised in the Chicago papers each day, promising to reveal the future for as little as twenty-five cents. Madame Zerapha, the Great Egyptian Prophetess of Wabash Avenue, claimed she could read fortunes and cure rheumatism, in person or by letter. But clairvoyants were not known to turn up at a doctor's office, unannounced, with news of a patient's death.

Despite Cream's condescending tone and the bizarre story about a fortune-teller, Dr. Whitman heeded his advice. He administered a spoonful of Stott's medicine to a dog. Within minutes the animal tumbled onto its side and went into spasms. Less than twenty-five minutes later, it was dead. He headed back to Garden Prairie to exhume the body. The stomach was removed, as Cream had suggested, and sent to a professor of chemistry and toxicology at Chicago's Rush Medical College for analysis. Dr. Walter Haines detected strychnine and estimated Stott had ingested more than three grains—"a quantity sufficient, several times over, to produce death," he reported. He tested the bottled medicine and found it contained about two and a half grains of the poison per fluid ounce.

There was no longer any doubt that Stott had been murdered. And Dr. Whitman and State's Attorney Coon were certain they knew who was responsible.

◇◇◇◇◇

DANIEL Stott had arrived in Garden Prairie at the end of the Civil War. He had been a merchant back in Canada, until his business failed. His second wife left him. His only son died young. He had come to Boone County to start over.

The district, which bordered on Wisconsin, still had a frontier feel. The first white settlers had trickled in less than fifty years earlier, making many residents older than the county. Villages clustered around depots after a railroad linked the area to Chicago in the 1850s. One of those stops got its name when a passenger stepped off a train, surveyed the tabletop fields stretching in all directions, and declared the spot "a garden on the prairie." A few miles west of Stott's new home was the county seat, Belvidere, a town of about three thousand.

Stott took charge of the Garden Prairie depot. He joined the Masonic Lodge. He had a large house with a veranda that was perfect for chatting with neighbors as they passed. "A man of good habits and genial temperament," by one account, "much liked and respected by all who knew him." He fit in. His third wife did not. Julia Abbey was born in England and had worked for local families as a maid. Marriage to the station agent catapulted her into the upper echelon of a small social circle, and she knew it. Dr. Whitman, the coroner, heard the gossip. "Julia was inclined to be snobbish with her neighbors," as he bluntly put it. Her tastes were too stylish, her manner too haughty. The couple had one child, Revel, a daughter born in 1871, but there was talk of a troubled marriage. Daniel Stott had been unwell for years and Julia was thirty-six years his junior. "Rumors, faint yet persistent, were abroad," Dr. Whitman recalled, "that she was tiring of her aging husband."

Stott consulted Cream in early 1881 and was pleased with the results. "I am improving Very Rapidly under your Treatment," he reported in a letter to his new doctor. Medication that Cream had prescribed had improved his digestion and "done wonders for the Kidneys," and he was sleeping better. Even his mood had improved—the medicine, he said, "makes me feel Happy." Cream examined him only once. Every ten days or so, Julia Stott would take the train into Chicago to visit Cream's office and pick up a prescription for a new batch of medicine. If the doctor was busy or she had other errands to run, Cream's landlady, a Mrs. Gridley, allowed her to use one of her extra rooms. On at least one visit, she stayed overnight. Her last trip to the city was on June 11, a Saturday, and she returned after midnight with the bottled medicine and capsules her husband took just before he died.

JULIA STOTT (*COMPLETE DETECTIVE CASES*, MAY 1940 / AUTHOR COLLECTION)

News of the suspected poisoning broke in the *Belvidere Standard* at the end of June in a back-page item that described Cream's demands for an inquest, the exhumation, and the experiment on the dog. "If further investigation should prove that poison had been administered to Mr. Stott, even if accidentally given, it will be a terrible affair."

The inquest was held in Dr. Whitman's office in Belvidere on the evening of July 14. James Rayner, a partner in the druggists Buck & Rayner, along with one of his dispensing clerks, had been summoned from Chicago. No error, they insisted, had been made in formulating Cream's prescription, which called for only a trace amount of strychnine. "All violent poisons are put in a dark closet by themselves," Rayner said, to ensure that clerks knew when they were handling dangerous substances. Mistakenly adding the large dose that had killed Stott was "an utter impossibility."

Julia Stott described her trip to Chicago to pick up the medicine and her husband's sudden death. She had walked to Buck & Rayner's—a round trip of more than three miles—to get the prescription filled, even though other drugstores were closer to Cream's office. Cream had not touched the bottled medicine when she returned to his office, she said, but he had broken open one of the capsules and tasted the contents.

Under questioning by Dr. Whitman and the state's attorney, her story began to unravel. She had left the package of medicine unattended in Cream's office, but she did not think it had been touched. She claimed she had not spoken to Cream since Stott's death, then admitted she had returned to Chicago to confront him about his letters and telegrams demanding an investigation.

"Do you think I gave the medicine wrong?" she had asked him.

"Mrs. Stott, the thing never entered my head," he had replied, according to her recollections of the exchange. "If you had given him an overdose it would not have killed him." Assuming, of course, "the medicine was right."

Cream's reputation took a beating. The clerk who filled the prescription was aware that the doctor had been "mixed up with disreputable cases." Eyebrows were raised as lawyers dissected the claim he had learned of Stott's death from a clairvoyant. Julia Stott mentioned that Cream had been in jail until the previous December. Had she ever seen him intoxicated? "I have seen him when I thought he had been drinking," she said, then added a punch line: "He was always smarter when he had been drinking a little."

Dr. Whitman proved to be the most damning witness. He read Cream's telegrams aloud and produced his letters as evidence. The doctor had been subpoenaed to testify at the inquest, he noted, but had failed to show up. And the coroner revealed information he had gleaned from his conversations with Julia Stott. Her husband, she had told the coroner, had once described Cream as a man who was "mighty tricky and needed watching."

The jurors exonerated the druggists and concluded that only one person could have laced the medicine with additional strychnine. "The evidence implicates one Thomas N. Cream," they announced in their verdict, "as the unlawful slayer of the deceased." Boone County's sheriff, Albert Ames, headed to Chicago with an arrest warrant. But Cream, who was facing prosecution for sending the obscene postcards—one of his telegrams to the coroner was sent on June 17, the day he mailed abusive messages to former patient Joseph Martin, the Chicago furrier—was long gone. He had skipped bail more than two weeks earlier.

Dr. Whitman and Ames continued to press Julia Stott for details of her dealings with Cream. They suspected the two had been lovers and had hatched a plot to get rid of her husband. Her story changed again. When she confronted Cream after the death, she now claimed, he had pressed her to give him power of attorney so that he could sue Buck & Rayner for putting too much strychnine in the medicine. "The druggists were responsible for the error and should be made to pay for it," he had told her, and a court might award thousands of dollars in damages. She had refused the offer.

Dr. Whitman went public with the new information in the last week of July. "It was a case of intentional poisoning," he told the *Belvidere Standard*, and "a put up job" to falsely accuse and sue the druggists. Cream, it now appeared, had planned the murder and poisoned Stott as part of a bizarre blackmail plot that had backfired; by demanding an exhumation and investigation, he had succeeded only in incriminating himself.

"Dr. Cream," the newspaper added, "is now the man badly wanted."

30

"CROOKED CREAM"

TWO MEN STEPPED OFF THE GREAT WESTERN RAILWAY'S train from Windsor, Ontario, on a July evening in 1881 and headed toward Gauthier's Hotel. Clouds drifting in from the northwest blocked the sinking sun in Belle River, a lakeside village of a few hundred about fifteen miles inside the Canadian border. A hotel employee pointed out the upstairs room of a guest who called himself Dr. Donald Ross. A ladder was propped against the side of the hotel, just outside his window. Their quarry seemed prepared to make a quick escape.

They worked out a plan. Sheriff Albert Ames, the one with the neatly trimmed hair and droopy mustache, would stand at the foot of the ladder in case the man tried to flee when William Bains went to his door. Bains was chief of police in Windsor, a town that stared warily across a wide river at Detroit, twenty times its size, and he was frequently enlisted to help US lawmen track down fugitives. A porous international border made Windsor a gateway for "crooks of all dyes" fleeing justice on the American side, a local paper grumbled, "a safety zone to safe blowers, hold-up men, thieves and vagabonds."

At one o'clock in the morning, when the guests were asleep, Bains rapped on the door. Cream opened it just as the officer was about to break it down. When an arrest warrant accusing him of murdering Daniel Stott was produced, he protested his innocence. Brought face-to-face with Ames, according to a press account, "he turned pale and trembled like a leaf."

He was arraigned the next day, July 28, before a magistrate in Windsor. Cream again denied any role in the murder. He had fled Chicago, he said, only to escape "the notoriety of the case" and to consult his father and other family members. It turned out his own carelessness had exposed his hiding place in Ontario—postal officials in Chicago had intercepted a letter he sent to someone in the city and alerted Ames.

"I don't see how they can implicate me in the affair," he told a reporter who turned up at his cell in Windsor's jail later that day. "I was the first person to demand an investigation."

"What made you skip out if you are so confident of being able to prove your innocence?" he was asked.

"I had some trouble, and was not doing very well, and went to look for a new place," he sputtered, leaving the reporter to fill in the details about the prosecution for sending obscene postcards and jumping bail. He had left Chicago in mid-June, he pointed out, weeks before he was accused of killing Stott.

Cream agreed to return to Illinois to face trial. He was out of money and options. He had arrived in Canada with thirty-five dollars in his pocket and had been forced to pawn his jewelry to top up his whisky glass as he lay low at the hotel. Fighting extradition would, at best, delay the inevitable for two or three weeks. Safe-blowing and theft were not among the crimes covered under the extradition treaty between the two countries. Murder was.

A reporter for the *Daily Tribune* caught up with Cream at the

Michigan Central Railroad's lakefront depot at about eight o'clock on the morning of August 2, as he and Ames changed trains in Chicago for the last leg of a 350-mile journey to Belvidere. Cream, handcuffed and disheveled, had not shaved in a couple of weeks. He was innocent of "the Garden Prairie business," as he called it, and was confident his father would hire "the best criminal lawyer in the State" to defend him. He denied tampering with Stott's medicine. He denied plotting to blackmail or sue Buck & Rayner. Julia Stott was "the biggest liar unhung," and he was eager to face her in court.

Ames escorted him aboard a Chicago & North Western train that pulled out at quarter past nine. Fields of black soil, peppered with homesteads and towering stone silos, stretched to the horizon as they entered Boone County. Just before Belvidere, they rumbled past a freshly dug grave and the small wood-frame station building bearing the name Garden Prairie, where Daniel Stott had worked. By lunchtime Cream was in a cell at the county courthouse.

◇◇◇◇◇

CREAM was convicted in the press long before he stood trial. He was a "notorious Chicago abortionist" tried for murder the year before, editors reminded their readers. One newspaper described the case as "perfectly analogous" to Alice Montgomery's unsolved murder a few months earlier, though the alleged poisoning and attempted-blackmail scheme was actually a match for the Ellen Stack case. The *Daily Tribune* offered detailed accounts of the sordid tale emerging in its backyard. "The annals of crime have rarely furnished a stranger case of poisoning," the paper announced "Assuming that the evidence is correct, the crime of this man can hardly be paralleled for cruelty and infamy." It would be Cream's word against Julia Stott's when the case came to trial, and the *Tribune* had chosen its side. "There is nothing in Mrs. Stott's conduct to show that she was privy to any plot to poison her husband," it declared, and she had been merely "an easy tool in his hands."

The publicity was most damaging in Belvidere, where men who would serve on Cream's jury were offered a preview of the prosecution's case and insights into his shady past. "The general belief seems to be that Mrs. Stott was unwittingly the agent for administering the poison," the *Belvidere Standard* reported within days of the arrest. Cream had schemed to "fix the poisoning" on Buck & Rayner and had hoped to "make a handsome sum" through blackmail. The newspaper resurrected details of the Catharine Gardner case in Ontario. And when Sheriff Ames announced that Cream had murdered Alice Montgomery in Chicago, the *Standard* featured the news on its front page, along with a prediction: "the 'Dr.' will have a handful of murders to answer for." Headline writers again toyed with his name: one dubbed him "Crooked Cream"; another settled on "Bad Cream." "Such a cow-ardly man," the Belvidere newspaper wisecracked, "ought to be cream-ated."

◇◇◇◇

CREAM'S trial for murder—his second in less than a year—opened in Belvidere on Monday, September 19. Hundreds of people converged on the Boone County courthouse, two stories of redbrick civic pride embellished with arched windows and a soaring central tower. Many were witnesses or had been summoned for jury duty. Inside, a visitor noted, the sheriff's wife had decorated the hallways and freshly painted courtroom with house plants, "making it a really pleasant place"—for those who were not on trial for their lives, at least.

It took almost a day to empanel the jury. So many candidates were rejected, likely based on the adverse publicity, that court officials were ordered to round up more from the audience and surrounding streets. Most of those selected were from Belvidere and included some of the county's leading citizens—"men of sound judgment," said one observer, "conscientious and honest."

By the time the first witness testified on September 20, the nation was in mourning. President James Garfield, felled by an assassin's bullet weeks earlier, had died overnight. "Grief and sadness seemed to cover the entire country like a cloud," noted an item in the Belvidere paper. Stores were hung in black bunting. Offices closed. Cream's prosecutors, however, pressed on with their case. Their key witness was Julia Stott. She was in custody and facing a murder charge for her suspected role in her husband's death. But separate trials had been ordered, and she had agreed to testify against Cream. Her testimony was expected to delve into matters too delicate for the women in the gallery. They were asked to leave.

CREAM STOOD TRIAL FOR THE MURDER OF DANIEL STOTT IN THE BOONE COUNTY COURTHOUSE IN BELVIDERE, ILLINOIS. (AUTHOR COLLECTION)

Petite and rail thin, Stott was nervous as she faced Cream across the crowded courtroom. Her voice was weak, her responses timid, and her testimony damning. "She turned States' evidence," the *Chicago*

Daily Tribune's correspondent noted, "and tried to convict Dr. Cream to save her own neck." She abandoned the story she had told at the coroner's inquest. Cream had instructed her to have Buck & Rayner fill his prescription, she said, and had escorted her to the store. When they were back in his office, he had handled the medicine. "She saw him tampering with it," one newsman reported, "though she did not see him put anything into it." She confirmed the widely reported story that Cream had tried to pressure her to sue the druggists for damages. And she admitted, for the first time, that she and Cream had been lovers—"criminally intimate," in the phrasing of the time. Her daughter, Revel, had tagged along for at least one visit to Cream's office. "Dr. Cream told me he loved my mother," the ten-year-old disclosed when she was called to testify, "and would like her as his own."

Mary McClellan, Cream's former landlady, buried him even deeper. Cream had visited her on June 12, the day Stott died, and had made an extraordinary prediction—apparently without the assistance of a clairvoyant. "He expected to hear of Daniel Stott's death at any time," she recalled, "as he had been poisoned." And, she claimed, he had made an even more incriminating statement in her presence: he said he had told Julia Stott "he could mix a medicine that would kill her husband in twenty minutes."

The prosecution presented the findings of Dr. Walter Haines of Chicago's Rush Medical College, who had detected strychnine in Stott's remains and in the medicine bottle. In Britain, laboratory mistakes and conflicting opinions had made jurors hesitant to accept the opinions of experts; Americans held an even lower opinion of physicians and scientists summoned to the witness stand in criminal cases. "The public has no confidence in expert testimony," was the blunt assessment of a contributor to the prestigious *Journal of the American Medical Association*. Disputes over procedures and findings made experts "the subject of everybody's sneer, and the object of everybody's derision." They were accused in the press of "gaudy and unembarrassed lying" or dismissed as "an unmitigated joke." But

Cream, the first to allege that Stott had died of strychnine poisoning, could not do an about-face and dispute laboratory tests that proved he had been correct. His lawyer, Daniel Munn, summed up the defense position to the jurors: Stott has been poisoned, but they were "trying the wrong person."

Cream had bragged of hiring the best criminal lawyer in the state, but his father had refused to fund his defense. Instead, Daniel Cream and his sisters had pooled their resources and sent three hundred dollars to help with the legal bills, and Munn, who had acted for Cream on the obscenity charges, took on the murder case. It was an uphill battle. He was an outsider from Chicago, pitted against a team of prominent local lawyers acting for the prosecution—State's Attorney Reuben Coon; his brother, Amos; and Charles Fuller, a state senator whose "fighting qualities" were said to be admired by supporters and political opponents alike. Munn grilled Stott for hours, but she stuck stubbornly to her new version of events. McClellan admitted her "hard feelings" for Cream—he had jilted her daughter and she was still on the hook for the twelve hundred dollars she posted as his bail—but she, too, survived Munn's cross-examination.

Cream would have to save himself. He was sworn in as a witness on the trial's third day. "A homely, coarse-looking man," the *Belvidere Standard*'s reporter thought, with receding dark hair "and very little of it." He was thirty-one but looked ten years older. His deep voice echoed through the courtroom. His denials were so loud and emphatic, the reporter felt certain they could be heard outside the courthouse.

Julia Stott had asked him for strychnine, he said. He had refused to supply it, but she somehow managed to procure the poison. She had shown it to him, vowing to "fix a dose" for her husband. He denied killing Daniel Stott. "In my prescription," he said, "there was nothing to cause death." He denied having sexual relations with Julia Stott, denied sending her to Buck & Rayner, denied handling Stott's medicine.

Why, he was asked, had he demanded an inquest?

"I suspected Mrs. Stott had poisoned him."

The state's attorney made short work of him. Under cross-examination, Cream "admitted many things against him," the *Chicago Times* reported, "and his denials did not cover near all the people's case." Cream's telegrams and letters were produced, exposing some of his testimony as "exactly contrary" to his earlier assertions.

Closing arguments lasted more than seven hours, extending the trial into a fourth day. Munn was "brilliant, able and eloquent" on Cream's behalf, the press reported. Fuller, a mesmerizing speaker with intense, deep-set eyes, presented "a masterly and convincing argument" of his own. The judge reviewed the law and the evidence before the jurors filed out at about five o'clock. As they deliberated, rain pattered on the arched windows of the courthouse. Spectators took bets on the outcome; the odds favored a hung jury.

They returned at about nine with a verdict: guilty.

The first ballot, reporters discovered, had been nine to three to convict. Four hours of debate had won over the holdouts. The jurors also dictated Cream's punishment. Only three had voted to send him to the gallows. His punishment would be life in prison, with one day of each year spent in solitary confinement. A journalist glanced at Cream to see his reaction. "Not a muscle of his face moved as he heard his dreadful sentence."

Munn considered an appeal to the state supreme court, but winning a new trial carried an enormous risk: a second jury might impose the death penalty. Speaking to the press after the trial, Fuller was confident justice had been done. "If ever a man had a fair trial and an able defence, Dr. Cream is that man," he claimed. "There can be no possible doubt of the guilt of the defendant."

◇◇◇◇◇

WHEN he arrived in Chicago in 1892, Inspector Frederick Smith Jarvis interviewed Dr. Walter Haines, the chemist who had found strychnine in Daniel Stott's stomach. Then he traveled north to Belvidere, to find out more about the case that had culminated in Cream's conviction for murder. He met with Boone County's sheriff, Albert Ames, who briefed him on the Stott investigation and trial. Oddly, Ames did not alert him to another homicide that, like Stott's, involved tainted medicine, strychnine poisoning, and false accusations that echoed the Lambeth murders. Back in 1881, the sheriff had been convinced Cream had poisoned Alice Montgomery not long before he killed Stott; he had even declared him guilty of her murder in the press. But for some reason, all these years later, he did not bring her death to Jarvis's attention. The inspector made no mention of Montgomery's poisoning in his reports to Scotland Yard.

◇◇◇◇◇

JULIA Stott spent six months in the Boone County jail, but she never stood trial. Many suspected she had been part of the murder plot, and even Fuller publicly declared them "equally guilty of the crime of murder." But prosecutors had agreed to release her if she revealed what she knew about her husband's death, and she had held up her end of the bargain. She was released in February 1882.

Cream, meanwhile, was transferred to the Illinois State Penitentiary on November 1, 1881, to begin serving his life sentence. "End of a Dangerous Career," a headline assured readers of the *Chicago Daily News*.

The prediction would prove to be premature.

31

INMATE NO. 4374

{JOLIET, ILLINOIS • 1881–1885}

FRESH FISH," INMATES CALLED NEW ARRIVALS TO THE
Illinois State Penitentiary in Joliet. While repeat offenders
barely flinched at the sight of its forbidding walls, "comparative
novices in crime," noted Sidney Wetmore, the prison's records clerk,
recoiled in terror and dread. "Their cheeks blanch, their frames trem-
ble nervously as they look at that vast pile, where for years, possibly
for life, their hopes, their ambitions, their very selves will lie buried."
Thomas Neill Cream had been behind bars before as he awaited trial
for the murders of Mary Anne Faulkner and Daniel Stott, but this was
different. He knew he might never come out alive.

Sheriff Albert Ames delivered Cream to the prison on the first
day of November 1881. Once inside, Cream was led to the receiving
department, where he was ordered to strip. A clerk, likely Wetmore,
noted the date and carefully recorded his identifying features. He was
182 pounds, with a solid build and "massive jaws and chin." The clerk
noted the duration of his sentence—"*His Natural Life*"—emphasizing
each word. Cream's "Legitimate Occupation" was recorded as phys-

ician. His "mental culture" was considered good; his "Habits of Life," such as chewing tobacco, were "moderate." He described himself as a widower, but no one asked what had happened to his wife. Prison officials were more interested in the deep scar on the left side of his abdomen. He had undergone surgery, Cream told them, but he did not explain the reason for the operation.

He was ordered to bathe in a tub in an open room, then issued a coat, vest, peaked cap, and a pair of pants, all emblazoned with black-and-white horizontal bands. The zebra stripes would make him easy to spot if he tried to escape. The uniform was also intended to humiliate—one woman, visiting for the first time, thought her husband looked like a circus clown. Cream's face was shaved clean and his hair cropped short, further marking him as a convict at a time when most men had long hair and mustaches or beards. His photograph was taken for the "rogues gallery" the prison maintained, to help track him down if he managed to scale the high walls and evade the sharpshooters who patrolled them. And he was issued a new identity. He was now inmate no. 4374.

The Illinois State Penitentiary—Joliet Prison, as it was better known—was one of the country's toughest and most notorious prisons. Its nine hundred cells housed "the most eminent rascals and hardened criminals in America," in Wetmore's words, "who have graced and disgraced all grades of society." Opened in 1869, it was a sprawling collection of cellblocks and shops enclosed within a wall erected by an earlier generation of inmates, who had built their own prison. About fifteen hundred men were serving time when Cream arrived.

The last decades of the nineteenth century were "the dark ages for America's prisons," a historian would one day note. Conditions were primitive. Cramped cells designed for one man usually held two. Cellblocks were poorly heated and dimly lit. Prisoners spent ten-hour days quarrying rock or toiling in silence in prison shops; it was believed that hard work and discipline would cure them of their criminal ways. When inmates disobeyed orders or prison rules, wardens could choose between punishing offenders or reforming them—and usually came down on the side of punishment. By the time Cream was locked up in Joliet, whipping, gagging, dousing with cold water, and other archaic practices had been abandoned in favor of a stint in solitary confinement. "My idea of punishment," explained Joliet's reform-minded warden, Robert McClaughry, "is to restrict the man from further wrong doing without inflicting pain upon him or doing anything in the nature of retribution, but at the same time to grip him with sufficiently firm hold to let him know that he is in the hands of the law."

A CELLBLOCK AT THE ILLINOIS STATE PENITENTIARY IN JOLIET AND THE CORRIDOR OUT-SIDE THE SOLITARY CONFINEMENT CELLS (AUTHOR COLLECTION)

Cream spent his first night sleeping in a wide passageway that faced the cells in the prison's solitary confinement building. This rite of passage not only fulfilled the sentencing requirement of one day a year in segregation, but it also reminded newcomers where malcontents were sent. Then the prison chaplain read him Joliet's rules. He was not allowed to speak—to guards, to visitors, or even to fellow inmates—without the permission of the prison's staff. He could chat with his cellmate "in a low tone" in the evenings but not with those in neighboring cells. Lights out at nine o'clock. He would take a bath once a week in the summer, every second week in the winter. He would attend chapel services each Sunday, unless ill or excused. As a sign of respect, he would touch his cap or forehead before speaking to any prison official. The list seemed endless. If he disobeyed or misbehaved, he could lose his weekly ration of tobacco and candles or wind up in solitary confinement. The chaplain handed him a card outlining the rules, for easy reference. If he soiled or defaced it, he was warned, he would be "severely punished."

Cream was taken to his cell, a closet-sized stone coffin seven feet high, seven feet deep, and just four and a half feet wide. An iron-framed bunk bed, a couple of stools, and a shelf to hold books and papers were the only furnishings. It was barely big enough for one man, but only a few hundred inmates had a cell to themselves. He would sleep on a thin straw mattress, beneath a rough woolen blanket that matched the stripes on his uniform. He was issued two buckets, one for washing and one to use as a toilet. He would grow accustomed to the stench of urine and feces. There was no window, just a small hole leading to the roof for ventilation. A strip of wood attached to the iron-barred cell door bore his name and inmate number.

Every morning except Sundays a bell jarred Cream awake at quarter till six to signal the start of the workday. Men scrambled to dress, wash, and make their beds. Fifteen minutes later, guards opened the cell doors and escorted them across the yard to sewer openings, where they dumped their toilet buckets. They marched there and back, and to and from work and meals, in single file and in lockstep. Each morning Cream would grab a breakfast of coffee, bread, and stew or hash and wolf it down in his cell. At quarter till seven the steam whistle of the boilerhouse screeched, and Cream marched to his workplace. He worked from seven o'clock in the morning until six in the evening with a forty-minute break for lunch, usually a large helping of meat and potatoes. After a light supper of bread and coffee or tea in his cell, he could rest or read by candlelight until nine o'clock.

Each night, as darkness fell, coughs punctured the cellblock's eerie silence. Exhausted men drifted into sleep. Then a guard pushed a button. The morning bell rang. The routine was repeated.

⬦⬦⬦⬦

CREAM was assigned to the stone-carving shop, where monuments and decorative elements for buildings were crafted—an eagle to adorn a customs house in Terre Haute, Indiana, was a typical commission. Prison officials likely thought his stout build made him suitable for such heavy work. His coworkers included an embezzler extradited from his South American refuge and a former police officer serving twenty-five years for murder. They worked alongside one another ten hours a day, six days a week, month after month, in silence. A man who spoke or looked up from his work risked being reported and punished. "Silence, obedience and strict attention to labor," noted Wetmore, "is the rigid law of the place."

A crackdown on repeat offenders brought a wave of new admissions as Cream began serving his sentence. "The prison is rapidly filling up with the hardest kind of crooks," the *Chicago Daily Tribune* noted, "most of whom are coming back for their second, third and fourth terms." Bank robbers marched in lockstep with safe-blowers; rapists, thieves, and killers worked side by side in the shops. A threat of sudden violence pervaded the prison. Inmates turned on one another or attacked guards; guards lashed out at stubborn, unruly prisoners. Eighteen months after Cream's arrival, Mike Mooney, who was serving time for theft, methodically sharpened a stolen metal file, waited for his cellmate, John Anderson, to fall asleep, and stabbed him to death. Frank Rande, a Wild West desperado thought to have murdered more than ten men, was seven years into a life sentence in 1884 when he attacked and nearly killed a deputy warden.

Some tried to escape. Wetmore reckoned only one in a hundred succeeded, and most of those who managed to scale the walls or bolt from a work gang were quickly recaptured. One man removed a prisoner's corpse from a coffin, climbed in, and ran off once the casket was carried outside the prison walls. Another burrowed into a wagonload of horse manure but was discovered. There was another means of escape. Thirty-nine inmates died in 1885 alone—"freed by death," as one newspaper put it—most of them victims of tuberculosis. Others were shipped off to insane asylums. Some men gave up and hanged themselves in their cells; one used a kitchen knife to slice open a vein in his leg and bled to death. When an inmate died and no family member claimed the body, burial was in a cemetery on a hill a half mile east of the prison. Hundreds of upright pine boards, bearing the man's name, prison number, age, and date of death painted in black letters, marked their graves for a few years, until the wood rotted away.

Inmates lived dual lives, recalled Franklin Hollingrood, who served time with Cream. After a "monotonous semi-conscious existence by day," many devoured periodicals and books in their cells before they were told to blow out their candles. For a few hours each evening their minds, at least, were free. Inmates could borrow books from the prison library or subscribe to newspapers or magazines. The library offered more than eight thousand volumes when Cream arrived, including works on history, religion, science, art, and philosophy. There were a few books on medical subjects and a chemistry text titled *The Narcotics We Indulge In; The Poisons We Select; The Odors We Enjoy*. Cream could escape into the novels of Jane Austen, Charles Dickens, Victor Hugo, Herman Melville, and Mark Twain. In an unintended cruelty, men with nowhere to go had access to more than six hundred travel books.

Cream was entitled to see one visitor every two months. His brother Daniel made the thousand-mile trip to Joliet several times, even though he could stay for only a half hour. The topic of conversation was always the same. "On every occasion," Daniel recalled, Cream "professed his innocence of the crime saying he had been committed on perjured evidence." Only one other family member appears to have stayed in touch. He corresponded with a cousin who lived in Brooklyn during his time in Joliet.

ILLINOIS STATE PENETENTIARY, JOLIET, ILL., PRISONERS MARCHING

JOLIET INMATES MARCHING IN LOCKSTEP (AUTHOR COLLECTION)

The warden, McClaughry, got to know Cream. He saw him most days, at least from a distance, until he resigned in 1888 to become warden at another prison. "A model officer," Wetmore said of his boss, "respected, feared and admired by every criminal." Years later, a journalist would have reason to inquire about one of those criminals—Dr. Cream. "He was a smart fellow," McClaughry recalled, "always claiming that he had been convicted on perjured testimony."

⬦⬦⬦⬦

THE small advertisement in the classified columns of the *Belvidere Standard* in March 1885 would have been easy to overlook. "NOTICE IS HEREBY GIVEN," it announced, "that the undersigned intends to apply to the Governor of Illinois for a pardon." The undersigned was Thomas N. Cream.

Since his arrival at Joliet, Cream had dispatched a steady stream of letters to his father, proclaiming his innocence and pleading for help. William Cream agreed to back the application to Governor Richard Oglesby for a pardon. To defray legal fees, he sent the equivalent of about five thousand dollars in today's US currency to Joliet's warden in the summer of 1885. The elder Cream "did not take much stock in his son's claim of innocence," noted Warden McClaughry, who read and approved every inmate's correspondence, "but was willing, if there was any probability that his son's innocence could be established, to furnish money to that end."

A life sentence in nineteenth-century Illinois was not necessarily imprisonment for life unless an inmate died behind bars. The governor could issue a pardon or shorten the sentence to a specific number of years, and political pressure was often the deciding factor. A successful bid for early release "was not so much a recognition of the prisoner's rehabilitation," one study of the state's penal system noted, "as proof of the sympathy that he was able to arouse among influential citizens." If an inmate had well-connected supporters and could convince enough people to sign a petition, freedom might be within his grasp. Of the 153 killers handed life terms in Illinois between 1818 and 1885, 42 were pardoned, a few after serving as little as a year. A dozen more had their sentences commuted to fixed terms. The odds for Cream's early release were about one in three.

He had already retained a lawyer. Omar Wright of Belvidere, who also served in the state legislature, took the case even though he had represented Julia Stott at the coroner's inquest into her husband's death. It was an astute choice, and not just because they both believed that Julia Stott had committed perjury. Wright was a Republican; so was Governor Oglesby, who had recently appointed Wright to serve as one of the three commissioners who oversaw the Illinois prison system.

Wright teamed up with John Jennison, a Chicago attorney, to gather evidence. Jennison collected sworn statements from several people who had overheard Cream's conversation with Mary McClellan. None recalled remarks about Stott's imminent death or an offer to "mix a medicine" that would kill him in twenty minutes. Jennison also spoke to McClellan. It turned out she had several possible motives for embellishing her testimony. She believed Cream had planned to poison her and her daughter, Lena, after they married, so that he could inherit their property. "He got what he deserved," she said. And it turned out she had not lost the twelve hundred dollars she had posted as bail before Cream fled to Canada. McClellan, who was in a chatty mood, volunteered that Sheriff Ames had assured her it would be "for her benefit" to testify against Cream. Apparently, it was. "She got out of it," Jennison reported, "and would not have to pay anything" to honor the bail bond. The lawyer added a sworn statement of his own, with details of his conversation with Cream shortly after Stott's death, when the doctor reported Julia Stott's threat to poison her husband. Acting on his advice, Jennison confirmed, Cream had contacted the Boone County coroner and insisted on the exhumation.

Wright, a white-bearded former school principal—opposing counsel called him the "teacher lawyer" behind his back—focused his attack on Julia Stott. He had refused to represent her after the coroner's inquest, he told the governor, and felt he could disclose his confidential dealings with her because he was convinced she had murdered her husband and acted alone. She had perjured herself either at the inquest, when she testified that Cream had not touched her husband's medicine, or at the trial, when she said he had tampered with it. The trial itself had been unfair—rumors and news reports condemned Cream in advance, and worse, the bailiff who had summoned jurors now admitted that the panel was "packed" with people likely to convict. Wright also circulated a petition supporting a pardon, with a preamble portraying Cream as the victim

of prejudice and perjured evidence and asserting that the real murderer "went Scott free by turning States Evidence." More than 170
people signed the petition, including neighbors of the Stott family
in Garden Prairie.

Cream did his part. That May he drafted a rambling, five-page
petition for a pardon. He attacked the evidence against him as flawed
and proclaimed he was "not guilty in any degree or manner, either in
word, deed or thought." Two months later he asked the Canadian government to intervene on his behalf. Canada had been a self-governing
nation for less than twenty years in 1885, and Britain still handled its
relations with foreign countries. The request was referred to the British
consulate in Chicago. The vice consul, John Dunn, met with Wright
several times and agreed to present Cream's petition and supporting
documents—including transcripts of hearings and the affidavits containing fresh evidence—to the governor. "I have no doubt that the
man was wrongly convicted and is innocent of the offence charged,"
Dunn declared in a covering letter when he submitted the materials to
Oglesby in early November.

Cream, meanwhile, had spent a week in solitary confinement
in April 1885 for ruining some of his stonework. Four months later,
he was sent back for eight days for what prison records described
as "not doing reasonable work." He would do two more stints in
solitary for breaches of discipline. Time in the "hole" was a horrific,
soul-destroying ordeal that threatened a man's health and sanity. The
cells of this prison-within-a-prison were empty—a plank on the cold
stone floor served as a bed. A small skylight admitted some light,
but a heavy wooden door shut out the world. Inmates subsisted on a
daily ration of half a slice of bread and a small cup of water. Cream
was handcuffed to the cell's barred inner door each day, forcing him
to stand for the ten hours he should have been at work. Those who
resisted were beaten with clubs. Those who screamed for release
were gagged with a leather strap.

Warden McClaughry believed in the power of segregation to

correct an inmate's behavior. "The terrible loneliness oppresses them," he told a Chicago audience in 1882, "and they always give in." A former inmate who served time with Cream in the 1880s alleged that many prisoners had gone mad in the solitary cells. One, who had been locked up for fifteen days, "came out at the end of that time a physical wreck," the former inmate claimed, and died within eighteen months.

The governor was unaware of Cream's misconduct—his prison disciplinary record was not included in the pardon file. But Charles Fuller, the prosecutor at trial, weighed in to defend the murder conviction. He was now a member of the Illinois House of Representatives and another prominent Republican who could command Oglesby's attention. "I never dreamed that I was aiding in sending an *innocent* man to the Penitentiary for Life," he assured the governor, and he was certain he had not. The evidence presented at Cream's trial "was sufficient to establish his guilt beyond even the *possibility* of a doubt." After meeting with Wright, however, Fuller softened his stance and told Oglesby he would not object to Cream's life sentence being commuted to a fourteen-year term.

Other, more strenuous objections reached the governor's desk in the capital, Springfield. James Rayner of the Chicago druggists Buck & Rayner, the target of Cream's failed blackmail plot after Daniel Stott's death, submitted four letters protesting a possible pardon. "Cream is too dangerous a man to be let loose upon the Public," he warned. Stott's murder "was one of the blackest on record: entirely unprovoked and coolly and craftily premeditated, designed and executed," noted one of the letters. "There are men in Chicago," added another, "who have good reason to think it is not the first crime of the same nature for which he is responsible." As well, the trial judge, jurors, and other Boone County officials were expected to sign a counterpetition, still in circulation in December 1885, objecting to a pardon. The final word was left to Dr. Frank Whitman, the coroner who had exhumed Stott's body at Cream's request. There should be no pardon, he told the gov-

ernor, for the man responsible for "one of the most premeditated, diabolical and fiendish murders ever perpetuated" in Boone County.

◇◇◇◇◇

ON the final day of 1885, as he cleared the decks and prepared for
the year ahead, Oglesby scribbled a single-page decision and inserted
it into the thick file labeled "Pardon Case No. 613." Cream's conviction and life sentence would stand. While inmate no. 4374 and his
supporters had raised questions about the motives and statements of
key witnesses, Julia Stott had insisted she was telling the truth when
she accused the doctor of tampering with her husband's medicine.
Oglesby did not consider the prisoner "sufficiently cleared of doubt"
to justify a pardon. "If Cream be really innocent of the crime it is not
improbable proofs may come to light to establish such fact," he wrote.
This evidence had yet to emerge, and it would be "a grave mistake" to
allow a man who might be "conscious of his guilt" to escape punishment "under the pretence of innocence."

Cream would have been devastated. Wright's troubling evidence
of possible perjury and jury tampering, combined with growing support for a pardon—even the British government was in his corner—
must have raised his hopes. But months of work and lobbying were
dismissed with a few strokes of Oglesby's pen. Cream had been locked
up in Joliet for four years and two months. He might remain there,
entombed in a tiny cell, or carving stone in silence, for the rest of his
life. His hatred for Julia Stott, the traitor who had put him behind
bars, grew more intense. His belief that prostitutes were a scourge and
must be eliminated had time to take deeper root in his mind. His
loathing for all women festered.

The rejection of the pardon application came as no surprise to
Robert McClaughry. He had seen hundreds of men come and go in
his decade as Joliet's warden. He prided himself on being able to dis-
tinguish between hardened criminals and the offenders who could be
reformed and reintegrated into society. "Some men are born criminals,

some achieve crime," he declared during a lecture on criminal behavior in Chicago, paraphrasing Shakespeare's *Twelfth Night*, "and some have crime thrust upon them."

Cream, he believed, was "a man of criminal instincts and propensities" who was capable of committing more horrific crimes.

32

"AS INNOCENT AS THE CHILD UNBORN"

{1886–1891}

O NE HUNDRED SEVENTEEN MEN, CREAM AMONG THEM, filled the front rows of Joliet's cavernous chapel in June 1886. Each wore a spray of white flowers pinned to the breast of his striped jacket and faced the pulpit and the sobering Bible teachings painted on the wall above. "When the wicked man turneth away from his wickedness that he hath committed, and doeth that which is lawful and right," the Old Testament prophet Ezekiel promised in Gothic script, "he shall save his soul alive." Music played, compliments of the twelve-member prison orchestra. Bouquets of fresh-cut flowers injected life into a gloomy room where once a week a congregation of murderers, rapists, robbers, and thieves gathered to worship.

"The Belvidere Poisoner," as the *Chicago Daily Tribune* now called him, came forward to confirm his conversion to Catholicism. Archbishop Patrick Feehan of Chicago marked him with the sign of the cross and lightly slapped him on the cheek—a reminder, an observer noted, that in future he was to "suffer with patience and even die for Christ."

Cream had abandoned the Presbyterian faith years earlier. When asked his religion for the prison intake form, he had replied, "None." He converted to Catholicism, he later admitted, to improve his chances of procuring a pardon. The salvation he was seeking was not the spiritual kind—he wanted to be saved from spending the rest of his life in prison. And about a year after the ceremony, he received news that promised to speed up his release.

◇◇◇◇◇

THE bitter Quebec City winters were not kind to William Cream. He suffered from respiratory problems, and each fall, as cold weather set in and ice blocked timber shipments to Europe, he headed south. He sought out resorts with spas and hot springs that would ease his condition, with Little Rock, Arkansas, becoming his preferred destination. With time on his hands and money to invest, he began to dabble in the real estate market there and at one point considered opening a bank. Soon he was being described as "a heavy owner" of properties in Little Rock and in Conway, a county north of the city. He returned to Quebec each spring, but his acrimonious partnership with timber exporter James Maclaren ended in 1882, after a falling out over the division of profits. He continued to buy and sell lumber, and groomed his second son, Daniel, to take over the business. William Cream was in Dansville, a spa town in western New York State, when he died on May 12, 1887, at age sixty-four.

Executors valued his estate—a portfolio of properties in Canada and Arkansas, stock in Quebec banks, and other investments—at about sixty thousand dollars. Under the terms of his will, drafted in 1885, five of his six children received five thousand dollars each— about one hundred and forty thousand dollars in today's US currency. Thomas Cream, however, would inherit nothing. His eldest child, "having received nearly Five thousand Dollars from me is not entitled to anything from my Estate," the will stipulated. William Cream had put him through medical school and likely paid the legal bills for his first trial for murder in 1880; he would do no more.

The balance of the estate was to be used to support the missionary work of the Presbyterian Church and other religious causes. One provision struck a Little Rock newspaper as odd enough to warrant a mention in its columns. The "eccentric old gentleman," it reported, left money to support "some society laboring for the conversion of Jews." Another bequest made it clear he would not have approved of his son's embrace of Catholicism—money was earmarked to support an American clergyman engaged in "the evangelisation of Roman Catholics." But his eldest son was not completely shut out. "I wish to leave his case to the good sense of the Executors," his father had noted as he drafted the will. "If they at any time think it desirable to give him some financial assistance they may do so." Any further payments, however, were to be of "a moderate extent."

One of the executors, Quebec City businessman Thomas Davidson, began to wonder if something could be done to free his old friend's imprisoned son. He contacted the authorities in Illinois and gathered copies of documents and evidence related to the Stott case. The more he read, the more convinced he became that Cream was innocent and had been convicted solely on Julia Stott's perjured testimony. And there was another injustice to correct. Davidson was certain that William Cream had died before his time, worn down by "the crushing weight of this great sorrow." He was determined, he explained later, "to use all the influence he could" to persuade Illinois politicians to set Thomas Neill Cream free. Daniel Cream, who had been subjected to his brother's pleas of innocence every time he visited him in Joliet, backed the effort.

Davidson collected letters from William Cream's friends and former business associates, attesting to the family's religious devotion and solid reputation. The Creams "were and are most respectable people," wrote one supporter, "I should even say bearing the very highest character." Former employers and other Quebec City residents remembered Cream as an honest, hardworking young man, but they had lost contact with him when he left to attend medical school. Davidson, in a letter of his own, spoke for many when he expressed disbelief that "the worthy son of such Godfearing parents" had "become as in a moment, the murderous criminal which the jury's verdict branded him."

Davidson also found an unlikely new ally. Charles Fuller, who had helped put Cream in prison, was enlisted to get him out. "I have investigated this matter very thoroughly," Fuller advised the governor's office in late 1888, and the people of Boone County "believe that he has been punished enough." A new petition, calling for Cream's sentence to be commuted to fourteen years, garnered the signatures of some of the most powerful men in the community—Belvidere's mayor and three aldermen, high-ranking city and county officials, newspaper publishers, businessmen, and lawyers.

Cream's fate was now in the hands of a new Republican governor. Joseph Fifer, who replaced Oglesby in January 1889, was a Civil War veteran and a former prosecutor who believed pardons and reduced sentences should be based on an inmate's background, conduct, and the fairness of the trial, not on popularity or political influence. Some juries meted out harsh punishments, while others—"acquitting juries," he called them—imposed the lightest penalties possible. "To me that didn't seem fair," he once noted, and the governor's power to intervene should be used to level the playing field, to "temper stern justice with rational mercy."

He was soon asked to consider a case that seemed tailor-made for the exercise of executive clemency—an inmate who claimed to be the innocent victim of perjury and a biased jury. Fuller, a close friend of the governor, acted as go-between. He forwarded Davidson's letters and other documents to the governor's office and fielded questions about the file. When Fifer sought assurances that Cream would leave Illinois if released, Fuller passed along the request to Daniel Cream. "You may promise the Governor that my brother will leave the State when free," he replied in June 1889. "It is likely that he will go to England or Scotland, where he has some relations and begin life anew."

ILLINOIS GOVERNOR JOSEPH FIFER USED HIS POWER TO COMMUTE PRISON SENTENCES TO "TEMPER STERN JUSTICE WITH RATIONAL MERCY." (AUTHOR COLLECTION)

Davidson kept up the pressure. He wrote to the governor directly in March 1890, pleading that Cream had been the victim of an unfair prosecution. "Utter the word," he urged, "that would set the captive at liberty and bid the oppressed go free." Next, he appealed to Frances Willard, the Illinois-based president of the Woman's Christian Temperance Union and a tireless advocate for prohibition, women's suffrage, and other reform causes. Cream was "as innocent as the child unborn," Davidson insisted, and within days the merits of Cream's conviction were being considered in Washington. Willard lobbied US senator Shelby Moore Cullom, a former Illinois governor, who agreed to raise the matter with Fifer. If, as Davidson, Wright, and now Willard believed, "Dr. Cream is innocent," Cullom told Fifer in July 1890, "of course he ought to be pardoned."

Davidson, however, was holding something back from this growing circle of supporters. He was beginning to have doubts about Cream's mental state. Some of the letters he received from Joliet were alarming, written "in a most extraordinary and incoherent style." Cream's mind, he feared, "had become unhinged."

A breakthrough came in the spring of 1891, when Daniel Cream convinced James Rayner, the Chicago druggist, to end his opposition to Cream's release. Fuller, meanwhile, kept up the pressure on Fifer. "The ends of justice," he told him that June, "have been satisfied by the punishment already inflicted."

Fifer finally relented on June 12—by chance, the tenth anniversary of Daniel Stott's death. "In view of the uncertain character of the evidence and the doubts existing as to the guilt of the petitioner," the governor wrote, Cream was "a fit and proper subject for Executive clemency." The life sentence was commuted to seventeen years. It was a pardon by another name, entitling him to be released within weeks. Good behavior during his time in Joliet, despite the infractions that had landed him in solitary confinement, reduced his new sentence to time served. He would be released on July 31.

Allegations that Cream had bought his freedom would surface in the press. "The judicious use of $5,000 among some politicians," the *St. Louis Post-Dispatch* reported, "secured Dr. Cream's release." Alfred Trude, the Chicago lawyer who had successfully defended the doctor at his 1880 trial for murdering Mary Anne Faulkner, believed "the free use of money" had facilitated Cream's "escape," as he put it, from Joliet. The five thousand "was placed in the hands of a well known politician," he told a journalist, "who made good use of it." While he did not name the politician, Trude was a prominent Democrat, and with Republicans in power at the state capital, he likely relished the chance to attack his rivals. Daniel Cream later acknowledged it cost his family one thousand dollars—the equivalent of twenty-eight thousand dollars in today's US currency—to get his brother out of prison, but he did not reveal who demanded or received this payment. Executor Thomas Davidson, for his part, denied any wrongdoing. Cream's family and the executors had "exerted every legitimate influence," he insisted, nothing more. The pious Davidson may have considered the payment of as much as five thousand a "legitimate" means of ending what he considered a grave injustice.

If Fifer had read the pardon file closely, he knew Cream had stood trial for murder—and was a suspect in other Chicago homicides—in the year leading up to Stott's death. Even if he were innocent of the Belvidere poisoning, Cream had a reputation as a dangerous man. A shocking number of women who sought him out for medical treatment or an abortion had wound up dead.

THE ORDER RELEASING CREAM IN 1891, AFTER HE HAD SERVED ALMOST TEN YEARS OF HIS LIFE SENTENCE FOR MURDER (ILLINOIS STATE ARCHIVES)

Arthur Conan Doyle, after his foray into detective fiction with his Sherlock Holmes character, was beginning to think about crime and punishment. Some men, he concluded, were so dangerous—and so likely to commit more crimes—that they should never be set free. If a killer were let loose and killed again, "was the State not an accomplice in the crime," he asked, "even as a keeper who deliberately opened a cage and let out a tiger would be responsible for that tiger's victims?"

◇◇◇◇◇

ONE of Cream's first stops after his release from Joliet on July 31 was the Chicago office of the Pinkerton's National Detective Agency. He had hired the famous private detectives a year earlier to track down Julia Stott, who had left Garden Prairie after the trial; an admission she had lied at his trial, hc had explained, would bolster his bid for early release. Pinkerton's had followed up on rumors she had remarried or was living "a disreputable life" in St. Louis but could not find her. Now Cream urged Frank Murray, the superintendent of the Chicago office, to keep looking, even though he no longer needed her to recant her testimony.

"The task was an impossible one," the detective told Cream, "and would simply have been a waste of money." The agency, he said, would make no further inquiries. If Cream wanted revenge—if he planned to confront or harm the woman who had put him behind bars—Murray wanted nothing more to do with the case. "He seemed very anxious to find Mrs. Stott," he recalled, "but at last gave up the job."

Cream was only passing through Chicago. He was on his way to Quebec City, where he spent the rest of that summer before heading to England. He never found out what happened to Julia Stott. But he would remember Murray's name. And when he created a detective to further one of his many blackmail schemes in London, this phantom sleuth would be christened W. H. Murray.

33

CHASING SHADOWS

{UNITED STATES AND CANADA • JUNE–SEPTEMBER 1892}

WHILE IN ILLINOIS DURING THE SUMMER OF 1892, Inspector Frederick Smith Jarvis reviewed Cream's prison file and confirmed that Scotland Yard's suspect had been released from Joliet barely two months before the Lambeth poisonings began. He immediately dispatched a copy of the records to Inspector John Bennett Tunbridge in London. Former Joliet warden Robert McClaughry, who championed the use of the Bertillon system of measurements to identify repeat offenders, prided himself on being able to spot inmates likely to commit more crimes once released. He was not surprised to learn that prisoner no. 4374 was once again a murder suspect. "He remembers Cream well," Jarvis noted in a summary of his Chicago inquiries, "as he saw him almost daily." Cream, in McClaughry's opinion, was "a licentious man" and "one apt to be in just such scrapes."

Meanwhile, back in London, a Canadian named John Cantle walked into the headquarters of Scotland Yard and announced he had information that might help the officers investigating the Lambeth murders. Cantle had seen Cream's picture in the newspapers and recognized him as the drunken, drug-addled passenger he had met the previous January on board the liner SS *Sarnia*, when Cream was headed back to Quebec City to collect money and strychnine. Cream, he said, had shown him a box of empty pill capsules and had claimed to have information about a woman poisoned in London. A sergeant took his statement and jotted down the names and addresses of other Canadian passengers on the crossing. Cantle was certain they would remember Cream.

The information was cabled overseas to Jarvis in Chicago, who backtracked to Canada to interview Rev. Robert Caswell, the prison chaplain who had heard Cream brag of his womanizing during the voyage. He also tracked down William Sellar, the salesman who had endured Cream's drunken, late-night visits to his stateroom. Sellar "believed he was guilty of poisoning the women," Jarvis reported. Quebec City's chief of police, Leon Vohl, was reluctant to discuss his experiences with Cream, with good reason—he had dined with an erratic man who confessed to performing illegal abortions and claimed to have made a "special study" of poisons. It was a month before Vohl agreed to give a formal statement. Cream, it turned out, had dropped by his office several times during his sojourn at Blanchard's Hotel. Vohl had even asked him to pick up some neckties for him at a London tailor shop, and they arrived after Cream's return to England. Cream, who would toy with Sergeant McIntyre and amateur sleuth John Haynes upon his return to London, must have been delighted to befriend the top law enforcement officer in his hometown.

Tunbridge also directed Jarvis to investigate the death of Daniel Cream's mother-in-law. Louisa Mary Read had died on August 29, 1891, at age sixty-three, while the family was spending the summer at a cottage near Quebec City. Cream, newly released from prison and soon to leave for England, was also staying at the cottage, and there were rumors Read had been seen in his company, and in good health, less than two days before she died. Jarvis tracked down Dr. Henry Russell, who had treated her for a form of cholera. The official cause of death, he discovered, was a brain hemorrhage. Read was weak and the doctor "positively assures me there was nothing suspicious about the death," Jarvis told Tunbridge. Dr. Russell, one of Quebec's leading physicians, knew Cream had served a prison term for poisoning, so he had been "on his guard," he told the detective. There were no symptoms of strychnine or other poisoning, and no exhumation was planned or required. "There is not the slightest ground for suspecting foul play," Jarvis concluded.

Other inquiries went nowhere, or the allegations were never pursued. Jarvis had journeyed to Hamilton and Kingston after reading in the newspapers that Cream had practiced in these Ontario cities, but he concluded the reports were false. Then Edward Levi, an innkeeper in England who had known Cream when they both lived in Chicago, came forward and said the doctor had spoken of poisoning two women in Quebec in the late 1870s. One might have been his wife, Flora Brooks. While Tunbridge considered asking Quebec police to investigate, no action was taken in response to Levi's allegation.

In Montreal, Jarvis learned of another possible poisoning. He interviewed Emily Turner, who had worked at London's Royal Aquarium the previous winter and was back in the city. A man she met at the aquarium, a Major Hamilton, had taken her to dinner several times. He was in his forties, had "a peculiarity about his eyes," and had offered to rent her a room on Lambeth Palace Road—the street where Cream had been a lodger—if she would agree to live with him. The man had given her gelatin capsules that burned her tongue and made her ill. Jarvis showed her a sample of Cream's handwriting, and she thought it resembled notes the man had sent to her. Convinced he had found a star witness, Jarvis produced Cream's photograph. No, Turner said, he was not Major Hamilton. Jarvis suspected she was lying, perhaps to avoid embarrassment or having to face Cream in court. "I am of the opinion this young woman knows more than she wants to mention," he told his superiors. But since she was adamant Cream was not the man who had given her the pills, "it appears useless to carry inquiry further." When the pills were tested, they were found to contain only quinine, a safe and common medicine with a bitter taste. Since the pills were harmless, Tunbridge noted after reviewing Jarvis's report, the possibility she had received them from Cream was "of no consequence."

Jarvis's next task was to trace Cream's drug samples. He took a train to Saratoga Springs in Upstate New York to interview the president of the G. F. Harvey Company, George Harvey, who described his meeting with Cream and his reluctance to make him the firm's London agent. Jarvis reviewed records of the company's sales of medicine and ingredients to Cream, including the strychnine and other poisons shipped to Blanchard's Hotel. Harvey showed him a case used to carry sample bottles of the firm's products. "It is precisely similar," Jarvis reported, "to the one found in Neill's possession."

But Jarvis's biggest breakthrough came when a man contacted the Montreal police, claiming he had important information about the case. John McCulloch met with Jarvis and revealed what Cream had told him during their stay at Blanchard's earlier that year. The salesman repeated Cream's comments about giving women poison in pills "to get them out of the family way" and described the bottle of poison Cream had shown him. Jarvis was instructed to make immediate arrangements to send McCulloch to England to testify.

Jarvis had expected to return to England by mid-July. But there were fresh leads to pursue and repeated requests from his superiors for further investigation. Scotland Yard wanted to ensure Cream had not obtained poison from sources other than the Harvey Company. The detective canvassed retail druggists and wholesale suppliers in Montreal, Quebec City, and New York—cities Cream had visited after his release from prison. It was a herculean task, and Jarvis enlisted the help of police forces in each city. He visited many stores and wholesalers in person, flashing Cream's photograph at each stop. An advertisement was inserted in Quebec newspapers offering a twenty-five-dollar reward for information about where Cream might have purchased strychnine. And Jarvis oversaw a second round of checks in each city after Scotland Yard learned that Cream might have bought or stolen the poison from a doctor or veterinarian. "It is of the utmost importance that this Strychnine should be traced to Neill if possible," Inspector Tunbridge noted after conferring with prosecutors. Despite the intensive search, no other source of Cream's strychnine was found.

Scotland Yard finally recalled Jarvis in mid-September. He walked down the gangway of the Allan Line steamer *Mongolian* in Liverpool on September 28, after more than three months of "exhausting enquiry," as he put it. His interviews and discoveries told the story of a promising young Canadian physician who, like some real-life Dr. Jekyll, had been transformed into a monster. He was an abortionist. A blackmailer. A devious poisoner. A cold-blooded killer. Jarvis's detailed reports would give prosecutors the ammunition they needed if Cream tried, once again, to portray himself as a respected professional who was wrongly accused of heinous crimes. Jarvis returned to London, the *Chicago Daily Tribune* reported, with the evidence needed "to present a strong and emphatic rebuttal of any defense that Neill, or Cream . . . may make."

VI

"JACK THE POISONER"

LONDON • OCTOBER–NOVEMBER 1892

34

"A Systematic and Deliberate Course of Action"

CREAM'S TRIAL OPENED ON THE AFTERNOON OF OCTOBER 17, 1892, in London's Central Criminal Court. For more than two centuries some of Britain's most notorious criminals had faced justice at the Old Bailey, as the fortress-like courthouse was known, among them William Palmer, the 1850s pioneer of strychnine poisoning and a doctor as infamous in his time as Cream was becoming in his own. Cream stood in a wood-paneled courtroom packed with lawyers and spectators as the indictments against him were read. Chatter in the overhanging gallery evaporated into silence. Justice Henry Hawkins, his scarlet robes trimmed in white fur, a shoulder-length wig dangling on either side of his head, scowled from the bench. In the jury box sat the twelve men who would decide Cream's fate, as motionless and impassive, one onlooker thought, as the wax effigies in Madame Tussaud's. Daylight filtered through a bank of tall windows that faced the gloomy walls of Newgate Prison, where he was being held during the trial.

Journalists put Cream under a magnifying glass. A reddish-brown beard, grown during four months in captivity, covered his square jaw. Gold-rimmed glasses corrected his incriminating crossed eyes. He wore a dark coat and vest, with a white necktie done up in a sailor's knot. Newgate guards said he was nervous, irritable, and sleeping poorly. But once in the courtroom, he was as impassive as the jurors, leaning forward now and then to whisper something to his lawyers. Only a slight twitching of his mouth and an occasional squirm in his seat seemed to betray any inner turmoil. Offenders charged with petty crimes, thought one veteran journalist, looked more fearful and distraught than this accused multiple murderer facing the gallows.

"THOMAS NEILL CREAM IN THE DOCK AT THE OLD BAILEY" (*BLACK AND WHITE: A WEEKLY ILLUSTRATED RECORD AND REVIEW*, OCTOBER 29, 1892 / AUTHOR COLLECTION)

Cream retreated to a corner of the prisoner's dock, as far from the jury and Newgate as possible, as Sir Charles Russell rose to open the prosecution's case. Irish born, with deep-set, piercing eyes and a commanding presence, Russell had been one of London's top corporate lawyers before entering politics in 1880. He was knighted a few years later and would one day be Lord Russell of Killowen. His personal handling of the prosecution as attorney general—he had been sworn in two months earlier, when Prime Minister William Gladstone formed his fourth administration—underlined the gravity of the allegations. Thorough in his preparations for trial and ruthlessly efficient when cross-examining witnesses, he was considered one of the leading British advocates of his time. "Russell," a colleague noted, "produced the same effect on a witness that a cobra produces on a rabbit." His legal arguments were just as simple, direct, and persuasive. "His method may be described in a sentence," wrote another colleague: "a clear statement driven home with the hammer of Thor."

By now Cream faced seven indictments. After the coroner's inquest found him responsible the previous July for the death of Matilda Clover, a preliminary hearing before a Bow Street magistrate had added charges of murdering Ellen Donworth, who had collapsed outside Waterloo Station, and Alice Marsh and Emma Shrivell, the women poisoned in the room they shared on Lambeth's Stamford Street. Cream was also charged with attempting to murder Louisa Harvey, who had fooled him into thinking she had swallowed his poisoned pills, and two counts of blackmail. But for now, Russell explained to the jury, the doctor would stand trial only on the charge of murdering Clover.

It had been a year, almost to the day, he noted, since Clover's "wretched and obscure life" had come to a sudden, horrible end. And for months, Russell admitted, not even the Scotland Yard detectives investigating the poisonings of other Lambeth prostitutes had known she had been murdered. But someone had known all along, he continued, driving home the crux of the prosecution's case: "Only one person living could know that a fearful tragedy has been enacted in her case, and that person was the one who had administered to her the fatal dose of strychnine." And that man, Russell was determined to prove, was seated in the prisoner's dock, leaning against the rail and holding his forehead in his right hand as if deep in thought.

∞∞∞∞

PEOPLE stood outside the Old Bailey for hours each morning, hoping to claim a seat in the courtroom. Barricades were erected to prevent a stampede when the doors opened. Court officials pocketed a shilling or two from spectators willing to pay to get inside—"idle men," in the haughty opinion of the *New York Times* correspondent assigned to the trial, "attracted by idle curiosity to witness two men fight for a fellow-man's life." Women, too, jostled for access and their broad, feathered hats mixed with the powdered wigs of junior lawyers eager to see legal heavyweights in action. A far larger audience could indulge in the latest criminal sensation in the pages of London's major newspapers, which offered daily, verbatim accounts of the testimony.

Cream had retained four lawyers for the trial, and his lead counsel began to poke holes in the prosecution's case. Gerald Geoghegan was a veteran advocate, reputed to have defended more murderers than any other barrister in the country. The son of an admired Irish poet, he spoke in a soothing brogue and wooed jurors with his charm and wit. In his hands, a fellow barrister recalled, "the very 'deadest' case always had a chance of an acquittal." He was "one of the greatest natural orators at the Bar," agreed another, "but, like most such men, exceedingly hard to stop." Outside the courtroom, Geoghegan found it hard to stop when he had a glass in his hand. He was constantly pestering colleagues to join him for a drink, and he drank even more when he feared one of his clients was about to be convicted. Alcohol was slowly destroying a brilliant legal career. A few years before he accepted Cream's brief he had withdrawn as lead counsel on the eve of a major murder trial, likely because he was on a drinking binge.

The client, a Polish immigrant named Israel Lipski who was accused of forcing acid down the throat of a young woman, had been found guilty and hanged.

But Geoghegan was at the top of his game—and apparently sober—as he mounted Cream's defense. He grilled Elizabeth Masters and Elizabeth May, the Lambeth women who had watched Cream follow Clover into her rooming house—and the only witnesses who could link her to the doctor. He raised doubts about the fairness of the identification lineups staged at the Bow Street Police Station, noting that Cream, unable to shave in prison, was the only bearded man in the group they had been shown. He marshaled legal arguments to block Russell from revealing Clover's dying words about being given poisoned pills by a man named Fred. To sow seeds of doubt in the minds of the jurors, he asked Francis Coppin, the medical assistant, and Dr. Robert Graham to repeat their assertions that Clover had died from excessive drinking, not strychnine poisoning.

◇◇◇◇◇

THEN Dr. Thomas Stevenson, the renowned chemist who had detected strychnine in Clover's remains, took the stand. He had been in the spotlight three years earlier, when all eyes in Britain were fixed on Florence Maybrick's sensational trial for poisoning her husband, a wealthy Liverpool merchant. His tests had confirmed another chemist's discovery of a lethal dose of arsenic in the victim's remains—a finding that led to Maybrick's conviction for murder despite evidence that James Maybrick was a hypochondriac who took an array of medicines containing arsenic and other poisons. For all his experience and expertise, Dr. Stevenson was never comfortable on the witness stand. Visibly nervous, especially when facing cross-examination, he was curt with his responses and spoke, recalled one journalist, with "a curiously defensive air." He clearly dreaded being summoned from the ordered, private world of the laboratory to explain and defend his findings in this most public of forums.

Geoghegan went on the offensive, relentlessly chipping away at the prosecution's only expert medical witness—and the only direct evidence that Clover had been murdered. Strychnine was a fast-acting poison, Geoghegan noted. The tetanic convulsions typically began a half hour after it was ingested, and death followed within an hour or two. Yet Clover had been in bed for several hours before her convulsions began. "If a patient has been asleep," Dr. Stevenson offered, the action of strychnine "may be retarded for two or three hours."

Geoghegan was incredulous. Was he suggesting the deadly poison's effects could be delayed by sleep alone?

Dr. Stevenson backtracked. If the victim had taken opium or morphine as well, yes, this was possible.

Had he found evidence of these drugs in Clover's remains?

No, he admitted. But there were cases, he added, of strychnine victims surviving for five or six hours after the onset of convulsions.

Clover was a chronic alcoholic in poor health, Geoghegan reminded the jurors. If she had been poisoned with strychnine, how could she survive for close to six hours?

"If a person were on the verge of delirium tremens I should think it would render the person more susceptible to the effect of strychnine," the doctor conceded. "I think a person like that would be affected sooner than a person living a temperate and healthy life."

Geoghegan suggested another possible cause of death. Could a disease affecting the spine cause the violent spasms Clover suffered?

Dr. Stevenson agreed it could. And while his examination of the spine had revealed no evidence of disease, he acknowledged, such afflictions were difficult to detect in a body exhumed many months after death.

Geoghegan zeroed in on the laboratory tests. The fluid extracted from Clover's remains had been injected under the skin of a frog, killing it. Would it not have been more appropriate, Geoghegan wondered, to test the fluid on a rabbit or a dog—a warm-blooded animal, more like a human?

Frogs were preferred for poisoning tests, Dr. Stevenson explained, because they so readily display symptoms. "The frog is a very delicate animal," he noted.

Geoghegan sensed an opening. Perhaps a frog was too delicate, too susceptible to such an injection?

The witness backtracked again. "I don't know that it is very susceptible."

Alkaloid poisons such as strychnine were difficult to detect?

They were, Dr. Stevenson acknowledged.

The color test used to detect strychnine in fluid recovered from the body—was it reliable? Was it not true the results of such tests could be "uncertain and fallacious"?

"An inexperienced person may make a mistake in the colour test if the drugs are not pure," Dr. Stevenson shot back. "The colour I rely on is a purple-violet, which then passes through a play of colours. . . . I know nothing else that gives that precise play of colours."

Geoghegan stopped there to remind the jury that the evidence Clover had died of strychnine poisoning boiled down to a dead frog, a few shades of color, and the opinion of a single doctor.

Russell, eager to repair the damage, returned to his feet. He invited Dr. Stevenson to summarize his findings and conclusions. The positive color test. The discovery of a sixteenth of a grain of strychnine in Clover's remains, which suggested she had ingested a much higher, lethal dose. The convulsions and swift death after the frog was injected with fluid taken from the victim's body. "I arrived at the result that strychnine was the cause of death, not taking each matter as isolated," Dr. Stevenson explained, "but as cumulative and supporting each other."

John McCulloch and John Haynes, Cream's former confidants, also faced sharp cross-examination. McCulloch, the salesman who had met Cream at Blanchard's Hotel in Quebec City, had trouble explaining why he had remained on friendly terms with a man who boasted of distributing poisoned pills to women. Geoghegan accused Haynes of trying to curry favor with Scotland Yard in hopes of being hired as a detective—incentive enough, jurors might think, to embellish his story. But the lawyer opted not to challenge the prosecution's new hand-writing expert, Walter de Grey Birch of the Manuscripts Department of the British Museum, who replaced the disgraced George Smith Inglis. Birch was confident the letter accusing Dr. William Broadbent, the physician to the royal family, of murdering Clover was in Cream's writing. Geoghegan was willing to concede that his client was a black-mailer, even if he was not a particularly successful one.

Inspector Tunbridge, when he testified on the third day of the trial, acknowledged that Scotland Yard had failed to follow up on the Broadbent letter, other than trying to set a trap for the blackmailer.

Justice Hawkins was incredulous. "No inquiry was made about the girl Clover?" he bellowed from his bench.

"None whatsoever," Tunbridge confirmed. The document was written off as the work of "an insane person," he added, and the police often received similar letters that were bogus.

The explanation did not satisfy the judge. "Here is a real person who actually lived at 27 Lambeth Road, and it is said that this person was poisoned by strychnine. This information comes to Scotland Yard, within a quarter of an hour's walk of the place. How comes it that no one took the trouble to make an inquiry at Lambeth Road?"

"Well, it was not done, my lord."

"My surprise remains," Justice Hawkins replied. The police clearly had deemed it more important to try to catch Dr. Broadbent's black-mailer than to investigate whether a woman had been murdered, as the letter appeared to reveal. Would inquiries have been made about Clover, he asked, if the blackmailer had been arrested?

"I presume so, my lord."

"I should presume not," Hawkins replied tartly, "from what happened."

The judge had opened a door. Geoghegan seized the opportun-ity to embarrass the Yard. Telegraph lines linked Metropolitan Police headquarters with its outlying stations, Tunbridge admitted as he was cross-examined.

Had anyone, Geoghegan asked, sent a telegram to Kennington Lane—the station nearest Lambeth Road—inquiring about Clover? "No," Tunbridge said. "The fault, if fault there be, rests with Scotland Yard."

◇◇◇◇◇

CREAM's fate could hinge on how Justice Hawkins ruled on an issue that remained unsettled under English law. Did the prosecution have the right to bolster its case with "similar-fact evidence"—to put a defendant on trial, in effect, for similar crimes that were not on the indictment before the court? Could Russell present evidence implicating Cream in the other three poisonings and the attempt to kill Louisa Harvey? The defense was suggesting Clover died of natural causes, Russell argued, and this should permit him to establish a pattern of behavior—"a systematic and deliberate course of action"—that pointed to Cream as her killer. The additional witnesses would show that Cream possessed strychnine, provided pills to women, and was linked to similar homicides.

Henry Warburton, another member of the defense team, objected. Considered a rising star in the tight-knit universe of Old Bailey barristers, he argued it would be tantamount to forcing Cream to stand trial on all seven indictments at once. A defendant was entitled to have a jury "decide each case on its merits." Similar-fact evidence should be admissible only if a defendant claimed a death was accidental or unintentional, and neither defense was being advanced on Cream's behalf. While Russell had cited precedents to support his motion, in every case, Warburton pointed out, the defendant had provided food to a victim and claimed not to have known it contained poison. In Cream's case, there was no need for further proof he had possessed "a comparatively common drug like strychnine" that doctors and druggists could easily obtain. His most serious concern was the impact the evidence of other crimes would have on the jury. It could endanger the fairness of the trial.

The decision rested with one of Britain's most accomplished and celebrated judges. To defendants and police officers alike, Sir Henry Hawkins was also among the most feared. "A cold, deliberate, experienced man of the world," in the opinion of the reporter covering Cream's trial for the *New York Times*. Scotland Yard's Frederick Wensley remembered him as "that stern judge," and Tunbridge, the latest target of his wrath, no doubt shared that assessment. Seventy-five years old, he had been a judge since the 1870s, when his stellar performance in the sensational case of the Tichborne Claimant, an impostor who posed as the missing heir to a fortune, catapulted him to the top of the legal profession. He became known as "Hanging Hawkins"—a label many judges earned in an era when a murder conviction carried an automatic death sentence—and he once condemned four offenders to the gallows in the same week. Beneath the gruff exterior he was a bit of an eccentric. He insisted that his flowing wig, which covered a head as bald on top as Cream's, must be freshened with pomade and powder every day. And he doted on his dog, a fox terrier named Jack, sometimes bringing him into the courtroom to sit with him on the bench. When he published his memoirs years later, he incorporated several bizarre chapters written as if from Jack's point of view. The dog was said to growl when legal arguments became tedious, alerting lawyers, on his master's behalf, that it was time to wrap up.

Justice Hawkins brushed aside the defense concerns. Similar-fact evidence could be useful in establishing motive, and "the more uncommon, the more rare, the more unaccountable the motive," he observed, "the more necessity there is to give sub-evidence." He clearly believed the random poisonings of four women, and an attempt to kill a fifth, fit within this rarified category of crimes. The attorney general could produce the evidence, and the jury would ultimately decide whether it was relevant to Clover's death. "The admissibility of evidence is one thing," he pointed out, "and the weight of evidence is another." Warburton pleaded with the judge to refer the issue to the Court of Crown Cases Reserved—an early form of appeals court—for a final ruling. There was no need, Justice Hawkins assured Cream's defenders. He was confident of "the soundness" of his decision.

◇◇◇◇◇

IT was the turning point in the trial. Louisa Harvey testified about Cream's attempt to ply her with pills on the evening they met on the Embankment near Charing Cross Station—"damning evidence," the London *Standard* noted, that put the murder weapon in the defendant's hands. The horrible deaths of Donworth, Marsh, and Shrivell were described to the jury. Laura Sabbatini identified blackmail letters she had written at her former fiancé's behest.

ATTORNEY GENERAL SIR CHARLES RUSSELL PRESENTED EVIDENCE IMPLICATING CREAM IN ALL FOUR LAMBETH POISONINGS. (AUTHOR COLLECTION)

Geoghegan's swagger vanished. He posed few questions and offered no objections as witness after witness exposed his client's lies, blackmail threats, and links to the other murdered women. When Russell closed his case on day four of the trial, Geoghegan announced he would call no witnesses to face the attorney general's cobra-like glare. No medical experts would challenge Dr. Stevenson's findings. If Geoghegan had dared to suggest the newspapers were wrong, that his client had a good reputation and was a competent medical man, it would open the door to rebuttal evidence from the prosecution—and unleash Inspector Frederick Smith Jarvis's damning findings.

An expected insanity defense never materialized. Perhaps Geoghegan could find no alienists, as psychiatrists were known at the time (the mentally ill were thought to be alienated from their normal selves), who believed that such a calculating, cold-blooded killer was not responsible for this actions. In Illinois Cream had twice taken the witness stand to assert he was innocent of murder, but in Britain he had no right to testify on his own behalf. Criminal defendants were certain to lie, it was thought, and it would be another six years before British law allowed them to be sworn in as witnesses. Some judges permitted defendants to make a statement to the jury after the evidence had been heard. Cream said nothing.

Geoghegan rallied for his closing argument, which lasted for most of the afternoon. Thousands of respectable men with mustaches, wearing dark coats and top hats, could be found on the streets of London. Could the witnesses who identified Cream be mistaken? And how could Clover have survived for so long if, as Dr. Stevenson asserted, she had been poisoned with fast-acting strychnine? He made no apologies for his client's drug-fueled, sex-obsessed lifestyle and reminded the jurors his client was on trial for murder, not immorality. And it was possible Cream had learned of Clover's death through conversations with the Lambeth prostitutes he knew so well. As a doctor, he had recognized her symptoms as consistent with strychnine poisoning and had used his suspicions to threaten Dr. Broadbent. Cream's abuse of opium and morphine, he argued, could explain his amateurish blackmail attempts and the "absurd statements" he made in his letters. And Geoghegan scoffed at the tests used to confirm the presence of strychnine in Clover's remains, claiming it was ludicrous to compare the symptoms of a frog to those of a human being. "Science, represented here by Dr. Stevenson, did not assist them," he told the jurors, and no conclusions "on which a man's life might depend, could be drawn from the experiment which had been conducted."

There was scattered applause when Geoghegan sat down, more likely in appreciation of his passionate performance than to show support for his repulsive client. The judge gruffly ordered those responsible to stop.

Russell needed little time to sum up his case. Witnesses linked Cream to Clover, and a letter in his handwriting showed he had known she had been poisoned with strychnine months before her body was exhumed. "Was it conceivable that an innocent man, becoming suspicious of such a murder, should have written a blackmailing letter to Dr. Broadbent," he asked, "instead of communicating with the police?" Geoghegan had barely mentioned Louisa Harvey's damning testimony; Russell believed her "remarkable story" of the incident on the Thames Embankment, confirming that Cream induced women to take pills, "threw a strong light on the case." If giving her medicine to improve her complexion had been "a kindly and not murderous act," the defendant could have written her a prescription. Instead, he had arranged for a nighttime rendezvous and had insisted that she swallow the capsules on the spot. Russell defended the prosecution's forensic evidence, stressing the "scientific attainments" of his expert witness and the "definite conclusions" that Clover had ingested a lethal dose of poison. "Dr. Stevenson had no interest to serve except the interest of truth," he contended, "and it might be assumed that he had used the best-known modes of analysis." If the evidence left them with "a solemn conviction that this man is guilty," the attorney general reminded the jurors, there was only one possible verdict.

35

"A Murder So Diabolical"

I T WAS NOT TO BE EXPECTED," JUSTICE HAWKINS TOLD THE jurors when the trial resumed the following morning, "that there should be mathematical proof of the commission of a crime." And often, the judge added, as in this case, there were no eyewitnesses to the act. The jurors would have to navigate a maze of circumstantial evidence to determine whether there was sufficient proof that Cream was a murderer.

There had been a rush for seats when the courtroom doors opened, as people scrambled to witness the final act of the Lambeth tragedy. "Not an inch of space unoccupied," the *Morning Post*'s reporter noted as he surveyed the courtroom, and latecomers stood in the passage-ways between tables and seats. Laura Sabbatini was there, to learn the fate of the man she had almost married. It was so quiet that the rustle of paper could be heard as journalists' notes were passed to messengers waiting to whisk them to newspaper offices on nearby Fleet Street. It was a year to the day since Matilda Clover's death.

Cream took up his post in a corner of the dock. While he looked paler and slightly less at ease than the day before as he was brought into the courtroom, he had assured one of his lawyers that he had slept well—his best night's sleep in months. He seemed certain he would be

JUSTICE HENRY HAWKINS, "A COLD, DELIBERATE" TRIAL JUDGE KNOWN AS HANGING HAWKINS, WAS CONVINCED OF CREAM'S GUILT. (AUTHOR COLLECTION)

acquitted. He had asked the lawyer if he was likely to be prosecuted for blackmail once he was cleared of the Clover murder.

The judge had another verdict in mind as he issued his instructions to the jury. Windows had been opened to let air into the stifling courtroom, and as he began his remarks, one of them guillotined closed with a crash. It was an ominous sign. If Justice Hawkins was certain a suspect was guilty, Old Bailey watchers knew, he would do his utmost to ensure a conviction. For three hours, without once looking at his notes, the judge painstakingly reviewed the evidence, patching up holes in the prosecution's case and highlighting every scrap of evidence that pointed to Cream's guilt. If the jury believed Elizabeth Masters and Elizabeth May, who had seen Cream with Clover, then the man in the dock—he turned and pointed to him with his pencil, to emphasize the point—had known and visited the victim. He agreed with Russell's contention that the writer of the Broadbent letter, Cream, must have poisoned Clover.

Justice Hawkins was well aware of Dr. Stevenson's expertise and reputation—he had been on the bench at Dr. George Henry Lamson's murder trial a decade before, when the analyst supplied crucial evidence that the victim, the defendant's young brother-in-law, had been killed with the rare poison aconitine. He also knew there was a lingering distrust of forensic medical experts; jurors were reluctant to send an offender to the gallows based on scientific experiments and opinions few of them could begin to understand. He was determined to erase any doubts Geoghegan may have planted in the minds of the men in the jury box. Dr. Stevenson, the judge assured them, was "a gentleman of great scientific attainments, of vast experience, and of untiring perseverance in discovering the truth." His laboratory tests should leave no doubt that Clover had died from a lethal dose of strychnine.

There was one final point to be made. The jury had heard details of the other Lambeth poisoning deaths, Justice Hawkins explained, because it would have been "impossible to come to anything like a satisfactory conclusion" without this corroborating evidence. Cream was entitled to the benefit of any doubts they might have about his guilt, he added, almost as an afterthought. "But if they were satisfied that he was the man who did commit the crime, then it was their duty to say so, fearlessly and firmly."

The jurors filed out of the courtroom at a quarter till two. Onlookers had barely begun to discuss the judge's comments when the twelve men returned with a verdict. Justice Hawkins struggled through the crowd to reclaim his place on the bench. Cream had already descended into the underground passage to Newgate, and his guards did an about-face, rushing him back to the courtroom. He stood and faced the jury, leaning casually against the ledge of the prisoner's dock.

A clerk posed the question: Was the prisoner guilty or not guilty of the murder of Matilda Clover?

Guilty, the foreman replied.

Cream did not flinch or betray any reaction. The passive, unconcerned facade he had projected through four months of court appearances remained intact. For the second time in a little more than a decade, he stood convicted of murder.

A few sobs were heard amid the spectators. Somewhere in the gallery, a woman screamed. There was a scuffle of feet as people rushed to spread the news to the large crowd assembled outside under a darkened sky that threatened rain. Everyone in the courtroom knew what came next.

"Have you anything to say why the Court should not give you judgment to die according to law?" a clerk asked.

Cream slowly shook his head. Guards entered the dock to stand beside him. A chaplain slipped through the crimson curtain behind the bench and took up a position to the judge's left. An assistant came forward and placed a square of black cloth—the feared "sentencing cap"—on the freshly greased and powdered wig. Cream had been convicted of a "most terrible crime," Justice Hawkins declared, "a murder so diabolical in its character, fraught with so much cold-blooded cruelty, that one dare hardly trust oneself to speak of the details." The "torture" inflicted on Clover was "an unparalleled atrocity," he told Cream, a crime that "can be expiated only by your death." He ordered Cream returned to Newgate to await execution.

"And may the Lord have mercy upon your soul."

36

"Insane in No Legal Sense"

N OT LONG AFTER CREAM'S TRIAL, JUSTICE HENRY Hawkins called on Melville Macnaghten, the chief constable of the Metropolitan Police at Scotland Yard. In a tailored suit, with his remaining gray hair trimmed almost to the scalp, he looked much smaller than he did on the bench. And shorn of his wig and scarlet robes, he could have passed for a businessman on an errand to report a burglary or an embezzling employee. The judge, however, had weightier matters to discuss.

Justice Hawkins considered himself an authority on how the police should do their jobs. He was known to cross-examine officers as if he were still an advocate. "Woe betide a policeman," noted one journalist, "who made any slips in his evidence before him." A speech on police conduct he had delivered a decade earlier, offering his views on everything from the proper way to question suspects to the evils of gossip and idleness, was included in a manual issued to members of the Metropolitan force. An officer's duty was not just to arrest offenders, he believed; by being alert and vigilant, officers could also ensure that criminals were not tempted to break the law. "When many crimes are

THE CASE OF THE MURDEROUS DR. CREAM

committed in any particular district," he noted in the manual, "one is apt to suspect that there has been something defective in the amount of vigilance exercised over it."

Four poisonings committed under Scotland Yard's nose, in a small area of London and within the span of six months, suggested a shocking lack of vigilance. By failing to investigate the Clover murder in late 1891, when Dr. Broadbent complained of blackmail, Scotland Yard had squandered a chance to nab Cream before he claimed more victims. Worse, the police had ignored a second letter, accusing Earl Russell of murdering Clover, an investigative lapse that was never mentioned at the trial. Countess Mabel Russell had been too ill to testify, and Justice Hawkins did not appear to know that another valuable lead had been squandered.

The judge's sharp exchange with Tunbridge and a reference, in his summation to the jury, to the "faint endeavour" made to find Dr. Broadbent's blackmailer, had encouraged the London press to mount its own attacks. "Four unfortunates had been killed," the *Pall Mall Gazette* complained, "and yet the police had no clue to the identity of the murderer." Scotland Yard, in the opinion of the *Daily News*, was guilty of "extraordinary and inexplicable neglect" for mishandling the Broadbent letter. The *Times of London*, while more restrained in its criticism, made it clear the public would not tolerate such lapses in future investigations. *Reynolds's Newspaper* weighed in with a letter to the editor, published under the headline "Crime and the Police." The author, using the pseudonym Northumbrian, made no mention of Cream's capture but insisted a new type of detective was needed to combat crime in London. "To detect criminals you must have a race of men of intelligence and special training in the ways of the criminal classes," Northumbrian argued, "cool, active, athletic men; well educated, and capable of standing any amount of fatigue, or privation, or hardship." The writer could have been describing Sherlock Holmes, the infallible detective who would never have overlooked such vital clues.

Justice Hawkins had already tried to repair the damage to Scotland Yard's reputation. When his court convened to hear a new case on October 22, the day after he sentenced Cream to die, he offered what amounted to an apology. He had conferred with the police, obtained a "most satisfactory explanation" of how the Broadbent letter was handled, he said, and wished to erase "any unfavourable impression" his comments had created. "So far from wishing to cast anything like a censure on them, I think that the conduct of the police from the commencement to the end of the case is admirable." The conduct of Inspector Tunbridge and the officers of the Lambeth Division, he added, was "most creditable."

The judge's visit to Macnaghten's office may have been a further attempt to mend fences. They discussed the case, and Justice Hawkins mentioned something he found puzzling: Why did Cream write the letters that sealed his fate? Macnaghten had a theory. Cream, he said, was "a hopelessly depraved individual" who, after gratifying his "mad lust for cruelty," had suffered fits of depression. "As a kind of salve to his conscience, he then sat down and wrote to *someone*, detailing the facts that a murder had been committed." Blackmail was almost incidental, perhaps explaining why he appeared to have made no attempt to collect the money he demanded. "Cream," Macnaghten suggested, "felt he must impart his guilty secrets to somebody."

◇◇◇◇◇

"Dr. Thomas Neill Cream," London's *News of the World* proclaimed, "must surely be the greatest monster of iniquity the century has seen." In the *Standard*, an outraged editor denounced Clover's murder as a "pitiless atrocity . . . almost unparalleled in the black annals of human crime." The London magazine *Black and White* christened him "the most cruel and the meanest among all the murderers of this age." Jack the Ripper, for all his savagery, never tortured his victims or tried to profit from their deaths, the magazine pointed out, and Cream had chosen a poison he knew would produce a slow, agonizing death. The

Daily Chronicle, the newspaper Cream had enlisted as an unwitting ally in his schemes to blackmail Dr. Broadbent and Dr. Joseph Harper, chalked up his crimes to a toxic combination of "sordid greed, low cunning, ruthless brutality and fiendish cruelty."

A NEWSPAPER ARTIST IMAGINED HOW THE "MONSTER OF INIQUITY" MIGHT RECALL "HIS AWFUL PAST" AS HE AWAITED EXECUTION. (*ILLUSTRATED POLICE NEWS*, NOVEMBER 5, 1892)

Were Cream's brutal crimes the work of a madman? Britain's legal definition of insanity, formulated a half century earlier in the case of Daniel M'Naghten, a man who tried to assassinate the prime minister, Robert Peel, demanded evidence that an offender was delusional and suffering from a severe mental illness. The key factors were whether murderers realized they were taking a life and understood that it was wrong to kill another human being. The attorney general, Sir Charles Russell, had taken the precaution of having four medical experts in attendance at Cream's trial, all taking notes and ready to testify if needed. There was evidence for Geoghegan to work with, including Cream's wild behavior during visits with friends and relatives in Canada, the mind-destroying years in Joliet Prison, and the stints in solitary confinement, an ordeal that had driven other inmates mad. Even his eye condition may have taken a toll on his mental state; James Aitchison, the optician Cream had consulted in London, believed his lifelong vision problems and constant headaches had made him a morphine addict, which in turn had "produced changes in his moral nature both startling and repulsive." Half a world away, in Chicago, the lawyer who had successfully defended Cream on a murder charge in 1880 expressed surprise that his mental state was never mentioned at the trial. "There are a dozen people in Chicago who would testify to his homicidal mania," Alfred Trude said in an interview republished in Britain, "and I am one of them."

An insanity plea, however, would have been futile. The M'Naghten Rules, as they were known, imposed a legal standard that did not align with some medical definitions of insanity. "All manner of wholly deranged persons, quite irresponsible for their behaviour," one legal scholar would note, "could be found guilty." Cream's bizarre murder-and-blackmail schemes seemed to have sprung from the mind of a lunatic. And what rational person would circulate letters, in his own handwriting, exposing himself as a killer? But his were not the uncontrolled acts of a madman. He had chosen his targets at random, but there was a pattern to his killings and a possible motive, money. He drew on his professional knowledge of poisons and, over time, refined his methods of administering strychnine. He knew what he was doing. His attempts to incriminate others and evade arrest were proof that he knew it was wrong to kill. A prison doctor at Newgate, in a report submitted on the eve of the trial, assured prosecutors he had not seen "any indication of insanity" during Cream's four months' incarceration. The respected *British Medical Journal*, which kept a close eye on the case, believed his mental condition fell within the M'Naghten definition of sanity. "Morally, without doubt, the man is insane," its editors argued, "but he is insane in no legal sense."

Cream appeared to be a new kind of monster. But there were more like him, the *Times of London* warned, "utterly devoid of moral sense" and capable of similar, ghastly crimes. "Their one object in life is to gratify their own evil passions, and they pursue that object wholly regardless of the sufferings of their fellows, without scruple and without remorse." It would be decades before the terms needed to properly classify Cream—*psychopath* and *serial killer*—came into common use. Scotland Yard's Melville Macnaghten believed Cream was a sexual maniac with "a craving for blood." A *Daily News* editorial echoed Macnaghten's assessment of this particular maniac's habit of writing letters to draw attention to his murders: "It was part of his mania that his crimes should create a sensation, even though that sensation should involve his own ruin."

With Cream scheduled to hang on November 8, his lawyers finally played the insanity card. The Home Office agreed to delay the execution until documents arrived from Canada—affidavits from relatives and friends that promised to shed light on his mental state. It might be enough to convince H. H. Asquith, Home Office secretary and a future prime minister, to commute the death sentence and dispatch Cream to an asylum for the criminally insane. The execution was delayed for one week.

Newspaper editors balked at the notion of sparing the life of such a callous killer. "There must be no thought of mercy for Neill" was the bottom line for the *Pall Mall Gazette*. "Such a man is doing acts of war against the race," London's *Spectator* noted solemnly, "and may justly be deprived of any possibility of doing any more." The *Standard*, too, demanded that the death sentence stand. "Cream belongs to that 'tribe of human vermin,'" the paper was certain, "which every civilized community is obliged, in its own protection, to trap and destroy." Even hardened criminals, it seemed, believed he deserved to hang for his cowardly use of poison. "Neill's a bloomin' skunk," one told London's *Illustrated Police News*, "and I'll give a cheer for 'Enery 'Awkins."

CREAM's world was now a fourteen-by-eight-foot stone box. Coconut matting shielded his feet from the cold floor. The only furnishings were a small table, a stool, a bed, a Bible, and a hymn book. A window was set high in the wall, so prisoners could not look into the prison courtyard and see the shed where condemned men were hanged. The shed where, at nine o'clock on the morning of November 15, Cream was scheduled to die.

"They shall never hang me!" he had proclaimed to his guards not long after the verdict. He was put on suicide watch, in case he tried to cheat the hangman. His gold-framed glasses were confiscated and replaced with a horn-rimmed pair to prevent him from swallowing or cutting himself with a piece of jagged metal. He ate with wooden utensils. When he asked for writing materials, he was handed a quill instead of a steel pen. One of the officers who investigated the poisonings thought the precautions unnecessary. "He is utterly reckless of other people's lives," a journalist was assured, "but he is particularly careful of his own neck."

He slept well—up to twelve hours a day—and washed down his meals with a daily ration of two pints of stout. He was taken from his cell only when he asked to walk in the exercise yard. His lawyer, John Waters, and Newgate's chaplain became regular visitors. He sent messages asking Sabbatini to visit as well, but she did not respond. Cream, the former Sunday school teacher turned killer, knew his Bible and recited the Gospel of St. Matthew from memory. Guards found Cream's calmness surprising, and unnerving. "If I had only served God as well as I have served my lusts and evil inclinations," he blurted out at one point, "I should never have been here now." He even seemed to forgive Justice Hawkins for hobbling his defense. "The Judge was dead against me," he said on another occasion. "But, perhaps, that was his duty."

Cream remembered his medical training at McGill, where he had learned how quickly a man died when hanged. "If it should come to the worst," he told Waters, "it means only a struggle of a few seconds, and then all will be over." He seemed to have hope, however, that he would avoid the gallows, as he had twice before. When told of the one-week reprieve, he sang and danced in his cell. He called it "a good omen," a witness claimed. "He felt sure his life would be spared."

Day after day, the newspapers offered fresh evidence of his callousness and depravity. In letters written to Sabbatini from prison—intercepted by the authorities and leaked to the press after the trial—Cream proclaimed his innocence and tried to convince his former fiancée that an unnamed member of Parliament had assembled two hundred witnesses who could clear his name. The correspondence also revealed his attempts to pressure her to destroy evidence and to lie for him. "I was perfectly safe till you swore against me," he complained in one of the missives. She must recant her testimony about writing blackmail letters for him, he said, and swear that she could not identify his handwriting. He disguised his penmanship in the letters to avoid handing the police additional evidence, only to discover Sabbatini had given his will and other samples of his writing to Inspector Tunbridge. Her betrayal was met with outrage and threats. "If you annoy me in any way or do me any injury . . . you are going to get into terrible trouble," he warned. "When I think of the harm you have done me," he added, menacingly, in another letter, "it makes me wild."

The most damning revelation came from John Haynes. Unemployed and subsisting on handouts from Scotland Yard—Tunbridge, who needed his testimony and feared he was suicidal, had authorized the payments—Haynes continued to give interviews to the press, likely for a fee. He recounted an incriminating exchange he had neglected to mention in court. He claimed he had once scolded Cream for chatting with prostitutes in broad daylight.

"Pshaw! I have killed lots of that cattle."

"Do you really say you have killed women?"

"Yes," Cream had replied. "All of that class are to be killed!"

A cry was soon heard from London's newsboys: "Full Confession of Dr. Neill." The *News of the World* reported that he had admitted to poisoning three of the Lambeth victims—all but Ellen Donworth. The report was quickly exposed as bogus. London's Central News Agency then distributed a news flash claiming Cream had admitted killing "a large number of women" in Canada during the late 1870s. Like Clover, they had been "buried without any suspicion of foul play." It, too, was found to be false.

Telegraph lines and subsea cables—the original worldwide communications network—made the Lambeth poisonings an international sensation. Reports of Cream's trial flashed from the Old Bailey to newspaper offices throughout Britain, rumbled off presses in cities and towns across the United States and Canada, clacked from Morse code receivers in distant Australia. Readers of the *Herald* in Glasgow, near his birthplace, learned that he did not flinch as the death sentence was passed. "Is Neill a Lunatic?" the Toronto *Globe* wondered in a headline. In Montreal, the city where he had earned his medical degree, the *Gazette* offered a detailed next-day account of the trial's final moments and hailed Justice Hawkins's summation as "a masterpiece of clearness and conciseness." The impending execution was front-page news in the Minnesota capital, St. Paul. The editor of the *True Republican* in Sycamore, Illinois, population three thousand, was of the opinion that the condemned man "well deserves his fate." In Australia, brief items on Cream's purported confession appeared in the Melbourne *Argus* and in the Adelaide *Observer*. A synopsis of his trial found its way into the London News column of the *Tasmanian*.

"All of Neill's life was marked with crime," observed the *New York Times*. "There was not the slightest doubt in anyone's mind that the verdict was a just one." Another New York paper, the *Sun*, considered Cream "the most dangerous, the most artful, the most depraved" murderer of the age, "and one of the most notable in history." There was hand-wringing in Belvidere, Illinois, over a Boone County jury's failure to condemn Cream to death in 1881. "The world would have got rid of a monster," noted an editorial in the *Belvidere Standard*, "and Gov. Fifer would not have made the worst mistake in his life by pardoning him." In Chicago, where the authorities had failed to bring Cream to justice for as many as three murders, the focus was on the killer, not the shortcomings of local police and prosecutors. "There was no redeeming feature in the man's character," concluded the *Chicago Times*. "He had been a criminal from the moment he was free to practice medicine." The editors of one of the city's papers sought to deflect blame and set the record straight. While many news reports described Cream as hailing from America, "he is a Canadian," the *Daily Inter Ocean* wanted it known, "and not an American in the ordinary and accepted sense of that term."

Some tried to cash in on Cream's notoriety. Londoner H. J. Meech, who crafted replica heads of the famous and infamous, advertised "a First-class and Life-like Model of Dr. Neill and his Victim Matilda Clover." The *Illustrated Police News*, gambling that there would be no further reprieve, announced that its November 19 issue would include a full-page illustration of the execution, based on the descriptions of prison officials since no journalists would be allowed to attend. Readers were advised to preorder copies, for a penny each, as "an enormous sale" was anticipated. Phrenologists asked the Home Office for permission to make a cast of Cream's head before he died, so its shape could be observed and studied in "the interests of science." A government official dismissed them as "quacks" and denied access. There was a bidding war for his clothing and effects. Madame Tussaud's balked at the asking price—two hundred pounds—and a showman in Glasgow emerged as the winner. The proceeds were expected to defray Cream's legal bills. Undaunted, Tussaud's had a wax likeness on display within four days of his conviction, as part of its Chamber of Horrors. General admission was one shilling, but children under twelve could see the next-best thing to the real Lambeth Poisoner for sixpence.

MADAME TUSSAUD'S EXHIBITION.
BAKER-STREET STATION.
THE LAMBETH POISONING CASE.—Portrait Model
of THOMAS NEILL CREAM, NOW ON VIEW in
the CHAMBER OF HORRORS. Admission, 1s. Children
under twelve, 6d. Extra Rooms, 6d.
Open 10 a.m. to 10 p.m.

MADAME TUSSAUD'S LONDON WAX MUSEUM ADDED A LIKENESS OF CREAM TO ITS

CHAMBER OF HORRORS WITHIN DAYS OF HIS CONVICTION FOR MURDER.

(*REYNOLDS'S NEWSPAPER*, JANUARY 1, 1893)

The Home Office amassed a stack of documents on the case, including clippings of the *Times of London*'s extensive coverage of the court proceedings and Justice Hawkins's detailed notes of the trial evidence. Newspaper accounts and Inspector Jarvis's findings in America, Godfrey Lushington, undersecretary at the Home Office, noted in a memo, revealed "a terrible career of crime, abortion & murder." The expected affidavits sworn by a few relatives and friends arrived from Canada, describing Cream's erratic behavior after his release from Joliet Prison. "They could not have thought seriously of his insanity," a Home Office official pointed out after reviewing the statements, "if they trusted him to come to England alone." No medical assessments or doctors' opinions were offered. Cream submitted a handwritten petition in which he disputed much of the evidence against him and denied doing "anything in the way of committing murder."

Secretary Asquith's decision was made public on November 11. "There is not the least ground for supposing that Neill was not fully responsible for his acts," he explained in a notation to his staff. "The law must take its course."

37

DEAD MAN'S WALK

CREAM ROSE FROM BED ABOUT SEVEN O'CLOCK ON November 15. He looked pale and haggard after a night of little sleep. He picked at a breakfast of eggs, bread, and tea, then slipped on the black coat and brown trousers he had worn at trial. He was wrapping a shirt collar around his neck when a voice piped up. "I wouldn't put that on this morning, if I were you," a guard said. Cream thought for a moment and tossed it aside.

The prison chaplain arrived about eight, clad in a white vestment, and invited him to seek God's forgiveness. They huddled for forty-five minutes in the gloomy gas-lit cell. Cream said little, then finally broke his silence. He made a short statement that sounded like a confession but offered no specifics. He "prayed God to forgive the crimes," the Home Office was later told, "which he without any extenuating circumstances committed."

Heavy footsteps were heard in the corridor. Newgate's governor entered at three minutes till nine, accompanied by other prison officials and guards. James Billington, London's executioner, moved swiftly to secure Cream's arms behind his back with leather straps. As he worked, Cream thanked the governor and his guards for their kindness. "You all have made the last two days amongst the happiest of my life."

The chaplain and a guard led the entourage through a dark passageway. Dead Man's Walk, it was called. Executed criminals were buried beneath the flagstone floor. A single letter carved in the wall—the initial of the surname—served as a grave marker for each one.

It took about a minute to reach the gallows shed on the opposite side of the courtyard. A fine, soaking rain fell on them. Outside Newgate's high walls, people had begun to gather an hour earlier, even though they would not be allowed to witness Cream's final moments. Their numbers swelled to as many as five thousand—the biggest crowd to assemble in London for a hanging, it was said, since public executions were banned in the 1860s. Most were "drink-sodden men" and "repulsive females," noted a journalist who joined their ranks. Bobbies struggled to keep the street clear for traffic to pass. More people filled the windows of nearby houses. The mood was festive, as if a carnival had set up shop in central London. No one seemed to mind the rain and bone-chilling dampness. "It's better hanging about out here," one man quipped, "than hanging up inside."

Cream, flanked by guards, reached the shed shortly before nine. Inside, a hemp rope, an inch in diameter and tied into a noose, dangled from links of heavy chain bolted to a beam. "I am the resurrection and the life," the chaplain recited as they entered the brick-lined room. Billington strapped Cream's legs and pulled a white hood over his face, then slipped on the noose. The prison bell tolled. At nine, the chimes of nearby St. Paul's Cathedral and St. Sepulchre Church clanged to mark the hour.

"In the midst of life," the chaplain continued, "we are in death." Billington pulled a lever. The trapdoor under Cream's feet slammed open with a thud that reverberated through the prison. His body fell five feet before the rope pulled tight, snapping his neck. The prison doctor descended into the pit below the scaffold and checked the left wrist for a pulse. There was none.

A black flag was hoisted above the prison, signaling that the executioner's work was done. The crowd erupted in cheers, applause, and laughter. "Now 'ee's a danglin'," someone shouted. The celebration could be heard inside the execution shed. The body remained suspended for another hour. By early afternoon, it would be interred beneath the flagstones of Dead Man's Walk, and soon a new letter would be chiseled into the wall.

THE *ILLUSTRATED POLICE NEWS* APPEARED WITHIN DAYS OF THE EXECUTION WITH SKETCHES CAPTURING CREAM'S FINAL MOMENTS. (NOVEMBER 19, 1892)

The crowd dispersed. The following day, a few people loitered in the rain outside Newgate's iron doors, where official announcements, written on bright blue and yellow paper, were posted. The notice confirming the execution of Thomas Neill Cream was soon too soggy to read, the words melting away into inky streaks and botches. The rampage of the "wretched murderer of lost women," as one news report called him, was over.

38

"I AM JACK . . ."

CREAM'S CONVICTION AND EXECUTION SAVED SCOTLAND Yard from a repeat of the battering its reputation had taken in the wake of the Ripper killings. The missteps that almost derailed the Lambeth Poisoner investigation—blackmail letters misplaced or ignored, an innocent man accused of murdering Ellen Donworth—were papered over as the Metropolitan Police closed the file on the case. Superintendent James Brannan of L Division, in his final report to Assistant Commissioner Robert Anderson, commended the officers who had identified and captured "one of the most monstrous and subtle criminals of the age." His men had been on the case day and night for weeks, Brannan noted. They had interviewed scores of prostitutes and patrolled the Strand and the main streets of Lambeth, on the lookout for a man matching the description of the assailant. "The turning point of the whole investigation," he wrote, was the discovery of Cream's letter to Coroner Wyatt, which was in his handwriting and ultimately led investigators to Dr. Harper and his son. He made no mention of the blackmail threats Scotland Yard had dismissed as the work of pranksters or lunatics or of the most serious blunder of all—the failure to investigate whether a woman named Matilda Clover had been poisoned, as some of the letters claimed.

Anderson was just as eager to focus on the outcome rather than the mistakes. Days before Cream's execution, Anderson circulated a memo praising the officers who had brought the killer to justice. Scotland Yard had a tradition of distributing rewards when major cases were solved, and Inspectors Tunbridge, Jarvis, and Harvey, and six others who had helped crack the case, shared about twenty pounds—roughly twenty-seven hundred US dollars today. Tunbridge, in recognition of his role as lead investigator, received the largest reward, five pounds. "In his conduct of the case," Anderson noted, "he has increased the high reputation he had already earned." He was promoted to chief inspector in 1894 and three years later sailed to New Zealand to command the national police, with a mandate to reform the country's scandal-plagued constabulary. He held the post until 1903, when he retired and returned to England.

Solving the Lambeth poisonings mystery would be touted as one of the finest moments in the history of the Metropolitan Police, a much-needed triumph after the failure to track down Jack the Ripper. "A striking example of the ceaseless care and vigilance which characterises Scotland Yard," the journalist W. Teignmouth Shore claimed in the 1920s. When *Reader's Digest* compiled accounts of the force's "great cases" in the 1970s, Cream's sordid tale led the pack. The Scotland Yard historian Douglas Browne, however, was unable to fathom how the blackmail letters could have been filed away and forgotten. "Normally it is a matter of routine to follow up all such accusations," he noted, "however improbable."

Scotland Yard had reason to be proud of the work done to convict Cream. The door-to-door inquiries and long hours had paid off. Dr. Stevenson's lab tests to detect strychnine had withstood the scrutiny of one of London's top defense lawyers. Jarvis had done impressive legwork to confirm Cream's crimes in the United States and Canada. "Inspector Luck" and "Sergeant Chance" had been on the case, leading Tunbridge to Benjamin Priest's drugstore and to the discovery of the blackmail letter that Cream had carelessly sent to Dr. Joseph Harper in his own handwriting. And the police could not be blamed for the failure to investigate Clover's death when it occurred—Dr. Robert Graham's certificate, attributing her seizures to natural causes, had ensured there would be no inquest in the fall of 1891. His negligence did not go unpunished. He stood trial in January 1893 on a charge of issuing a false death certificate and was convicted and ordered to post a bond of one hundred pounds, to be forfeited if he was again found guilty of misconduct. Accurate death certificates, one newspaper reminded the profession after his trial, were essential "to prevent the commission of crime with impunity."

The Cream case burnished Dr. Thomas Stevenson's reputation and helped build public confidence in the laboratory tests used to detect strychnine and other poisons. The Home Office called on him to analyze samples or testify in at least two dozen major poisoning cases over three decades—more than any other analyst or chemist in the country. He was knighted in 1904 and hailed in headlines as "The Poison-Finder" and a "Master of Poisons" when he died in 1908. "British justice has lost one of its most able allies," lamented one report of his death, "perhaps the most successful unraveller of poison mysteries of modern times." Two years later a team of analysts that included Dr. Bernard Spilsbury—Dr. Stevenson's successor as Britain's most renowned forensic scientist—detected the toxic alkaloid hyoscine in body parts buried in a London cellar, then linked the remains to the missing wife of an American doctor, Hawley Harvey Crippen. Crippen's dramatic 1910 trial and conviction were watershed moments for forensic science, which had been struggling to win over the skeptics since Dr. Alfred Taylor's time. The crime-fighting alliance we take for granted today, between scientists and detectives, was finally on a solid foundation.

But some hard truths remained. Scotland Yard had been oblivious to Cream's murderous spree for months, and Dr. Graham's negligence was only partly to blame. L Division had been quick to assume Ellen Donworth had committed suicide to escape her life on the streets, even though it was unclear how she could have obtained strychnine. It had been easy for Cream to deflect suspicion and dupe investigators with his tall tales about his fellow lodger, Walter Harper. Too easy. His medical credentials and his case of drug samples had been enough to convince some high-ranking officers that he was an innocent man with his ear to the ground and guilty only of a fondness for prostitutes. His status as a doctor had almost enabled him, once again, to escape justice

The police officers on Cream's trail had dismissed Lambeth's prostitutes as "unreliable." And the traps Scotland Yard set to try to catch the man blackmailing prominent Londoners exposed bias and double standards. Such vigilance was lacking, as Justice Hawkins pointed out during the trial, when it came to making routine inquiries to confirm whether an "unfortunate" woman named Matilda Clover had died in Lambeth. But four women proved to be instrumental in identifying and convicting Cream. Elizabeth Masters and Elizabeth May were the only witnesses able to place him in Clover's company. Laura Sabbatini, despite the shock and humiliation of discovering she had almost married a monster, summoned the courage to come forward to identify his handwriting and to admit her role as an unwitting accomplice to blackmail. And Louisa Harvey had been just as determined to tell a jury how Cream had poisoned his victims—crucial testimony that sealed his fate.

Scotland Yard had been lucky. Unlike the Ripper, Cream had seemed determined to help his pursuers. He sent blackmail letters in his distinctive handwriting. He flaunted his samples of drugs and poisons. He struck up friendships with a police officer, Sergeant Patrick McIntyre, and a would-be detective, John Haynes. He made clumsy attempts to convince them that someone else had committed the murders. The real mystery is why it took Scotland Yard so long to realize the Lambeth Poisoner was hiding in plain sight—a drug-addicted doctor who consorted with prostitutes, had access to strychnine, and knew far too much about the gruesome deaths of four women.

◇◇◇◇◇

THE *ILLUSTRATED POLICE NEWS* REVIEWED CREAM'S LONDON CRIMES IN THE WAKE OF
HIS SENTENCING. (OCTOBER 29, 1892)

"I AM Jack . . ."

Three words have fueled more than a century of speculation that Cream was Jack the Ripper. Newspaper reports, which surfaced a decade after Cream's execution, claimed that these were his last words, uttered as the trap was sprung in the execution shed of Newgate Prison. Was it a last-second confession, cut off in midsentence, to the Whitechapel murders?

The similarities between the two killers are obvious and were noted at the time of the Lambeth poisonings. Both preyed on women in a downtrodden area of London, with no apparent motive other than an urge to kill. "The points of resemblance," the *Pall Mall Gazette* acknowledged the day after Cream's conviction, "are remarkable." But the Lambeth Poisoner had been locked up in an Illinois prison when the Ripper stalked his victims. He had an iron-clad alibi.

Unless. Could Cream have bribed his way out of Joliet Prison before 1888 and made his way to London? A Canadian writer, Don Bell, advanced this theory in the 1970s, ignoring the weight of documentary evidence confirming that inmate no. 4374 was not released until 1891. The idea gained traction, and Cream was added to a long list of Ripper suspects, joining such unlikely candidates as Prince Albert Victor, the Duke of Clarence, an heir to the throne who died in 1892. A bizarre new theory was advanced to explain away the prison records confirming his incarceration—Cream may have had a double, who served his sentence in his place as he roamed free and claimed more victims.

The purported gallows confession first appeared in a few American newspapers in January 1902. A brief item attributed to the *London Chronicle* reported that Cream's executioner, James Billington, had heard the words "I am Jack . . ." and had claimed to be the man who hanged the Ripper. The reports appeared after Billington's death and attracted little attention at the time. No other witness to the execution came forward to corroborate the claim, but the story was repeated over the years in accounts of Cream's crimes.

Most Ripperologists, as students of the Whitechapel murders are known, have dismissed Cream as a suspect, and not only because he was locked up in an American prison in 1888. "Different method, different place, different time, different man," noted the editors of one compilation of Ripper-related documents and theories. A "knife-wielding disemboweller" like the Ripper, they argued, "does not become the cautious poisoner."

There remains a possible link between the most notorious serial killers of the Victorian Age: the Ripper's murders may have inspired Cream to cross the Atlantic to launch his attack on London's prostitutes. The dubious confession, however, has been enough to earn him a place in the mythology surrounding the Whitechapel murders. Today, when guides leading tours of Jack the Ripper's London review the names of possible culprits, chances are the list will include Dr. Thomas Neill Cream.

EPILOGUE

"AN ELIZABETHAN TRAGEDY OF HORRORS"

THE FUTURE HISTORIAN OF THE LATTER PART OF THIS nineteenth century," the *British Medical Journal* predicted in an editorial on the Lambeth poisonings, "cannot fail to note the present epidemic of homicide." It had been barely three years since the Ripper terrorized Whitechapel. In Fall River, Massachusetts, that August, as Cream awaited trial, a young woman named Lizzie Borden was charged with hacking her father and stepmother to death with an ax. And in the early months of 1892, the conviction and execution of Frederick Deeming in Australia made headlines around the world. English born and a gas fitter by trade, he was convicted of murdering a woman in Melbourne and implicated in the deaths of two wives and his four children. But it would be another decade before Britain saw another monster of Cream's ilk—George Chapman, who poisoned three women in London and was hanged in 1903. Decades later, when George Orwell pondered the elements of a classic, crowd-pleasing English murder—greed, sex, or both as the motive, poison as the weapon—he counted Cream among the killers "whose reputation has stood the test of time."

As recently as the 1950s one anthology of famous murder cases suggested the awkward terms "series-murder" or "multicide" to designate a succession of murders committed by the same person. References to "serial killers" did not begin to appear in media reports until the 1980s, and scholars and law enforcement officials continue to debate an exact definition. The US Federal Bureau of Investigation casts a broad net and considers anyone who murders two or more people, in separate events, as a serial murderer. They kill for money, for sex, or for the perverse pleasure of inflicting pain on others. Unlike mass murderers who kill in a hail of gunfire, serial killers seek out their victims, carefully plan how and when to act, and kill over a period of months or years. Cream's murders displayed each of these characteristics, and, in common with many serial killers, he appears to have committed at least one act of arson as a young man. There was a pattern in eight of his killings: he tampered with a prescription or laced capsules with strychnine, then accused druggists or prominent persons of being the poisoner. His victims took the pills or medication he offered without hesitation. He was a doctor, the "trusted hand," and his profession shielded him from suspicion or bought him the time he needed to accuse others and plot an escape.

The magnitude of Cream's crimes will never be known with certainty. In a span of fifteen years he was convicted of two murders, stood trial for a third, and faced charges of killing three more people. He was the prime suspect in four other poisonings. Surviving court records and press reports make a convincing case that he was guilty of all ten of these homicides. He likely tried to kill Louisa Harvey and people who were sickened after taking medicine he provided. Cream began his life of crime as an arsonist and an abortionist, graduated to murder, then used forgery and blackmail to cover his tracks or to try to profit from the deaths, even though there's no evidence he followed through on any of his blackmail schemes. By the time he arrived in London in 1891, he had perfected his technique. Enclosing strychnine in gelatin capsules masked its bitter taste and delayed the poison's effects until after he had fled. He had become a killing machine. Had he not spent almost a decade in prison, or if Scotland Yard had taken weeks or months longer to identify him as the Lambeth Poisoner, there's little doubt he would have claimed more lives.

Nine of Cream's ten known or suspected victims were women. The sexism and hypocrisy of the late nineteenth century served as his unseen accomplices, driving the vulnerable and the desperate into his clutches. Canadian academic Angus McLaren produced the definitive scholarly study of Cream's crimes in the 1990s, digging deep into Scotland Yard's archives to explore why he killed and how he was caught. He considered Cream "a sick product of his society." Britain's marriage and divorce laws imposed double standards that were telling. A man could seek a divorce on the grounds of adultery, but a woman needed additional cause—desertion, cruelty, even rape—to escape a bad marriage. Before 1870, a woman surrendered all her property to her husband's control on her wedding day. Prostitution offenses singled out women for punishment, as if they alone were to blame for the immoral behavior of men. Thousands were charged in London every year with "annoying male persons for the purposes of prostitution," but action was rarely taken against their clients. Until the mid-1880s, British police operating in neighborhoods near military bases had the power to arrest suspected prostitutes and force them to be examined and treated for sexually transmitted diseases. The Contagious Diseases Acts were designed to protect soldiers and sailors, yet nothing was done to identify infected men or to prevent them from spreading disease.

The pervasive sexism and inequality of the times isolated prostitutes and pregnant, unwed women alike, relegating them to the margins of society. Women came to Cream seeking an illegal abortion or medicine to induce a miscarriage in order to escape the stigma, or "the living death," of having a child out of wedlock. Poverty, unemployment, and the limited opportunities available for unmarried women drove or lured other women into prostitution. They were "unfortunates" or "degraded women," as the newspapers described them, objects of pity and scorn. In Cream's twisted mind, however, prostitutes were not just offensive or immoral. They were less than human—"cattle" to be killed, a "menace" to be eradicated. The "degradation and defenceless condition" of Cream's Lambeth victims, the *South London Chronicle* noted with a tinge of guilty conscience, "appealed in vain for protection." Little was offered. Some of the Scotland Yard officers pursuing Cream privately condemned the "character" and "habits" of his victims, blaming them when the police investigation stalled.

Behind the names of each of Cream's known or suspected female victims was a story of hardship, struggle, or despair. Flora Brooks's pregnancy hastened her marriage to the man who was likely her killer. Catharine Gardner, Mary Anne Faulkner, and Alice Montgomery were young, single women toiling at low-paying jobs as maids or waitresses when they discovered they were pregnant. Ellen Stack, the Chicago maid who sought out Cream for abortion-inducing drugs, apparently believed she was pregnant as well. Matilda Clover, a chronic alcoholic at age twenty-seven, was struggling to raise a child on her own and thought she had found a generous man willing to help her. Alice Marsh had quit her job as a maid and moved to London with a friend, Emma Shrivell, ostensibly to work in a biscuit factory. Shrivell had lived with a man for a year before arriving in Lambeth, even though she was only eighteen. Ellen Donworth was pregnant at sixteen, but her child died soon after it was born; she turned to prostitution when she lost her job in a bottling plant. Nine women who deserved protection, understanding, and sympathy but endured only indifference and shame. Nine lives cut short.

Serial killers continue to target those living on the margins—sex workers, the homeless, transients, drug addicts, teenage runaways. Many lead lives filled with desperation and risk, and their lifestyles make them wary of the police and vulnerable to attack. If they disappear—and assuming there is anyone to report the disappearance— police may have few leads to go on and little incentive to investigate.

American criminologist Steven Egger has described victims such as these as "less-dead"—people of little worth or value to society, whose deaths are deemed less important than those of victims living mainstream, middle-class lives. In the midst of Jack the Ripper's rampage, the *Times of London* published an astonishing letter to the editor that commended the killer for "clearing the East-end of its vicious inhabitants." Cream's victims, like the Ripper's, were seen as expendable. "Women had no voice, and few rights, and the poor were considered lazy and degenerate," the historian Hallie Rubenhold has noted of the age that spawned these killers. "To have been both of these things was one of the worst possible combinations." Such attitudes have persisted. Peter Sutcliffe murdered thirteen women—and likely more—in northern England between 1975 and 1980. Many of the victims of the man who became known as the "Yorkshire Ripper" were sex workers, but his crimes drew more police attention and public outrage when he began to attack "respectable" women. Cream's shocking crimes resonate in a time when murderous predators still lurk in the shadows and in a culture obsessed, like that of our Victorian ancestors, with tales of crime and detection. Serial killers continue to prey on the "less-dead" and evade capture, despite DNA evidence, criminal profiling, and other advances in forensic science. And investigators continue to struggle to connect seemingly motiveless crimes and random victims to a single murderer.

Cream, unwittingly, made it easier to convict other serial killers. The prosecution's use of damning evidence of each one of his London murders became a model for the admission of similar-fact evidence in cases of multiple murder or where there is a pattern to a series of attacks or assaults. Justice Henry Hawkins's decision was cited in the Australian courts in 1893 when a couple was convicted of murdering a baby. The bodies of a dozen other infants were found buried at their previous residences, and this evidence was ruled admissible. When George Joseph Smith stood trial in the Old Bailey in 1915 for drowning his wife in a bathtub, the Cream precedent allowed prosecutors to show he had disposed of two other women in the same manner. Smith, known as the "Brides in the Bath" killer, was convicted and hanged. Similar-fact evidence remains an option in criminal cases under the evidentiary rules in use in the United States, Britain, Canada, and other common-law countries.

⬦⬦⬦⬦⬦

CREAM's infamy was assured in 1923 when the transcript of the Old Bailey proceedings was published as a volume in the Notable British Trials series, a collection of sensational cases that includes two fellow Victorian era doctors turned poisoners, William Palmer and Edward Pritchard. "The whole story is like the plot of an Elizabethan tragedy of horrors," W. Teignmouth Shore, who edited the volume, remarked in an introductory essay as he struggled to understand what drove Cream to kill. "He may have had a half-crazy delight in feeling that the lives of the wretched women whom he slew lay in his power," he wrote, "that he was the arbiter of their fates." Two pioneers of the true-crime genre zeroed in on whether Cream was insane. Edmund Pearson, an American writer best known for his account of the Lizzie Borden case, was convinced the murders were too well planned to be the work of a madman. "He was cool and calm in the transaction of business," he argued in 1927. "He would not have murdered had he not believed that he could again outwit the law and escape its penalty." To F. Tennyson Jesse, the great-niece of the poet Alfred, Lord Tennyson, and the author of numerous accounts of British murder cases, his crimes "seemed mad and yet were not without method." Shore added his voice to the consensus that Cream met the legal threshold for sanity: knowing what he was doing and knowing it was wrong. "He utilized his medical knowledge to attain his ends, and he understood clearly that his acts were illegal."

These were the deliberate acts of a sadist who reveled in playing God. "In Cream we see the god-complex wrought to mania," was the assessment of an Australian writer, Philip Lindsay, in the 1950s. "He found his satisfaction purely in the thought of others dying by his invisible hand." When Cream was a medical student in Montreal, one of his instructors had urged doctors to be "useful and God-like." He chose instead to use the God-like powers of a medical man not to save lives but to decide who lived and who died. He killed some of the women he encountered and spared others, as if acting on a whim. He left Mary Anne Faulkner to die after a botched abortion. He almost certainly held chloroform to Catharine Gardner's face until she died. But these were exceptions to his pattern of killing from afar. He sent most of his victims to their deaths with ticking time bombs of lethal pills, delivering death with an unseen hand.

Cream's story found its way into true-crime anthologies and resurfaced from time to time in newspaper and magazine features. Dr. Frank Whitman, the Illinois coroner who was instrumental in convicting Cream of the murder of Daniel Stott, went public with his story in 1940 in the pages of the pulp magazine *Complete Detective Cases*. Some accounts created or perpetuated myths. The too-good-to-be-true Jack the Ripper confession has been irresistible and is frequently repeated as fact. Many versions of the story confidently state that Cream was forced to marry Flora Brooks at gunpoint or that he inherited the bulk of his father's estate. One writer added a melodramatic twist, claiming his last request was to be given a vial of strychnine.

Fictionalized accounts have also appeared. *The Gentleman from Chicago*, published in the 1970s, presented the lurid, self-serving confession Cream could have written while awaiting execution. Canadian playwright David Fennario gave the story an operatic flourish— an approach that might have appealed to the musically inclined Cream—complete with a chorus of prostitutes and a song lyric "I want to kill, kill, kill." The British author and screenwriter David Pirie imagined Arthur Conan Doyle and his mentor, Dr. Joseph Bell, as crime-fighting partners in a series of novels and the BBC series *Murder Rooms: Mysteries of the Real Sherlock Holmes*, which first aired in 2000. One installment sends them in pursuit of Cream, someone they know from his medical studies in Edinburgh and "the only man I have ever met," claims the Conan Doyle character, "who deserves worse than the description 'evil.'"

Cream embodies the stereotype of the Victorian villain, a shadowy figure complete with top hat, hollow laugh, and sinister, cross-eyed stare. The Jack the Ripper of poisoners. A Mr. Hyde for the ages. Evil and depravity in human form. In the Netflix series *River*, released in 2015, a ghostly "angel of death"—Cream, portrayed by the actor Eddie Marsan—torments a London detective who's struggling to cope with the murder of a colleague. "Have no fear of robbers or murderers. They are external dangers, petty dangers," says a menacing Lambeth Poisoner, quoting Victor Hugo. "We should fear ourselves. The great dangers are within us."

◇◇◇◇◇

For more than seven decades, Cream's wax figure was a fixture in the Chamber of Horrors at Madame Tussaud's in London. The doppelganger was posed with pen and paper in his hands, as if he were jotting one of the blackmail notes that would help send him to the gallows. He stood shoulder-to-shoulder with Deeming, Chapman, and other notorious English murderers. Millions of visitors were reminded of Cream and his crimes until 1968, when the figure was withdrawn from the exhibit to make way for new generations of murderous fiends.

Few remnants of Cream's world have survived. In Quebec City, Chalmers Church still stands, and a notation in the parish records reminds researchers that "the unfortunate and notorious son" of William Cream once worshipped and taught Sunday school there. Brooks House is gone, but Flora Brooks's headstone is just inside the chain-link fence surrounding what French-speaking residents of Waterloo, Quebec, call the "English Cemetery." Cream remains on the list of graduates of Montreal's McGill University, despite the unwelcome attention he draws to his alma mater. In Chicago, redevelopment has swept away the West Madison Street neighborhood where he practiced and killed. The Boone County Courthouse, the scene of his trial for murdering Daniel Stott, however, still commands a hilltop in Belvidere, Illinois. Joliet Prison closed in 2002, but its unguarded walls and empty cells serve as a monument to the folly of unleashing him on the world to kill again.

Time and World War II bombings have obliterated many of the landmarks of Cream's Lambeth. St. Thomas' Hospital, damaged in the Blitz, has been modernized, but the medical wing where Cream studied in the 1870s still stands, vacant and crumbling. The Wellington pub and hotel, across from Waterloo Station, bears silent witness to the last moments of Ellen Donworth, who collapsed on the opposite side of the street. Another survivor is the building that housed the Mason's Arms pub, four doors down from the long-demolished house where Matilda Clover lived and died. The townhouse at 103 Lambeth Palace Road, where Cream lodged, and the houses where his other three victims died are also gone. A visitor can follow his route on Hercules Road, though, and stand at the corner where Elizabeth Masters and Elizabeth May witnessed his encounter with Clover, or cross Westminster Bridge and imagine him stopping, midspan, and refusing to accompany Sergeant Patrick McIntyre to Scotland Yard. "As one walks through the drab streets of Lambeth," W. Teignmouth Shore wrote in the 1920s, "the shadow of this sinister man still haunts them." Retracing his steps today, some 130 years after his crimes, leaves an eerie feeling that his crimes will haunt them forever.

In central London, the King Lud pub at Ludgate Circus, where he treated Elizabeth Masters to a drink, is now a trendy restaurant. The Northumberland Arms, where he shared a glass of wine with Louisa Harvey before trying to kill her, survives as a pub and has been rechristened the Sherlock Holmes, complete with a second-floor room displaying artifacts that could have adorned the Great Detective's Baker Street flat. When Newgate Prison closed in 1902, shortly before its demolition to make way for a new building to house the Central Criminal Court—the Old Bailey of today—the remains of executed prisoners were disinterred and moved to London's municipal cemetery, northeast of the city center in Manor Park. Cream now lies in an unmarked grave in section 339. Two of Jack the Ripper's victims— Catherine Eddowes and Mary Ann Nichols—are also buried in the cemetery's expansive grounds. The case of drug samples that Cream brought with him from America, including a vial of strychnine, went on public display in London in 2015 as part of an exhibit of artifacts stored in Scotland Yard's Black Museum.

DANIEL STOTT'S WEATHERED HEADSTONE
IN GARDEN PRAIRIE, ILLINOIS (AUTHOR PHOTO)

The most chilling reminder of Cream's horrific crimes, however, can be found in a windswept cemetery in Garden Prairie, Illinois. A weathered headstone marks Daniel Stott's grave, erected, it is claimed, by his friends long ago, under cover of darkness. "Poisoned," the inscription declares, "by his wife & Dr. Cream."

CAST OF CHARACTERS

—

THE LAMBETH POISONER
- » Thomas Neill Cream, doctor, abortionist, blackmailer, serial killer

KNOWN AND SUSPECTED VICTIMS
- » Flora Eliza Brooks, Cream's wife, Waterloo, QC
- » Matilda Clover, London, England
- » Ellen Donworth, London, England
- » Mary Anne Matilda Faulkner, Chicago
- » Catharine Hutchinson Gardner, London, ON
- » Alice Marsh, London, England
- » Sarah Alice Montgomery, Chicago
- » Emma Shrivell, London, England
- » Ellen Stack, Chicago
- » Daniel Stott, Garden Prairie, IL

TARGETS OF ATTEMPTED OR SUSPECTED POISONINGS
- » Violet Beverly, London, England
- » Louisa Harvey, also known as Louisa Harris, London, England
- » Matilda Nadeau, Quebec City
- » Louisa Mary Read, mother of Cream's sister-in-law, Jessie Read, Quebec City
- » Emily Turner, London, England

The Cream Family

- » Daniel Cream, brother; husband of Jessie Read
- » Mary Cream, sister
- » Mary Elder Cream, mother
- » William Cream, father; timber merchant in Quebec City
- » Elizabeth Harbeson, stepmother

Police Investigators

Chicago
- » John Rehm, sergeant
- » Edward Steele, lieutenant

Belvidere, IL
- » Albert T. Ames, sheriff of Boone County

London, England
- » Robert Anderson, assistant commissioner, Metropolitan Police (Scotland Yard)
- » James Brannan, superintendent, L Division (Lambeth)
- » Colin Chisholm, chief inspector, L Division
- » George Comley, constable, L Division
- » George Harvey, inspector, L Division
- » Frederick Smith Jarvis, inspector, Metropolitan Police
- » George Lowe, inspector, L Division
- » Melville Macnaghten, chief constable, Metropolitan Police
- » Patrick McIntyre, sergeant, Metropolitan Police
- » John Mulvany, chief inspector, L Division
- » John Bennett Tunbridge, inspector, Metropolitan Police
- » Alfred Ward, sergeant, L Division

Coroners and Forensic Investigators

London, ON
- » Dr. John R. Flock, coroner
- » Dr. James Niven, physician

Chicago
» Dr. Theodore Bluthardt, Cook County physician
» Dr. Walter Haines, professor of chemistry and toxicology, Rush Medical College
» Canute Matson, Cook County coroner
» Major W. E. Waite, Cook County deputy coroner

Belvidere, IL
» Dr. Frank Whitman, Boone County coroner

London, England
» A. Braxton Hicks, coroner for mid-Surrey
» Dr. Thomas Kelloch, house physician, St. Thomas' Hospital
» Dr. Thomas Stevenson, chemist and Home Office analyst
» George Percival Wyatt, coroner for the counties of London and Surrey
» Dr. Cuthbert Wyman, house physician, St. Thomas' Hospital

KEY WITNESSES
Canada
» Lyman Brooks, hotel owner and father of Flora Brooks, Waterloo, QC
» John Cantle, salesman, Toronto
» Robert Caswell, prison chaplain, Toronto
» Robert Gardner, brother of Catharine Gardner
» David Lindsay, archdeacon and rector of St. Luke's Anglican Church, Waterloo, QC
» Sarah Long, hotel maid, London, ON
» John McCulloch, salesman, Toronto
» Dr. Cornelius Phelan, Waterloo, QC
» Dr. Herbert Reddy, Cream's McGill Medical School classmate, Montreal
» William Sellar, salesman, Montreal
» Leon Vohl, chief of police, Quebec City

United States
» George Harvey, president, G. F. Harvey Company, drug manufacturer, Saratoga Springs, NY
» Martin Kingman, salesman for G. F. Harvey Company
» Joseph Martin, target of obscene postcards, Chicago
» Robert McClaughry, warden, Illinois State Penitentiary, Joliet; later, chief of police, Chicago
» Mary McClellan, Cream's landlady and mother of his fiancée, Lena, Chicago
» Frank Murray, superintendent, Pinkerton's National Detective Agency, Chicago
» Julia Stott, wife of Daniel Stott; Cream's mistress and co-accused, Garden Prairie

England
» Francis Coppin, physician's assistant, London
» Robert Graham, doctor, London
» John Haynes, ship's engineer and former British government agent, London
» Elizabeth Masters, London
» Elizabeth May, London
» Emma Phillips, Matilda Clover's landlady, London
» Lucy Rose, Emma Phillips's maid, London
» Laura Sabbatini, Cream's fiancée; dressmaker, Berkhamsted
» Emily Sleaper, daughter of Cream's landlady, London
» Charlotte Vogt, landlady of Alice Marsh and Emma Shrivell, London

TARGETS OF BLACKMAIL THREATS
» Dr. William Broadbent, physician, London, England
» Dr. Joseph Harper, physician, Barnstaple, England
» Walter J. Harper, Joseph Harper's son; medical student, St. Thomas' Hospital, London, England

» Frank Pyatt, druggist, Chicago
» James Rayner, druggist, Chicago
» Countess Mabel Russell, wife of Earl Russell, London, England
» William Frederick Danvers Smith, bookseller and member of Parliament, London, England

PROSECUTORS
» Amos Coon, lawyer, Belvidere, IL
» Reuben Coon, state's attorney, Belvidere, IL
» Charles Fuller, lawyer and state senator, Belvidere, IL
» George Ingham, Cook County assistant state's attorney, Chicago
» Sir Charles Russell, attorney general, London, England

CREAM'S LAWYERS
» Gerald Geoghegan, barrister, London, England
» John Jennison, Chicago
» Daniel Munn, Chicago
» Alfred Trude, Chicago
» Henry Warburton, barrister, London, England
» John Waters, lawyer, London, England
» Omar Wright, Belvidere, IL

JUDGES AND MAGISTRATES
» Sir John Bridge, magistrate, London, England
» Joseph Eaton Gary, circuit court, Chicago
» Sir Henry Hawkins, High Court of Justice, London, England
» Horace Smith, magistrate, London, England

KEY FIGURES IN CREAM'S CLEMENCY APPEAL
» Shelby Moore Cullom, US senator from Illinois
» Thomas Davidson, executor of William Cream's will and family friend, Quebec City

CAST OF CHARACTERS

» John Dunn, vice consul, British consulate, Chicago
» Joseph Fifer, governor of Illinois
» Richard Oglesby, governor of Illinois
» Frances Willard, president, Woman's Christian Temperance Union

ACKNOWLEDGMENTS

Inspector Frederick Smith Jarvis of Scotland Yard worked alone in the summer of 1892 when he tracked a serial killer's movements in the United States and Canada. My efforts to trace Thomas Neill Cream's crimes and to re-create his world would have been impossible without the generous assistance of archivists, librarians, museum curators, court officials, and researchers in three countries.

In Quebec City, David Rourke and Matt Bircher at Chalmers-Wesley United Church, *Quebec Chronicle-Telegraph* editor Shirley Nadeau, and Deborah van der Linde, manager of the Morrin Centre's Library of the Literary and Historical Society of Quebec, helped me to document Cream's early life. Lori Podolsky, Melissa Como, and Isabelle Morissette of the McGill University Archives in Montreal and Christopher Lyons and Lily Szczygiel at McGill's Osler Library assembled records relating to his medical studies. Lyz Damansa Falaise of the McCord Museum in Montreal provided the Notman Studio photographs of Cream as a medical student. At the Bibliothèque et Archives nationales du Québec, Nathalie Vaillancourt, Sylvie Bédard, Yvan Carette, Rénald Lessard, Joanie Levasseur, Eric Beaudin, and Rénald Lessard fielded my requests for records and images. I researched the Quebec community of Waterloo in Cream's time with the assistance of staff members of two local museums—Arlene Royea Ayotte and Cari Ensio of the Brome County Historical Society in

Lac-Brome/Knowlton and Cecilia Capocchi of Granby's Société d'histoire de la Haute-Yamaska.

I found records related to Cream's year in London, Ontario, with the help of Theresa Regnier, Anne Daniel, and Connie Sutherland at Western University's Archives, Arthur McClelland at the London Public Library, and Jennifer Grainger and Jennifer Robertson of the London and Middlesex Historical Society. Local historian Daniel Brock graciously guided my research when I visited London and helped with follow-up requests for information. And thanks to the staff of the Archives of Ontario in Toronto and to Peggy Perdue, who oversees the Arthur Conan Doyle Collection at the Toronto Public Library, a mecca for fans of Sherlock Holmes.

The day I contacted Julie Kleive at the office of the Boone County Circuit Court in Belvidere, Illinois, I was astonished to discover the case file on Cream's prosecution for the 1881 murder of Daniel Stott was on her desk—by chance, she was consulting it for her own work on the court's history. Circuit Court clerk Linda J. Anderson and Anna Pivoras and Lonna Bentley of the Boone County Museum of History also aided my research in Belvidere. In Chicago, Douglas Bicknese at the National Archives; Justin Cochran, Paul Hughes, and William Wojtkiewicz of the Illinois Regional Archives; and Phil Costello in the Archives Department of the Circuit Court of Cook County helped me track down trial and inquest records. Staff of the Chicago History Museum's research center, the Harold Washington Library, and the Newberry Library provided access to newspaper coverage, images, and other information. John Reinhardt of the Illinois State Archives in Springfield located Cream's prison file and records of his bid for early release.

Staff at the National Archives in Kew, the British Library, and the London Metropolitan Archives fielded my inquiries about records and were of invaluable assistance during my visits to London. Jon Newman, Zoe Darani, and Stefanie Anderson of the Lambeth Archives helped me to reconstruct the neighborhood in Cream's time and directed me to the Victorian era street guides and maps I needed to pinpoint murder scenes. I obtained records of Cream's medical training at St. Thomas' Hospital with the assistance of Joel Haley, Adam Cox, and Diana Manipud of the King's College London Archives. Geraldine O'Driscoll of the Royal College of Surgeons, London, confirmed his failed bid for certification in England. Aaron Fleming at the Royal College of Surgeons of Edinburgh, Estela Dukan and Daisy Cunynghame of the Royal College of Physicians of Edinburgh, and Alice Doyle at the Edinburgh University Library supplied details of his licenses to practice medicine. Richard Buteux, bereavement services officer for the City of London, helped me find Cream's gravesite. Hugh Alexander at the National Archives; Chris Rawlings, Andrew Gough, and Zoe Stansell of the British Library; and Justin Hobson, Tracy Tran, and Jasmine Rodgers of London's Science and Society Picture Library helped me obtain images.

I assembled newspaper coverage with the assistance of Charles André Nadeau and University of King's College student researchers Emma Meldrum, Rebecca Cooke, and Cory Funk. Jamie Gaetz helped with archival research in Ontario and research on the Cream family. In Halifax, Patricia Chalmers of the University of King's College Library and Helen Wojcik of Dalhousie University's Killam Memorial Library located hard-to-find books. Mary Rostad produced the maps. Others who helped with my research include Roger Johnson of the *Sherlock Holmes Journal*; Crime Museum curator Paul Bickley; authors Adam Selzer, Paul Willetts, and Trevor Cole; Sherlock Holmes expert Mattias Boström; and Nona Stancheva, Sedi Kukwikila, and Claire Treacy of Madame Tussauds London.

No writer could ask for a better champion and ally than Hilary McMahon of Westwood Creative Artists, my agent. And no writer could have a more supportive editor than Amy Gash of Algonquin Books of Chapel Hill. Amy helped me to reimagine how to tell this story and I'm grateful for her guidance, insights, and friendship. Thanks as well to members of the Algonquin team—Elisabeth

Scharlatt, Abby Muller, Brunson Hoole, Jude Grant, Steve Godwin, Anne Winslow, and Michael McKenzie—who helped to bring this book into the world. And thanks to my editors at HarperCollins Canada, Jim Gifford and Janice Zawerbny, and to Noelle Zitzer, Alan Jones, and Michael Millar for their work on the Canadian edition.

Unlike Inspector Jarvis, I was never alone as I unearthed Cream's crimes and the long struggle to bring him to justice. Kerry Oliver was involved at every stage, from research to proofreading, as this book took shape. I am grateful, most of all, for her enthusiasm and unwavering support for everything I do.

SOURCES

EACH LETTER HAS BEEN CAREFULLY PASTED ONTO A SHEET of thin cardboard, to keep it from crumbling. Time has mellowed the paper to a sepia tone and the edges are frayed from handling, but the words are as chilling and sinister as when they were written 130 years ago. In the serene, light-filled reading room of Britain's National Archives in Kew, an hour by train from the congestion of central London, the Lambeth Poisoner once again utters his threats and spins his lies. The blackmail letters that helped convict Thomas Neill Cream of the murder of Matilda Clover—some in his distinctive, left-sloping handwriting—are preserved in the thick file that the Home Office compiled before deciding to send him to the gallows.

It takes a moment to sink in. These are not copies. One of history's most prolific serial killers handled these sheets of paper. He picked up a pen and carefully composed the missives that slipped a noose around his neck. A researcher who opens the scuffed tan boxes indexed as HO 144/245 and 144/246 opens a window on the past—and comes face-to-face with a killer.

When George Orwell published his essay "Decline of the English Murder" in 1946, a half century after the Lambeth murders, he doubted Thomas Neill Cream would ever be forgotten. Like other notorious killers of the Victorian Age—Jack the Ripper and Dr. William Palmer top the list—his story of cruelty and depravity would be "known in its general outline," Orwell wrote, "to almost everyone." He was, after all, among the criminals notorious enough to rate a volume in the Notable British Trials series in the 1920s. But Cream has faded from memory, along with the names of his victims. Even the exact number of people he killed or tried to poison is unknown and, at this distance, unknowable.

This is the first complete account of Cream's crimes and the Scotland Yard manhunt that ultimately brought him to justice. It reveals how the sexist attitudes and prejudices of the Victorian Age allowed this monster to poison vulnerable and desperate women, many of whom had turned to him for help. It exposes the flawed police and forensic investigations in three countries that allowed him to evade suspicion and detection and how, even after he was convicted and imprisoned for one murder, he was set free to kill again. And it recounts the months of relentless detective work—the missteps, the setbacks, and the stunning breakthroughs—that ended his murderous rampage. In an age when death came suddenly, from disease and other natural causes, a doctor offering help and medicine could kill almost with impunity. Cream cruelly betrayed the trust of his victims and did just that.

The Case of the Murderous Dr. Cream is a work of narrative nonfiction, as true to the historical record as I could make it. Nothing has been added or embellished. Every scene is based on a contemporary description of what occurred and where events unfolded; all quotations and dialogue are presented as they were recorded in newspaper reports, memoirs, police reports, and transcripts of court proceedings. I believe true stories draw their power—their ability to engage, to astonish, to educate—not from layers of invention but from their authenticity. There is one undeniable truth at the heart of this book: all this really happened.

The endnotes that follow document the sources used to re-create Cream's crimes and his nineteenth-century world. Some of this material has never been published until now. My goal was to locate as many original records as possible, and this took me on a journey

SOURCES

through the Canadian provinces of Quebec and Ontario, to Illinois, and, ultimately, to London. Scotland Yard's investigation file at the National Archives—hundreds of pages of reports and memoranda—revealed how the Lambeth murders were solved and includes Inspector Frederick Smith Jarvis's meticulous reports on Cream's murders in the United States and Canada. A collection of maps and street directories at the Lambeth Archives made it possible to turn back time and pinpoint murder scenes and victims' lodgings. A file on Cream's application for release from Joliet Prison, preserved at the Illinois State Archives in Springfield, yielded fresh insights into his early life, his time behind bars, and the years-long effort to commute his life sentence. I discovered paperwork relating to Cream's prosecution for the murder of Mary Anne Faulkner in a box of miscellaneous files in the archives of the Circuit Court of Cook County in Chicago; it includes the text of the judge's instructions to the jury. Information gleaned from these records and the original documents and transcripts of the Daniel Stott murder case, still housed at the Boone County courthouse in Belvidere, Illinois, are reproduced here for the first time.

The full transcript of Cream's 1892 trial, documenting the London murders, is available online as part of the *Proceedings of the Old Bailey, London's Central Criminal Court, 1674 to 1913* (www.oldbaileyonline. org). Another version of the trial transcript, with the addition of the opening and closing statements of counsel and the judge's instructions to the jury, was reproduced in journalist W. Teignmouth Shore's *Trial of Thomas Neill Cream*, which joined the Notable British Trials series in 1923. The first stop for anyone seeking to understand Cream's crimes, however, is Canadian historian Angus McLaren's thorough study of the murders and their context, *A Prescription for Murder: The Victorian Serial Killings of Dr. Thomas Neill Cream*, which appeared in 1993.

In addition to the sources cited below, I used census and genealogical records available through the website Ancestry (www.ancestry .com) to gather information about Cream's immediate family and his

SOURCES

Scottish origins. Weather conditions on a particular day were confirmed using newspaper reports and forecasts and, for Canada, the Historical Climate database (www.climate.weather.gc.ca). All monetary figures expressed in today's values were converted using tools available through the website MeasuringWorth (www.measuringworth.com) and are presented in US dollars. I pored over nineteenth-century photographs and maps to capture the look and feel of the lost world described in this book. And I retraced Cream's murderous journey from Waterloo, Quebec, to the streets of Lambeth, to see for myself where this "monster of iniquity" lurked in the shadows as he decided who would live and who would die.

PROLOGUE: GHOSTS

1   **final day of July** Cream's release is recorded in Secretary of State, Executive Section, Convict Register, 1866–1887, Record Series 103.103, Illinois State Archives, Springfield. The armed guards patrolling along the walls are described in S. W. Wetmore, "Life in a Great Prison," *Illustrated American*, March 8, 1890, 58.

1   **a modest gift** Frank Morn, *Forgotten Reformer: Robert McClaughry and Criminal Justice Reform in Nineteenth-Century America* (Lanham, MD: University Press of America, 2011), 45.

1   **stuffed into a pillowcase** S. W. Wetmore, "Life in Joliet Prison" (manuscript), 2–3, MSS Alphar W, S. W. Wetmore Collection, Chicago History Museum, 158.

1   **entitled to a train** Morn, *Forgotten Reformer*, 88.

2   **marching day after day** The requirement to march in lockstep is noted in S. W. Wetmore, *Behind the Bars at Joliet: A Famous Prison, Its Celebrated Inmates and Its Mysteries* (Chicago: Western News, 1892), 27.

2   **The stripes** "Crime, Its Causes," *Chicago Daily Tribune*, April 14, 1882.

3   **based on eleven** Colin Beavan, *Fingerprints: The Origins of Crime Detection and the Murder Case that Launched Forensic Science* (New York: Hyperion, 2001), 80–81.

3   **odds of finding** Henry T. F. Rhodes, *Alphonse Bertillon: Father of Scientific Detection* (London: George G. Harrap, 1956), 82.

3   **renders the identification** Wetmore, *Behind the Bars at Joliet*, 213, 215.

3   **Police in Birmingham** Dominic Midgley, "World's First Ever Mugshots: An Early Rogues Gallery of 19th Century Criminals," *Daily Express* (London), June 14, 2018, www.express.co.uk/life-style/life/974039/mugshot-police-criminals-worlds-first-birmingham.

4   **repeat offenders be identified** Morn, *Forgotten Reformer*, 92. The increase in the prison population owing to the Illinois repeat offender law is noted in "Joliet Prison," *Chicago Daily Tribune*, July 4, 1884.

4   **grew weary of filing** Bertillon's background and the development of his anthropometric system is traced in Beavan, *Fingerprints*, 76–93.

4   **It substitutes certainty** Quoted in Morn, *Forgotten Reformer*, 93. While Cream's measurements must have been recorded—the system was in operation at Joliet for four years before his release—his prison file contains no Bertillon records. His mug shot is also missing.

4   **American police forces** Jürgen Thorwald, *The Century of the Detective* (New York: Harcourt Brace & World, 1965), 93.

5   **became the distinguishing** Raymond B. Fosdick, "The Passing of the Bertillon System of Identification," *Journal of Criminal Law and Criminology* 6, no. 3 (1915): 364.

5   **bertillonage had its drawbacks** Ibid., 364–65.

5   **no central registry** An American registry of Bertillon and other criminal records would be established in Washington, DC, in 1910. See Morn, *Forgotten Reformer*, 294.

5   **still years away** Beavan, *Fingerprints*, 13, 17, 40, 42–46, 186–87.

5   **No man can** Quoted in Morn, *Forgotten Reformer*, 255.

5   **simply for the sake** "Neill Committed for Murder," *Chicago Daily Tribune*, July 19, 1892.

6   **one of America's first** Erik Larson, *The Devil in the White City: Murder, Magic, and Madness at the Fair that Changed America* (New York: Crown, 2003). While Holmes confessed to twenty-seven murders, recent research suggests he may have committed no more than nine, all of them after 1891. See Adam Selzer, *H. H. Holmes: The True History of the White City Devil* (New York: Skyhorse, 2017), 375–76.

CHAPTER 1. "A GREAT SIN-STRICKEN CITY"

11   **clad in a mackintosh** Testimony of Emily Sleaper, "Trial of Thomas Neill," October 1892, *Proceedings of the Old Bailey, London's Central Criminal Court, 1674 to 1913*, 1430. The entire trial transcript is searchable online, www.oldbaileyonline.org.

12   **one of the scandals** Quoted in Jerry White, *London in the Nineteenth Century: "A Human Awful Wonder of God"* (London: Jonathan Cape, 2007), 301.

12   **a great sin-stricken city** Quoted in Leonard Piper, *Murder by Gaslight: True Tales of Murder in Victorian and Edwardian England* (London: Michael O'Mara Books, 1991), 50.

13   **confronted a group** Frederick Porter Wensley, *Forty Years of Scotland Yard: The Record of a Lifetime's Service in the Criminal Investigation Department* (Garden City, NY: Garden City, 1931), 2.

13   **well-known rookery** Peter Quennell, *London's Underworld: Henry Mayhew* (London: Bracken Books, 1983), 138, 188.

13   **Fagin, Bill Sikes** Simon Winchester, *The Professor and the Madman: A Tale of Murder, Insanity, and the Making of the Oxford English Dictionary* (New York: HarperCollins, 1998), 3.

13   **choked the air** This description of Lambeth's industries and railways is based on Hannah Renier, *Lambeth Past: Kennington, Vauxhall, Waterloo* (London: Historical Publications, 2006), 103–11, 118–23.

13 **was in every sense** Peter Ackroyd, *London: The Biography* (London: Chatto & Windus, 2000), 692.

13 **most lurid and beastly** Geoffrey Best, *Mid-Victorian England, 1851–75* (London: Fontana Press, 1979), 51.

13 **Whoreterloo** Renier, *Lambeth Past*, 123.

13 **dark, damp arches** Quoted in Janet Roebuck, *Urban Development in 19th-Century London: Lamheth, Battersea and Wandsworth, 1838–1888* (London: Phillimore, 1979), 121.

15 **unfortunates** The term appears in countless press reports of the era. For examples, see the *British Medical Journal*, October 29, 1892; the *South London Chronicle*, October 29, 1892; and quoted in Angus McLaren, *A Prescription for Murder: The Victorian Serial Killings of Dr. Thomas Neill Cream* (Chicago: University of Chicago Press, 1993), 74, 127.

15 **Life was precarious** See Janet Howarth, "Gender, Domesticity and Sexual Politics," in *The Nineteenth Century: The British Isles, 1815–1901*, ed. Colin Matthew (Oxford: Oxford University Press, 2000), 185; and Best, *Mid-Victorian England*, 121.

15 **the usual ways** Kathryn Hughes, *Victorians Undone: Tales of the Flesh in the Age of Decorum* (Baltimore: Johns Hopkins University Press, 2018), 235.

15 **workin' and slavin'** Quennell, *London's Underworld*, 53–55.

15 **more women** Quoted in Thomas R. C. Gibson-Brydon, *The Moral Mapping of Victorian and Edwardian London: Charles Booth, Christian Charity, and the Poor-but-Respectable* (Montreal: McGill-Queen's University Press, 2016), 65–66.

16 **He was most** Inspector Frederick Smith Jarvis Report, June 30, 1892 (Quebec City), Metropolitan Police Office Records, MEPO 3/144, National Archives, London.

16 **He wished and decided** Letter, Thomas Davidson to Rev. George Mathews, December 15, 1891, Home Office Records, HO 144/246 A 54360/25, National Archives, London.

16 **His actions at times** Affidavit of Jessie Read, October 29, 1892, HO 144/246 A 54360/23.

16 **mental derangement** Affidavit of Thomas Davidson, October 29, 1892, ibid.

16 **Daniel and Davidson withdrew a sum** Jarvis Report, June 30, 1892 (Quebec City), MEPO 3/144.

16 **considered sending him** Jarvis Report, July 7, 1892 (Montreal), ibid.

16 **We believed** Affidavit of Davidson. Davidson also discussed their rationale in Jarvis Report, June 30, 1892 (Quebec City), ibid.

17 **of sound mind** *Records Relating to the Will of Thomas Neill Cream*, September 9, 1891, Bibliothèque et Archives nationales du Québec, Quebec City.

17 **announcing his arrival** Jarvis Report, July 4, 1892 (Montreal), MEPO 3/144.

17 **The restaurant's decor** This description of the restaurant and its menu is drawn from Nathaniel Newnham-Davis, *Dinners and Diners: Where and How to Dine in London* (London: Grant Richards, 1899), 68–71.

17 **well informed and travelled** "The Poisoner Neill: A Study of His Crimes by One Who Knew Him," *St. James's Gazette* (London), October 24, 1892. This is the source of the comments that follow on Cream's statements, tastes, and habits.

18 **his left eye turned** Inspector John Bennett Tunbridge Report, May 28, 1892, MEPO 3/144.

18 **consult an eye specialist** Ibid.

18   **diagnosed his condition** "Neill's Eyesight," *Times of London*, October 27, 1892; and "The Convict Neill," *Standard* (London), November 12, 1892.
18   **He supplied two pairs** Testimony of James Aitchison, "Trial of Thomas Neill," 1418.
18   **not in the habit** Testimony of John George Kirkby, ibid., 1422–23.

CHAPTER 2. "DETECTIVE-FEVER"

20   **Do you feel** Wilkie Collins, *The Moonstone* (New York: Harper & Brothers, 1868), 151. The other quotations in this paragraph and the next appear on pp. 55, 57, and 73 of this edition.
20   **obsessions in the nineteenth** Examples of the popularity of crime and murder, unless otherwise noted, are drawn from Judith Flanders, *The Invention of Murder: How the Victorians Revelled in Death and Detection and Created Modern Crime* (London: HarperPress, 2011), chaps. 1–4.
20   **"Nothing," proclaimed** Quoted in Michael Diamond, *Victorian Sensation: Or, the Spectacular, the Shocking and the Scandalous in Nineteenth-Century Britain* (London: Anthem Press, 2003), 154.
20   **Readers craved "sensations"** Ibid., 1–3.
21   **form of pornography** Stephen Carver, *The 19th Century Underworld: Crime, Controversy & Corruption* (Barnsley, UK: Pen & Sword History, 2018), 135, 147.
21   **commonplace murders** Richard D. Altick, *Deadly Encounters: Two Victorian Sensations* (Philadelphia: University of Pennsylvania Press, 1986), 10.
21   **the week has been** *Spectator* (London), July 13, 1861, 738.
21   **hoping to catch** The intense interest in the 1840 murder of Lord William Russell, slain by a servant in his London home, was typical. See Claire Harman, *Murder by the Book: A Sensational Chapter in Victorian Crime* (London: Viking, 2018), 24, 91.
21   **Dear me!** Quoted in Diamond, *Victorian Sensation*, 5–6.
22   **Something more goes** Thomas De Quincey, *On Murder Considered as One of the Fine Arts* (London: Penguin Classics, 2015), 5, 53.
22   **"unusual intelligence" and their** Charles Dickens, "A Detective Police Party," *Household Words*, July 27, 1850.
22   **steady-looking, sharp-eyed** Charles Dickens, *Bleak House* (London: Chapman & Hall, 1868), 189.
22   **"Nothing," Dickens wrote** Ibid., 438.
22   **Sergeant Cuff was modeled** Kate Summerscale, *The Suspicions of Mr. Whicher: A Shocking Murder and the Undoing of a Great Victorian Detective* (New York: Walker, 2008), 87.
22   **Edgar Allan Poe** Julian Symons, *Bloody Murder: From the Detective Story to the Crime Novel* (Harmondsworth, UK: Viking, 1985), 39.
23   **Arthur Conan Doyle combined** Conan Doyle acknowledged that his detective fiction followed "the footmarks of Poe." See Richard Lancelyn Green, comp., *The Uncollected Sherlock Holmes* (Harmondsworth, UK: Penguin Books, 1983), 270.
23   **observational skills and** John Dickson Carr, *The Life of Sir Arthur Conan Doyle* (New York: Barnes & Noble Books, 1994), 44–45.

23 **a new idea** William Fox newsreel interview with Conan Doyle, 1927, posted by Objet D'Art, YouTube, May 1, 2016, www.youtube.com/watch?v=tVgN2-vNknw.

24 **the true detective** Quoted in Michael Sims, *Arthur & Sherlock: Conan Doyle and the Creation of Holmes* (London: Bloomsbury, 2017), 157.

24 **consulting detective** Arthur Conan Doyle, *A Study in Scarlet*, in *"A Study in Scarlet" and "The Sign of the Four"* (New York: Peebles Press, 1975), 23. This job title is repeated in other stories.

24 **They lay all** Ibid.

24 **Among detective stories** This is one of the reviews reproduced in *Sherlock Holmes and Conan Doyle in the Newspapers*, ed. Mattias Boström and Matt Laffey, vol. 1, *1881–1892* (Indianapolis: Gasogene Books, 2015), 54.

24 **out of their depths** Arthur Conan Doyle, *The Sign of the Four*, in *"A Study in Scarlet" and "The Sign of the Four"* (New York: Peebles Press, 1975), 149.

24 **You have brought** Conan Doyle, *Study in Scarlet*, 42.

25 **almost insatiable** John Curran, introduction to Israel Zangwill, *The Perfect Crime: Big Bow Mystery*, Detective Club Crime Classics (London: Collins Crime Club, 2015), vi. See also Clare Clarke, "Detective Fever: Why We Are Addicted to Sherlock Holmes and Victorian Crime," *Irish Times* (Dublin), January 6, 2016.

25 **The scenes** Quoted in Symons, *Bloody Murder*, 73.

25 **Libraries adjusted** Reginald Pound, *The Strand Magazine, 1891–1950* (London: Heinemann, 1966), 92.

25 **By one estimate** Christopher Sandford, *The Man Who Would Be Sherlock: The Real Life Adventures of Arthur Conan Doyle* (Stroud, UK: History Press, 2017), 28.

25 **Major newspapers** Sims, *Arthur & Sherlock*, 189–90. The American papers that republished the first story, "A Scandal in Bohemia," are listed in the *Arthur Conan Doyle Encyclopedia*, last edited November 6, 2019, www.arthur-conan-doyle.com/index.php?title=A_Scandal_in_Bohemia.

25 **less interested** Flanders, *Invention of Murder*, 294.

25 **all were on the shelves** *Catalogue of the Library of the Illinois State Penitentiary, Joliet, Illinois* (Joliet: Joliet Daily Republic Print, 1883), 140, 143, 167.

25 **last and highest court** Conan Doyle, *Sign of the Four*, 149.

26 **like a herd of buffalo** Arthur Conan Doyle, "The Boscombe Valley Mystery," in *The Adventures of Sherlock Holmes* (London: HarperPress, 2009), 88.

26 **official police** Arthur Conan Doyle, "A Scandal in Bohemia," in ibid., 2.

26 **defied the best talent** See the advertisement for *The Adventures of Sherlock Holmes* in the *Westminster Budget*, November 10, 1893. The quotation was reproduced from a review published in the *Liverpool Courier*.

26 **officers were portrayed** Diamond, *Victorian Sensation*, 75.

26 **Defective Department** Quoted in Haia Shpayer-Makov, *The Ascent of the Detective: Police Sleuths in Victorian and Edwardian England* (Oxford: Oxford University Press, 2011), 202.

26 **muddled-headed** Ibid., 212.

26 **inept bunglers** H. Paul Jeffers, *Bloody Business: An Anecdotal History of Scotland Yard* (New York: Barnes & Noble Books, 1992), 97.

26 **fools flourished** S. Theodore Felstead, *Shades of Scotland Yard: Stories Grave and Gay of the World's Greatest Detective Force* (London: John Long, 1950), 14.

26 **sarcasm at the expense** Quoted in Shpayer-Makov, *Ascent of the Detective*, 276.

26 **My experience** Letter, Conan Doyle to Mrs. Robert Barr, ca. 1917, Series 1: Arthur Conan Doyle Correspondence, 1888–1930, Box 1, Folder 34, C. Frederick Kittle Collection of Doyleana, Newberry Library, Chicago (emphasis in original).

26 **the exercise** Frederick Porter Wensley, *Forty Years of Scotland Yard: The Record of a Lifetime's Service in the Criminal Investigation Department* (Garden City, NY: Garden City, 1931), 68.

27 **When a doctor does** Arthur Conan Doyle, "The Adventure of the Speckled Band," in *The Adventures of Sherlock Holmes* (London: HarperPress, 2009), 186.

CHAPTER 3. ELLEN DONWORTH

28 **I want to get** This account of Donworth's death is drawn from "Death by Poisoning. Suicide," L Division Report, October 23, 1891, Metropolitan Police Office Records, MEPO 3/144, National Archives, London; "Suspicious Death of a Girl in Lambeth," *Morning Advertiser* (London), October 16, 1891; "Poisoning Mystery in Lambeth," *Lloyd's Weekly Newspaper* (London), October 18, 1891; and "The Poisoning Mystery in Lambeth," *Lloyd's Weekly Newspaper* (London), October 25, 1891.

29 **perfectly sensible** "Poisoning Mystery in Lambeth," *Lloyd's Weekly Newspaper* (London), October 25, 1891.

29 **A tall, dark, cross-eyed** Ibid.

29 **She had all the symptoms** Testimony of John Johnson, October 1892, "Trial of Thomas Neill," *Proceedings of the Old Bailey, London's Central Criminal Court, 1673 to 1913*, 1418–21, 1458, www.oldbaileyonline.org.

29 **Let me die** "Death by Poisoning. Suicide."

29 **She used to walk** The first day of the coroner's inquest was reported in "Suspicious Death of a Girl in Lambeth"; and "Poisoning Mystery in Lambeth," *Lloyd's Weekly Newspaper* (London), October 18, 1891.

29 **the proceeds** "Sad End of a Girl's Career," *North-Eastern Daily Gazette* (Middlesbrough, Yorkshire), October 17, 1891.

30 **opened a file** The first notation on File No. 73854 is dated October 19, 1891, MEPO 3/144.

30 **Police have ascertained** "Death by Poisoning. Suicide."

30 **more like a lady's** Testimony at the second day of the inquest was reported in "The Lambeth Poisoning Mystery," *Morning Advertiser* (London), October 23, 1891; "Mysterious Poisoning Case at Lambeth," *Pall Mall Gazette* (London), October 23, 1891; and "Poisoning Mystery in Lambeth," *Lloyd's Weekly Newspaper* (London), October 25, 1891.

31 **I am writing to say** The letter was read into evidence at Cream's 1892 trial, and a handwriting expert testified it was in his handwriting. "Trial of Thomas Neill," 1440, 1460.

31   **Deceased died from** "Lambeth Poisoning Mystery."

31   **There is little doubt** "Death by Poisoning. Suicide."

31   **I do not think** Ibid.

31   **"Clearly," he noted** Notation on report, ibid.

32   **This is the poison** "Supposed Capture of the Lambeth Poisoner," *Morning Advertiser* (London), November 4, 1891.

32   **attended Slater's arraignment** Inspector George Harvey Report, November 3, 1891, MEPO 3/144.

32   **That is the man** "The Charge of Attempting to Poison," *Daily News* (London), November 23, 1891.

32   **Supposed Capture** *Morning Advertiser* (London), November 4, 1891.

32   **police had failed** Harvey Report, L Division, November 23, 1891, MEPO 3/144.

32   **There was too much** "Charge of Attempting to Poison."

32   **merely guilty** Ibid.

32   **a ridiculous prosecution** "A Ridiculous Prosecution," *Daily News* (London), December 17, 1891. Slater complained of being "utterly ruined" by the prosecution and publicity, but the government denied his claim for compensation. See "This Morning's News," *Daily News* (London), June 30, 1892.

CHAPTER 4. MATILDA CLOVER

33   **all of a twitch** This account of Clover's death, unless otherwise noted, is based on the statements of Lucy Rose, Francis Coppin, and Emma Phillips, April 28, 1892, Metropolitan Police Office Records, MEPO 3/144, National Archives, London; Rose's testimony at the inquest into Clover's death, reported in "The Mysterious Poisoning Cases in Lambeth," *Daily News* (London), June 23, 1892; and "Trial of Thomas Neill," October 1892, *Proceedings of the Old Bailey, London's Central Criminal Court, 1674 to 1913*, 1423–29, 1432–37, www.oldbaileyonline.org.

35   **twisted and turned** Arthur Conan Doyle, *The Sign of the Four*, in *"A Study in Scarlet" and "The Sign of the Four"* (New York: Peebles Press, 1975). 187. The other quotations in this paragraph are from pp. 188 and 195.

35   **Dr. Graham had spoken** At the inquest into Clover's death, Rose testified she passed along this information to Graham. See "Mysterious Poisoning Cases in Lambeth"; and "The Mysterious Poisoning of Girls," *Reynolds's Newspaper* (London), June 26, 1892.

36   **When she sat** A drawing based on the photograph accompanied the article "The Charge of Poisoning in South London," *Penny Illustrated Paper* (London), July 23, 1892, 57. Clover was described in Report of Dr. Thomas Stevenson on Exhumation of Body of Matilda Clover deceased, and on Analysis of the Viscera, May 6, 1892, MEPO 3/144, as well as in Stevenson's reports reproduced in W. Teignmouth Shore, ed., *Trial of Thomas Neill Cream* (London: William Hodge, 1923), 197, 205.

37   **I noticed a peculiar** Testimony of Elizabeth Masters and Elizabeth May, "Trial of Thomas Neill," 1418–21.

38   **M. Clover, 27 years** Testimony of John Measures, ibid., 1429.

38 **Fourteen other caskets** Shore, *Trial of Thomas Neill Cream*, 26.

38 **Grave No 2215H** Chief Inspector John Mulvany and Inspector George Harvey Memo, April 28, 1892, MEPO 3/144.

38 **a miserable street outcast** *St. James's Gazette* (London), October 22, 1892, quoted in Angus McLaren, *A Prescription for Murder: The Victorian Serial Killings of Dr. Thomas Neill Cream* (Chicago: University of Chicago Press, 1993), 73.

CHAPTER 5. "A HUMAN 'WERE-WOLF'"

39 **London's nightmare** Unless noted, details of the Ripper murders are drawn from Maxim Jakubowski and Nathan Braund, eds., *The Mammoth Book of Jack the Ripper* (London: Robinson, 2008), 3–57. There continues to be debate over how many murders Jack the Ripper committed, but the victims described in this chapter are the "canonical five" that police investigators of the time, and most writers since, have attributed to a single assailant. See Stewart P. Evans and Donald Rumbelow, *Jack the Ripper: Scotland Yard Investigates* (Stroud, UK: History Press, 2006), 260.

39 **"Whitechapel," the panicked** Editorial, *Observer* (London), September 16, 1888.

39 **women of the unfortunate** These descriptions of the victims appeared in "The Shocking Murder in Whitechapel," *Observer* (London), September 2, 1888; "East End Outrages," *Observer* (London), September 9, 1888; and "The East End Murders," *Observer* (London), September 23, 1888.

40 **Hallie Rubenhold has made** Hallie Rubenhold, *The Five: The Untold Lives of the Women Killed by Jack the Ripper* (Boston: Houghton Mifflin Harcourt, 2019).

40 **Many are actually afraid** "The Whitechapel Panic," *Guardian* (Manchester), October 10, 1888.

40 **A massive police operation** These measures were reported in "The Shocking Murder in Whitechapel"; "The East End Murder: The Adjourned Inquest," *Guardian* (Manchester), September 14, 1888; "From Our London Correspondent," *Guardian* (Manchester), October 3, 1888; "The East-End Murders," *Times of London*, October 8, 1888; "The Murders in London," *Times of London*, October 21, 1888; and "Notes," *Observer* (London), November 11, 1888. See also Frederick Porter Wensley, *Forty Years of Scotland Yard: The Record of a Lifetime's Service in the Criminal Investigation Department* (Garden City, NY: Garden City, 1931), 4; and Douglas G. Browne, *The Rise of Scotland Yard: A History of the Metropolitan Police* (London: George G. Harrap, 1956), 208.

40 **The victims, without exception** Melville L. Macnaghten, *Days of My Years* (London: Edward Arnold, 1914), 56.

40 ***Punch* published** The cartoon is reproduced in Peter Stubley, *1888: London Murders in the Year of the Ripper* (Stroud, UK: History Press, 2012), among the images inserted after p. 140.

40 **a consummate master** "The Detection of Crime," *Times of London*, October 11, 1888.

40 **ignorance of the elementary** "The Whitechapel Fiend," *New-York Tribune*, November 11, 1888.

40   **Even if one fell** J. North Conway, *The Big Policeman: The Rise and Fall of America's First, Most Ruthless, and Greatest Detective* (Guilford, CT: Lyons Press, 2010), 5.

41   **All our methods** Editorial, *Times of London*, November 15, 1888.

41   **A young policeman** Wensley, *Forty Years of Scotland Yard*, 1.

42   **A detective must** W. C. Gough, *From Kew Observatory to Scotland Yard: Being Experiences and Travels in 28 Years of Crime Investigation* (London: Hurst & Blackett, 1927), 18.

42   **a visit to the Black** Gordon Honeycombe, *The Murders of the Black Museum 1870–1970* (London: Bloomsbury Books, 1992), 13.

42   **on landings and** Andrew Lansdowne, *A Life's Reminiscences of Scotland Yard* (London: Leadenhall Press, ca. 1890), 15.

42   **many detectives preferred** Ibid., 105; and Wensley, *Forty Years of Scotland Yard*, 19.

42   **The average criminal** Gough, *From Kew Observatory to Scotland Yard*, 20–21.

42   **Wensley once holed up** Wensley, *Forty Years of Scotland Yard*, 65, 80.

43   **The two finest detectives** Gough, *From Kew Observatory to Scotland Yard*, 47.

43   **When a murderer** George Dilnot, *Triumphs of Detection: A Book about Detectives* (London: Geoffrey Bles, 1928), 244.

CHAPTER 6. LOUISA HARVEY

47   **waited beneath the Gothic** This account of Harvey's encounters with Cream, which occurred between October 20 and 25, 1891, is based on her testimony at Cream's 1892 trial. "Trial of Thomas Neill," October 1892, *Proceedings of the Old Bailey, London's Central Criminal Court, 1674 to 1913*, 1452–54, www.oldbaileyonline.org. Additional details are drawn from W. Teignmouth Shore, ed., *Trial of Thomas Neill Cream* (London: William Hodge, 1923), 28–29; "The Lambeth Poisoning Cases," *Daily News* (London), July 8, 1892; "The Lambeth Poisoning Cases," *Standard* (London), July 8, 1892; and "The London Poisoning Cases," *Reynolds's Newspaper* (London), July 10, 1892. Her first name is shortened to Lou or Loo in many accounts of the Cream case.

47   **Now Illuminated Throughout** *London and Fashionable Resorts: A Complete Guide* (London: J. P. Segg, 1892), 117.

47   **World-Famed** Ibid.

47   **And the top hat** Robert C. K. Ensor, *England: 1870–1914* (Oxford: Oxford University Press, 1936), 337.

48   **massive Moorish-themed** The theater is described in "Alhambra Theatre," Cinema Treasures, cinematreasures.org/theaters/30493. Alhambra shows are described in "Vaudeville Theatre," *Times of London*, October 13, 1891; and "The London Music Halls," *Era* (London), October 17, 1891.

48   **High Class Variety Entertainment** *London and Fashionable Resorts*, 116.

48   **improper proposals** Tracy C. Davis, *Actresses as Working Women: Their Social Identity in Victorian Culture* (London: Routledge 1991), 82–83.

48   **brazen-faced women** Liza Picard, *Victorian London: The Life of a City, 1840–1870* (London: Phoenix, 2006), 246.

48   **women of the town** Davis, *Actresses as Working Women*, 151.

52 **If they ever become** The letters to Frederick Smith were read into the record at Cream's trial. See "Trial of Thomas Neill," October 1892, *Proceedings of the Old Bailey, London's Central Criminal Court, 1674 to 1913*, 1440, www.oldbaileyonline.org; and W. Teignmouth Shore, ed., *Trial of Thomas Neill Cream* (London: William Hodge, 1923), 97.

53 **notified the police** Shore, *Trial of Thomas Neill Cream*, 10.

53 **the man you have** The letter was reproduced in "The Lambeth Poisonings," *Daily News* (London), October 18, 1892; it is also noted in Shore, *Trial of Thomas Neill Cream*, 55.

53 **Magistrate Smith showed** Deposition of Frank Thorpe, Central Criminal Court Records, CRIM 1/38/1, National Archives, London.

54 **I am not humbugging** The Broadbent letter was reproduced in "Lambeth Poisonings"; and Shore, *Trial of Thomas Neill Cream*, 49.

54 **another trap was set** Testimony of Dr. William Broadbent, "Trial of Thomas Neill," 1421; and Angus McLaren, *A Prescription for Murder: The Victorian Serial Killings of Dr. Thomas Neill Cream* (Chicago: University of Chicago Press, 1993), 25.

54 **in the midst of** George Robb and Nancy Erber, eds., *Disorder in the Court: Trials and Sexual Conflict at the Turn of the Century* (London: Macmillan Press, 1999), 144.

54 **in a position** Shore, *Trial of Thomas Neill Cream*, 180; and McLaren, *Prescription for Murder*, 25, 152nn14–15.

54 **We treated the matter** Deposition of George Rich, CRIM 1/38/1.

55 **A business known** Charles Wilson, *First with the News: The History of W. H. Smith, 1792–1972* (London: Jonathan Cape, 1985), 4, 186. Smith took over the firm when his father died on October 6, and he was elected MP on October 27. McLaren, *Prescription for Murder*, 24, 152n17; "Election Intelligence," *Times of London*, October 22, 1891.

55 **His name appeared** See, for example, "The Illness of Prince George," *Daily News* (London), November 23, 1891. Biographical details are drawn from "Obituary: Sir William Broadbent," *Times of London*, July 11, 1907. The prince's illness is described in George Arthur, *King George V: A Sketch of a Great Ruler* (London: Jonathan Cape, 1929), 44–45. Broadbent suspected that press coverage of his treatment of the prince made him a target for the blackmail threat. See Jeffrey Bloomfield, "The Doctor Wrote Some Letters," *Criminologist* 15, no. 4 (Winter 1991): 233.

55 **The Russell divorce case** See "The Russell Matrimonial Suit," *Pall Mall Gazette* (London), November 26, 1892; and "Russell Matrimonial Case," *Lloyd's Weekly Newspaper* (London), November 29, 1891.

56 **To accuse a man** "England Is Called Blackmailer's Home," *Daily Inter Ocean* (Chicago), December 31, 1905.

56 **unaware of the letters** The lead investigator first referred to one of the letters—the one sent to Lady Russell—in June 1892. Inspector John Bennett Tunbridge Report, June 6, 1892, Metropolitan Police Office Records, MEPO 3/144, National Archives, London.

57 **Don't you know me?** Testimony of Louisa Harvey, "Trial of Thomas Neill," 1453.

Harvey also recounted their conversation, with slight changes of wording, in a letter to the Bow Street Magistrate's Court and when she testified at the coroner's inquest into the death of Matilda Clover in June 1892. See Shore, *Trial of Thomas Neill Cream*, 29, 187.

57 **a young woman** Sabbatini was described in "The Lambeth Poisoning Cases," *Daily News* (London), June 25, 1892.

57 **I shall be as faithful** December 1, 1892, letter to Sabbatini was reproduced in "Neill Still in Newgate," *Lloyd's Weekly Newspaper* (London), October 30, 1892. The brief courtship is described in Shore, *Trial of Thomas Neill Cream*, 117–18, 184–85; and Testimony of Laura Sabbatini, "Trial of Thomas Neill," 1451.

57 **She was aware** Testimony of Sabbatini, "Trial of Thomas Neill," 1451.

57 **free of all vicious** Statement of Mrs. Sabbatini, September 23, 1892, MEPO 3/144.

57 **placed under restraint** Inspector Frederick Smith Jarvis Report, July 4, 1892 (Montreal), ibid.

58 **He seems to have** Affidavit of Thomas Davidson, October 29, 1892, Home Office Records, HO 144/246 A 54360/23, National Archives, London.

58 **His friends here** Thomas Davidson to Rev. George Mathews, December 15, 1891, HO 144/246 A 54360/25.

58 **He told Sabbatini** Testimony of Sabbatini, "Trial of Thomas Neill," 1451; and Shore, *Trial of Thomas Neill Cream*, 118.

CHAPTER 8. "A BAD MAN WITH NO REFINEMENT"

59 **He was very restless** Sellar's account of the voyage is told in Inspector Frederick Smith Jarvis Report, September 2, 1892 (Montreal), Metropolitan Police Office Records, MEPO 3/144, National Archives, London.

60 **acted in every** Jarvis Report, July 15, 1892 (Toronto), ibid.; and Statement of William Fisher, July 21, 1892, ibid. Fisher, the steward for Cream's cabin, confirmed he was "more or less drunk" for the entire voyage and "was continually speaking about prostitutes and women."

61 **He constantly spoke about women** Jarvis Report, July 29, 1892 (New York), ibid. On Vohl's background, see William Cochrane, ed., *The Canadian Album: Men of Canada*, vol. 2 (Brantford, ON: Bradley, Garretson, 1893), 88.

61 **a woman who had** Sergeant John Craggs Memo, June 20, 1892, MEPO 3/144.

61 **Cream arrived** Cream's arrival date is recorded in Jarvis Report, June 30, 1892 (Quebec City), ibid.

61 **It is poison** Jarvis Report, July 19, 1892 (Montreal), ibid.; and Testimony of John Wilson McCulloch, "Trial of Thomas Neill," October 1892, *Proceedings of the Old Bailey, London's Central Criminal Court, 1674 to 1913*, 1438–39, www.oldbaileyonline.org.

62 **the rooms were cheap** *The Maritime Provinces: A Handbook for Travelers* (Boston: Houghton, Mifflin, 1890), 255.

62 **As matters now stand** Jarvis Report, June 30, 1892 (Quebec City), MEPO 3/144.

62 **Daniel Cream dropped by** Ibid.

62 **in a perfect stupor** Jarvis Report, July 19, 1892 (Montreal), ibid.

63 **a loose sort** Jarvis Report, July 21, 1892 (Saratoga, NY), ibid.

63 **array of deadly narcotics** Cream's order was reproduced in Jarvis Report, August 25, 1892 (Montreal), ibid.

63 **He expected to make** Jarvis Reports, July 4, 1892 (Montreal) and July 19, 1892 (Montreal), ibid.

63 **Take one at tea time** "The London Blackmailer," *Quebec Saturday Budget* (Quebec City), July 16, 1892.

64 **commissioned a local printer** Jarvis Reports, June 30, 1892 (Quebec City), July 4, 1892 (Montreal), and July 7, 1892 (Montreal), ibid.

64 **Ellen Donworth's Death** The circular is reproduced in W. Teignmouth Shore, ed., *Trial of Thomas Neill Cream* (London: William Hodge, 1923), facing p. 17.

64 **given a discount** Jarvis Reports, July 21, 1892 (Saratoga, NY) and August 25, 1892 (Montreal), MEPO 3/144.

65 **one of the 220** Jarvis Report, July 7, 1892 (Montreal), ibid. The *New York Times* noted Cream's name on the passenger list in an article titled "Off to Europe," March 24, 1892.

CHAPTER 9. ALICE MARSH AND EMMA SHRIVELL

66 **heard a door creak** Comley's description of Cream is based on his notes and his testimony in court. See "Trial of Thomas Neill," October 1892, *Proceedings of the Old Bailey, London's Central Criminal Court, 1674 to 1913*, 1455–56, www .oldbaileyonline.org; W. Teignmouth Shore, ed., *Trial of Thomas Neill Cream* (London: William Hodge, 1923), 189; and Constable George Comley Report, April 12, 1892, Metropolitan Police Office Records, MEPO 3/144, National Archives, London.

66 **swarming with brothels** Thomas R. C. Gibson-Brydon, *The Moral Mapping of Victorian and Edwardian London: Charles Booth, Christian Charity, and the Poor-but-Respectable* (Montreal: McGill-Queen's University Press, 2016), 65.

67 **There is one more inside** Comley Report, April 12, 1892, MEPO 3/144.

67 **some powerful poison** Police Constable William Eversfield Report, April 13, 1892, ibid.

67 **She held up** Details of Shrivell's statements are based on the officers' reports; court testimony; and Depositions of Comley and Eversfield, Central Criminal Court Records, CRIM 1/38/1, National Archives, London.

67 **Accidental poisoning** Inspector George Lowe Report, L Division, April 12, 1892, MEPO 3/144.

68 **The British Admiralty** "The Admiralty and the Tinned Fish," *Pall Mall Gazette* (London), May 6, 1892.

68 **Reports in the next** "Fatal Poisoning Case," *Times of London*, April 13, 1892; and "Mysterious Death of Two Girls," *Pall Mall Gazette* (London), April 13, 1892.

68 **specific, deadly poison** Testimony of Dr. Cuthbert Wyman, "Trial of Thomas Neill," 1456.

68 **Do you think** "The Poisoning of Two Girls in South London," *Daily News* (London), April 14, 1892. Evidence presented on the first day of the inquest was summarized in Lowe Report, April 13, 1892, MEPO 3/144.

68 **performed autopsies** Stevenson's notes on cases of Marsh and Shrivell, reproduced in Shore, *Trial of Thomas Neill Cream*, 192.

69 **This points** Chief Inspector John Mulvany and Inspector George Harvey Report, April 21, 1892, MEPO 3/144.

69 **No effort will be** Ibid.

69 **"*Clifton*, another"** Lowe Report, April 12, 1892, ibid. (emphasis in original).

69 **bore a good character** Letter, Detective Inspector Samuel Jupp and Chief Constable James Terry to Superintendent James Brannan, April 13, 1892, ibid.; and "Poisoning of Two Girls in South London."

70 **found work** Jupp and Terry to Brannan, April 13, 1892.

70 **Brannan sent a sergeant** Sergeant John McCarthy Report, April 21, 1892, and Mulvany and Harvey Report, April 21, 1892, MEPO 3/144.

70 **wreaths placed on their** Letter, Detective Inspector Samuel Jupp to Chief Constable James Terry, April 28, 1892, ibid.

70 **written on the letterhead** Copy of Letter Found at Lodgings of Deceased, dated April 10, 1892, ibid.

70 **The local constabulary** Mulvany and Harvey Report, April 16, 1892, ibid.; and Letter, Superintendent Edward Coppinger to Superintendent James Brannan, April 28, 1892, ibid.

70 **Every inquiry is now** Mulvany and Harvey Report, April 16, 1892, ibid.

70 **Slater was tall** Testimony of George Harvey, "Trial of Thomas Neill," 1447.

70 **Comley was reassigned** Mulvany and Harvey Report, April 21, 1892, MEPO 3/144.

70 **All efforts to trace** Mulvany and Harvey Report, April 28, 1892, ibid.

CHAPTER 10. BITTER MEDICINE

71 **I proceeded** Descriptions of Stevenson's tests and conclusions are based on his notes and report, reproduced in W. Teignmouth Shore, ed., *Trial of Thomas Neill Cream* (London: William Hodge, 1923), 192–96, 203–5, as well as on his trial testimony, recorded in "Trial of Thomas Neill," October 1892, *Proceedings of the Old Bailey, London's Central Criminal Court, 1674 to 1913*, 1456–57, www.oldbaileyonline.org.

72 **it was sold** Linda Stratmann, *The Secret Poisoner: A Century of Murder* (New Haven, CT: Yale University Press, 2016), 19–20.

72 *poudre de succession* John Emsley, *The Elements of Murder: A History of Poison* (Oxford: Oxford University Press, 2005), 142.

72 **Fatal Facility** *Punch*, September 8, 1849, reproduced in Katherine Watson, *Poisoned Lives: English Poisoners and Their Victims* (London: Hambleton & London, 2004), image 4 of insert between pp. 114 and 115.

72 **symptoms of a lethal** Arsenic's effects and widespread use in the nineteenth century are discussed in Kathryn Harkup, *A Is for Arsenic: The Poisons of Agatha Christie* (London: Bloomsbury Sigma, 2015), 22–30.

72 **laboratory test** The Marsh test for the presence of arsenic, named for its developer, the British chemist James Marsh, was first used in a criminal trial in 1840. Ibid., 24–25.

SOURCES

73   **Poison Book** Tony Hargreaves, *Poisons and Poisonings: Death by Stealth* (Cambridge: Royal Society of Chemistry, 2017), 13.

73   **out of fashion** Stratmann, *Secret Poisoner*, 188.

73   **variety of plant toxins** Watson, *Poisoned Lives*, 20–21; and Jürgen Thorwald, *Proof of Poison* (London: Camelot Press, 1966), 44–45.

73   **It attacks the central** Harkup, *A Is for Arsenic*, 239–40.

73   **as a muscle stimulant** Strychnine's uses are noted in Hargreaves, *Poisons and Poisonings*, 66.

73   **As little as half** Harkup, *A Is for Arsenic*, 246.

73   **In the present state** Quoted in Stratmann, *Secret Poisoner*, 144.

73   the whole frame shudders William Fuller Alves Boys, *A Practical Treatise on the Office and Duties of Coroners in Ontario*, 2nd ed. (Toronto: Hart & Rawlinson, 1878), 75.

74   **In the roster** Harkup, *A Is for Arsenic*, 241.

74   **first to use strychnine** The evidence that Wainewright was a serial poisoner is discussed in Andrew Motion, *Wainewright the Poisoner: The Confession of Thomas Griffiths Wainewright* (New York: Alfred A. Knopf, 2000), 153–54.

74   **Strychnine would not make** George R. Knott, "William Palmer—1856," in *Famous Trials 1*, ed. Harry Hodge (Melbourne, London, and Baltimore: Penguin Books, 1941), 140.

74   **drank brandy and coffee** Details of the Palmer case, unless otherwise noted, are drawn from Stephen Bates, *The Poisoner: The Life and Crimes of Victorian England's Most Notorious Doctor* (New York: Overlook Duckworth, 2014); and Stratmann, *Secret Poisoner*, 171–86.

75   **admitted at Palmer's trial** Taylor's conclusions and the defense position are discussed in Bates, *Poisoner*, 55, 199, 203–47.

75   **deadly cat and mouse** Deborah Blum, *The Poisoner's Handbook: Murder and the Birth of Forensic Medicine in Jazz Age New York* (New York: Penguin Books, 2010), 2.

76   **battery of chemical tests** Hargreaves, *Poison and Poisonings*, 226; and Thorwald, *Proof of Poison*, 63–64. The taste tests and animal experiments are described in Harkup, *A Is for Arsenic*, 247, and Watson, *Poisoned Lives*, 26–28.

76   **all poisonous vegetable alkaloids** Cited in Stratmann, *Secret Poisoner*, 217–18.

76   **could simply visit** Watson, *Poisoned Lives*, 145–46.

76   **able to buy thirty** The Edmunds case is recounted in ibid., 218–26; and Lisa Appignanesi, *Trials of Passion: Crimes Committed in the Name of Love and Madness* (New York: Pegasus Books, 2015), 13–134.

77   **So dangerous an article** Quoted in Stratmann, *Secret Poisoner*, 226.

77   **Almost two hundred doctors** Alannah Tomkins, *Medical Misadventure in an Age of Professionalisation, 1780–1890* (Manchester: Manchester University Press, 2017), 176–77.

77   **He is different** Rupert Furneaux, *The Medical Murderer* (London: Elek Books, 1957), 9–10.

77   **attributing the deaths** The Pritchard case is recounted in ibid., 55–61; "A Deadly Bedside Manner," *Scotsman*, November 18, 2005; and Emsley, *Elements of Murder*, 229–32.

77   **a brother medical man** Tomkins, *Medical Misadventure in an Age of Professionalisation*, 177.

77 **Of all types** Furneaux, *Medical Murderer*, 25.

77 **the hardest man** "Doctors as Criminals," *Cincinnati Medical Journal* 12, no. 7 (July 1895): 518.

78 **the most difficult** Boys, *Practical Treatise*, 81, 83–84, 88.

78 **with a scrupulous regard** Ibid., 138–40.

79 **The opinion of a distinguished** Stratmann, *Secret Poisoner*, 193.

79 **an absolute and blind** Alfred S. Taylor, *On Poisoning by Strychnia, with Comments on the Medical Evidence Given at the Trial of William Palmer for the Murder of John Parsons Cook* (London: Longman, Brown, Green, Longmans & Roberts, 1856), 4.

79 **Thomas Smethurst** Details of the Smethurst case are drawn from Stratmann, *Secret Poisoner*, 193–202; and Emsley, *Elements of Murder*, 156–58.

80 **brought an amount** Quoted in Douglas G. Browne and E. V. Tullett, *Bernard Spilsbury: His Life and Cases* (Harmondsworth, UK: Penguin Books, 1951), 20.

80 **In the eyes** Colin Evans, *The Father of Forensics: The Groundbreaking Cases of Sir Bernard Spilsbury, and the Beginnings of Modern CSI* (New York: Berkley Books, 2006), 3.

80 **joined the staff** Biographical information on Dr. Stevenson, unless otherwise noted, is drawn from Stratmann, *Secret Poisoner*, 241; Thorwald, *Proof of Poison*, 78–79; Watson, *Poisoned Lives*, 171–73; and "Sir Thomas Stevenson," *Guardian* (Manchester), July 29, 1908.

80 **He never jumped** "The Poison-Finder," *Guardian* (Manchester), July 29, 1908.

80 **To the guilty** "A Master of Poisons," *Washington Post*, August 16, 1908.

80 **with the pitiless** "Another Marathon Protest," *Sun* (New York), August 9, 1908.

80 **at least fifty** Thorwald, *Proof of Poison*, 78.

81 **George Henry Lamson** Details of the Lamson case are drawn from Hargrave L. Adam, "Dr Lamson—1882," in *Famous Trials* 5, ed. James H. Hodge (London: Penguin Books, 1955); and Stratmann, *Secret Poisoner*, 239–45.

82 **biting and numbing effect** Adam, "Dr Lamson—1882," 180.

82 **no known chemical test** Thorwald, *Proof of Poison*, 79.

CHAPTER 11. "A STRANGE CUSTOMER"

83 **death from strychnine** "The Stamford Street Poisoning Mystery," *Pall Mall Gazette* (London), May 6, 1892.

83 **The police had not** "The Stamford Street Poisoning Case," *Reynolds's Newspaper* (London), May 8, 1892.

84 **exhaustive enquiries** Chief Inspector John Mulvany and Inspector George Harvey Report, May 5, 1892, Metropolitan Police Office Records, MEPO 3/144, National Archives, London.

84 **Apparently there will be** "Stamford Street Poisoning Case." This report also noted the crowd in the hearing room.

84 **Superintendent James Brannan** Application for Special Enquiry to Be Made in Divisions, April 27, 1892, MEPO 3/144. The application was updated on May 2 with the notation "No information obtained."

84 **Police in Chatham** Superintendent Edward Coppinger to Superintendent James Brannan, May 1, 1892, ibid.

84 **a sea captain** This and the other quotations in this paragraph are from Statement of Charles Burdett, May 6, 1892, ibid.

84 **A ship's officer** Mulvany and Harvey Reports, May 7, 1892, and May 16, 1892, ibid.

84 **Police in Liverpool** Superintendent James Brannan to Chief Superintendent George Williams, May 9, 1892, ibid.; and Chief Inspector George Marsh to Superintendent James Brannan, May 18, 1892, ibid.

85 **going door to door** Testimony of George Comley and Alfred Ward, "Trial of Thomas Neill," October 1892, *Proceedings of the Old Bailey, London's Central Criminal Court, 1674 to 1913*, 1446–47, www.oldbaileyonline.org.

85 **Another case has come** Mulvany and Harvey Report, April 28, 1892, MEPO 3/144.

85 **authorized the exhumation** W. Teignmouth Shore, ed., *The Trial of Thomas Neill Cream* (London: William Hodge, 1923), 197.

85 **Without doubt** Brannan to Williams, May 9, 1892, MEPO 3/144.

86 **Musical Eccentrics** Classified advertisement on p. 27 of *Era*, May 7, 1892, and May 14, 1892.

86 **would recall Comley** Testimony of Comley and Ward, "Trial of Thomas Neill," 1455–58; and Mulvany and Harvey Report, May 16, 1892, MEPO 3/144.

86 **lived solely to indulge** Mulvany and Harvey Report, May 16, 1892, MEPO 3/144.

86 **It is important** Ibid.

86 **an American drink** Mulvany and Harvey Report, May 19, 1892, ibid. A photograph of the samples case was reproduced in Luke Spencer, "Getting in the Minds of Murderers at London's Hidden Crime Museum," *Atlas Obscura*, February 17, 2016, www.atlasobscura.com/articles/getting-in-the-minds-of-murderers-at-londons-hidden-crime-museum.

87 **Dr. Neal** Mulvany and Harvey Report, May 19, 1892, MEPO 3/144.

88 **exactly what a person** Mulvany and Harvey Report, May 23, 1892, ibid.

88 **He is an extremely** Ibid.

88 **a strange customer** Mulvany and Harvey Report, May 20, 1892, ibid.

88 **I know from experience** Notation on ibid.

88 **lodge a complaint** Mulvany and Harvey Report, May 19, 1892, ibid.

88 **had worked for** Testimony of Patrick McIntyre, "Trial of Thomas Neill," 1446.

89 **well known among** Haynes's account in this paragraph is drawn from Statement of John Patrick Haynes, May 23, 1892, MEPO 3/144; and Testimony of John Patrick Haynes, "Trial of Thomas Neill," 1441–43.

89 **Dear Sir** The letter was read into the record at Cream's trial. See "Trial of Thomas Neill," 1440.

89 **Wyatt had ignored** The Wyatt and Clarke letters and the connection to the Donworth circular were discussed in the Mulvany and Harvey Report, May 23, 1892, MEPO 3/144.

90 **provided the Coroner** Testimony of Laura Sabbatini, "Trial of Thomas Neill," 1459.

90 **may be guilty** Statement of Haynes, May 23, 1892, MEPO 3/144.

90 **as he is frequently** Mulvany and Harvey Report, May 23, 1892, ibid.

90 **a highly respectable person** Statement of Emily Sleaper, May 23, 1892, ibid.; and Testimony of Emily Sleaper, "Trial of Thomas Neill," 1431.

90 **Get a specimen** Notation on Statement of Haynes, May 23, 1892, MEPO 3/144.

CHAPTER 12. THE SUSPECT

---

91   **If Haynes can be** Notation on Chief Inspector John Mulvany and Inspector George Harvey Report, May 19, 1892, Metropolitan Police Office Records, MEPO 3/144, National Archives, London.

91   **in his fifteenth year** Register of Leavers from the Metropolitan Police, MEPO 4/353/62195.

91   **a St. Thomas's man** This description of McIntyre's dealings with Cream is based on Statement of Patrick McIntyre, May 30, 1892, MEPO 3/144; and Testimony of Patrick McIntyre, "Trial of Thomas Neill," October 1892, *Proceedings of the Old Bailey, London's Central Criminal Court, 1674 to 1913*, 1444–46, www.oldbaileyonline.org.

92   **He talked readily** This account of the interview at 103 Lambeth Palace Road is drawn from Mulvany and Harvey Report, May 24, 1892, MEPO 3/144; and Statement of McIntyre, May 30, 1892, ibid.

93   **Lambeth's "poisoner of prostitutes"** "The Case of Poisoning in Stamford Street," *British Medical Journal* 1, no. 1637 (May 14, 1892): 1042.

93   **Being a medical man** Testimony of McIntyre, "Trial of Thomas Neill," 1445.

93   **monitoring L Division's investigation** See his notation on "Death by Poisoning. Suicide," L Division Report, October 23, 1892, MEPO 3/144.

93   **when the secretary of state** Secretary of State's Office to Assistant Commissioner Robert Anderson, May 21, 1892, ibid.

93   **"These women," as one** Mulvany and Harvey Report, May 23, 1892, ibid. On other inquiries among Lambeth prostitutes, see Statement of Ida B. Houstine, May 23, 1892, ibid; Mulvany and Harvey Report, May 24, 1892, ibid.; Statement of Elizabeth Sullivan, May 25, 1892, ibid.; and Inspector George Harvey Report, May 26, 1892, ibid. The list of ships was noted in the May 24 report of Mulvany and Harvey.

93   **The officer sent** Sergeant John McCarthy Report, May 26, 1892, ibid.

93   **a search of London's death records** Sergeant John McCarthy and Inspector George Harvey Report, May 28, 1892, ibid.

93   **He had found strychnine** Dr. Thomas Stevenson to Sir Augustus Stephenson, May 23, 1892, ibid.

94   **As our client is not** Waters & Bryan to Sir Edward Bradford, May 26, 1892, ibid.

94   **I told him** Statement of McIntyre, May 30, 1892, ibid.

94   **He would not** Ibid.

94   **The stalled Lambeth investigation** Memo, "Rewards in Thos. Neill's Case: Murder," November 11, 1892, MEPO 3/144.

94   **I am anxious** Assistant Commissioner Robert Anderson to Waters & Bryan, May 27, 1892, ibid.

94   **Tunbridge was a rising** Biographical details are drawn from Register of Leavers from the Metropolitan Police, MEPO 4/340/52085; and "John Bennett Tunbridge," *Te Ara: The Encyclopedia of New Zealand*, teara.govt.nz/en/biographies/2t52/tunbridge-john-bennett.

94   **one of the smartest** Melville L. Macnaghten, *Days of My Years* (London: Edward Arnold, 1914), 274.

95   **As wary as a** "Alice Woodhall's Booty," *New York Times*, June 6, 1888.

SOURCES

95   **capable of a brilliant** George Dilnot, *Triumphs of Detection: A Book about Detectives* (London: Geoffrey Bles, 1928), 245.

95   **a process too "delicate,"** Colin Beavan, *Fingerprints: The Origins of Crime Detection and the Murder Case that Launched Forensic Science* (New York: Hyperion, 2001), 91.

96   **Assuming Haynes' statement** Inspector John Bennett Tunbridge Report, May 28–29, 1892, MEPO 3/144. This is also the source of the details that follow of Tunbridge's May 29 interview with Cream.

96   **Cream had been taking** His escalating drug use was noted in ibid; Testimony of John Patrick Haynes, "Trial of Thomas Neill," 1444; and "The Poisoner Neill: A Study of His Crimes by One Who Knew Him," *St. James's Gazette* (London), October 24, 1892.

Chapter 13. "You Have Got the Wrong Man"

98   **indisputable evidence** The letter was reproduced in "The Stamford Street Tragedy," *Observer* (London), June 5, 1892.

98   **He had consulted** "Charge of Blackmailing," *Illustrated Police News* (London), June 18, 1892.

99   **Someone's idea** This was Walter Harper's assessment when he testified at the Clover inquest. See "The Lambeth Poisoning Cases," *Daily News* (London), July 14, 1892.

99   **That Neill was the writer** Inspector John Bennett Tunbridge Report, June 3, 1892, Metropolitan Police Office Records, MEPO 3/144, National Archives, London.

100   **Otherwise we may be** Ibid.

100   **It was manufactured** The manufacturer was the Fairfield Paper Company of Salmon Falls, Massachusetts. See "Trade Items," *American Stationer*, July 26, 1888, 181.

100   **close & careful investigation** This and the quotations in the next paragraph are from Assistant Commissioner Robert Anderson to Home Office, June 4, 1892, MEPO 3/144.

101   **You have got** Cream's arrest was described in Tunbridge Report, June 6, 1892, ibid.; and Testimony of John Bennett Tunbridge, "Trial of Thomas Neill," October 1892, *Proceedings of the Old Bailey, London's Central Criminal Court, 1674 to 1913*, 1448–49, www.oldbaileyonline.org.

101   **Enquiry should be made** Tunbridge Report, June 11, 1892, MEPO 3/144.

102   **Care should be taken** Ibid.

102   **any clue they may** Home Office undersecretary Godfrey Lushington to Assistant Commissioner Robert Anderson, June 9, 1892, ibid.

Chapter 14. Jarvis of the Yard

105   **one of the shrewdest** "Inspector Jarvis's Mission," *New York Times*, June 29, 1892.

105   **biggest man at the Yard** "Bank Robbers Will Rejoice," *City Affairs* (London), August 28, 1897.

105 **helped round up** "The Dynamite Outrages," *Times of London*, February 3, 1885; "The Tower Explosion," *Guardian* (Manchester), February 6, 1885; and "The Dynamite Explosions," *Guardian* (Manchester), February 24, 1885.

105 **devoted all his energies** "A Famous Detective," *New York Times*, September 6, 1897 (reproducing a *Daily Telegraph* report).

105 **a rough fellow** Ibid.

105 **highly educated man** Ibid.

107 **A man of the world** Melville L. Macnaghten, *Days of My Years* (London: Edward Arnold, 1914), 274–75.

107 **once tracked a fraudster** "The United States," *Times of London*, January 14, 1889; and "The Charge against a Macclesfield Manufacturer," *Guardian* (Manchester), April 19, 1889.

107 **An earthquake** George Dilnot, *Triumphs of Detection: A Book about Detectives* (London: Geoffrey Bles, 1928), 137.

107 **Thousands of people** "Famous Detective."

107 **Jarvis's high-profile** See, for instance, "Jarvis, of Scotland Yard," *Evening World* (New York), June 28, 1892; "Inspector Jarvis's Mission"; "Feeling against Cream," *Montreal Daily Herald*, July 2, 1892; "Tracing Cream's Record," *Montreal Daily Witness*, July 15, 1892; and "The Cream Case," *Quebec Saturday Budget*, September 24, 1892.

107 **no suspicious deaths** Inspector Frederick Smith Jarvis to Scotland Yard, June 30, 1892, Metropolitan Police Office Records, MEPO 3/144, National Archives, London; Inspector Frederick Smith Jarvis Report, June 30, 1892 (Quebec City), ibid.; and "Inspector Jarvis's Mission."

107 **privileged upbringing** Jarvis Reports, June 30, 1892 (Quebec City) and July 4, 1892 (Montreal), MEPO 3/144.

108 **got over this matter** Jarvis Report, July 4, 1892 (Montreal), ibid.

CHAPTER 15. "A YOUNG MAN OF RARE ABILITY"

109 **Tourists in search** *Guide to Quebec and the Lower Saint-Lawrence, Compiled Expressly for This Season* (Quebec, 1882), 3. This description is also based on *The Canadian Handbook and Tourist's Guide* (Montreal: M. Longmoore, 1867), 17; and "Quebec," *New York Times*, September 20, 1867.

110 **away in a corner** Inspector Frederick Smith Jarvis Report, August 11, 1892 (New York City), Metropolitan Police Office Records, MEPO 3/144, National Archives, London.

110 **born in Ireland** Census records identify William Cream's birthplace as Ireland, and a close friend confirmed he was from Belfast. Thomas Davidson to Frances Willard, June 22, 1890, Secretary of State, Executive Section, Records of Commutations of Sentence, 1877–1928, Record Series 103.098, Illinois State Archives, Springfield.

110 **picturesque steep streets** Charles Dickens, *American Notes and Pictures from Italy* (Geneva: Edito-Service, n.d.), 249.

110 **Gibraltar of America** Ibid.

110   **Every stick** Arthur R. M. Lower, *Great Britain's Woodyard: British America and the Timber Trade, 1763–1867* (Montreal: McGill-Queen's University Press, 1973), 215. The timber rafts are described in J. E. Bernier, *Master Mariner and Arctic Explorer: A Narrative of Sixty Years at Sea from the Logs and Yarns of Captain J. E. Bernier* (Ottawa: Le Droit, 1939), 172–73, and in Dickens, *American Notes*, 248.

111   **the appearance of one** Eileen Reid Marcil, *The Charley-Man: A History of Wooden Shipbuilding at Quebec, 1763–1893* (Kingston, ON: Quarry Press, 1995), 123.

111   **major player** Ibid., 120. Details of Pollok, Gilmour & Company's operations are drawn from Frederick William Wallace, *In the Wake of the Wind-ships* (Toronto: Musson Book, 1927), 78–80, and David Macmillan, "Allan Gilmour (1805–1884)," in *Dictionary of Canadian Biography*, www.biographi.ca/en/bio/gilmour_allan_1805_84_11E.html.

111   **Cream may well** Cream was identified as a clerk at Wolfe's Cove as early as 1856 in the Cream Family Index Cards, Chalmers-Wesley United Church, Quebec City (I am indebted to the secretary of Chalmers-Wesley, David Rourke, for providing these records.) Cream is described as Gilmour's "cove manager" in George Gale, *Quebec: Twixt Old . . . and . . . New* (Quebec: Telegraph Printing, 1915), 68.

112   **The Creams moved into** Jarvis Report, June 30, 1892 (Quebec City), MEPO 3/144.

112   **in charge of timber** For examples of legal issues that Cream dealt with as manager, see *William Cain v. William Cream*, September 8, 1866; and *Narcisse Morency v. William Cream*, July 28, 1875. Archives des notaires du Québec, records of Romuald Couillard de Beaumont (1865–82) and Marcel Bourget (1865–94). Bibliothèque et Archives nationales du Québec, Quebec City. Both disputes were over timber shipments.

112   **It must be desperation** Quoted in Lorne F. Hammond, "Capital, Labour and Lumber in A. R. M. Lower's Woodyard: James Maclaren and the Changing Forest Economy, 1850–1906" (PhD diss., University of Ottawa, 1993), 85.

112   **an energetic, smart businessman** Richard M. Reid, "James Maclaren (1818–1892)," in *Dictionary of Canadian Biography*, www.biographi.ca/en/bio/maclaren_james_12E.html.

112   **They met in 1865** Details of Cream's role as agent and his relationship with Maclaren are drawn from Hammond, "Capital, Labour and Lumber," 162–66.

112   **In a recent letter** Ibid., 166.

113   **The layout** Marc Lafrance and David-Thierry Ruddel, "Physical Expansion and Socio-Cultural Segregation in Quebec City, 1765–1840," in *Shaping the Urban Landscape: Aspects of the Canadian City-Building Process*, ed. Gilbert A. Stelter and Alan F. J. Artibise (Ottawa: Carleton University Press, 1982), 148–72.

113   **rough, powerful men** Frederick William Wallace, *Wooden Ships and Iron Men* (London: White Lion, 1973), 99.

113   **thugs known as crimps** Judith Fingard, *Jack in Port: Sailortowns of Eastern Canada* (Toronto: University of Toronto Press, 1982), 212, 215.

113   **three out of four** Lafrance and Ruddel, "Physical Expansion and Socio-Cultural Segregation," 162.

113   **generous with his** In 1877 and 1878, for instance, he donated to a Presbyterian college and a missionary fund. *The Canadian Congregational Year Book 1877–8* (Toronto: Congregational Publishing, 1877), 136; and *The Canadian Congregational Year Book 1878–9* (Ottawa: Congregational Publishing, 1878), 107, 168.

113   **founding member** Gale, *Quebec*, 245.

114   **Godfearing** Thomas Davidson to Illinois governor Joseph Fifer, March 10, 1890, Records of Commutations of Sentence, 1877-1928, Record Series 103.098, Illinois State Archives, Springfield.

114   **hath fed me** Last Will and Testament, William Cream, November 1885, appended to the probate petition of Daniel Cream, May 25, 1887, Records of the Superior Court for the Province of Quebec, Bibliothèque et Archives nationales du Québec, Quebec City.

114   **Every one of them** Davidson to Fifer.

114   **neo-Gothic stone walls** Details about the church and its history are drawn from George W. Crawford, *Remember All the Way: The History of Chalmers-Wesley United Church, Quebec City* (Montreal: Price-Patterson, 2006), 145–68. A description from the *Quebec Gazette*, March 7, 1853, appears on p. 149.

115   **dissatisfied with choir** Cream Family Index Cards, Chalmers-Wesley United Church; Eileen Marcil, "John Munn (1788–1859)," in *Dictionary of Canadian Biography*, www.biographi.ca/en/bio/munn_john_1788_1859_8E.html. William Cream returned to Chalmers in November 1880. His son Daniel and daughter Rachel rejoined in 1882, when the Congregational church closed.

115   **school the Gilmour company** Jarvis Report, June 30, 1892 (Quebec City), MEPO 3/144.

115   **Thomas taught** Angus McLaren, *A Prescription for Murder: The Victorian Serial Killings of Dr. Thomas Neill Cream* (Chicago: University of Chicago Press, 1993), 33; and "Old London's Sensation," *Globe* (Toronto), June 28, 1892.

115   **incapable of anything disreputable** Letter, Thomas Davidson, October 18, 1888, Records of Commutations of Sentence, 1877-1928, Record Series 103.098, Illinois State Archives, Springfield.

115   **only three of five** The findings of a survey conducted in 1867, cited in Richard Gwyn, *John A., The Man Who Made Us: The Life and Times of John A. Macdonald,* vol. 1, *1815–1867* (Toronto: Random House Canada, 2007), 28.

115   **life expectancy in Canada** Lance W. Roberts, Rodney A. Clifton, Barry Ferguson, Karen Kampen, and Simon Langlois, eds., *Recent Social Trends in Canada, 1960– 2000* (Montreal: McGill-Queen's University Press, 2005), 23.

115   **One of the ways** J. K. Johnson, ed., *Affectionately Yours: The Letters of Sir John A. Macdonald and His Family* (Toronto: Macmillan of Canada, 1969), 11.

115   **The Cream family** The deaths of Christina and Hannah Cream are recorded in the Registrie d'inhumation du Mount Hermon Cemetery, Quebec City, 1846–1904, Bibliothèque et Archives nationales du Quebec, accessed through www.ancestry.com.

116   **His affection and anxiety** James Emslie to Thomas Davidson, October 18, 1888, Records of Commutations of Sentence, 1877-1928, Record Series 103.098, Illinois State Archives, Springfield.

116   **Brief newspaper** *Quebec Mercury*, January 18, 1870; and *Morning Chronicle and Commercial and Shipping Gazette* (Quebec City) January 18, 1870. Thomas was listed as one of the official witnesses to her burial: Burial Record, Mary Cream, January 19, 1870, Vital and Church Records 1621–1968, Drouin Collection, Institut généalogique Drouin, Montreal, accessed through www.ancestry.com. Frost often delayed internment until the spring, but unseasonably mild weather appears to have allowed for

an immediate burial for Mary Cream. There were, for instance, fifty-five burials in Montreal's cemeteries during the week ending January 15. "City Mortality," *Montreal Gazette*, January 18, 1870.

116 **third-generation shipbuilder** Eileen Marcil, "William Henry Baldwin (1827–1894)," *Dictionary of Canadian Biography*, www.biographi.ca/en/bio/baldwin_william_henry_12E.html.

116 **confidential clerk** Letter, William H. Baldwin, October 18, 1888, and Letter, Peter Baldwin, November 27, 1888, Records of Commutations of Sentence, 1877-1928, Record Series 103.098. Illinois State Archives, Springfield. When Thomas began work at the shipyard is unclear, but Peter Baldwin stated he had worked for William Baldwin for "a number of years previous" to 1870.

116 **a perfect young man** Letter, William H. Baldwin, October 18, 1888.

116 **gave every satisfaction** Letter, Peter Baldwin, November 27, 1888.

117 **prove that Quebec** Descriptions of the fire, efforts to save the Baldwin shipyard, and the impact on the industry are drawn from "Tremendous Conflagration," *Morning Chronicle and Commercial and Shipping Gazette* (Quebec City), May 24, 1870; "Great Fire in St. Roch's," *Quebec Mercury*, May 25, 1870; and "The Recent Conflagration," *Quebec Mercury*, May 26, 1870.

117 **continued to produce wooden** On the decline of the shipbuilding and timber industries, see Wallace, *Wooden Ships and Iron Men*, 263, 269, 310; Marcil, *Charley-Man*, 68–69; and Lower, *Great Britain's Woodyard*, 130–33.

117 **William Cream branched** *Sessional Papers of the Parliament of the Dominion of Canada*, 1869 3, no. 6 (Ottawa: Queen's Printer, 1869), 14; *Quebec Official Gazette* 4, no. 32 (August 10, 1872): 1318; "La poterie de Cap-Rouge . . . au fil du temps," La société historique du Cap-Rouge, June 16, 2015, shcr.qc.ca/chronique.php?no=172; and "Chroniques—Personnages—Joseph Bell Forsyth," La société historique du Cap-Rouge, June 16, 2015, shcr.qc.ca/chronique.php?no=11; *Returns from the Chartered Banks of the Dominion of Canada* (Ottawa: MacLean, Roger, 1875), 4, 154, 213; and *Report of the Superintendent of Insurance, Dominion of Canada (1878)* (Ottawa: MacLean, Roger, 1879), 291, 321.

117 **The ambitious curriculum** Descriptions of the academy and its offerings are drawn from Cyrus Thomas, *History of the Counties of Argenteuil, Québec, Prescott, Ontario* (Belleville, ON: Mika Publishing, 1981; originally published 1896), 233–36.

118 **steady, industrious, kindhearted** James Emslie to Thomas Davidson, October 18, 1888.

118 **expressed a desire** Jarvis Report, June 30, 1892 (Quebec City), MEPQ 3/144.

118 **a young man** Letter, James Robertson, October 26, 1888, Records of Commutations of Sentence, 1877-1928, Record Series 103.098, Illinois State Archives, Springfield.

CHAPTER 16. "THE ANIMAL SPIRITS WITHIN"

119 **brandishing body-snatching implements** *Daily Witness* (Montreal), November 12, 1875, quoted in Royce MacGillivray, "Body-Snatching in Ontario," *Canadian Bulletin of Medical History/Bulletin canadien d'histoire de la médicine* 5 (1988): 58.

The incident was also reported in "Resurrectioning," *McGill Gazette* (Montreal), December 1, 1875.

119 **shortage of cadavers** "College Items," *McGill Gazette* (Montreal), December 15, 1875.

119 **as many as three** "A Communication," *University Gazette* (McGill, Montreal), January 1, 1874.

119 **It is better** "My Last Experience of Resurrectionning," *University Gazette* (McGill, Montreal), January 1, 1874.

120 **Quebec introduced a law** MacGillivray, "Body-Snatching in Ontario," 56, 58. Quebec's Anatomy Act was introduced in 1883.

120 **fifty dollars for each** Francis J. Shepherd, *Reminiscences of Student Days and Dissecting Room* (Montreal, privately printed, 1919), 24.

120 **nearly every subject** Ibid., 25.

120 **May the morning** W. Wright, *Introductory Lecture Delivered at the Opening of the 49th Session—Medical Faculty of McGill University* (Montreal: George E. Desbarats, 1872). This and the other quotations in this paragraph and the next appear on pp. 1, 10, and 15.

120 **The arrival** Cream was one of the last to officially register. Student Register, Faculty of Medicine, McGill University, 1824–1876, RG 38, McGill University Archives, Montreal. The register confirms Cream's attendance for each of the three academic years that followed.

120 **solid and progressive** J. E. Pecher, *Flood's Guide Book of the Ottawa, St. Lawrence and Saguenay Rivers, Also Montreal and Quebec Cities* (Montreal: John Lovell, 1872), 27.

120 **new and elegant edifices** Ibid.

121 **Golden Square Mile** Jean-Claude Marsan, *Montreal in Evolution: Historical Analysis of the Development of Montreal's Architecture and Urban Environment* (Montreal: McGill-Queen's University Press, 1981), 191, 257–58.

121 **pioneering the use** These medical innovations are described in Paul Strathern, *A Brief History of Medicine from Hippocrates to Gene Therapy* (London: Constable & Robinson, 2005), 193–94, 280–83, 296–97.

121 **as an enormous fad** Arthur Conan Doyle, "The Romance of Medicine," in *Conan Doyle's Tales of Medical Humanism and Values: Round the Red Lamp: Being Facts and Fancies of Medical Life, with Other Medical Short Stories*, ed. Alvin E. Rodin and Jack D. Key (Malabar, FL: Krieger Publishing, 1992), 466.

121 **a dangerous innovation** Ibid., 19.

121 **Druggists still stocked jars** Shepherd, *Reminiscences of Student Days and Dissecting Room*, 21.

121 **most physicians realized** Thomas Neville Bonner, *Medicine in Chicago, 1850–1950: A Chapter in the Social and Scientific Development of a City* (Madison, WI: American History Research Center, 1957), 31.

121 **With the little cleanliness** Quotations and descriptions in this paragraph are drawn from Shepherd, *Reminiscences of Student Days and Dissecting Room*, 3, 5, 13, 15–16, 19–21.

122 **learned by watching and** Joseph Hanaway and Richard Cruess, *McGill Medicine*, vol. 1, *The First Half Century, 1829–1885* (Montreal: McGill-Queen's University Press, 1996), xxi–xxii, 18–9, 49–54, 59, 63–64; and Shepherd, *Reminiscences of Student Days and Dissecting Room*, 14–15.

SOURCES

122 **A lecture in obstetrics** These examples of subjects covered in McGill courses are drawn from the notebooks of one of Cream's fellow students, Robert Bell, who graduated in 1878. See "Operations to Save Life of Mother by Sacrificing Child," lecture delivered February 18, 1878, recorded in Notebook 6, *Obstetrics, Session 1877–78*, no. 2; "Abortion," lecture delivered November 13, 1877, recorded in Notebook 8, *Midwifery, Session 1877–78*; "Death by Hanging," portion of lecture delivered November 26, 1877, recorded in Notebook 8, *Medical Jurisprudence, Session 1877–78*. P078, John Bell Fonds, Folders 11 and 13, Osler Library of the History of Medicine, McGill University, Montreal. The "2 edged sword" comment was made in a November 25, 1875, lecture in the Practice of Medicine course, Folder 6, Notebook 2.

122 **sometimes necessary** "Cream's Case," *Chicago Times*, November 19, 1880.

122 **safe when used properly** Chloroform's effects and early use as an anesthetic are described in Joseph Lister, "Anaesthetics," in *System of Surgery, Theoretical and Practical*, vol. 3, ed. T. Holmes (Philadelphia: Henry C. Lea's Son, 1882), 525–59.

122 **would soon die** Linda Stratmann, *The Secret Poisoner: A Century of Murder* (New Haven, CT: Yale University Press), 250.

122 **formulated their own medicines** William Osler, "Introductory Lecture," *Canadian Medical & Surgical Journal* 6, no. 5 (November 1877): 199.

123 **blood-stained and reeking** Shepherd, *Reminiscences of Student Days and Dissecting Room*, 3.

123 **they tossed coins** Ibid., 20.

123 **abundance of fresh material** *Annual Calendar of McGill College and University, Session of 1872–73* (Montreal: J. C. Becket, 1872), 57.

123 **There is something** "My Last Experience of Resurrectionning."

123 **where they please** Inspector Frederick Smith Jarvis Report, July 4, 1892 (Montreal), Metropolitan Police Office Records, MEPO 3/144, National Archives, London.

123 **red-light district** Andrée Lévesque, "Éteindre le 'Red Light': Les réformateurs et la prostitution à Montréal, 1865–1925," *Urban History Review* 17, no. 3 (February 1989): 191. The prevalence of taverns and brothels is discussed in Craig Heron, *Booze: A Distilled History* (Toronto: Between the Lines, 2003), 106; Marcel Martel, *Canada the Good: A Short History of Vice since 1500* (Waterloo, ON: Wilfrid Laurier University Press, 2014), 55; and Micheline Dumont, Michele Jean, Marie Lavigne, and Jennifer Stoddart, *Quebec Women: A History* (Toronto: Women's Press, 1987), 170.

123 **What man** "Boarding Houses, &c.," *McGill Gazette* (Montreal), October 22, 1875.

124 **It would be another** Stanley Brice Frost, *McGill University: For the Advancement of Learning*, vol. 1, *1801–1895* (Montreal: McGill-Queen's University Press, 1980) 261, 285–86.

124 **Campus life revolved around** Ibid., 282, 287.

124 **the spirit of song** "College Items," *McGill Gazette* (Montreal), October 22, 1875.

124 **invitation to sing** Untitled news item, *McGill Gazette*, (Montreal), February 1, 1876, 69.

124 **the snares** Wright, *Introductory Lecture*, 14.

124 **Be almost anything** Ibid.

124 **switched to chewing tobacco** "Description of Convict," November 1, 1881, Secretary of State, Executive Section, Records of Commutations of Sentence, 1877–1928, Record Series 103.098, Illinois State Archives, Springfield.

124 **lawless, exuberant** "Medical Education in New York," *Harper's Magazine*, September 1882, 672.

124 **boozy dinners** Shepherd, *Reminiscences of Student Days and Dissecting Room*, 6–7.

124 **He always conducted himself** Jarvis Report, July 19, 1892 (Montreal), MEPO 3/144. Porter confirmed that Cream lodged with her from 1872 to 1876.

124 **They did not associate** Jarvis Report, July 4, 1892 (Montreal), ibid. Bell and Sutherland are identified in Hanaway and Cruess, *McGill Medicine*, 126–27.

125 **wild and fond** Jarvis Report, July 4, 1892 (Montreal), MEPO 3/144.

125 **optional courses** *Annual Calendar 1872–73*, 59–60.

125 **William Cream remarried** Marriage Record, William Cream and Elizabeth Ann Clements Harbeson, March 23, 1874, and Baptism Record, Elizabeth Harbeson (born September 6, 1834), July 14, 1836, Vital and Church Records 1621–1968, Drouin Collection, Institut généalogique Drouin, Montreal, accessed through www.ancestry. com; and Marriage Contract, William Cream and Elizabeth A. C. Harbeson, March 21, 1874, Contrats de mariage de la région de Québec, 1761–1946, Bibliothèque et Archives nationales du Québec, Quebec City.

125 **well supplied with money** Jarvis Report, July 4, 1892 (Montreal), MEPO 3/144.

125 **series of studio** Images I-96440.1 (1873–74), I-99946.1 (1874), I-99948.1 (1874), I-99949 (1874), II-16502.1 (1875), II-24646.1 (1876), and II-24647.1 (1876), McCord Museum, Montreal, collections.musee-mccord.qc.ca.

125 **Photographer to the Queen** *The Canadian Handbook and Tourist's Guide* (Montreal: M. Longmoore, 1867), 215; Stanley G. Triggs, "William Notman (1826–1891)," *Dictionary of Canadian Biography*, www.biographi.ca/en/bio/notman_william_12E.html.

125 **took out an insurance** Jarvis Report, July 7, 1892 (Montreal), MEPO 3/144.

126 **Stout solid build** "Description of Convict." His auburn whiskers are described in "The Abortionists," *Chicago Daily News*, August 24, 1880.

127 **gentle, kind, and genial** Wright, *Introductory Lecture*, 13.

127 **to devote their abilities** The account of the convocation in this paragraph is based on the following newspaper reports: "Convocation Day at the University," *Daily Witness* (Montreal), March 31, 1876; "McGill University" and "McGill University— Annual Meeting of Convocation," *Daily Witness* (Montreal), April 1, 1876; "McGill University," *Montreal Evening Star*, April 1, 1876; "McGill University," *Montreal Gazette*, April 1, 1876. McGill began conferring the degree of MD, CM in 1862. Hanaway and Cruess, *McGill Medicine*, 44.

128 **final examinations** *Annual Calendar of McGill College and University, Montreal, Session of 1876–77* (Montreal: J. C. Becket, 1876), 59.

128 **How do poisons** *Annual Calendar of McGill College and University, Session of 1873–74* (Montreal: J. C. Becket, 1874), 233–35; and *Annual Calendar 1876–77*, 190.

128 **Cream's thesis** Lori Podolsky, acting university archivist, McGill University Archives, Montreal, email communication with author, May 12, 2017. Most theses from Cream's time are believed to have been lost in a 1907 fire that destroyed the

medical building. David S. Crawford, "Theses in the Osler Library Including that of Pierre de Sales Laterrière," *Osler Library Newsletter*, no. 111 (2009), 2. The subject of Cream's thesis is listed in *Annual Calendar 1876–77*, 59.

128 **the art of medicine** Hanaway and Cruess, *McGill Medicine*, 43. The English translation appears on p. 199.

129 **Cream added his signature** Registry of Graduates, vol. 1, 1833–1961, Faculty of Medicine, RG 38 C12 File 290, McGill University Archives.

Chapter 17. Flora Eliza Brooks

130 **Brooks had operated** Brooks Family, File 429, Brome County Historical Society Archives, Lac-Brome (Knowlton), Quebec; Cyrus Thomas, *The History of Shefford: Civil, Ecclesiastical, Biographical and Statistical* (Montreal: Lovell Printing & Publishing, 1877), 119, 133; and *The Eastern Townships Business and Farmers Directory 1892* (Toronto: Might's Directory, 1892), 616–18. An item in the *Waterloo Advertiser and District of Bedford Times* (QC), October 14, 1892, noted his service with the militia's 79th Battalion and referred to him as "Capt. L. H. Brooks." The hotel's assessed value, seventy-five hundred dollars, made it one of the most valuable properties in the village: Rôle d'évaluation, 1869–1874, V008—Fonds Ville de Waterloo, 1867–1974, Société d'histoire de la Haute-Yamaska, Granby.

130 **As beautiful a tract** *The Canadian Handbook and Tourist's Guide* (Montreal: M. Longmoore, 1867), 47, 56.

131 **a stranger visiting** Thomas, *History of Shefford*, 122. Details of Waterloo's history and development are drawn from *Waterloo, Québec: The First Hundred Years/Le premier cent ans 1867–1967* (Waterloo: Gaudet Printing, 1967), 13, 21, 25–37; *Guide du patrimoine bâti de la MRC de La Haute-Yamaska* (Granby, QC: Société d'histoire de la Haute-Yamaska, 2015), 123–45; Mario Gendron and Richard Racine, *Waterloo: 125 ans d'histoire* (Granby, QC: Société d'histoire de Shefford, 1992), 105–19; and *Eastern Townships Gazetteer & Directory for the Years 1875–76* (Montreal: W. H. Irwin, 1875), 222–23.

131 **Flora Brooks had met** Inspector Frederick Smith Jarvis Report, July 7, 1892 (Montreal), Metropolitan Police Office Records, MEPO 3/144, National Archives, London.

131 **courtship rituals** Peter Ward, "Courtship and Social Space in Nineteenth-Century English Canada," *Canadian Historical Review* 68, no. 1 (March 1987): 35–62.

132 **the habit of coming** Jarvis Report, July 7, 1892 (Montreal), MEPO 3/144.

132 **He became a fixture** "Record of a Rascal," *Salt Lake (UT) Herald*, June 30, 1892.

132 **purchased skeletons, bones** Joseph Lister's personal collection, for instance, included a complete skeleton, a thorax, a bladder, and a severed head with the top of the spinal cord attached. Lindsey Fitzharris, *The Butchering Art: Joseph Lister's Quest to Transform the Grisly World of Victorian Medicine* (London: Allen Lane, 2017), 45.

132 **fire broke out** The fire and insurance claim detailed in the following paragraph are recounted in Jarvis Reports, July 7, 1892 (Montreal) and July 19, 1892 (Montreal), MEPO 3/144.

133 **almost unequalled** Details of the weather and local events in this paragraph and the next are drawn from reports and advertisements published in the *Waterloo Advertiser and District of Bedford Times* (QC), August 4, 11, 18, and 24, 1876.

133 **Cream promised** "Record of a Rascal."

134 **procured either by** Jarvis Report, July 7, 1892 (Montreal), MEPO 3/144.

134 **criminal offense** Samuel R. Clarke and Henry P. Sheppard, *A Treatise on the Criminal Law of Canada*, 2nd ed. (Toronto: Hart, 1882), 209–10.

134 **substances used** Angus McLaren, "Birth Control and Abortion in Canada, 1870–1920," *Canadian Historical Review* 59, no. 3 (1978): 329–30.

134 **a living death** Quoted in Constance Backhouse, *Petticoats and Prejudice: Women and Law in Nineteenth-Century Canada* (Toronto: Osgoode Society/Women's Press, 1991), 349n4.

134 **What does all this** "Record of a Rascal." Some press reports about Cream's early life included a dubious claim that Brooks showed up at the hotel armed with a revolver and threatened to shoot Cream if he refused to marry Flora, but this appears unlikely. An example is "The Conviction of Neill," *Pall Mall Gazette* (London), October 22, 1892.

135 **love and affection** Marriage Contract, Thomas N. Cream, M.D., and Flora E. Brooks, September 11, 1876, Archives des notaries du Quebec, District of Bedford, notary Thomas Brassard, no. 8589, Bibliothèque et Archives nationales du Québec, Sherbrooke.

135 **reclined on a lounge** "Record of a Rascal."

135 **never met Flora Brooks** Jarvis Report, July 4, 1892 (Montreal), MEPO 3/144.

135 **The *Advertiser* published** *Waterloo Advertiser and District of Bedford Times* (QC), September 15, 1876.

135 **He was going to England** Jarvis Report, July 7, 1892 (Montreal), MEPO 3/144.

Chapter 18. Student No. 2016

136 **I cannot think** Sir James Clark to Florence Nightingale, July 9, 1867, quoted in E. M. McInnes, *St. Thomas' Hospital*, 2nd ed. (London: Special Trustees for St. Thomas' Hospital, 1990), 111.

137 **It was common** Joseph Hanaway and Richard Cruess, *McGill Medicine*, vol. 1, *The First Half Century, 1829–1885* (Montreal: McGill-Queen's University Press, 1996), 65–69, 73.

136 **to qualify for membership** Classmate Herbert Reddy explained why he and Cream chose St. Thomas' in an interview with a Scotland Yard detective in 1892. Inspector Frederick Smith Jarvis Report, July 4, 1892 (Montreal), Metropolitan Police Office Records, MEPO 3/144, National Archives, London. Reddy is listed as a member of the class of 1876 in Hanaway and Cruess, *McGill Medicine*, 127.

137 **the finest hospital** "The New St. Thomas's Hospital and Medical School," *British Medical Journal* 1, no. 383 (May 2, 1868): 435. This description of the hospital and medical school also draws on "St. Thomas's Hospital Medical School," *British Medical Journal* 2, no. 2122 (August 31, 1901): 537; and McInnes, *St. Thomas' Hospital*, 110–11.

137 **admitting thirty-four hundred** Walter Rivington, *The Medical Profession: Being the Essay to which Was Awarded the First Carmichael Prize of £200 by the Council of the Royal College of Surgeons, Ireland, 1879* (Dublin: Fannin, 1879), 319.

137 **All students have** St. Thomas's Hospital Medical and Surgical College, Session 1872–1873, H01/ST/MS/A/05/001, St. Thomas' Hospital, Medical School Records, London Metropolitan Archives.

137 **was followed by** McInnes, *St. Thomas' Hospital*, 136. The early use of vaccination and chloroform are noted on pp. 137 and 148.

138 **As a charity hospital** "Hospital Wards for the 'Well-to-Do,'" *British Medical Journal* 1, no. 934 (November 23, 1878): 781. One building was set aside for paying patients in 1878, with the fees used to cover the cost of accepting more impoverished patients.

138 **The hospital should be** "Introductory Lectures: St. Thomas's Hospital," *British Medical Journal* 2, no. 145 (October 10, 1863): 395.

139 **that a little over-indulgence** "Medical Students at Work," *Graphic* (London), October 2, 1886, 367.

139 **confirmed Cream's connection** Inspector John Bennett Tunbridge Memos, June 21, 1892, and July 8, 1892, MEPO 3/144.

139 **student no. 2016** Index to Pupil Entry Books 1825–1930, TH/FP12, St. Thomas' Hospital, Medical School Records, King's College London Archives.

139 **cubs** McInnes, *St. Thomas' Hospital*, 75–76. In 1878 the school's enrollment stood at 187. Rivington, *Medical Profession*, 259.

139 **promising and wide-open field** This is discussed in Wendy Mitchinson, *The Nature of Their Bodies: Women and Their Doctors in Victorian Canada* (Toronto: University of Toronto Press, 1991), chap. 6.

139 **five hundred pregnant women** Chicago midwife Hattie Mack cited this figure when she and Cream were prosecuted for murder in 1880. See "Dr Cream's Crime," *Chicago Daily News*, August 23, 1880.

139 **assisted and advised others** He noted this in testimony at his 1880 trial for murder in Chicago. "Cream's Case," *Chicago Times*, November 19, 1880; and "Dr. Cream," *Chicago Daily Tribune*, November 19, 1880.

139 **Award of Honor** "Murderers' Row," *Chicago Daily Tribune*, November 17, 1880.

139 **served as a dresser** Registration of Pupils Attainment and Appointments 1869–1905, TH/FP13, St. Thomas' Hospital, Medical School Records, King's College London Archives. Many accounts of Cream's medical career state that he served as an obstetrics clerk while at St. Thomas'. See, for instance, Angus McLaren, *A Prescription for Murder: The Victorian Serial Killings of Dr. Thomas Neill Cream* (Chicago: University of Chicago Press, 1993), 34. The box where this appointment would be noted, however, is blank on Cream's student record.

139 **These assistants accompanied surgeons** Lindsey Fitzharris, *The Butchering Art: Joseph Lister's Quest to Transform the Grisly World of Victorian Medicine* (London: Allen Lane, 2017), 4.

139 **A good dresser** "Medical Students at Work," 367.

139 **Men who had already** W. Somerset Maugham, who studied at St. Thomas' in the early 1890s, recalled that the obstetrics clerk who supervised his work was "a young man recently qualified." Maugham, *Liza of Lambeth* (London: Vintage Books, 2000), vii.

139 **as much time as they** "Medical Students at Work," 364.

140 **Four other McGill graduates** Joel Haley, King's College London Archives, email communication with the author, September 4, 2017. Hanaway and Cruess's *McGill Medicine*, 127, identifies three of the four—Reddy, Alexander Munro, and Arthur Ritchie—as members of the class of 1876.

140 **knew about his scrapes** Jarvis Report, July 4, 1892 (Montreal), MEPO 3/144. Reddy "remembers Cream being at the Hospital for nearly a year," the detective noted, "but was not intimate with him and never knew where he resided in London."

141 **recognized the name** Jarvis Report, July 7, 1892 (Montreal), ibid. A press report, "Record of a Rascal," *Salt Lake (UT) Herald*, June 30, 1892, described Alexander as "rich and in a social position."

141 **pursuing the daughter** The description in this paragraph is based on Sergeant George Bush Memo, June 27, 1892, MEPO 3/144.

141 **bewildering multiplicity** Rivington, *Medical Profession*, 6, 9, 45.

141 **A board of examiners** *Calendar of the Royal College of Surgeons of England, 1876* (London: Taylor & Francis, 1876), 300–1. Professional standards and examination and other admission requirements are set out at pp. 43–46, 47–49. Exam results for that year, which the college's president described as typical, are reported on pp. 298–99 and 302.

142 **Cream paid** *Examination Book*, vol. 7, *1867–1877*, RCS-EXA/2/2/1/6. Royal College of Surgeons of England Archives, London. Cream's result is listed at line 100. (He is incorrectly identified as a graduate of the University of Toronto's medical school.) Archivist Geraldine O'Driscoll confirmed that "referred" signifies a failing grade on the examination in an August 2, 2016, email communication with the author.

142 **demanded a thorough understanding** Questions asked the year before Cream wrote the examination were reproduced in *Calendar of the Royal College of Surgeons of England, 1876*, 337–42.

142 **the police hesitated** "The Summing Up," in W. Somerset Maugham, *Mr. Maugham Himself* (Garden City, NY: Doubleday, 1954), 566. St. Thomas' staff and students attended at 1,620 home births in 1876. See *The Medical Directory for 1878, including the London and Provincial Medical Directory, the Medical Directory for Scotland, the Medical Directory for Ireland* (London: J. & A. Churchill, n.d.), 250.

CHAPTER 19. A PREMATURE DEATH

143 **Being sick of body** Last Will & Testament, Flora Eliza Brooks, July 25, 1877, Archives des notaries du Quebec, District of Bedford, notary Louis Jodoin, no. 2251, Bibliothèque et Archives nationales du Québec, Sherbrooke.

143 **fairly recovered** Inspector Frederick Smith Jarvis Report, July 7, 1892 (Montreal), Metropolitan Police Office Records, MEPO 3/144, National Archives, London.

144 **a half state** "Record of a Rascal," *Salt Lake (UT) Herald*, June 30, 1892.

144 **Phelan ordered her to stop** Jarvis Report, July 7, 1892 (Montreal), MEPO 3/144.

144 **he presented Lyman Brooks** Ibid.

145 **after a lingering illness** *Waterloo Advertiser and District of Bedford Times* (QC), August 15, 1877.

145 **Lung diseases** Mario Gendron, "Mourir en 1870," Société d'histoire de la Haute-Yamaska, November 30, 2010, www.shhy.info/sante/mourir-en-1870.

145 **the stroke was received** Samuel R. Clarke and Henry P. Sheppard, *A Treatise on the Criminal Law of Canada*, 2nd ed. (Toronto: Hart, 1882), 194–95.

145 **Dr. Eric Sparham** See *A Defence of Dr. Eric Benzel Sparham, Charged and Convicted of the Crime of Murder: Being a Medico-Legal Inquiry into the Cause of the Death of Miss Sophia Elizabeth Burnham, His Supposed Victim* (Brockville, ON: Leavitt & Southworth, 1876).

146 **never saw any** Jarvis Report, July 7, 1892 (Montreal), MEPO 3/144.

Chapter 20. The Licentiate

147 **The fees are moderate** Walter Rivington, *The Medical Profession: Being the Essay to which Was Awarded the First Carmichael Prize of £200 by the Council of the Royal College of Surgeons, Ireland, 1879* (Dublin: Fannin, 1879), 46–47.

147 **Athens of the North** Robert Crawford, *On Glasgow and Edinburgh* (Cambridge, MA: Belknap Press/Harvard University Press, 2013), 27.

147 **Auld Reikie** Ibid., 17.

148 **the largest in Britain** Rivington, *Medical Profession*, 258–59.

148 **The operating table** Conan Doyle described operating techniques during his student days in "His First Operation," in *Conan Doyle's Tales of Medical Humanism and Values: Round the Red Lamp: Being Facts and Fancies of Medical Life, with Other Medical Short Stories*, ed. Alvin E. Rodin and Jack D. Key (Malabar, FL: Krieger Publishing, 1992), 29–32.

148 **two rounds of written examinations** *The Medical Directory for 1878, including the London and Provincial Medical Directory, the Medical Directory for Scotland, the Medical Directory for Ireland* (London: J. & A. Churchill, n.d.), 943–44, provides details of the examinations and the subjects covered.

149 **labouring under disease** Helen M. Dingwall, *"A Famous and Flourishing Society": The History of the Royal College of Surgeons of Edinburgh* (Edinburgh: Edinburgh University Press, 2005), 171.

149 **completing his second year** Conan Doyle appears to have been in Edinburgh until at least late April, when he traveled south to work as a doctor's assistant in Sheffield for three weeks. See his May 26 and May 29, 1878, letters to his mother, Mary Doyle, in Jon Lellenberg, Daniel Stashower, and Charles Foley, eds., *Arthur Conan Doyle: A Life in Letters* (London, HarperPress, 2007), 102–4. In his memoirs, however, Conan Doyle mistakenly recalled completing his stint in Sheffield in "the early summer of '78." Arthur Conan Doyle, *Memories and Adventures and Western Wanderings* (Newcastle upon Tyne: Cambridge Scholars Publishing, 2009), 16.

149 **a favorite haunt** Rodin and Key, *Conan Doyle's Tales of Medical Humanism and Values*, 37. Conan Doyle later befriended writers Robert Louis Stevenson and J. M. Barrie, who also attended Edinburgh University about this time, and suspected he had "brushed elbows" with them during his university days. See Conan Doyle, *Memories and Adventures*, 185.

149 **ability to size up** See Conan Doyle, *Memories and Adventures*, 15–16; and Irving Wallace, *The Fabulous Originals: Lives of Extraordinary People Who Inspired Memorable Characters in Fiction* (Millwood, NY: Krause Reprint, 1972), 22–23.

149 **His intuitive powers** Harry How, "A Day with Dr. Conan Doyle," *Strand Magazine* 4, no. 20 (August 1892): 186.

150 **The scars** Ibid., 188.

150 **the vast importance** "The Original of 'Sherlock Holmes': An Interview with Dr. Joseph Bell," *Pall Mall Gazette* (London), December 28, 1893.

150 **His inquiries cracked** Wallace, *Fabulous Originals*, 36–38. See also Ely M. Liebow, *Dr. Joe Bell: Model for Sherlock Holmes* (Madison, WI: Popular Press, 2007), 119–22.

150 **It would be** "Original of 'Sherlock Holmes.'"

150 **One in three candidates** Results of both examinations for 1878 were reported in "Return, by the Registrar, of Results of Professional Examinations for Degrees, Diplomas, and Licenses granted in 1878 by the Bodies in Schedule (A.) of the 'Medical Act (1858),'" appended to the *Special Report from the Select Committee on the Medical Act (1858) Amendment (No. 3) Bill [Lords]*, reproduced in *Parliament of Great Britain, Reports from Committees*, vol. 12 (1878–79), 415.

150 **Dr. Bell was among** "Minutes of the Royal College of Surgeons of Edinburgh," vol. 16 (1878), 713, Royal College of Surgeons of Edinburgh Archives, Edinburgh. For Bell's role as secretary-treasurer, his service as an examiner, and the requirement to submit educational records and pay fees at 20 Melville Street, see *Medical Directory for 1878*, 941, 943–44. *Transactions of the Royal Society of Edinburgh*, vol. 29 (1878–80) (Edinburgh: Robert Grant & Son, 1880), 692, confirms this was Bell's home address in the late 1870s. In 1884 he moved to nearby 2 Melville Crescent, where a plaque records his link to the character of Sherlock Holmes. Michael Sims, "The scene of the crime . . . Sherlock Holmes and the indelible link to Edinburgh," *National* (Glasgow), March 6, 2017.

151 **skill in Anatomy** "Minutes of the Royal College of Surgeons of Edinburgh," 713–14. Cream's double qualification was recorded on the same day, April 13, 1878, in the "List of Licentiates," vol. 2 (1877–51), RCP/EXA/6/6, Records of the Royal College of Physicians of Edinburgh. Angus McLaren asserted that Cream was granted a license in midwifery, and this appears to be based on newspaper advertisements promoting Cream's early medical practice in Canada. While midwifery was among the subjects covered in the Edinburgh examinations, the records of these colleges make no mention of this specific qualification. See Angus McLaren, *A Prescription for Murder: The Victorian Serial Killings of Dr. Thomas Neill Cream* (Chicago: University of Chicago Press, 1993), 35.

151 **entitled to display** W. S. Craig, *History of the Royal College of Physicians of Edinburgh* (Oxford: Blackwell Scientific Publications, 1976), 307.

151 **should entitle its holder** Rivington, *Medical Profession*, 44, 47.

151 **Cream never lost** His accent could still be detected when he was in his thirties. See "The Abortionists," *Chicago Daily News*, August 24, 1880.

CHAPTER 21. CATHARINE HUTCHINSON GARDNER

152 **Catharine Hutchinson Gardner** While her name was widely reported in the press as Kate Lorne Gardner, her brother Robert eventually pointed out that Catharine Hutchinson Gardner was her correct name. See "Inquest File—Kate or Kitty Gardner," May 3, 1879, Middlesex County Coroner Investigations and Inquests, RG 22-3395, Archives of Ontario, Toronto; and "The Katie Gardner Case!" *London (ON) Free Press*, May 14, 1879.

152 **walked toward the privy** This description of the discovery of Gardner's body is based on the following press reports: "A Case of Suicide," *London (ON) Free Press*, May 3, 1879; "A Case of Suicide," *London (ON) Free Press*, May 5, 1879; and "Mysterious Death," *Daily Advertiser* (London, ON), May 5, 1879.

153 **a sweetish, insidious scent** Arthur Conan Doyle, "The Curse of Eve," in *Conan Doyle's Tales of Medical Humanism and Values: Round the Red Lamp: Being Facts and Fancies of Medical Life, with Other Medical Short Stories*, ed. Alvin E. Rodin and Jack D. Key (Malabar, FL: Krieger Publishing, 1992), 116.

153 **Not liking the place** "The Abortionists," *Chicago Daily News*, August 24, 1880.

153 **a miniature Pittsburgh** Orlo Miller, *A Century of Western Ontario: The Story of London, "The Free Press," and Western Ontario, 1849–1949* (Westport, CT: Greenwood Press, 1972), 175.

153 **raw newness and impermanence** Orlo Miller, *This Was London: The First Two Centuries* (Westport, ON: Butternut Press, 1988), 135. The future Edward VII's stay at the Tecumseh House is noted on p. 97.

154 **Advertisements for Cream's practice** They first appeared in the *Free Press* on September 11, 1878, and in the *Daily Advertiser* (London, ON), on September 16, 1878

154 **one of the city's finest** *History of the County of Middlesex, Canada* (Toronto: W. A. & C. L. Goodspeed, 1889), 228.

155 **He registered to vote** Ontario, Canada Voter Lists, 1867–1900, City of London, Ward 4 (August 29, 1879), 82, accessed through www.ancestry.com.

155 **a "pillar" of the congregation** All material attributed to James Reid is drawn from an 1892 newspaper interview in "Dr. Cream's Career," *London Free (ON) Press*, June 29, 1892, republished in "The Murdered Women," *Globe* (Toronto), June 29, 1892.

155 **He taught Sunday school** Ibid.

155 **helping children improve** The role of Sunday schools is described in Michael Paterson, *Life in Victorian Britain: A Social History of Queen Victoria's Reign* (London: Robinson, 2008), 173.

155 **He joined the local** Cream's YMCA membership and Sunday school teaching are noted in "Dr. Cream," *Chicago Daily Tribune*, August 23, 1880; and "Dr Cream's Crime," *Chicago Daily News*, August 23, 1880.

155 **a safe Christian environment** J. William Frost, "Christianity and Culture in America," in *Christianity: A Social and Cultural History*, 2nd ed. (Upper Saddle River, NJ: Prentice Hall, 1998), 476.

155 **sporting events and camping** Miller, *This Was London*, 140. The camping excursions were noted in Jennifer Grainger, *Early London: A Photographic History from the Orr Collection 1826–1914* (Windsor, ON: Biblioasis, 2016), 114.

155 **social intercourse and moral** *History of the County of Middlesex, Canada*, 358. Cream's attendance at club gatherings was noted in press coverage of the inquest into Gardner's death.

155 **He was on the program** "Social Entertainment," *London (ON) Free Press*, March 14, 1879; and "Sociable," *Daily Advertiser* (London, ON), March 14, 1879.

155 **respectable people did not** Geoffrey Best, *Mid-Victorian England, 1851–75* (London: Fontana Press, 1979), 283–84.

156 **professed allegiance** Karen Halttunen, *Confidence Men and Painted Women: A Study of Middle-Class Culture in America, 1830–1870* (New Haven, CT: Yale University Press, 1982), xiii.

156 **thorough and primitive duality** Robert Louis Stevenson, *Dr. Jekyll & Mr. Hyde and Other Strange Tales* (London: Arcturus Publishing, 2009), 56–59. The story was first published in 1886.

156 **charged under Ontario's Medical Act** "Practising without a License," *London (ON) Free Press*, February 24, 1879.

156 **paid his registration fees** The *Daily Advertiser* (London, ON) report, published on February 28, 1879, was reproduced in "Local Court Fined Victorian Poisoner," *London (ON) Free Press*, May 25, 1983. See also "Personal," *London (ON) Free Press*, February 28, 1879.

156 **remained active for months** Notations in Lawrason's minute book and other court records relating to the Medical Act case were reproduced in "Local Court Fined Victorian Poisoner." This source confirms there was no further press coverage of the prosecution.

157 **The general opinion is** "Case of Suicide," *London (ON) Free Press*, May 3, 1879.

157 **It is indeed desirable** William Fuller Alves Boys, *A Practical Treatise on the Office and Duties of Coroners in Ontario*, 2nd ed. (Toronto: Hart & Rawlinson, 1878), 7. Boys's background is drawn from "Judge Boys passed away on Sunday," *Barrie (ON) Examiner*, December 3, 1914.

157 **practicing medicine for two** Biographical information on Flock is drawn from George Maclean Rose, ed., *A Cyclopaedia of Canadian Biography* (Toronto: Rose Publishing, 1886), 417; and *Medical Chronicle Appointments* (October 2, 1858), *or Montreal Monthly Journal of Medicine and Surgery* 6, no. 5 (1858): 239.

157 **violence or unfair means** "Coroner's Bill for Upper Canada," *British American Medical and Physical Journal* 6, no. 8 (December 1850): 380–82; and J. C. E. Wood, "Discovering the Ontario Inquest," *Osgoode Hall Law Journal* 5, no. 2 (1967): 246–48.

157 **quarrels approaching to fights** "Coroner's Inquests," *Ottawa Daily Citizen*, October 28, 1879. There were similar altercations between rival coroners in New York and New Jersey during this era. See Colin Evans, *Blood on the Table: The Greatest Cases of New York City's Office of the Chief Medical Examiner* (New York: Berkley Books, 2008), 10–11.

157 **there would be no** "Coroner's Inquests," *Ottawa Daily Citizen*, November 8, 1879.

158 **whilst the body** These duties are listed in Boys, *Practical Treatise*, 6, 123–27, 155. This was considered an essential reference work for Ontario coroners in 1879. See the letter of J. G. Scott to Julius P. Bucke, September 16, 1879, Deputy Attorney General Letterbooks, vol. 17, RG 4-26, Archives of Ontario, Toronto.

158 **While most** Guy St-Denis, "The London District and Middlesex County, Ontario, Coroner's Inquests, 1831–1900," *Archivaria* 31 (Winter 1990–91): 143.

158 **of sound mind** Boys, *Practical Treatise*, 2–3.

159 **with great caution** Ibid., 126.

159 **her stomach was removed** J. G. Scott to W. H. Ellis, June 7, 1879; J. G. Scott to Julius P. Bucke, June 7, 1879; and J. G. Scott to Julius P. Bucke, September 16, 1879, Deputy Attorney General Letterbooks, vol. 17, RG 4-26, Archives of Ontario. The woman, Sarah Shingles, died on April 28. Procedures for preserving and shipping autopsy samples were outlined in Boys, *Practical Treatise*, 139–40.

159 **had established detective branches** See, for instance, Matthew Pearl, "The Incredible Untold Story of America's First Police Detectives," *Boston Globe Magazine*, April 28, 2016, www.bostonglobe.com/magazine/2016/04/28/the-incredible-untold-story-america-first-police-detectives/jewdTrdVzkQZJuVZEEc9TJ/story.html.

159 **upon who gets possession** Rachael Griffin, "Detective Policing and the State in Nineteenth-Century England: The Detective Department of the London Metropolitan Police, 1842–1878" (PhD diss., University of Western Ontario, 2016), 55–61, ir.lib.uwo.ca/cgi/viewcontent.cgi?article=4896&context=etd.

159 **officers played** In the Gardner case, the constable who discovered the body testified at the inquest. Another officer tracked down a witness who had moved to a neighboring town. See "The Katie Gardner Mystery," *London (ON) Free Press*, May 12, 1879.

160 **about half the men** Toronto, for instance, had almost twice as many officers per capita in 1878. Mark Richardson, *On the Beat: 150 Years of Policing in London Ontario* (London: London Police Service/Museum London, 2005), 26. The need for more constables was noted in "The Police Force," *London (ON) Free Press*, January 8, 1879.

160 **We can't hire gentlemen** Quoted in Miller, *Century of Western Ontario*, 198.

160 **accounted for almost half** "The Police Force."

160 **The animals roam around at night** "The Cow By Law," *Daily Advertiser* (London, ON), May 8, 1879.

160 **If possible the body** Boys, *Practical Treatise*, 124–25.

CHAPTER 22. BY SOME PERSON UNKNOWN

161 **lawful and honest men** William Fuller Alves Boys, *A Practical Treatise on the Office and Duties of Coroners in Ontario*, 2nd ed. (Toronto: Hart & Rawlinson, 1878), 112, 116.

161 **down-hearted** Testimony from the first day of inquest is based on "Inquest File— Kate or Kitty Gardner," May 3, 1879, Middlesex County Coroner Investigations and Inquests, RG 22-3395, Archives of Ontario, Toronto; "A Case of Suicide," *London (ON) Free Press*, May 5, 1879; and "Mysterious Death," *Daily Advertiser* (London, ON), May 5, 1879.

162 **were required to delegate** Boys, *Practical Treatise*, 134.

162 **No stains of chloroform** This account of the second day of the inquest is based on "Inquest File—Kate or Kitty Gardner"; "The Katie Gardner Case," *London (ON) Free Press*, May 8, 1879; and "Mystery," *Daily Advertiser* (London, ON), May 8, 1879.

162 **London was rife** Public interest in the case was noted in "Inquest," *Daily Advertiser* (London, ON), May 7, 1879; and "London," *Hamilton (ON) Spectator*, May 8, 1879.

163 **she was** Presbyterian Registrations of Deaths, 1869–1938, MS935, reel 22, "Deaths—City of London, County of Middlesex, 1879," no. 134, p. 549, Archives of Ontario, Toronto.

164 **would recognize her handwriting** "The Katie Gardner Mystery," *London (ON) Free Press*, May 9, 1879.

164 **administered to her** "Inquest File—Kate or Kitty Gardner." The jury's exoneration of Birrell was reported in "The Katie Gardner Case!" *London (ON) Free Press*, May 14, 1879.

164 **cognizant of some details** "Murder or Suicide—Which?" *London (ON) Free Press*, May 15, 1879.

164 **extremely one-sided** "The Kate Gardner Mystery," *London (ON) Free Press*, May 16, 1879.

165 **he had administered** "Dr. Cream," *Chicago Daily Tribune*, August 23, 1880.

165 **Handwriting analysis had played** Paul Collins, *Blood & Ivy: The 1849 Murder that Scandalized Harvard* (New York: W. W. Norton, 2018), 197–200; and C. Ainsworth Mitchell, *The Expert Witness and the Applications of Science and of Art to Human Identification, Criminal Investigation, Civil Actions and History* (Cambridge: W. Heffer & Sons, 1923), 141.

165 **if witnesses familiar** Boys, *Practical Treatise*, 106–7.

165 **The culprit** Ibid., 127.

166 **pleaded guilty** "Local Court Fined Victorian Poisoner," *London (ON) Free Press*, May 25, 1983. The minimum fine of twenty-five dollars for the offense is referred to in "Fined," *Daily Advertiser* (London, ON), May 6, 1879.

166 **a sweltering day** The London area's heat wave is noted in Greg Stott and Glenn Stott, eds., *"Passing into Oblivion": The Diaries of William Porte, Lucan, Ontario, 1864–1898* (Anokra, ON: Anokra Press, 2009), 94.

166 **he left the city** Cream revealed his departure date in a newspaper interview. See "The Other Side," *Daily Inter Ocean* (Chicago), November 19, 1880.

166 **The chloroform had been** Inspector Frederick Smith Jarvis Report, July 14, 1892 (Toronto), Metropolitan Police Office Records, MEPO 3/144, National Archives, London.

167 **Then a letter arrived** Frank Murray to Robert Pinkerton, June 12, 1892, and Robert Pinkerton to Superintendent John Shore, June 14, 1892, ibid. Scotland Yard's receipt of the Pinkerton's letters on June 20 is confirmed in Superintendent John Shore Memo, June 20, 1892, ibid.

167 **with the least possible** Inspector John Bennett Tunbridge Memo, June 21, 1892, ibid.

CHAPTER 23. MISSING LINKS

171 **Strangely enough** The quotations in this paragraph and next are from Inspector John Bennett Tunbridge Report, May 28, 1892, Metropolitan Police Office Records, MEPO 3/144, National Archives, London (emphasis in original).

171 **The fact that Clover** Tunbridge Report, June 6, 1892, ibid.

171 **Tunbridge interviewed Laura Sabbatini** Ibid.

174 **slip of paper** Tunbridge Report, June 11, 1892, ibid.

174 **took a long look** Tunbridge Report, May 28, 1892, ibid.

174 **also failed to recognize** Efforts to have Linfield and Burdett identify Cream are outlined in Tunbridge Report, June 11, 1892, ibid.

175 **like the man I saw** "The Stamford Street Poisoning Case," *Reynolds's Newspaper* (London), June 12, 1892.

175 **There were previous cases** "The Stamford Street Tragedy," *Observer* (London), June 5, 1892.

175 **The man was not named** See, for example, "The Mysterious Poisoning Cases in London," *Guardian* (Manchester), June 10, 1892; and "The Lambeth Poisoning Mysteries," *Pall Mall Gazette* (London), June 9, 1892. On British legal restrictions on news coverage of court cases in the nineteenth century, see Galia Schneebaum and Shai J. Lavi, "The Riddle of *Sub-judice* and the Modern Law of Contempt," *Critical Analysis of Law: An International & Interdisciplinary Law Review* 2, no. 1 (2015): 191–93.

175 **one paper cleverly reported** "The South London Poisoning Cases," *Standard* (London), June 10, 1892.

175 **pointing to systematic poisoning** "Lambeth Poisoning Mysteries."

175 **discovery of the missing** "South London Poisoning Cases."

175 **He is suffering** "The Lambeth Poisoning Case," *Daily News* (London), June 7, 1892.

176 **under the most serious** "Strychnine Given to Immoral Girls," *Cincinnati Inquirer*, June 12, 1892. The Philadelphia press reports were "Was Neall the Poisoner?" *Philadelphia Inquirer*, June 11, 1892; and "London's Poisoning Case," *Times* (Philadelphia), June 11, 1892.

176 **The general impression** "Singular Blackmail Case," *New York Times*, June 21, 1892. This report also appeared as "Thomas Neill's Case," *Baltimore Sun*, June 21, 1892.

176 **Jack the Poisoner** *Buffalo Morning Express*, June 27, 1892.

176 **determined to find** Tunbridge Report, June 11, 1892, MEPO 3/144.

176 **bloated and unrecognizable** The condition of Clover's body was described in the report and lab notes of Dr. Stevenson, reproduced in W. Teignmouth Shore, ed., *Trial of Thomas Neill Cream* (London: William Hodge, 1923), 197, 205. The viewing by the jury was noted in "The London Poisoning Mysteries," *Guardian* (Manchester), June 23, 1892.

177 **I will do my best** Coroner A. Braxton Hicks to Assistant Commissioner Robert Anderson, June 17, 1892, MEPO 3/144.

177 **The hall could accommodate** *County of London: Theatres and Music Halls* (London: London County Council, 1904), 15.

177 **chattering and laughing crowd** "The Mysterious Poisoning Cases in Lambeth," *Daily News* (London), June 24, 1892.

177 **A coroner's court** "The Mysterious Poisoning Cases in Lambeth," *Daily News* (London), June 23, 1892.

177 **I received instructions** Ibid. Cream's demeanor was noted in "The Poisoning Mysteries," *Illustrated Police News* (London), July 9, 1892.

178 **If you had any** "The Mysterious Poisoning of Girls," *Reynolds's Newspaper* (London), June 26, 1892.

178 **In the future** Ibid.

178 **points to the administration** Stevenson's testimony at the inquest was reported in ibid. His June 10, 1892, report and lab notes were reproduced in Shore, *Trial of Thomas Neill Cream*, 197–203, 205–6. His handwritten report, titled Report of Dr. Thomas Stevenson on Exhumation of Body of Matilda Clover deceased, and on Analysis of the Viscera, is in the Scotland Yard investigation file, MEPO 3/144. His tests and findings were described in detail at Cream's trial in October 1892. See Testimony of Thomas Stevenson, "Trial of Thomas Neill," October 1892, *Proceedings of the Old Bailey, London's Central Criminal Court, 1674 to 1913*, 1432–38, www.oldbaileyonline.org.

178 **Lucy Rose, however** The testimony of Rose, Taylor, and Phillips was reported in "Mysterious Poisoning Cases in Lambeth," *Daily News* (London), June 23, 1892.

178 **Cream appeared** This paragraph is based on the following press reports: "The Stamford Street Poisoning Case," *Pall Mall Gazette* (London), June 10, 1892; "The Mysterious Poisoning Cases," *Guardian* (Manchester), June 11, 1892; "Stamford Street Poisoning Case," *Reynolds's Newspaper* (London); and "Charge of Blackmailing," *Illustrated Police News* (London), June 18, 1892. The description of Cream in the prisoner's dock is based on "The Poisoning Mysteries," *Lloyd's Weekly Newspaper* (London), June 26, 1892.

179 **They are all written** "Poisoning Mysteries," *Lloyd's Weekly Newspaper* (London).

179 the first amongst Harry How, "An Expert in Handwriting," *Strand Magazine* 8, no. 3 (September 1894): 293–94.

179 **I was convinced** Tunbridge Report, June 25, 1892, MEPO 3/144.

180 **They picked him out** Ibid.

180 **I know a girl** Sleaper's testimony was reported in "The Lambeth Poisoning Case," *Morning Post* (London), June 25, 1892; "The Lambeth Poisoning Cases," *Times of London*, June 25, 1892; and "The Lambeth Poisoning Cases," *Daily News* (London), June 25, 1892.

181 **Then Laura Sabbatini** Her arrival and testimony were reported in "Lambeth Poisoning Cases," *Daily News* (London); "Lambeth Poisoning Case," *Morning Post* (London); and "Poisoning Mysteries," *Lloyd's Weekly Newspaper* (London). Cream's "nonchalant attitude" during the hearing was noted in "Mysterious Poisoning of Girls."

181 **He appeared much relieved** Tunbridge Report, May 28, 1892, MEPO 3/144. Haynes's testimony was reported in "Lambeth Poisoning Case," *Morning Post* (London); "Lambeth Poisoning Cases," *Daily News* (London); and "Poisoning Mysteries," *Lloyd's Weekly Newspaper* (London). The prosecution of the theater agent was reported in "The Stamford-Street Road to Ruin," *Daily News* (London) June 25, 1892; and "The Alleged Assaults on Stage Pupils," *Reynolds's Newspaper* (London), June 26, 1892.

182 **Hoots and jeers greeted him** The scene outside the hall was described in "Lambeth Poisoning Cases," *Daily News* (London); and Tunbridge Report, July 4, 1892, MEPO 3/144. An illustration of the scene, with the caption "The Poisoning Mysteries," appeared on the front page of the *Illustrated Police News* (London), July 9, 1892.

Chapter 24. Resurrection

183 **I was struck** Harvey's letter to the magistrate was reproduced in W. Teignmouth Shore, ed., *Trial of Thomas Neill Cream* (London: William Hodge, 1923), 28–29. This description of her testimony at the inquest on July 7 is drawn from these press reports: "The Lambeth Poisoning Cases," *Daily News* (London), July 8, 1892; "The Lambeth Poisoning Case," *Morning Post* (London), July 8, 1892; "The Lambeth Poisoning Cases," *Standard* (London), July 8, 1892; and "The London Poisoning Cases," *Reynolds's Newspaper* (London), July 10, 1892.

184 **perhaps the most mysterious** "The Lambeth Poisoning Cases," *Daily News* (London).

184 **sunny Brighton** "London Poisoning Cases."

184 **reluctant to become embroiled** She failed to appear for a later hearing, forcing police to issue a subpoena. This incident and Scotland Yard's efforts to have her search for the missing letter were recorded in Inspector John Bennett Tunbridge Reports, June 14 and 19, 1892; July 1, 1892; and August 2, 1892, Metropolitan Police Office Records, MEPO 3/144, National Archives, London.

185 **His theme was solely** The interview was republished in "The Poisoning Mysteries," *Lloyd's Weekly Newspaper* (London), June 26, 1892.

185 **Neill was crazy** "Neill's Life in London," *Lloyd's Weekly Newspaper* (London), July 10, 1892.

185 **While at first his manners** "Poisoning Mysteries."

185 **career of crime** "The Poisoning Mysteries," *Illustrated Police News*, July 9, 1892.

185 **Charges of a more** The Waters and Bridge quotations in this paragraph are from "Poisoning Mysteries" *Lloyd's Weekly Newspaper* (London).

186 **have the right** "The Mysterious Poisoning of Girls," *Reynolds's Newspaper* (London), June 26, 1892.

187 **publishing images of Cream** "Poisoning Mysteries," *Lloyd's Weekly Newspaper* (London).

187 **analysis of the pills** Stevenson's July 11, 1892, report of his tests on the sample pills was reproduced in Shore, *Trial of Thomas Neill Cream*, 206–7.

187 **He was smiling** "Prisoner at Bow-Street," *Lloyd's Weekly Newspaper* (London), July 17, 1892.

187 **Thank God** "Neill's Life in London," *Lloyd's Weekly Newspaper* (London), July 10, 1892.

187 **I'm having a fair** Ibid.

187 **Dear Sir** This account of the July 13 hearing, the "Jack the Ripper" letter, and the verdict is based on these press reports: "The Poisonings in South London," *Standard* (London), July 14, 1892; "The Poisoning Mystery," *Morning Post* (London), July 14, 1892; "The Lambeth Poisoning Cases," *Daily News* (London), July 14, 1892;

"The Lambeth Poisoning Case," *Times of London*, July 14, 1892; "London Poisoning Mysteries," *Lloyd's Weekly Newspaper* (London), July 17, 1892; and "The Poisoning Mysteries," *Reynolds's Newspaper* (London), July 17, 1892.

189 **faced a crowd** "Lambeth Poisoning Cases," *Daily News* (London), July 14, 1892.

189 **Bit by bit** "Lambeth Poisoning Cases," *Daily News* (London), July 8, 1892.

CHAPTER 25. MARY ANNE MATILDA FAULKNER

193 **Footsteps drummed** Descriptions of the night Faulkner died, the discovery of her body, the arrests of Cream and Mack, and their statements to police were reported in "A Horrible Case," *Chicago Daily News*, August 21, 1880; "Dr Cream's Crime," *Chicago Daily News*, August 23, 1880; "The Abortionists," *Chicago Daily News*, November 17, 1880; "Double Murder," *Chicago Daily Tribune*, August 22, 1880; "Murderous Malpractice," *Daily Inter Ocean* (Chicago), August 23, 1880; and "Cream's Crime," *Daily Inter Ocean* (Chicago), November 18, 1880.

194 **One identified** Letter marked Exhibit B, filed in *People of the State of Illinois v. Thomas Cream et al.*, Case No. 10926, Box 46, Nineteenth-Century Felony Case Files, Criminal Court of Cook County, Circuit Court of Cook County, archives room 1113, Richard J. Daley Center, Chicago.

194 **Dr. Cream** Ill not Letter marked Exhibit B, filed in ibid.

195 **A Brutal Case** *Chicago Daily News*, August 21, 1880.

195 **a massive fire** Details of the Great Fire's destruction are drawn from Dominic A. Pacyga, *Chicago: A Biography* (Chicago: University of Chicago Press, 2009), 77.

195 **The city has risen** Lady Duffus Hardy, *Through Cities and Prairie Lands: Sketches of an American Tour* (Chicago: Belford, Clarke, 1882), 76–77.

195 **the pulse of America** Reproduced in Stuart Shea, comp., *Chicago in Quotations* (Oxford: Bodleian Library, 2016), 26.

195 **I wish I could** Quoted in Donald L. Miller, *City of the Century: The Epic of Chicago and the Making of America* (New York: Simon & Schuster, 1996), 131.

195 **full of energy** Hardy, *Through Cities and Prairie Lands*, 79.

196 **one million across** Thomas J. Schlereth, *Victorian America: Transformations in Everyday Life, 1876–1915* (New York: HarperCollins, 1991), 71.

196 **Faulkner, twenty-nine** Details about Faulkner are drawn from "Double Murder" and "Murderous Malpractice."

196 **added his name** Certificate of Thomas N. Cream (No. 4290), Register of Licensed Physicians and Surgeons, 1877–1952, Department of Professional Regulation, Record Series 208.028, Illinois State Archives, Springfield.

196 **frequent outbreaks** Thomas Neville Bonner, *Medicine in Chicago, 1850–1950: A Chapter in the Social and Scientific Development of a City* (Madison, WI: American History Research Center, 1957), 23, 25. The state's regulation of the medical profession after 1877 is noted on p. 59.

196 **summer complaint** "Cream a Tartar," *Chicago Times*, August 24, 1880.

197 **relocated his office** One of his offices was at 807 West Madison. His frequent moves were noted in "Churning Cream," *Chicago Times*, August 25, 1880.

SOURCES

197 **considerable difficulty** "Abortionists."

197 **above a barbershop** Neighboring buildings and businesses were identified using newspaper reports and the *United States Federal Census 1880*, Chicago Cook County Illinois, enumeration district 106, p. 12, accessed through www.ancestry.com.

197 **shabby tenements** "House Inspection," *Chicago Daily Tribune*, February 8, 1881. On belief odors spread disease, see "Sanitary Subjects," *Chicago Daily Tribune*, August 17, 1879; and "The Death-Rate," *Chicago Daily Tribune*, May 17, 1881.

197 **crammed with new arrivals** Myriam Pauillac, "Near West Side," in *Encyclopedia of Chicago*, www.encyclopedia.chicagohistory.org/pages/878.html.

197 **nursery for criminals** *Chicago Daily News*, July 7, 1877, quoted in Pacyga, *Chicago*, 70.

197 **Vagrants and gangs roamed** John Flinn and John Wilkie, *History of the Chicago Police from the Settlement of the Community to the Present Time* (Chicago: Police Book Fund, 1887), 152.

197 **All tastes** Paul Durica and Bill Savage, eds., *Chicago by Day and Night: The Pleasure Seeker's Guide to the Paris of America* (Evanston, IL: Northwestern University Press, 2013), 3. Originally published in 1892.

197 **operate openly** Herbert Asbury, *The Gangs of Chicago: An Informal History of the Chicago Underworld* (New York: Thunder's Mouth Press, 2002), 93, 100–103.

197 **bribed the police** "The Gamblers' Triumph," *Chicago Daily Tribune*, January 28, 1875. On police corruption in this era, see Richard C. Lindberg, *To Serve and Collect: Chicago Politics and Police Corruption from the Lager Beer Riot to the Summerdale Scandal, 1855–1960* (Carbondale: Southern Illinois University Press, 1998), chap. 6.

197 **Chicago is in a terrible** Quoted from a letter written in 1874 in Richard C. Lindberg, *The Gambler King of Clark Street: Michael C. McDonald and the Rise of Chicago's Democratic Machine* (Carbondale: Southern Illinois University Press, 2017), vii. Lindberg's book also documents McDonald's gambling empire and political power.

197 **cast adrift** "Doing a Good Work," *Boston Daily Globe*, May 6, 1887.

198 **If a girl didn't** Quoted Joanne J. Meyerowitz, *Women Adrift: Independent Wage Earners in Chicago, 1880–1930* (Chicago: University of Chicago Press, 1988), 27.

198 **They will be left** Quoted in ibid., 48. The association's boardinghouse was noted in "Christian Women," *Chicago Daily Tribune*, November 11, 1881.

198 **tenth of what** "City Slave Girls," *Chicago Times*, July 30, 1890.

198 **scores of self styled** "Lifting the Lid," *Pantagraph* (Bloomington, IL), August 28, 1880.

198 **as little as two dollars** "Irregular M.D.s," *Chicago Daily Tribune*, February 7, 1880.

198 **going rate of ten dollars** Schlereth, *Victorian America*, 274.

198 **quickening** Constance Backhouse, *Petticoats and Prejudice: Women and Law in Nineteenth-Century Canada* (Toronto: Osgoode Society/Women's Press, 1991), 147.

198 **Homemade concoctions** Alison Prentice, Paula Bourne, Gail Cuthbert Brandt, Beth Light, Wendy Mitchinson, and Naomi Black, *Canadian Women: A History* (Toronto: Harcourt Brace Jovanovich, 1988), 164.

199 **female irregularities** Ibid.

199 **Ladies who have reason** Angus McLaren, "Birth Control and Abortion in Canada, 1870–1920," *Canadian Historical Review* 59, no. 3 (1978): 329.

199   **When you are solicited** Quoted in Backhouse, *Petticoats and Prejudice*, 149.

199   **frequent reports** See "Medical Malpractice," *Chicago Daily Tribune*, July 12, 1880; "Another Abortion," *Chicago Daily Tribune*, November 6, 1880; and "Refused to Prosecute," *Chicago Daily Tribune*, November 23, 1880.

199   **diseases of the womb** "The Cream Murder Trial," *Belvidere (IL) Standard*, September 27, 1881.

199   **Producing abortions** "Churning Cream."

199   **over their troubles** "Neill's Last Moments," *Illustrated Police News* (London), November 26, 1892.

199   **as many as fifteen** Mack made this allegation at the coroner's inquest into Faulkner's death. "The Faulkner Inquest," *Chicago Daily Tribune*, August 24, 1880. A claim that brothel keepers retained Cream for abortion services is noted in Vincent Starrett, "The Chicago Career of Dr. Cream—1880," in *Chicago Murders*, ed. Sewell Peaslee Wright (New York: Duell, Sloan & Pearce, 1945), 16.

199   **So long as passion** "A Hideous Crime," *Chicago Daily Tribune*, August 29, 1880.

200   **Dr. Cream cautioned me** This account of the inquest, unless otherwise noted, is based on Hattie Mack's written statement, filed in Inquest No. 1420, Mary A. Faulkner, Cook County Coroner's Inquest Records, 1872–1911, Illinois Regional Archives Depository, Northeastern Illinois University, Chicago, and the following press reports: "The Faulkner Inquest," *Daily Inter Ocean* (Chicago), August 24, 1880; "Cream a Tartar"; "Dr Cream's Crime"; and "The Faulkner Inquest," *Chicago Daily Tribune*. These reports identify Waite only by his title, but his rank and initials appear in "Sheriff Mann's Appointments," *Daily Inter Ocean* (Chicago), November 19, 1880.

201   **Dr. Donald Fraser** Fraser graduated from McGill in 1869. Joseph Hanaway and Richard Cruess, *McGill Medicine*, vol. 1, *The First Half Century, 1829–1885* (Montreal: McGill-Queen's University Press, 1996), 124.

202   **following an abortion committed** Verdict, Inquest No. 1420, Mary A. Faulkner, Cook County Coroner's Inquest Records, 1872–1911.

202   **Under Illinois law** "Hideous Crime."

202   **The Doctor's Record** "Dr Cream's Crime."

203   **to palm off** "Dr. Cream," *Chicago Daily Tribune*, August 23, 1880.

203   **no educated physician** "Abortionists," *Chicago Daily News*, August 24, 1880.

203   **inexperienced and non-professional** Ibid.

203   **general opinion** "Dr. Cream," *Daily Advertiser* (London, ON), August 31, 1880.

203   **Cream's Crime** See "Dr Cream's Crime"; "Cream's Crime," November 18, 1880, *Chicago Times*; and "Cream's Crime," *Daily Inter Ocean* (Chicago).

203   **labeled him a quack** "Murderous Malpractice"; "'Dr.' Cream," *Daily Inter Ocean* (Chicago), November 17, 1880; and "Dr Cream's Crime."

203   **fatal and revolting case** "Murdered by Malpractice," *New York Times*, August 22, 1880.

203   **poor, but honest** "Murderous Malpractice."

203   **scribbled a note** The note was filed as Exhibit A in *People of the State of Illinois v. Thomas Cream et al.*

203   **When a notorious abortionist** "Dr. Earll: The Notorious Abortionist at His Accursed Business Again," *Chicago Daily News*, August 25, 1880. He was convicted

of the lesser offense of attempted abortion and sentenced to a five-year prison term. See "For Five Years," *Chicago Daily News*, December 10, 1880.

203 **fiendish practice** "Hideous Crime" (emphasis in original).

203 **one-year prison term** "The Murder Record," *Daily Inter Ocean* (Chicago), April 26, 1884.

204 **merciless prosecution** "Hideous Crime" (emphasis in original).

204 **Cream wound up sharing** "Murderers' Row," *Daily Inter Ocean* (Chicago), November 17, 1880.

204 **a good deal of comfort** "Electric Brieflets: United States," *Daily Advertiser* (London, ON), August 31, 1880; and "The Two Abortionists," *Chicago Daily News*, August 28, 1880.

204 **Why should I** "Murderers' Row," *Chicago Daily Tribune*, November 17, 1880.

204 **money supplied** There is no direct evidence that William Cream funded his son's defense, but Cream had little money of his own and had received almost $5,000— about $140,000 today—from his father before the latter's death in 1887. See Last Will and Testament, William Cream, November 1885, appended to the probate petition of Daniel Cream, May 25, 1887, Records of the Superior Court for the Province of Quebec, Bibliothèque et Archives nationales du Québec, Quebec City.

204 **more murderers, thieves** "Attacking Mr. Trude," *Chicago Daily Tribune*, December 22, 1894. Trude's career is reviewed in "Alfred S. Trude, Famed Lawyer, Is Dead at 87," *Chicago Daily Tribune*, December 13, 1933.

204 **defended about thirty** O. E. Turner, *Sturla-Stiles Tragedy* (Chicago: O. E. Hammond, 1883), 80.

204 **McDonald, who relied** Lindberg, *Gambler King of Clark Street*, 45.

205 **He could fine me** "How Armour Gave A. S. Trude a Start," *Chicago Daily Tribune*, March 3, 1901.

205 **He is a good judge** Turner, *Sturla-Stiles Tragedy*, 81. His crime scene visits are noted on p. 80.

205 **an unprincipled series** *Chicago Herald*, March 25, 1883, quoted in Lindberg, *Gambler King of Clark Street*, 46.

CHAPTER 26. "PURE CREAM"

206 **combined intelligence and power** Descriptions of Cream and details of jury selection, opening statements, and other early proceedings are drawn from the following press reports: "Will Be Tried Separately," *Daily Inter Ocean* (Chicago), November 16, 1880; "The Criminal Court: The Murder of Mary Faulkner," *Chicago Times*, November 17, 1880; "The Abortionists," *Chicago Daily News*, November 17, 1880; "The Cream Case," *Chicago Journal*, November 17, 1880; "'Dr.' Cream," *Daily Inter Ocean* (Chicago), November 17, 1880; "Cream's Crime," *Daily Inter Ocean* (Chicago), November 18, 1880; and "Dr. Cream," *Chicago Daily Tribune*, November 18, 1880.

206 **attractive in its new** "Echoes of a Dead Past," *Chicago Globe*, June 30, 1892; and John Moses and Joseph Kirkland, eds., *History of Chicago Illinois: Aboriginal to Metropolitan*, vol. 1 (Chicago: Munsell, 1895), 215.

207 **bridge of sighs** "Echoes of a Dead Past."

207 **Men who are not** "Old-Fashioned Judge Gary," *Chicago Daily Tribune*, December 25, 1897. Biographical details are drawn from "Gallery of Local Celebrities: No. XII—Joseph Easton Gary," *Chicago Daily Tribune*, April 15, 1900; "Judge Gary Dies 'in the Harness,'" *Chicago Daily Tribune*, November 1, 1906; and James Green, *Death in the Haymarket: A Story of Chicago, the First Labor Movement and the Bombing that Divided Gilded Age America* (New York: Pantheon Books, 2006), 210–11, 217.

207 **Irrelevant oratorical flights** "This Is My Birthday," *Chicago Daily Tribune*, July 9, 1903.

208 **from the blunt** Mack's testimony is drawn from these press reports: "Cream's Crime"; "Cream's Crime," *Chicago Times*, November 18, 1880; "Dr. Cream," *Chicago Journal*, November 19, 1880; and "Dr. Cream," *Chicago Daily Tribune*, November 19, 1880.

208 **Cream's evasions** The police testimony was reported in "Abortionists"; "Cream's Crime," *Daily Inter Ocean* (Chicago); and "Dr. Cream," *Chicago Daily Tribune*, November 18, 1880.

208 **an ignorant and reckless** The medical evidence was reported in "The Cream Case," *Chicago Daily News*, November 18, 1880; "Cream's Case," *Chicago Times*, November 19, 1880; "The Other Side," *Daily Inter Ocean* (Chicago), November 19, 1880; and "Dr. Cream," *Chicago Daily Tribune*, November 19, 1880.

209 **a thorough knowledge** Cream's testimony was reported in "Dr. Cream," *Chicago Journal*; "Cream's Case"; "Dr. Cream," *Chicago Daily Tribune*, November 19, 1880; "The Cream Case," *Chicago Daily News*, November 19, 1880; and "Other Side."

209 **the Greatest Physician** "Doubtful Doctors," *Chicago Daily Tribune*, February 20, 1880; and "Presumably a Fraud," *Chicago Daily Tribune*, August 3, 1880.

209 **waging a well-publicized** See, for instance, "Irregular M.D.s," *Chicago Daily Tribune*, February 7, 1880; "State Board of Health," *Chicago Daily Tribune*, April 11, 1880; "Illinois State Medical Society," *Chicago Daily Tribune*, May 20, 1880; and "Quacks," *Chicago Daily Tribune*, July 24, 1880.

210 **coached and drilled** The closing arguments were reported in "Cream Case," *Chicago Daily News*, November 19, 1880; "Dr. Cream," *Chicago Journal*; "Dr. Cream," *Chicago Daily Tribune*, November 20, 1880; "Who Did It?" *Daily Inter Ocean* (Chicago), November 20, 1880; and "Pure Cream," *Chicago Times*, November 20, 1880.

210 **conscientious, hard-working** "Death of George C. Ingham," *Chicago Legal News*, February 28, 1891, 217.

210 **a fierce glitter** "Cream Case," *Chicago Daily News*, November 19, 1880.

211 **the work of a skillful** Judge's Instructions to the Jury for the Defendant, filed in *People of the State of Illinois v. Thomas Cream et al.*, Case No. 10926, Box 46, Nineteenth-Century Felony Case Files, Criminal Court of Cook County, Circuit Court of Cook County, archives room 1113, Richard J. Daley Center, Chicago.

211 **We the jury find** Verdict, ibid.

211 **jumped to his feet** Cream's reaction was recorded in "The Cream Case," *Chicago Daily News*, November 20, 1880; "Who Did It?"; and "Pure Cream."

211 **In these days** Editorial Page Note, *Chicago Daily News*, December 11, 1880.

211 **dropped the murder charge** "Fourteen Years," *Chicago Daily Tribune*, November 21, 1880.

212   **Pure Cream** *Chicago Times*, November 20, 1880.
212   **He was a most** "A Psychological Wonder," *St. Louis Post-Dispatch*, November 15, 1892; and "Cream Executed," *Montreal Star*, November 15, 1892.
212   **left free to spread** "The Trinity of Sin," *Chicago Times*, April 16, 1881.
212   **talked incessantly** "A Psychological Wonder."
212   **O'Hara briefed him** Inspector Frederick Smith Jarvis Report, July 14, 1892 (Toronto), Metropolitan Police Office Records, MEPO 3/144, National Archives, London.

CHAPTER 27. ELLEN STACK AND SARAH ALICE MONTGOMERY

213   **tossing about** Details of Stack's death and Cream's comments, unless otherwise noted, are drawn from "Died of Colic," *Chicago Daily Tribune*, March 11, 1881; and "The Coroner's Work," *Daily Inter Ocean* (Chicago), March 11, 1881.
214   **with his character unblemished** "Not an Abortionist," *Decatur Herald*, November 20, 1880.
214   **he might testify in defense** "Dr. Earll," *Chicago Daily Tribune*, December 4, 1880; "Waiting for the Verdict," *Daily Inter Ocean* (Chicago), December 9, 1880; and "Around Town," *Daily Inter Ocean* (Chicago), December 4, 1880. Earll's conviction and sentence were reported in "For Five Years," *Chicago Daily News*, December 10, 1880.
214   **DR. CREAM, Graduate** *Chicago Daily Tribune*, January 23, 1881. The advertisement appeared on p. 7. On the Illinois State Board of Health's prosecution of quacks, see "Irregular M.D.s," *Chicago Daily Tribune* February 7, 1880; "Local Crime," *Chicago Daily Tribune*, March 6, 1880; and "State Board of Health," *Chicago Daily Tribune*, April 11, 1880.
214   **forms that touted** This is noted in a copy of the prescription he wrote for Ellen Stack in March 1881. See Home Office Records, HO 144/245 A 54360/3, National Archives, London.
214   **Terror District** Richard C. Lindberg, *Gangland Chicago: Criminality and Lawlessness in the Windy City* (Lanham, MD: Rowman & Littlefield, 2016), 122.
214   **soon engaged to marry** Cream's fiancée is identified in "Skipped Out: The Notorious Dr. Cream," *Chicago Daily Tribune*, June 28, 1881. See also Vincent Starrett, "The Chicago Career of Dr. Cream—1880," in *Chicago Murders*, ed. Sewell Peaslee Wright (New York: Duell, Sloan & Pearce, 1945), 23.
215   **It was found** "Coroner's Work."
215   **Some rumors were afloat** "Sudden Death," *Chicago Times*, March 11, 1881.
215   **The girl had every** "Coroner's Work." Cases of smallpox were noted in press reports, and fifty people died of the disease that July. See "Contagious Diseases," *Chicago Daily News*, April 21, 1881; "The Small-Pox Again," *Chicago Daily News*, April 28, 1881; and "The Deaths during July," *Chicago Daily News*, August 6, 1881.
216   **Cases of accidental** See "Probably a Druggist's Mistake," *Chicago Daily Tribune*, July 27, 1880, a report on a Minnesota poisoning; and "A Druggist's Blunder," *Chicago Daily Tribune*, August 10, 1880, on a similar case in New Jersey. On the New York ordinance, see "Poison in Prescriptions," *Chicago Daily News*, September 8, 1880.

216 **mistakenly added morphine** "A Druggist's Blunder," *Chicago Daily Tribune*,
January 30, 1881.

216 **no inquest was held** There is no record of an inquest in the archives of the Cook
County Coroner's Office. Paul M. Hughes, intern at Illinois Regional Archives
Depository, Northeastern Illinois University, Chicago, telephone communication
with the author, July 27, 2017.

216 **Stack was interred** See the note from Stack's relatives and friends, thanking the
Bowler family for "aiding in giving the remains a decent burial," published in "The
City: In General," *Chicago Daily Tribune*, March 13, 1881; and "Chicago Brevities,"
Daily Inter Ocean (Chicago), March 14, 1881. Her burial is recorded in *Cook County
Illinois Deaths Index, 1878–1922*, accessed through www.ancestry.com.

216 **There is no question** "The City: In General," *Chicago Daily Tribune*, March 12, 1881.

217 **I understand you are** Copies of Cream's March 13 and March 24 letters are in HO
144/245 A 54360/3 (emphasis in original).

218 **I asked him if** "Murdered by Poison: Astounding Criminal Career of Dr. T. N.
Cream," *Chicago Daily Tribune*, June 28, 1892.

218 **by changing the medicines** Pyatt's allegation is contained in the July 26, 1892, letter
of J. Hayes Sadler of the British Consulate in Chicago to the Foreign Office, HO
144/245 A 54360/3. Some press reports later identified Cream as Stack's killer. See
"A Study of His Crimes: By One Who Knew Him," *St. James's Gazette* (London),
October 24, 1892; and "Well Known over Here," *Daily Review* (Decatur, IL),
November 16, 1892. Stack's death is also linked to Cream in W. Teignmouth Shore,
ed., *Trial of Thomas Neill Cream* (London: William Hodge, 1923), 4.

219 **A death surrounded** "Mysterious Death," *Chicago Daily Tribune*, April 10, 1881.
Unless otherwise cited, this description of Montgomery, her movements, and her
death are based on this and the following press reports: "Was It Suicide?" *Chicago
Times*, April 10, 1881; "Alice Montgomery," *Chicago Daily Tribune*, April 11, 1881;
"Death's Mystery," *Chicago Times*, April 11, 1881; "Alice Montgomery," *Chicago
Daily News*, April 11, 1881; and "Alice Montgomery's Fate," *Chicago Morning News*,
April 11, 1881.

220 **an autopsy revealed** The postmortem's results were reported in "Alice
Montgomery," *Chicago Daily News*; "Alice Montgomery's Death," *Daily Inter Ocean*
(Chicago), April 12, 1881; "Alice Montgomery," *Chicago Daily Tribune*, April 12, 1881;
and "Suicide of an Illiopolis Girl," *Decatur (IL) Weekly Republican*, April 14, 1881.

220 **Somebody committed** "Pith of the News," *Daily Inter Ocean* (Chicago), April 12, 1881.

220 **produced letters** The text of the letters was reproduced in news coverage of
the inquest. See "The Dead Speak," *Chicago Times*, April 24, 1881; and "Very
Unsatisfactory," *Chicago Daily Tribune*, April 24, 1881.

220 **We further find** Inquest No. 316, Sarah Alice Montgomery, April 11, 16, and 23, 1881,
Cook County Coroner's Inquest Records, 1872–1911, Control No. 7/0044/01, vol. 7,
p. 1. Illinois Regional Archives Depository, Northeastern Illinois University, Chicago.

220 **did the strychnine** "Very Unsatisfactory."

220 **Could Alice have got** "Dead Speak."

221 **a regular abortionist** Inspector Frederick Smith Jarvis Report, July 14, 1892 (Toronto),
Metropolitan Police Office Records, MEPO 3/144, National Archives, London.

221 **One jostles the elbow** Quoted in Herbert Asbury, *The Gangs of Chicago: An Informal History of the Chicago Underworld* (New York: Thunder's Mouth Press, 2002), 92.

221 **A ten-dollar bribe** Frank Morn, *Forgotten Reformer: Robert McClaughry and Criminal Justice Reform in Nineteenth-Century America* (Lanham, MD: University Press of America, 2011), 155.

221 **patronized saloons and brothels** Ibid., 139.

221 **McDonald made regular payments** Richard C. Lindberg, *To Serve and Collect: Chicago Politics and Police Corruption from the Lager Beer Riot to the Summerdale Scandal, 1855–1960* (Carbondale: Southern Illinois University Press, 1998), 42; and Curt Johnson with R. Craig Sautter, *The Wicked City: Chicago from Kenna to Capone* (New York: Da Capo Press, 1998), 110.

222 **in an exceedingly bad box** "Dead Speak."

222 **The mystery of Alice** "Very Unsatisfactory."

222 **"Cream," he assured** News item from *Rockford (IL) Register*, reproduced in the *Belvidere (IL) Standard*, September 13, 1881. Chicago author and historian Adam Selzer appears to be the first writer to link Cream to Montgomery's murder. See "Did Dr. Thomas Neill Cream Kill Alice Montgomery?" *Mysterious Chicago: History at Its Coolest*, posted September 4, 2015, mysteriouschicago.com/did-dr-thomas-neill-cream-kill-alice-montgomery.

CHAPTER 28. A DESPICABLE SCHEME

223 **I am obliged** Indictment, November 22, 1881, *United States v. Thomas N. Cream*, Criminal Case 686, Record Group 21 (Criminal Cases 1873–1939), Records of the US Circuit and District Courts, Northern District of Illinois, Eastern Division, Chicago, National Archives at Chicago. The text of the postcards was reproduced in "'Dr.' Cream: In the Toils for Sending Scurrilous Postal-Cards," *Chicago Daily Tribune*, June 19, 1881.

223 **two threatening letters** "'Dr.' Cream."

224 **a fine** Newspaper accounts of the case incorrectly reported the maximum fine as five hundred dollars in 1881. See the report on the Kentucky case of *United States v. Smith* in the *Internal Revenue Record and Customs Journal* 28 (October 16, 1882): 327.

224 **People over in Canada** "Off-Color 'Cream,'" *Chicago Daily Tribune*, June 21, 1881.

224 **the notorious Dr. Cream** See "Dr. Cream's Artifice," *Chicago Daily News*, June 22, 1881; "Skipped Out: The Notorious Dr. Cream," *Chicago Daily Tribune*, June 28, 1881; and "Doctor Cream's Crime," *Chicago Morning News*, June 20, 1881.

224 **a prospect of being rewarded** "'Dr.' Cream."

224 **enclosed his title in quotation marks** See ibid; "Whipped Cream: The Public Lash Is Again Wrapped around the Recreant Legs," *Daily Inter Ocean* (Chicago), June 20, 1881; and "Off-Color 'Cream.'"

224 **was granted a one-week adjournment** Transcript of Proceedings, July 2, 1881, *United States v. Thomas N. Cream*, Criminal Case 686, Record Group 21 (Criminal Cases 1873–1939), Records of the US Circuit and District Courts, Northern District of Illinois, Eastern Division, Chicago.

224 **resorted to** "'Dr.' Cream."
225 **ordered to forfeit her bond** Transcript of Proceedings; and "Dr. Cream Did Not Appear," *Chicago Daily News*, June 27, 1881.
225 **The case against Cream** "Skipped Out."

CHAPTER 29. DANIEL STOTT

226 **His upper lip** Julia Stott described her husband's death in Transcript of Evidence before the Coroner's Jury, July 14, 1881, 6–7, 12, filed in *People of the State of Illinois v. Thomas N. Cream and Julia A. Stott*, Case No. 4580, Circuit Court, Boone County, IL.
227 **Want you to have** The originals of Cream's telegrams and letters to Whitman and Coon, and their responses, are on file in ibid.
227 **His skill and marked** *Belvidere Illustrated: Historical, Descriptive and Biographical* (Belvidere, IL: Daily Republican, 1896), 88–89.
228 **was endeavoring** Frank S. Whitman and R. Lehman Neff, "Hidden Horror of the Pink Pills," *Complete Detective Cases* 2, no. 3 (May 1940): 55. Whitman described his reaction to the telegrams and his search for the names Crame and Cram in this article.
228 **He died of one** Transcript of Evidence before the Coroner's Jury, July 14, 1881, 45–46, 49.
230 **As many as a dozen** See, for instance, classified advertisements under the heading "Clairvoyants" on p. 3 of the *Chicago Daily News*, August 11, 1880.
230 **Within minutes the animal** Transcript of Evidence before the Coroner's Jury, July 14, 1881, 49.
230 **a quantity sufficient** Letter, Walter Haines, ibid., July 8, 1881.
231 **frontier feel** Background on Garden Prairie, Belvidere, and Boone County is drawn from *Images of America: Belvidere and Boone County* (Charleston, SC: Arcadia Publishing, 2015), 7–9, 17, 116.
231 **A man of good habits** "Doctor Cream," *Chicago Daily Tribune*, August 1, 1881. This is the source of other biographical information on Daniel and Julia Stott.
231 **Julia was inclined** Whitman and Neff, "Hidden Horror of the Pink Pills," 40.
231 **Rumors, faint yet persistent** Ibid.
231 **I am improving** Daniel Stott to Thomas Neill Cream, March 18, 1881, filed in *People of the State of Illinois v. Thomas N. Cream and Julia A. Stott*.
232 **ten days or so** Transcript of Evidence before the Coroner's Jury, July 14, 1881, 1–2, 8–9, 13.
232 **If further investigation** "Local Items," *Belvidere (IL) Standard*, June 28, 1881.
232 **The inquest was held** All quotations and testimony in this account of the inquest are drawn from Transcript of Evidence before the Coroner's Jury, July 14, 1881.
234 **The druggists were responsible** This exchange and the additional questioning of Julia Stott were reported in "Doctor Cream."
234 **It was a case** "Crooked Cream," *Belvidere (IL) Standard*, July 26, 1881.

CHAPTER 30. "CROOKED CREAM"

235 **crooks of all dyes** Quoted in C. H. Gervais, *The Border Police: One Hundred and Twenty-Five Years of Policing in Windsor* (Waterloo, ON: Penumbra Press, 1992), 22.

236 **he turned pale** "Dr. Cream Nabbed," *Belvidere (IL) Standard*, August 2, 1881. Details of Cream's arrest are drawn from this article and "Alleged Murder," *Detroit Free Press*, July 28, 1881. Cream used the name Thomas Creighton when he crossed the border but was registered at the Belle River hotel as Dr. Ross. See "Doctor Cream," *Chicago Daily Tribune*, August 1, 1881.

236 **the notoriety of the case** "Alleged Murder."

236 **to consult his father** Thomas Davidson to Frances Willard, June 22, 1890, Records of Commutations of Sentence, 1877–1928, Record Series 103.098, Illinois State Archives, Springfield.

236 **postal officials in Chicago** "Dr. Cream Nabbed."

236 **I don't see how** "The Notorious Cream," *Chicago Daily Tribune*, July 29, 1881.

236 **He had arrived** "Doctor Cream."

236 **not among the crimes** Samuel R. Clarke and Henry P. Sheppard, *A Treatise on the Criminal Law of Canada*, 2nd ed. (Toronto: Hart, 1882), 10, 19–20.

237 **the Garden Prairie business** "Dr. Cream," *Chicago Daily Tribune*, July 3, 1881.

237 **notorious Chicago abortionist** *Pantagraph*, July 28, 1881. His trial for the murder of Mary Anne Faulkner was noted in "Notorious Cream."

237 **perfectly analogous** "Dr. Cream Again," *Daily Advertiser* (London, ON), June 28, 1881

237 **The annals of crime** "The Cream Poisoning Case," *Chicago Daily Tribune*, August 2, 1881.

238 **The general belief** "Dr. Cream Nabbed."

238 **fix the poisoning** "Local Items," *Belvidere (IL) Standard*, August 2, 1881.

238 **When Sheriff Ames announced** "Local Items," *Belvidere (IL) Standard*, August 16, 1881; and news item from *Rockford (IL) Register*, reproduced in *Belvidere (IL) Standard*, September 13, 1881.

238 **along with a prediction** "Local Items," *Belvidere (IL) Standard*, August 16, 1881.

238 **Crooked Cream** "Local Items," *Belvidere (IL) Standard*, July 26, 1881.

238 **Bad Cream** *Pantagraph*, July 28, 1881

238 **Such a cow-ardly man** "Local Items," *Belvidere (IL) Standard*, August 9, 1881.

238 **making it a really** "Circuit Court," *Belvidere (IL) Standard*, September 13, 1881.

238 **It took almost a day** "Cream's Trial," *Chicago Times*, September 21, 1881.

238 **men of sound judgment** "Criminal News," *Chicago Daily Tribune*, October 19, 1881. Five of the first nine selected were from Belvidere. See "The Cream Murder Trial—Latest," *Belvidere (IL) Standard*, September 20, 1881.

239 **Grief and sadness** "How the News Was Received," *Belvidere (IL) Standard*, September 27, 1881.

239 **matters too indelicate** "The Cream Murder Trial," *Belvidere (IL) Standard*, September 27, 1881. This is also the source of the description of Julia Stott as she testified.

239 **She turned States' evidence** "Criminal News," *Chicago Daily Tribune*, September 22, 1881.

240 **She saw him tampering** "Cream's Trial," *Chicago Times*, September 22, 1881.

240 **criminally intimate** Ibid.

240 **Dr. Cream told me** "Criminal News," *Chicago Daily Tribune*, September 22, 1881.

240 **He expected to hear** Ibid.

240 **he could mix** Transcript of the Evidence of Mary McClellan (September 1881), Records of Commutations of Sentence, 1877-1928, Record Series 103.098, Illinois State Archives, Springfield.

240 **The public has no confidence** Quoted in Mark Essig, "Poison Murder and Expert Testimony: Doubting the Physician in Late Nineteenth-Century America," *Yale Journal of Law and the Humanities* 14, 1 (2002): 206.

240 **the subject of everybody's** Quoted in ibid.

240 **gaudy and unembarrassed lying** Quoted in ibid.

240 **an unmitigated joke** Quoted in ibid.

241 **trying the wrong person** "Criminal News," *Chicago Daily Tribune*, September 22, 1881.

241 **refused to fund his defense** Inspector Frederick Smith Jarvis Report, July 4, 1892 (Montreal), Metropolitan Police Office Records, MEPO 3/144, National Archives, London.

241 **fighting qualities** *Belvidere Illustrated: Historical, Descriptive and Biographical* (Belvidere, IL: Daily Republican, 1896), 81.

241 **Munn grilled Stott** "Cream Murder Trial."

241 **hard feelings** "Criminal News," *Chicago Daily Tribune*, September 23, 1881.

241 **A homely, coarse-looking** "Cream Murder Trial."

241 **fix a dose** Ibid.

241 **In my prescription** "Criminal News," *Chicago Daily Tribune*, September 23, 1881.

241 **I suspected Mrs. Stott** Ibid.

242 **admitted many things** "Cream's Case," *Chicago Times*, September 23, 1881.

242 **exactly contrary** Ibid.

242 **brilliant, able and eloquent** "Criminal News," *Chicago Daily Tribune*, September 24, 1881.

242 **a masterly and convincing** "Cream Sentenced for Life," *Chicago Times*, September 25, 1881.

242 **Spectators took bets** "Cream Murder Trial."

242 **nine to three** "Cream Sentenced for Life."

242 **Not a muscle** "Circuit Court."

242 **might impose the death penalty** This point was made in "Criminal News," *Chicago Daily Tribune*, October 18, 1881.

242 **If ever a man** "Criminal News," *Chicago Daily Tribune*, October 19, 1881.

242 **Jarvis interviewed Dr. Walter Haines** The detective's findings in Chicago and Belvidere are recorded in Jarvis Reports, July 11, 1892 (Chicago), and July 14, 1892 (Toronto), MEPO 3/144.

243 **equally guilty** "Criminal News," *Chicago Daily Tribune*, September 24, 1881.

243 had agreed to release "Mrs. Stott Released," *Belvidere (IL) Standard*, February 21, 1882.

243 **End of a Dangerous** "Prison for Life," *Chicago Daily News*, September 24, 1881.

CHAPTER 31. NO. 4374

---

244 **Fresh fish** S. W. Wetmore "Life in Joliet Prison" (manuscript), 2–3, MSS Alpha1 W, S. W. Wetmore Collection, Chicago History Museum; and "In Convict Garb," *Chicago Daily Tribune*, November 20, 1885. Descriptions of the admission process are based on these sources unless otherwise noted.

244 **massive jaws and chin** "Description of Convict," November 1, 1881, Records of Commutations of Sentence, 1877–1928, Record Series 103.098, Illinois State Archives, Springfield. Cream's mug shot is missing from his prison file.

245 **looked like a circus clown** Frank Morn, *Forgotten Reformer: Robert McClaughry and Criminal Justice Reform in Nineteenth-Century America* (Lanham, MD: University Press of America, 2011), 45, 88.

245 **the most eminent rascals** Wetmore, "Life in Joliet Prison," 4, 8.

245 **About fifteen hundred men** Within six months of Cream's arrival, the number stood at 1,504. "Crime, Its Causes," *Chicago Daily Tribune*, April 14, 1882.

245 **the dark ages** Edgardo Rotman, "The Failure of Reform: United States, 1865–1965," in *The Oxford History of the Prison: The Practice of Punishment in Western Society*, ed. Norval Morris and David J. Rothman (New York: Oxford University Press, 1995), 170.

246 **My idea of punishment** Morn, *Forgotten Reformer*, 67.

246 **solitary confinement building** "In Convict Garb"; and Wetmore, "Life in Joliet Prison," text of address dated April 15, 1892.

246 **Joliet's rules** The rules are reproduced in Morn, *Forgotten Reformer*, 69n45. They were issued in 1876 but still in force when Cream arrived. See *Catalogue of the Library of the Illinois State Penitentiary, Joliet, Illinois* (Joliet: Joliet Daily Republic Print, 1883), 4–5.

247 **closet sized stone coffin** The cells are described in S. W. Wetmore, *Behind the Bars at Joliet: A Famous Prison, Its Celebrated Inmates and Its Mysteries* (Chicago: Western News, 1892), 21–23.

247 **He would grow accustomed** The "atmosphere" emanating from the cells is noted in Everett J. Murphy, Warden, *Report of the Commissioners of the Illinois State Penitentiary at Joliet for the Two Years Ending Sept. 30, 1900* (Springfield: State of Illinois, 1901), 11–12.

247 **start of the workday** For the daily routine, see Wetmore, "Life in Joliet Prison," 6–8; and "Convict Life," *Chicago Daily Tribune*, February 23, 1884. The menu is reproduced in Morn, *Forgotten Reformer*, 49n12. On the practice of marching in lockstep, see David J. Rothman, "Perfecting the Prison: United States, 1789–1865," in Morris and Rothman, *Oxford History of the Prison*, 122.

248 **Cream was assigned** "Description of Convict."

248 **eagle to adorn** "Joliet Jots," *Chicago Daily Tribune*, August 23, 1885. This article also identified his coworkers.

248 **Silence, obedience** Wetmore, "Life in Joliet Prison," 7.

248 **The prison is rapidly** "Joliet Prison," *Chicago Daily Tribune*, July 4, 1884.

248 **sharpened a stolen** "Killed by His Cell-Mate," *Chicago Daily Tribune*, June 1, 1883; Wetmore, *Behind the Bars at Joliet*, 129–32.

248 **a Wild West desperado** "Frank Rande," *Chicago Daily Tribune*, March 3, 1884; "Rande's Hand," *Cairo (IL) Bulletin*, March 8, 1884; Wetmore, *Behind the Bars at Joliet*, 108–10.

248 **only one in a hundred** Wetmore, *Behind the Bars at Joliet*, 89–100.

249 **One man removed** Henri Le Caron, *Twenty-Five Years in the Secret Service: The Recollections of a Spy* (London: William Heinemann, 1893), 49–52.

249 **Thirty-nine inmates** died "Within Stone Walls," *Chicago Daily Tribune*, January 18, 1886. Tuberculosis as the leading cause of death is noted in "Joliet Prison," *Daily Inter Ocean* (Chicago), December 29, 1886.

249 **freed by death** "From Joliet," *Chicago Daily Tribune*, August 8, 1885.

249 **one used a kitchen knife** Morn, *Forgotten Reformer*, 59. Wetmore described other suicides in "Life in Joliet Prison," 15.

249 **cemetery on a hill** S. W. Wetmore, "Life in a Great Prison," *Illustrated American*, March 8, 1890, 58; and Wetmore, "Life in Joliet Prison," 20–21.

249 **monotonous semi-conscious existence** Wetmore, *Behind the Bars at Joliet*, 51, 54.

249 **subscribe to newspapers** Ibid., 76, 101–2.

249 **The library offered** *Catalogue of the Library of the Illinois State Penitentiary*. The twenty-page "Voyages and Travels" section begins on p. 65. The book *The Narcotics We Indulge In; The Poisons We Select; The Odors We Enjoy* is listed on p. 87.

249 **he could stay for only** Wetmore, "Life in Joliet Prison," 26.

249 **On every occasion** Inspector Frederick Smith Jarvis Report, July 4, 1892 (Montreal), Metropolitan Police Records Office, MEPO 3/144, National Archives, London.

250 **He corresponded** Ibid.

250 **A model officer** Wetmore, "Life in Joliet Prison," 3.

250 **He was a smart fellow** "McClaughry Talks of Cream," *Chicago Daily Tribune*, June 27, 1892.

250 **The small advertisement** The notice was reproduced in a "Proof of Publication" form filed as part of the pardon application. Records of Commutations of Sentence, 1877–1928, Record Series 103.098, Illinois State Archives, Springfield.

251 **did not take much** "McClaughry Talks of Cream." On the monitoring of inmate mail, see Morn, *Forgotten Reformer*, 45.

251 **was not so much** William Robert Greene, "Early Development of the Illinois State Penitentiary System," *Journal of the Illinois State Historical Society* 70, no. 3 (August 1977): 192.

251 **Of the 153 killers** "'Lifers,'" *Chicago Daily Tribune*, September 19, 1885. Wetmore recorded similar statistics in *Behind the Bars at Joliet*, 137.

251 **one of the three commissioners** The state senate approved the April 16, 1885, nomination on May 28 of that year. *Journal of the Senate of the Thirty-Fourth General Assembly of the State of Illinois* (Springfield, IL: Journal, State Printers, 1885), 570, 627, 825.

252 **remarks about Stott's imminent** Affidavits of Fredericke Martin, Samuel Martin, and Eva Adams, March 26, 1885, Records of Commutations of Sentence, 1877–1928, Record Series 103.098, Illinois State Archives, Springfield.

252 **He got what he deserved** Affidavits of John Jennison, July 21, 1884, and April 21, 1885, ibid. McClellan may have had an additional motive to seek revenge. She appar-

ently told Sheriff Albert Ames that Cream had seduced her daughter and made her pregnant. He had performed an abortion, she added, and "she had got over it all right." Jarvis Report, July 11, 1892 (Chicago), MEPO 3/144.

252 **teacher lawyer** *Belvidere Illustrated: Historical, Descriptive and Biographical* (Belvidere, IL: Daily Republican, 1896), 129–30.

252 **focused his attack** Affidavit of O. H. Wright, July 19, 1884; O. H. Wright to Governor Richard Oglesby, November 4, 1885; Petition to Governor Oglesby, October 1, 1885. Records of Commutations of Sentence, 1877–1928, Record Series 103.098, Illinois State Archives, Springfield.

252 **refused to represent her** Affidavit of O. H. Wright, August 18, 1887, ibid.

253 **not guilty in any degree** Petition of Thomas N. Cream, May 1885, ibid.

253 **he asked the Canadian government** "Thomas N. Cream—Asks Interference of Dominion Government to Secure His Release from Illinois State Prison, July 1885," Department of Justice files, RG13-A-2, vol. 63, file 1885-744, Library and Archives Canada, Ottawa. The record itself is missing from the archive's collections. Email of Alison Pier, Reference Services, Library and Archives Canada, to author, May 17, 2017.

253 **I have no doubt** John Dunn to Governor Richard Oglesby, November 9, 1885, Records of Commutations of Sentence, 1877–1928, Record Series 103.098, Illinois State Archives, Springfield.

253 **not doing reasonable work** Warden's Office Form on Convict Conduct, May 27, 1889, and May 22, 1891, ibid.

253 **a horrific, soul-destroying ordeal** Conditions in solitary confinement were described in Wetmore, "Life in Joliet Prison," 20; and *Behind the Bars at Joliet*, 50.

254 **The terrible loneliness** "Crime, Its Causes."

254 **many prisoners had gone mad** "Revealed: An Ex-Convict, Just from Joliet, Tells Interesting Tales," *Chicago Daily Globe*, October 21, 1892.

254 **I never dreamed** Charles Fuller to Governor Richard Oglesby, November 17, 1885, Records of Commutations of Sentence, 1877–1928, Record Series 103.098, Illinois State Archives, Springfield (emphasis in original).

254 **Fuller softened his stance** Charles Fuller to Governor Richard Oglesby, January 1, 1886, ibid.

254 **Cream is too dangerous** Buck & Rayner to Governor Richard Oglesby, March 21, 1885, November 20, 1885, and November 30, 1885, ibid.

254 **were expected to sign** Buck & Rayner to Governor Richard Oglesby, January 2, 1886, ibid.; and Frank S. Whitman to James B. Rayner, December 31, 1885, ibid.

255 **one of the most premeditated** Frank S. Whitman to Governor Richard Oglesby, January 3, 1886.

255 **sufficiently cleared of doubt** Letter, Governor Richard Oglesby, December 31, 1885, ibid.

255 **Some men are born** "Crime, Its Causes."

256 **a man of criminal** "McClaughry Talks of Cream."

CHAPTER 32. "AS INNOCENT AS THE CHILD UNBORN"

257 **When the wicked man** See photographs of the chapel's interior in Joliet Prison Photograph Collection, 1987.0129 PPL, Chicago History Museum.

258 **suffer with patience** "Confirming Convicts," *Chicago Daily Tribune*, June 7, 1886. The sprays of white flowers are described in "Convicts Confirmed," *Daily Review* (Decatur, IL), June 8, 1886.

258 **When asked his religion** "Description of Convict," November 1, 1881, Records of Commutations of Sentence, 1877–1928, Record Series 103.098, Illinois State Archives, Springfield.

258 **chances of procuring** "Hanged at Newgate," *Chicago Daily Tribune*, November 15, 1892.

258 **He suffered from** Lorne F. Hammond, "Capital, Labour and Lumber in A.R.M. Lower's Woodyard: James Maclaren and the Changing Forest Economy, 1850–1906" (PhD diss., University of Ottawa, 1993), 165–67. Information on Cream's health problems, his journeys south, his Little Rock investments, and his break with Maclaren are drawn from this source. Street directories for Quebec City list Daniel Cream as a lumber merchant, replacing William Cream, after 1886.

258 **a heavy owner** "Died," *Daily Arkansas Gazette* (Little Rock), June 4, 1887.

258 **Executors valued his estate** Executor William Brown offered this estimate of the estate's value in an 1892 interview with Scotland Yard detective Frederick Jarvis. Inspector Frederick Smith Jarvis Report, June 30, 1892 (Quebec City), Metropolitan Police Office Records, MEPO 3/144, National Archives, London.

258 **having received** Last Will and Testament, William Cream, November 1885, appended to the probate petition of Daniel Cream, May 25, 1887, Records of the Superior Court for the Province of Quebec, Bibliothèque et Archives nationales du Québec, Quebec City. After Cream's arrest, many newspapers erroneously reported that he had inherited $16,000, a quarter of the entire estate—almost $445,000 today. One of the earliest of these reports originated in Chicago. See "O'Neill Is Not His Name," *Chicago Daily News*, June 28, 1892.

259 **eccentric old gentleman** "Local Items," *Daily Arkansas Gazette* (Little Rock), June 22, 1887.

259 **I wish to leave** Last Will and Testament, William Cream, November 1885.

258 **the crushing weight** Thomas Davidson to Governor Joseph Fifer, March 10, 1890, Records of Commutations of Sentence, 1877–1928, Record Series 103.098, Illinois State Archives, Springfield.

259 **to use all** Jarvis Report, June 30, 1892 (Quebec City), MEPO 3/144; and Affidavit of Thomas Davidson, October 29, 1892, Home Office Records, HO 144/246 A 54360/23, National Archives, London.

259 **backed the effort** Jarvis Report, July 4, 1892 (Montreal), MEPO 3/144.

259 **were and are most** James Emslie to Thomas Davidson, October 18, 1888, Records of Commutations of Sentence, 1877–1928, Record Series 103.098, Illinois State Archives, Springfield.

260 **Former employers and other** Letter, William H. Baldwin, October 18, 1888; Letter, Rod Davison, October 20, 1888; Letter, James Robertson, October 26, 1888; and Letter, Peter Baldwin, November 27, 1888, ibid.

260 **the worthy son** Davidson to Fifer, March 10, 1890, ibid.
260 **I have investigated** Charles Fuller to Governor Richard Oglesby, November 28, 1888, ibid.
260 **A new petition** Petition to Governor Joseph Fifer, n.d., ibid.
260 **acquitting juries** James O'Donnell Bennett, *"Private Joe" Fifer* (Bloomington, IL: Pantagraph Printing & Stationery, 1936), 80.
260 **To me that didn't** Ibid. Biographical information on Fifer is drawn from pp. 69–70, 78–79; and "Private Joe Dies in His 98th Year; Victim of a Fall," *Chicago Daily Tribune*, August 7, 1938.
260 **Fuller, a close friend** *Belvidere Illustrated: Historical, Descriptive and Biographical* (Belvidere, IL: Daily Republican, 1896), 81.
260 **You may promise** Daniel Cream to Charles Fuller, June 4, 1889, and Charles Fuller to Governor Joseph Fifer, June 8, 1889, Records of Commutations of Sentence, 1877–1928, Record Series 103.098, Illinois State Archives, Springfield.
261 **Utter the word** Davidson to Fifer, March 10, 1890, ibid.
261 **as innocent as** Thomas Davidson to Frances Willard, June 22, 1890, ibid.
261 **Dr. Cream is innocent** Senator Shelby Moore Cullom to Governor Joseph Fifer, July 3, 1890, ibid.
261 **in a most extraordinary** Jarvis Report, June 30, 1892 (Quebec City), MEPO 3/144.
262 **Cream convinced James Rayner** James Rayner to Charles Fuller, May 4, 1891, Records of Commutations of Sentence, 1877–1928, Record Series 103.098, Illinois State Archives, Springfield.
262 **The ends of justice** Charles Fuller to Governor Joseph Fifer, June 12, 1891, ibid.
262 **In view of** Quoted in H. Kenneth Scatliff, "Medical Lore in Chicagoland: A Mistress Foils the Master Plot," *Chicago Medicine* 68, no. 24 (November 27, 1965): 1063.
262 **a fit and proper** Order to Commute the Sentence of Thomas N. Cream, June 12, 1891, Department of Corrections, Penitentiary Mittimus Files, 1857–1916, Record Series 243.202, Illinois State Archives, Springfield.
262 **Good behavior** Warden's Office Form on Convict Conduct, May 22, 1891, Records of Commutations of Sentence, 1877–1928, Record Series 103.098, Illinois State Archives, Springfield. The formula used to reduce an inmate's sentence—up to six months was deducted from a fixed prison term for each year of good behavior—is outlined in "Friend of Felons," *Chicago Daily Tribune*, October 7, 1893.
262 **The judicious use** "Anarchist Neebe: He Will Leave Prison a Free Man on Thanksgiving Day," *St. Louis Post-Dispatch*, November 20, 1892.
262 **the free use of money** Trude discussed the payments in "Cream Executed," *Montreal Star*, November 15, 1892; and "Execution of Neil," *Illustrated Police News*, November 19, 1892.
262 **it cost his family** Daniel Cream to Rev. George Mathews, May 14, 1892, HO 144 /246 A 54360/25. Wright, in contrast, appears to have been paid only forty dollars—about $1,100 in today's terms—for his extensive efforts on Cream's behalf. "McClaughry Talks of Cream," *Chicago Daily Tribune*, June 27, 1892.
262 **exerted every legitimate influence** Affidavit of Thomas Davidson, October 29, 1892, HO 144/246 A 54360/23.

263 **was the State not** Arthur Conan Doyle, *Memories and Adventures and Western Wanderings* (Newcastle upon Tyne: Cambridge Scholars Publishing, 2009), 299.

264 **The task was** "O'Neill Is Not His Name," *Chicago Daily News*, June 28, 1892. Murray also described his dealings with Cream in a June 12, 1892, letter to Robert Pinkerton, who ran the firm's New York office, in MEPO 3/144.

CHAPTER 33. CHASING SHADOWS

265 **He remembers** Cream well Details of the Chicago investigation are drawn from Inspector Frederick Jarvis Reports, July 11, 1892 (Chicago) and July 14, 1892 (Toronto), Metropolitan Police Records Office, MEPO 3/144, National Archives, London; and Letter, Inspector Frederick Smith Jarvis to Superintendent John Shore, July 19, 1892, ibid.

265 **a licentious man** "McClaughry Talks of Cream," *Chicago Daily Tribune*, June 27, 1892.

265 **John Cantle walked** Report, Sergeant John Craggs to Inspector John Bennett Tunbridge, June 20, 1892, MEPO 3/144.

266 **The information was cabled** Superintendent John Shore directed that the information about *Sarnia*'s passengers be passed along to Jarvis. See his notation on Inspector John Bennett Tunbridge Memo, June 21, 1892, ibid.

266 **interview** Rev. Robert Caswell Jarvis Report, July 15, 1892 (Toronto), ibid.

266 **believed he was guilty** Jarvis Report, September 2, 1892 (Montreal), ibid.

266 **Leon Vohl, was reluctant** Jarvis Reports, June 30, 1892 (Quebec City) and July 29, 1892 (New York City), ibid.

266 **died on August 29, 1891** Quebec, Vital and Church Records, 1621–1968, Drouin Collection, Institut généalogique Drouin, accessed through www.ancestry.com. Brain hemorrhage as the official cause of death is noted in Mount Hermon Cemetery Index, 1846–1904, Quebec City, accessed through www.ancestry.com.

266 **Read had been seen** Police suspicions and details of Read's death are outlined in Tunbridge Memo, September 6, 1891, MEPO 3/144; and Jarvis Report, September 12, 1892 (Quebec City), ibid.

267 **positively assures me** Jarvis Report, September 12, 1892 (Quebec City), ibid.; Tunbridge Memo, September 6, 1892, ibid.; Telegram, Superintendent John Shore to Inspector Frederick Smith Jarvis, September 7, 1892, ibid.; and Letter, Jarvis to Shore, September 10, 1892, ibid.

267 **journeyed to** Hamilton and Kingston Jarvis Report, July 19, 1892 (Montreal), ibid.

267 **poisoning two women** Tunbridge Memo, July 12, 1892, and July 14, 1892, ibid.; and Testimony of Edward Levi, "Trial of Thomas Neill," October 1892, *Proceedings of the Old Bailey, London's Central Criminal Court, 1674 to 1913*, 1417, www.oldbaileyonline.org.

267 **a peculiarity** Jarvis Report, August 29, 1892 (Montreal), MEPO 3/144.

267 **I am of the opinion** Ibid.

267 **it appears useless** Ibid.

268 **of no consequence** Tunbridge Memo, September 8, 1892, ibid.

268 **It is precisely similar** Jarvis Report, July 21, 1892 (Saratoga Springs, NY), ibid.

268 **McCulloch met with Jarvis** Jarvis Report, July 19, 1892 (Montreal), ibid.

268 **Jarvis was instructed** Telegram, Shore to Jarvis, August 10, 1892; and Jarvis Report, August 16, 1892 (Montreal), ibid. Scotland Yard agreed to pay McCulloch two hundred dollars a month. See Jarvis Report, August 11, 1892 (New York City); and Telegram, Jarvis to Scotland Yard, August 10, 1892, ibid.

268 **Jarvis had expected** Letter, Jarvis to Shore, July 11, 1892, ibid.

269 **It is of the utmost** Tunbridge Memo, September 6, 1892, ibid. Steps taken to find the source of the strychnine are outlined in Jarvis Reports, June 30, 1892 (Quebec City), August 11, 1892 (New York City), August 16, 1892 (Montreal), and August 25, 1892 (Montreal), ibid. On the reward and the checks with doctors and veterinarians, see Telegram, Shore to Jarvis, September 7, 1892, ibid.; Jarvis to Shore, September 10, 1892, ibid.; and Jarvis Report, September 12, 1892 (Quebec City), ibid. On the Brooklyn search, see "Where Did Neil Buy the Poison?" *New York Times*, September 18, 1892.

269 **exhausting enquiry** Jarvis Report, September 29, 1892 (London), ibid.; and Telegram, Jarvis to Shore, September 27, 1892, ibid.

269 **to present a strong** "Inspector Jarvis Ready to Take Up the Cream Poisoning Case," *Chicago Daily Tribune*, August 11, 1892. The newspaper mistakenly believed that the detective would sail home from New York in mid-August.

Chapter 34. "A Systematic and Deliberate Course of Action"

273 **some of Britain's** This list of offenders is drawn from Walter Thornbury, "The Old Bailey," in *Old and New London: A Narrative of Its History, Its People and Its Places*, vol. 2 (London: Cassell, Petter & Galpin, 1878), 461–77, www.british-history.ac.uk/old-new-london/vol2/pp461-477.

273 **evaporated into silence** "The Lambeth Poisonings," *Daily News* (London), October 18, 1892. The silence in the courtroom during the reading of the indictment was noted in "Neill Put on Trial," *New York Times*, October 18, 1892.

273 **as motionless and impassive** "On Trial for Poisoning," *New York Times*, November 9, 1892. Descriptions of the courtroom during Cream's trial, unless otherwise noted, are drawn from this article.

274 **nervous, irritable** "The Lambeth Poisonings," *Daily News*, October 20, 1892.

274 **looked more fearful** "The Lambeth Poisonings," *New York Times*, October 18, 1892. Cream's demeanor was also described in "Lambeth Murders" and "Lambeth Poisoning Cases," *Daily Telegraph* (London), October 18, 1892.

275 **"Russell," a colleague noted** R. Barry O'Brien, *The Life of Lord Russell of Killowen* (New York: Longmans, Green, 1901), 101.

275 **His method may** O'Brien, *Life of Lord Russell*, 102.

275 **wretched and obscure life** Russell's opening statement was reproduced in W. Teignmouth Shore, ed., *Trial of Thomas Neill Cream* (London: William Hodge, 1923), 45–59.

276 **idle men** This description of the crowds inside and outside the courtroom is drawn from "On Trial for Poisoning"; "Lambeth Murders"; "The Lambeth Murders," *Morning Post* (London), October 19, 1892; and "Lambeth Poisonings," *Daily News* (London), October 20, 1892.

276 **defended more murderers** Martin L. Friedland, *The Trials of Israel Lipski: A True Story of a Victorian Murder in the East End of London* (London: Macmillan, 1984), 24.

276 **the very "deadest" case** Samuel Ingleby Oddie, *Inquest* (London: Hitchinson, 1941), 103.

276 **one of the greatest** Edward Marjoribanks, *For the Defence: The Life of Sir Edward Marshall Hall* (New York: Macmillan, 1947), 37. His eloquence was also noted in "Irishmen at the Bar of England," *Irish Law Times and Solicitors' Journal* 30, no. 1517 (February 22, 1896): 89.

276 **He was constantly pestering** Friedland, *Trials of Israel Lipski*, 30.

276 **on a drinking binge** This was the conclusion of Friedland, author of the definitive account of the case. See ibid., 30–31.

277 **He grilled** Geoghegan's cross-examinations and legal arguments, unless otherwise noted, are drawn from Shore, *Trial of Thomas Neill Cream*, 61–65, 70–72, 76, 78, 87–91, 102–4, 107–8, 118.

277 **in the spotlight** Dr. Stevenson's role in the case is described in Kate Colquhoun, *Did She Kill Him? A Victorian Tale of Deception, Adultery and Arsenic* (London: Little, Brown, 2014), 200, 249–53.

277 **a curiously defensive air** "The Poison-Finder," *Guardian* (Manchester), July 29, 1908.

278 **If a patient** This account of Stevenson's cross-examination and his summary of his findings is drawn from "Trial of Thomas Neill," October 1892, *Proceedings of the Old Bailey, London's Central Criminal Court, 1674 to 1913*, 1435–37, www.oldbaileyonline.org.

280 **No inquiry was made** Shore, *Trial of Thomas Neill Cream*, 111.

280 **Geoghegan seized the opportunity** Ibid., 115.

281 **a systematic and deliberate course** The legal arguments on similar-fact evidence and Hawkins's ruling are drawn from ibid., 118–20; "Trial of Thomas Neill," 1451–52; "Lambeth Poisonings," *Daily News* (London), October 20, 1892; and "The Lambeth Murders," *Morning Post* (London), October 20, 1892.

281 **Considered a rising star** "Reviews," *Law Magazine and Review* no. 306 (November 1897): 157.

282 **A cold, deliberate** "On Trial for Poisoning."

282 **that stern judge** Frederick Porter Wensley, *Forty Years of Scotland Yard: The Record of a Lifetime's Service in the Criminal Investigation Department* (Garden City, NY: Garden City, 1931), 29.

282 **Hanging Hawkins** On Hawkins's career, see "Mr. Justice Hawkins," *London Illustrated News*, November 18, 1876; "Sir Henry Hawkins," *Spectator*, November 5, 1904; "Sir Henry Hawkins," *New York Times*, December 10, 1904; "Good Legal Stories," *New York Times*, February 10, 1906; and "Lord Brampton Dead," *New York Times*, October 7, 1907;

282 **and he once condemned** Wensley, *Forty Years of Scotland Yard*, 31.

282 **freshened with pomade and powder** "English Judge's Outfit," *New York Times*, August 31, 1895.

282 **as if from** Jack's Richard Harris, ed., *The Reminiscences of Sir Henry Hawkins, Baron Brampton*, vol. 2 (London: Edward Arnold, 1904), chaps. 44–46.

282 **The dog was said** "Sir Henry Hawkins," *New York Times*.

283 **damning evidence** Editorial, *Standard* (London), October 22, 1892.

284 **no right to testify** Friedland, *Trials of Israel Lipski*, 96.

284 **Geoghegan rallied** The defense summation was reproduced in Shore, *Trial of Thomas Neill Cream*, 137–48.

285 **There was scattered applause** "No Witnesses for the Defense," *New York Times*, October 21, 1892.

285 **Was it conceivable** For Russell's closing argument, see Shore, *Trial of Thomas Neill Cream*, 148–52.

CHAPTER 35. "A MURDER SO DIABOLICAL"

286 **It was not to be** Hawkins's charge to the jury was published in W. Teignmouth Shore, ed., *Trial of Thomas Neill Cream* (London: William Hodge, 1923), 153–64.

286 **Not an inch** "The Lambeth Murders," *Morning Post* (London), October 22, 1892.

286 **he had assured** Ibid.

287 **one of them guillotined** The window's slamming closed was noted in "Lambeth Poisonings," *Lloyd's Weekly Newspaper* (London), October 23, 1892.

287 **If Justice Hawkins was certain** Walter Preston Armstrong, "A Famous English K.C.," *Yale Law Journal* 29, no. 7 (May 1920): 722.

287 **without once looking** Miscellaneous news item, *Pall Mall Gazette* (London), October 22, 1892, p. 6.

288 **The jurors filed out** This description of the verdict's announcement and reaction in the courtroom is drawn from the following press reports: "Lambeth Murders"; "The Lambeth Poisonings," *Daily News*, October 22, 1892; "The Murders in Lambeth," *Guardian* (Manchester), October 22, 1892; "Neill Sentenced to Death," *New York Times*, October 22, 1892; "Lambeth Poisonings," *Lloyd's Weekly Newspaper* (London); and "Lambeth Poisoning Mystery Solved," *Reynolds's Newspaper* (London), October 23, 1892.

289 **An assistant came forward** This part of the ritual is described in "English Judge's Outfit," *New York Times*, August 31, 1895.

289 **most terrible crime** A transcript of the sentencing was published in Shore, *Trial of Thomas Neill Cream*, 161.

CHAPTER 36. "INSANE IN NO LEGAL SENSE"

290 **called on Melville** Macnaghten described the meeting and their conversation in Melville L. Macnaghten, *Days of My Years* (London: Edward Arnold, 1914), 115–16.

290 **Woe betide a policeman** "Lord Brampton Dead," *New York Times*, October 7, 1907.

290 **When many crimes** Sir Henry Hawkins, "The Duties of Police Constables," reproduced in *Irish Law Times and Solicitors' Journal* 16, no. 823 (November 4, 1882): 534–36.

291 **Countess Mabel Russell had** Inspector John Bennett Tunbridge Report, October 14, 1892, Metropolitan Police Office Records, MEPO 3/144, National Archives, London. Cream's prosecutor, Sir Charles Russell, was not related to the couple.

291 **faint endeavour** W. Teignmouth Shore, ed., *Trial of Thomas Neill Cream* (London: William Hodge, 1923), 159.

291 **Four unfortunates** "Unparalleled Atrocity," *Pall Mall Gazette* (London), October 22, 1892.

291 **extraordinary and inexplicable neglect** "The Lambeth Poisonings," *Daily News* (London), October 22, 1892.

291 **the public would not tolerate** Editorial, *Times of London*, October 22, 1892.

291 **To detect criminals** "Crime and the Police," *Reynolds's Newspaper* (London), October 23, 1892.

292 **most satisfactory explanation** Shore, *Trial of Thomas Neill Cream*, 169. Hawkins's mea culpa was widely reported in the press. See "The Conviction of Neill," *Pall Mall Gazette* (London), October 22, 1892; and "Lambeth Poisoning Mystery Solved," *Reynolds's Newspaper* (London), October 23, 1892.

292 **Dr. Thomas Neill** "Neill's Career," *News of the World* (London), October 23, 1892.

292 **pitiless atrocity** Editorial, *Standard* (London), October 22, 1892.

292 **the most cruel** News item, *Black and White: A Weekly Illustrated Record and Review* (London), October 29, 1892, 488.

293 **sordid greed** Quoted in Leonard Piper, *Murder by Gaslight: True Tales of Murder in Victorian and Edwardian England* (London: Michael O'Mara Books, 1991), 50.

293 **four medical experts** Reported in "The Convict Neill," *Standard* (London), October 24, 1892; and "Neill Still in Newgate," *Lloyd's Weekly Newspaper* (London), October 30, 1892.

294 **produced changes** "Neill's Fate—the Law to Take Its Course," *Pall Mall Gazette* (London), November 12, 1892.

294 **There are a dozen** Ibid.

294 **All manner** F. A. Whitlock, *Criminal Responsibility and Mental Illness* (London: Butterworths, 1963), 3.

294 **any indication of insanity** Letter, Dr. Philip Francis Gilbert, October 14, 1892, Home Office Records, HO 144/245 A 54360/10, National Archives, London. His assessment was reported in "Respite of Neill," *Lloyd's Weekly Newspaper* (London), November 6, 1892.

294 **Morally, without doubt** "The Case of Thomas Neill," *British Medical Journal* 2, no. 1661 (October 29, 1892): 961.

295 **utterly devoid** Editorial, *Times of London*.

295 **came into common use** Peter Vronsky, *Sons of Cain: A History of Serial Killers from the Stone Age to the Present* (New York: Berkley, 2018), 11–14, 266–67.

295 **a craving for blood** Macnaghten, *Days of My Years*, 100–101, 115.

295 **It was part of** "Lambeth Poisonings."

295 **There must be no thought** "Unparalleled Atrocity."

295 **acts of war** "Thomas Neill," *Spectator*, October 29, 1892.

295 **Cream belongs to** Editorial, *Standard*.

295 **Neill's a bloomin' skunk** "Passing Notes," *Illustrated Police News* (London), November 12, 1892.

296 **a fourteen-by-eight-foot** The cell was described in "The Condemned Poisoner in Newgate," *Pall Mall Gazette* (London), October 24, 1892; and "Neill Still in Newgate."

296 **They shall never hang me!** "Neill's Prison Life," *Illustrated Police News* (London), November 5, 1892. Cream's routine and the steps taken to prevent a suicide attempt were noted in this article, "Respite of Neill," and "Neill's Fate—the Law to Take Its Course."

296 **He is utterly reckless** Quoted in Shore, *Trial of Thomas Neill Cream*, 36.

296 **If I had only served** "Neill's Last Moments," *Illustrated Police News* (London), November 26, 1892.

296 **The Judge was dead** "Convict Neill."

296 **If it should come** "Execution of Neill," *Reynolds's Newspaper* (London), November 20, 1892.

297 **a good omen** "Respite of Neill." Later writers appear to have mistaken the timing of Cream's celebration, recording that he sang and danced in his cell after Geoghegan's persuasive closing argument at the trial. See, for instance, Shore, *Trial of Thomas Neill Cream*, 34, 36.

297 **newspapers offered fresh evidence** For examples of reporting on his previous crimes, see "The Lambeth Poisoning Cases: Neill's Career," *Reynolds's Newspaper* (London), October 23, 1892; and "Neill's Career."

297 **I was perfectly safe** "Neill Still in Newgate." The claim he had the support of a member of Parliament was made in a letter dated July 26, 1892, and reproduced in Shore, *Trial of Thomas Neill Cream*, 31.

297 **If you annoy me** Letter dated June 28, 1892, published in the *Daily Telegraph*, October 24, 1892, and also reproduced in Shore, *Trial of Thomas Neill Cream*, 29–30.

297 **When I think of** Letter dated August 5, 1892, reproduced in Shore, *Trial of Thomas Neill Cream*, 31–32.

297 **feared he was suicidal** Tunbridge Report, September 26, 1892, MEPO 3/144.

297 **Pshaw!** "Neill Still in Newgate." The interview first appeared in *Morning*, a London newspaper founded earlier that year. See "The Lambeth Poisoner," *Aberdeen Weekly Journal*, October 29, 1892.

298 **Full Confession** "The Condemned Poisoner in Newgate."

298 **a large number of women** "The Convict Neill," *Morning Post* (London), October 28, 1892. The confessions were refuted in "The Convict Cream," *Guardian* (Manchester), October 25, 1892; "The Neill Case," *Daily News* (London), October 25, 1892; and "The Convict Neill," *Standard* (London), October 29, 1892.

298 **Reports of Cream's trial** The articles noted in this paragraph appeared in the following newspapers: "The Poisoning of Girls in London," *Glasgow Herald*, October 22, 1892; "General London Cables," *Globe* (Toronto), November 1, 1892; "Sentenced to Be Hanged," *Gazette* (Montreal), October 22, 1892; "Neil Will Be Hanged," *Daily Globe* (St. Paul, MN), October 22, 1892; "Local," *True Republican* (Sycamore, IL), October 29, 1892; "The Lambeth Poisoning Cases," *Argus* (Melbourne), October 28, 1892; "The Lambeth Poisoning Cases," *Observer* (Adelaide), October 29, 1892; and "Miscellaneous," *Tasmanian* (Launceston), October 29, 1892.

298 **All of Neill's life** "Thomas Neill Hanged," *New York Times*, November 16, 1892.

298 **the most dangerous** "Cream Hanged at Newgate," *Sun* (New York), November 16, 1892.

299 **The world would have** "Dr. Cream to Be Hung," *Belvidere (IL) Standard*, October 26, 1892.

299 **There was no redeeming feature** "Cream's Day of Doom," *Chicago Times*, November 15, 1892.

299 **he is a Canadian** "Popular King Oscar," *Daily Inter Ocean* (Chicago), November 6, 1892.

299 **a First-class** Advertisement, *Era* (London), November 12, 1892.

299 **an enormous sale** "Execution of Dr. Neill," Advertisement, *Illustrated Police News* (London), November 12, 1892.

299 **the interests of science** Francis Thorburn, phrenologist, to Home Office secretary H. H. Asquith, October 29, 1892, HO 144/246 A 54360/13; Home Office undersecretary Lushington Memo, October 29, 1892, ibid.; and Lorenzo N. Fowler, phrenologist, to Home Office secretary H. H. Asquith, November 4, 1892, HO 144/246 A 54360/18.

299 **Madame Tussaud's balked** "The Value of Murderer's Relics," *Pall Mall Gazette* (London), October 28, 1892; and "Neill's Prison Life." Using the proceeds to pay Cream's legal bills was noted in "Condemned Poisoner in Newgate."

299 **Tussaud's had a wax** Advertisement, *Standard* (London), October 24, 1892.

300 **The Home Office amassed** HO 144/245 and 144/246.

300 **a terrible career** Lushington Memo, November 2, 1892, HO 144/246 A 54360/15.

300 **They could not have** Memo, November 9, 1892, HO 144/246 A 54360/23.

300 **anything in the way** Petition of Thomas Neill, October 23, 1892, and November 2, 1892, HO 144/245 A 54360/11.

300 **There is not the least** Notation, dated November 11, to November 9, 1892, Memo, HO 144/246 A 54360/23. The decision was announced in that day's evening newspapers. See "The Fate of Neill," *Daily News* (London), November 11, 1892.

CHAPTER 37. DEAD MAN'S WALK

301 **I wouldn't put that on** Details of Cream's execution, unless otherwise noted, are based on "Execution of Neill in Newgate," *Pall Mall Gazette* (London), November 15, 1892; "Execution of Neill," *Standard* (London), November 16, 1892; "Execution of Neill," *Reynolds's Newspaper* (London), November 20, 1892; and "Neill's Last Moments," *Illustrated Police News* (London), November 26, 1892.

301 **prayed God** Everard Milman, governor of Newgate, to Home Office, November 15, 1892, Home Office Records, HO 144/246 A 54360/32, National Archives, London.

301 **You all have made** "Execution of Neill" *Standard* (London).

302 **Dead Man's Walk** "The Condemned Poisoner in Newgate," *Pall Mall Gazette* (London), October 24, 1892.

302 **drink-sodden men** Details about the crowd gathered outside Newgate were reported in "Execution of Neill in Newgate"; and "Execution of Neill," *Morning Post* (London), November 16, 1892.

304 **A few people loitered** "The Last of a Murderer," *Pall Mall Gazette* (London), November 17, 1892.

304 **inky streaks and blotches** Ibid.

304 **wretched murderer** "Execution of Neill," *Reynolds's Newspaper* (London).

CHAPTER 38. "I AM JACK . . ."

305 **one of the most monstrous** Superintendent James Brannan Report, October 22, 1892, Metropolitan Police Office Records, MEPO 3/144, National Archives, London.

306 **In his conduct** Memo, "Rewards in Thos. Neill's Case: Murder," November 11, 1892, ibid. Tunbridge was promoted to chief inspector shortly before his retirement in 1895. See Richard S. Hill, "Tunbridge, John Bennett," *Dictionary of New Zealand Biography/Te Ara: The Encyclopedia of New Zealand*, teara.govt.nz/en/biographies/2t52/tunbridge-john-bennett.

306 **A striking example** W. Teignmouth Shore, ed., *Trial of Thomas Neill Cream* (London: William Hodge, 1923), 169.

306 **great cases** Elizabeth Jenkins, "Thomas Neill Cream, Poisoner," *Great Cases of Scotland Yard*, vol. 1 (London: Reader's Digest Association, 1978), 15–106. The Cream investigation was also touted as one of Scotland Yard's successes in Norman Lucas, *The CID* (London: Arthur Barker, 1967), 36–37.

306 **Normally it is** Douglas G. Browne, *The Rise of Scotland Yard: A History of the Metropolitan Police* (London: George G. Harrap, 1956), 240.

307 **to prevent the commission** Editorial, *Liverpool Mercury*, January 14, 1892. The trial was reported in "Central Criminal Court," *Standard* (London), January 14, 1893.

307 **British justice has lost** "Man Who Detected Many Poisons," *Victoria (BC) Daily Times*, August 20, 1908. See also "The Poison-Finder," *Guardian* (Manchester), July 29, 1908; "Sir Thomas Stevenson," *Guardian* (Manchester), July 29, 1908; and "A Master of Poisons," *Washington Post*, August 16, 1908.

307 **watershed moments** Colin Evans, *The Father of Forensics: The Groundbreaking Cases of Sir Bernard Spilsbury, and the Beginnings of Modern CSI* (New York: Berkley Books, 2006), 31. On the Crippen case, see Douglas G. Browne and E. V. Tullett, *Bernard Spilsbury: His Life and Cases* (Harmondsworth, UK: Penguin Books, 1951), 35–54.

310 **The points of resemblance** "The Conviction of Neill," *Pall Mall Gazette* (London), October 22, 1892.

310 **advanced this theory** Don Bell, "Jack the Ripper: The Final Solution?" *Criminologist* 9, no. 33 (Summer 1974): 40–51. See also "Montreal This Morning," *Montreal Gazette*, January 6, 1975; "The Judge Called him 'Diabolical, Wicked,'" *Montreal Gazette*, February 24, 1979, and "McGill Grad Took His Secret to the Gallows," *Montreal Gazette*, February 26, 1979.

310 **such unlikely candidates** For a list of Ripper suspects, see Donald Rumbelow, *The Complete Jack the Ripper* (London: Virgin Books, 2013), 136–280.

310 **A bizarre new theory** See Jay Robert Nash, *Almanac of World Crime* (New York: Bonanza Books, 1986), 293. The eminent British barrister Edward Marshall Hall gave some credence to this theory when he recalled his defense of a man accused of bigamy in the London courts in the mid-1880s. The charge was dismissed when his client proved he had been in prison in Australia at the time of the marriages, and Hall suspected the man had used a "'double' in the underworld" to give him an alibi. A few years later, Hall attended Cream's trial at the Old Bailey and was convinced he was the man he had defended in the bigamy case. But Hall had a poor memory for faces, and his suggestion that Cream had been freed from

prison before 1891 and had enlisted another criminal in distant Australia to lie for him is as far-fetched as the theory that he was Jack the Ripper. See Edward Marjoribanks, *For the Defence: The Life of Sir Edward Marshall Hall* (New York: Macmillan, 1947), 35–36, 249.

310 **The purported gallows confession** "The Last of Jack the Ripper," *Marion (OH) Star*, January 11, 1902, appears to be the earliest report of the "I am Jack . . ." statement, citing the *London Chronicle*. The item was republished in the *Baltimore Sun* and smaller papers in Connecticut, Pennsylvania, Kansas, Louisiana, and California in the weeks that followed. The statement was repeated in 1913 in a news article on last words spoken on the gallows, then appears to have been forgotten until the 1950s. See "Scaffold Good-Bys: Dramatic Last Words," *Times-Democrat* (New Orleans), June 22, 1913; and "Jack the Ripper!" *Chicago Sunday Tribune*, January 14, 1951.

310 **reports appeared after Billington's death** There is "no official source and no independent witness," Billington's biographer has noted, to confirm either the statement attributed to Cream or that his executioner later boasted of hanging Jack the Ripper. See Alison Bruce, *Billington: Victorian Executioner* (Stroud, UK: History Press, 2009), 62–63.

310 **was repeated over the years** Three of numerous examples are Grierson Dickson, *Murder by Numbers* (London: Robert Hale, 1958), 86; Roy Harley Lewis, *Victorian Murders* (Newton Abbot, UK: David & Charles, 1988), 188; and Leonard Piper, *Murder by Gaslight: True Tales of Murder in Victorian and Edwardian England* (London: Michael O'Mara Books, 1991), 50.

311 **Different method, different place** Maxim Jakubowski and Nathan Braund, eds., *The Mammoth Book of Jack the Ripper*, 459, 462. Claims that Cream was the Ripper have also been refuted in Donald Rumbelow, *The Complete Jack the Ripper* (London: Robinson, 2008), 209–11; Jeffrey Bloomfield, "Gallows Humor: The Alleged Ripper Confession of Dr. Cream," *Ripper Notes: The International Journal for Ripper Studies*, no. 23 (July 2005): 50–58; and more recently in Bruce Robinson, *They All Love Jack: Busting the Ripper* (New York: HarperCollins, 2015), 164.

311 **Today, when guides** When the author joined the popular Jack the Ripper Walk conducted by the firm London Walks, on March 25, 2018, Cream was mentioned as a possible suspect.

EPILOGUE: "AN ELIZABETHAN TRAGEDY OF HORRORS"

312 **The future historian** "The Case of Poisoning in Stamford Street," *British Medical Journal* 1, no. 1637 (May 14, 1892): 1042.

312 **In Fall River** "Lizzie Borden Charged with Murder," *Chicago Daily Tribune*, August 12, 1892.

312 **made headlines around the world** Maurice Gurvich and Christopher Wray, *The Scarlet Thread: Australia's Jack the Ripper, A True Crime Story* (Sydney, NSW: Fairfax Books, 2007).

312 **another monster of Cream's ilk** David Wilson, *A History of British Serial Killing* (London: Sphere, 2009), 8. On the Chapman case, see Helena Wojtczak, *Jack*

the Ripper at Last? The Mysterious Murders of George Chapman (East Sussex, UK: Hastings Press, 2014).

312 **whose reputation has stood** George Orwell, *Decline of the English Murder* (London: Penguin Books, 2009), 15.

313 **"series-murder" "multicide"** Grierson Dickson, *Murder by Numbers* (London: Robert Hale, 1958), 13. Peter Vronsky's research suggests the term "serial killer" first appeared in the *New York Times* in 1981. See his *Sons of Cain: A History of Serial Killers from the Stone Age to the Present* (New York: Berkley, 2018), 13.

313 **anyone who murders** Robert J. Morton and Mark A. Hilts, eds., *Serial Murder: Multi-Disciplinary Perspectives for Investigators* (Federal Bureau of Investigation, National Center for the Analysis of Violent Crime, 2005), 9, www.fbi.gov/stats-services/publications/serial-murder#two. See also Berit Brogaard, "What Defines a Serial Killer?" *Psychology Today*, May 31, 2017, www.psychologytoday.com/ca/blog/the-superhuman-mind/201705/what-defines-serial-killer.

313 **They kill for** See Eric W. Hickey, *Serial Murderers and Their Victims*, 4th ed. (Belmont, CA: Thomson Wadsworth, 2006), 16–19, 22–23. The connection between acts of arson and serial murder is noted on pp. 31–22.

314 **a sick product** Angus McLaren, *A Prescription for Murder: The Victorian Serial Killings of Dr. Thomas Neill Cream* (Chicago: University of Chicago Press, 1993), 140.

314 **A man could seek a divorce** Geoffrey Best, *Mid-Victorian England, 1851–75* (London: Fontana Press), 303.

314 **a woman surrendered all** Ibid., 304.

314 **annoying male persons** McLaren, *Prescription for Murder*, 65, 67–68.

314 **power to arrest suspected prostitutes** Mary Lyndon Shanley, *Feminism, Marriage, and the Law in Victorian England, 1850–1895* (Princeton, NJ: Princeton University Press, 1989), 82–86.

315 **degradation and defenceless condition** *South London Chronicle*, October 29, 1892, quoted in McLaren, *Prescription for Murder*, 127.

316 **less-dead** Quoted in Vronsky, *Sons of Cain*, 80–83.

316 **clearing the East-end** E. Fairfield, "To the Editor of the Times," *Times of London*, October 1, 1888.

316 **Women had no voice** Hallie Rubenhold, *The Five: The Untold Lives of the Women Killed by Jack the Ripper* (Boston: Houghton Mifflin Harcourt, 2019), 12.

316 **his crimes drew more** See Wilson, *History of British Serial Killing*, 161–91.

316 **cited in the Australian courts** See *R. v. Makin* (1893) 14 LR (NSW) 1 (30 March 1893), 40; and *Makin v. Attorney General for New South Wales* (1893) UKPC 56 (12 December 1893), 56.

316 **drowning his wife** Eric R. Watson, ed., *Trial of George Joseph Smith* (Glasgow: William Hodge, 1922), 34–35.

317 **The whole story** W. Teignmouth Shore, ed., *Trial of Thomas Neill Cream* (London: William Hodge, 1923), 32, 40.

317 **He was cool and calm** Edmund Pearson, *Murder at Smutty Nose and Other Murders* (Garden City, NY: Doubleday, Page, 1927), 146–47.

317 **seemed mad** F. Tennyson Jesse, *Murder and Its Motives* (London: George G. Harrap, 1924), 195.

SOURCES

317 **He utilized his medical knowledge** Shore, *Trial of Thomas Neill Cream*, 37.

317 **In Cream we see** Philip Lindsay, *The Mainspring of Murder* (London: John Long, 1958), 75, 79.

318 **useful and God-like** W. Wright, *Introductory Lecture Delivered at the Opening of the 49th Session—Medical Faculty of McGill University* (Montreal: George E. Desbarats, 1872), 15.

318 **Cream's story found its way** Examples are Jay Robert Nash, *Almanac of World Crime* (New York: Bonanza Books, 1986), 22, 292–93, 318–19; and John Marlowe, *The World's Most Evil Psychopaths: Horrifying True Life Cases* (London: Arcturus Publishing, 2007), 43–50.

318 **went public with his story** Frank S. Whitman and R. Lehman Neff, "Hidden Horror of the Pink Pills," *Complete Detective Cases* 2, no. 3 (May 1940): 38–41, 55–58.

318 **Jack the Ripper confession** The confession is reported as fact in Nash, *Almanac of World Crime*, 239, 319. While recent anthologies concede that Cream may never have uttered the words, they assume his executioner, Billington, was the source of the purported confession, not newspaper stories published after his death. See Marlowe, *World's Most Evil Psychopath*, 50; and Jenni Davis, *Poison, a History: An Account of the Deadly Art & Its Most Infamous Practitioners* (New York: Chartwell Books, 2018), 88.

318 **forced to marry Flora Brooks** See, for example, Dickson, *Murder by Numbers*, 75.

318 **inherited the bulk** One of many examples is Max Haines, "Wicked Doctor Cream," in *The Collected Works of Max Haines* (Toronto: Toronto Sun Publishing, 1985), 114.

318 **vial of strychnine** Frank Adams, "Dr. Cream: The Elegant Killer from Canada," *Globe and Mail* (Toronto), April 17, 1962.

318 **the lurid, self-serving confession** John Cashman, *The Gentleman from Chicago: Being an Account of the Doings of Thomas Neill Cream, M.D. (M'Gill), 1850–1892* (London: Hamish Hamilton, 1974). For a more recent fictional account told from Cream's perspective, see A. J. Griffiths-Jones, *Prisoner 4374* (London: Austin Macauley Publishers, 2015).

318 **I want to kill, kill, kill** David Fennario, *Doctor Thomas Neill Cream (Mystery at McGill)* (Vancouver: Talon Books, 1993), 126.

319 **the only man I have** David Pirie, *The Dark Water* (London: Arrow Books, 2005), 4.

319 **Have no fear** "Episode 1," *River*, directed by Richard Laxton, Netflix, 2015. Hugo's actual words were "Have no fear of robbers or murderers. Such dangers are without, and are but petty. We should fear ourselves. . . . The great dangers are within us." Victor Hugo, *Les Misérables*, vol. 1 (Ware, UK: Wordsworth Editions, 1994), 20.

319 **Cream's wax figure** *Madame Tussaud's Exhibition: Official Guide & Catalogue* (July 1932), babel.hathitrust.org/cgi/pt?id=umn.319510020934977. This description is based on a photograph reproduced in Richard D. Altick, *Victorian Studies in Scarlet* (London: J. M. Dent & Sons, 1970), 160–61.

319 **withdrawn from the exhibit** Email communication with Sedi Kukwikila, spokesperson for Madame Tussaud's, June 13, 2018.

319 **the unfortunate and notorious son** Cream Family Index Cards, Chalmers-Wesley United Church, Quebec City.

319 **Cream remains on the list** Suggestions that Cream's medical degree was revoked after his conviction and execution appear to be in error. See Edward H. Bensley, "McGill University's Most Infamous Medical Graduate," *Canadian Medical Association Journal* 109 (November 17, 1973): 1024. The list of frequently asked questions on the website of the McGill archives includes a reference to the university's infamous graduate. See "Did 'Jack the Ripper' attend McGill University?" www.mcgill.ca/library/branches/mua/archival-resources/archives-faqs.

320 **As one walks** Shore, *Trial of Thomas Neill Cream*, 32.

320 **rechristened the Sherlock Holmes** Nicholas Utechin, "The Sherlock Holmes at 60," *Sherlock Holmes Journal* 33, no. 2 (Summer 2017): 64–8.

321 **an unmarked grave** Email communication with Richard Buteux, bereavement services officer, City of London Cemetery and Crematorium, June 27, 2016.

321 **The case of drug samples** "The Secret of Scotland Yard's Black Museum," *Daily Mail*, September 4, 2015, www.dailymail.co.uk/femail/article-3222439.

322 **erected, it is claimed** "Old Murder Tale Revived in Story of Marble Shaft," *Belvidere (IL) Daily Republican*, October 7, 1929; and Whitman and Neff, "Hidden Horror of the Pink Pills," 58.

INDEX

Page numbers in italics refer to illustrations.

Maclaren, James, 112, 258
Macnaghten, Melville, 40, 290, 292, 295
Madame Tussaud's, 21–22, 299, 300, 319
maps, 14, 106
marriage law, 314
Marsan, Eddie, 319
Marsh, Alice, 69, 69–70, 315
    false accusations concerning, 89,
      98, 181
    inquest, 68, 83–84
    investigation, 67–70, 72–73, 84–85,
      96, 174 (*see also* "Fred," search for)
    murder charge laid, 275
    testimony presented in Clover trial,
      283
Martin, Deborah, 223
Martin, Joseph, 223–24, 224
Masons' Arms (pub), 36, 178, 320
mass murder, 313
Masters, Elizabeth, 37, 38, 179–80, 277,
    287, 308
Mathews, George, 57–58
Matson, Canute, 220, 221
Matthews, Henry, 93
Maugham, W. Somerset, 142
May, Elizabeth, 37, 38, 179–80, 277, 287, 308
Maybrick, Florence, 277
Maybrick, James, 277
Mayhew, Henry, 13, 15
McClaughry, Robert, 2, 4, 5, 250, 251,
    253, 54
    and Cream, 255–56, 265
McClellan, Lena, 214, 241, 252
McClellan, Mary, 214, 224, 225, 240,
    241, 252
McCulloch, John, 61–62, 268, 279
McDonald, Mike, 197, 204, 221
McGill Gazette, 123, 124
McGill University Medical School,
    107, 119–20, 121–24, 125, 127–29,
    318, 319

McIntyre, Patrick, 91, 92–93, 94, 100,
    308
McLaren, Angus, 314
Medical Act (Ontario), 156
medical licensing, 141–42, 147, 148–49,
    150. *See also under* Cream, Thomas
    Neill
medical training, 119–20, 121–23, 137–38.
    See also under Cream, Thomas
    Neill
medicine, as a science, 121
Meech, H. J., 299
merits, decisions on, 281–83, 316–17
Metropole Hotel, 64
Metropolitan Police. *See also* Scotland
    Yard
    creation of, 22
    E Division, 53, 56
    errors by, 189, 280–81, 290–93, 305,
      307–8
    in fiction, 24, 25–26
    L Division, 30, 56, 292, 307–8
mice, 76, 82
miscarriage, induced, 134, 198, 199. *See
    also* abortion
M'Naghten, Daniel, 293
M'Naghten Rules, 294
monkshood, 73
Montgomery, Sarah Alice, 218–22, 237,
    238, 243, 315
Montreal, 115, 120–21, 123. *See also*
    McGill University Medical
    School
Mooney, Mike, 248
Moonstone, The (Collins), 20, 22
Moore, Dr. Charles, 162
Morning Post, 286
morphine, 30, 63, 73, 216, 278
    taken by Cream, 18, 60, 61, 62, 96,
      284, 294
motivation for murder, 41, 43